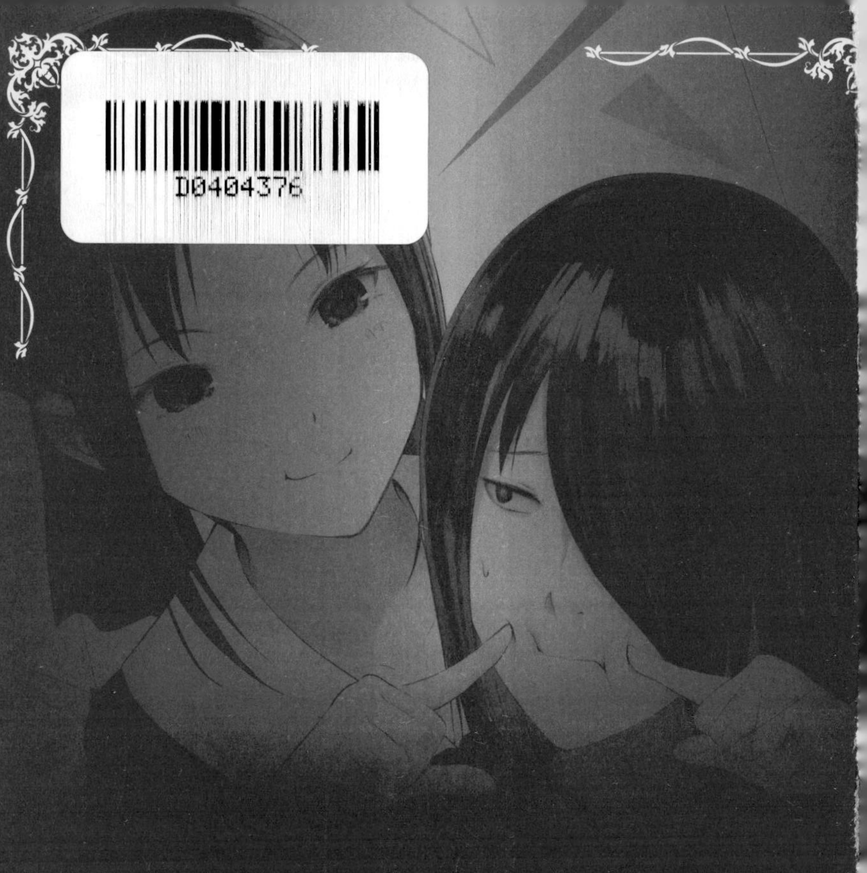

KAGUYA-SAMA
LOVE IS WAR

18

AKA AKASAKA

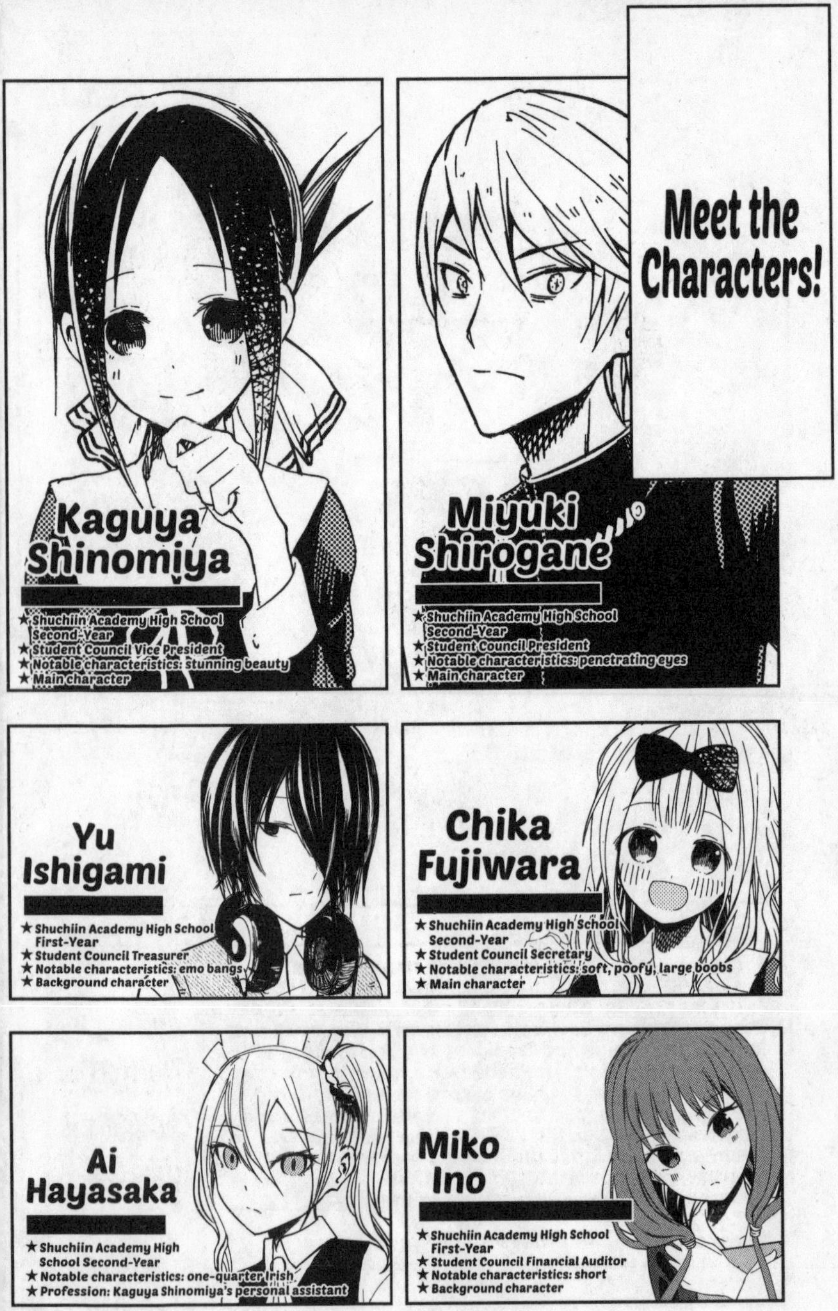
Meet the Characters!
Miyuki Shirogane
[redacted]
★Shuchiin Academy High School Second-Year
★Student Council President
★Notable characteristics: penetrating eyes
★Main character
Kaguya Shinomiya
[redacted]
★Shuchiin Academy High School Second-Year
★Student Council Vice President
★Notable characteristics: stunning beauty
★Main character
Chika Fujiwara
[redacted]
★ Shuchiin Academy High School Second-Year
★ Student Council Secretary
★ Notable characteristics: soft, poofy, large boobs
★ Main character
Yu Ishigami
[redacted]
★ Shuchiin Academy High School First-Year
★ Student Council Treasurer
★ Notable characteristics: emo bangs
★ Background character
Miko Ino
[redacted]
★ Shuchiin Academy High School First-Year
★ Student Council Financial Auditor
★ Notable characteristics: short
★ Background character
Ai Hayasaka
[redacted]
★ Shuchiin Academy High School Second-Year
★ Notable characteristics: one-quarter Irish
★ Profession: Kaguya Shinomiya's personal assistant

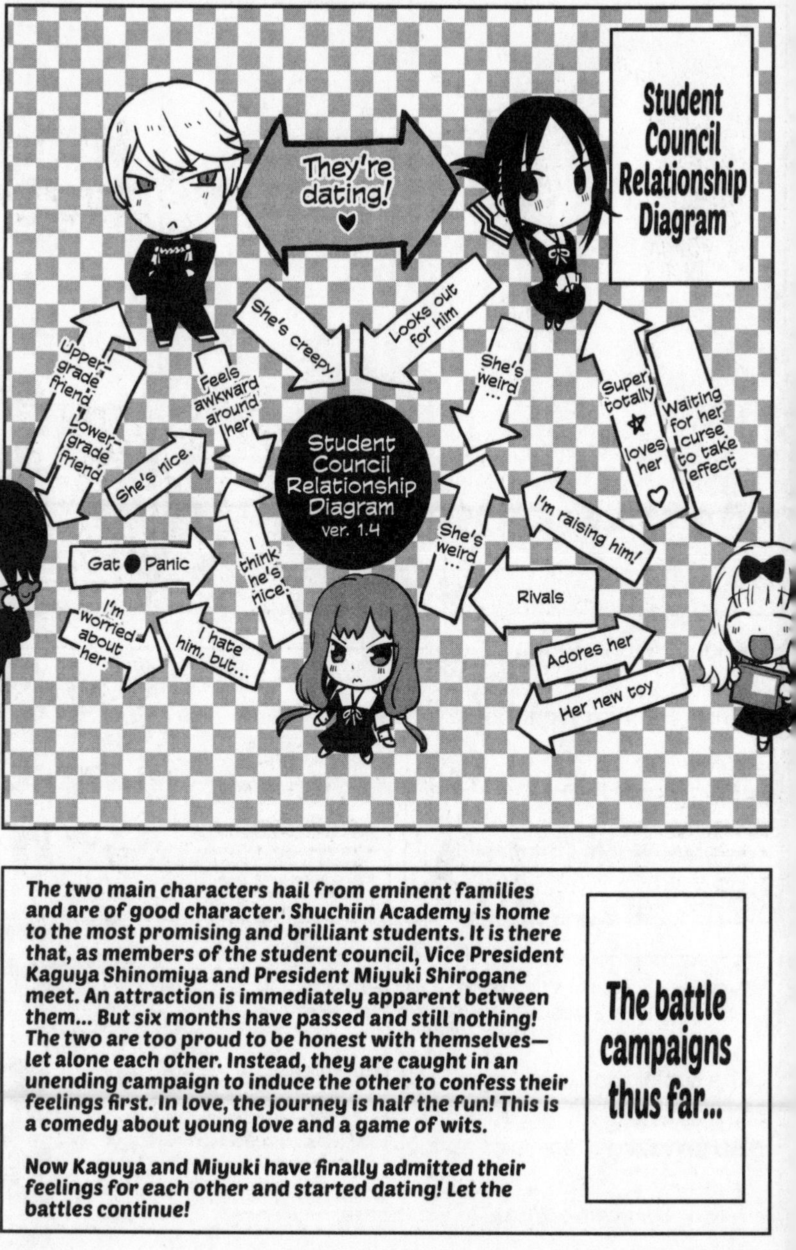
Student Council Relationship Diagram
They're dating!
She's creepy.
Looks out for him
Upper-grade friend
Lower-grade friend
Feels awkward around her
She's weird...
Super totally ☆ loves her ♡
Waiting for her curse to take effect
Student Council Relationship Diagram ver. 1.4
She's nice.
I'm raising him!
Gat ● Panic
I think he's nice.
She's weird...
Rivals
I'm worried about her.
I hate him, but...
Adores her
Her new toy

The two main characters hail from eminent families and are of good character. Shuchiin Academy is home to the most promising and brilliant students. It is there that, as members of the student council, Vice President Kaguya Shinomiya and President Miyuki Shirogane meet. An attraction is immediately apparent between them... But six months have passed and still nothing! The two are too proud to be honest with themselves—let alone each other. Instead, they are caught in an unending campaign to induce the other to confess their feelings first. In love, the journey is half the fun! This is a comedy about young love and a game of wits.

Now Kaguya and Miyuki have finally admitted their feelings for each other and started dating! Let the battles continue!

The battle campaigns thus far...

KAGUYA-SAMA LOVE IS WAR

BATTLE CAMPAIGNS 18

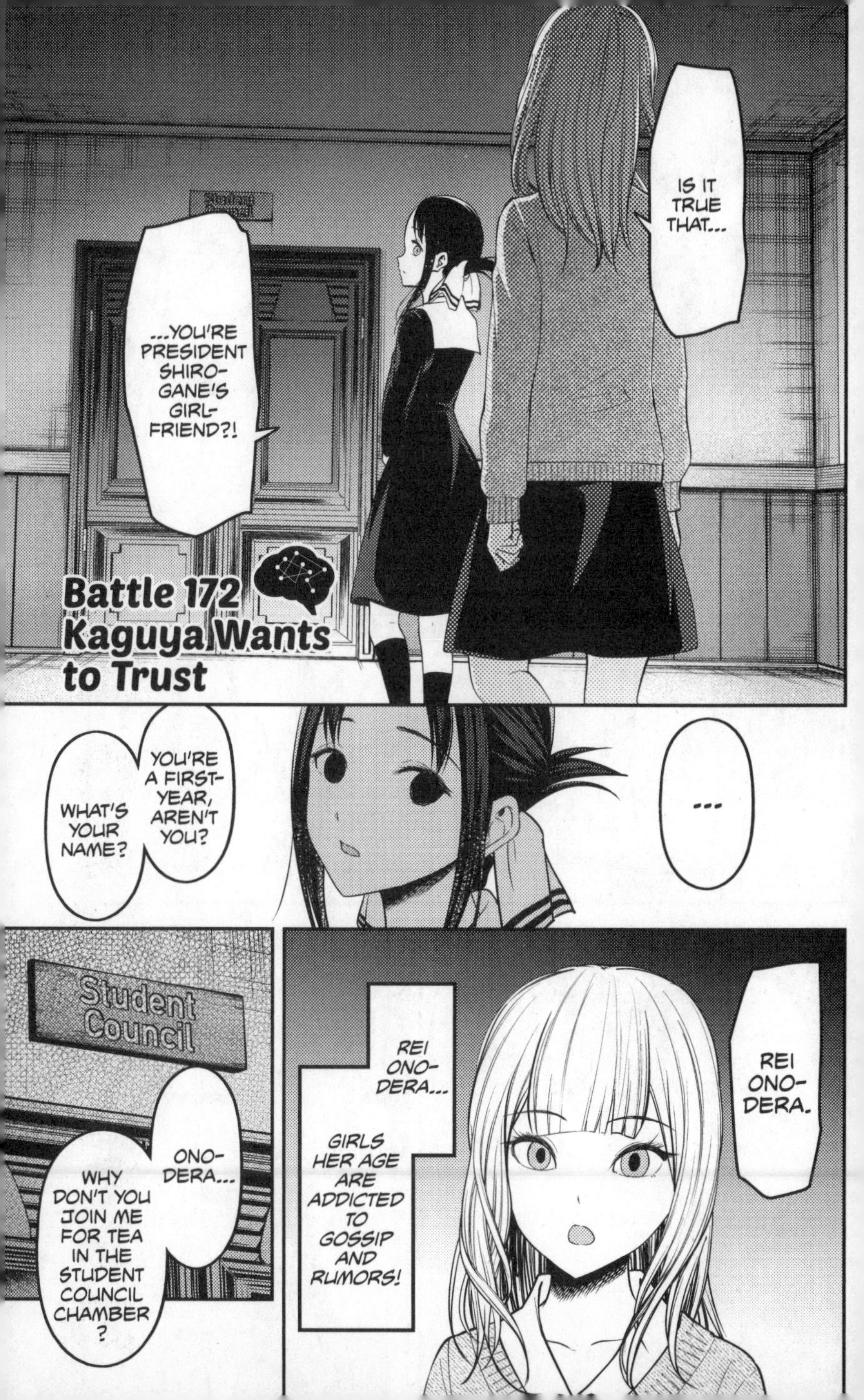
IS IT TRUE THAT...
...YOU'RE PRESIDENT SHIROGANE'S GIRLFRIEND?!
Battle 172 Kaguya Wants to Trust
...
YOU'RE A FIRST-YEAR, AREN'T YOU?
WHAT'S YOUR NAME?
REI ONODERA.
REI ONODERA...
GIRLS HER AGE ARE ADDICTED TO GOSSIP AND RUMORS!
Student Council
ONODERA...
WHY DON'T YOU JOIN ME FOR TEA IN THE STUDENT COUNCIL CHAMBER?

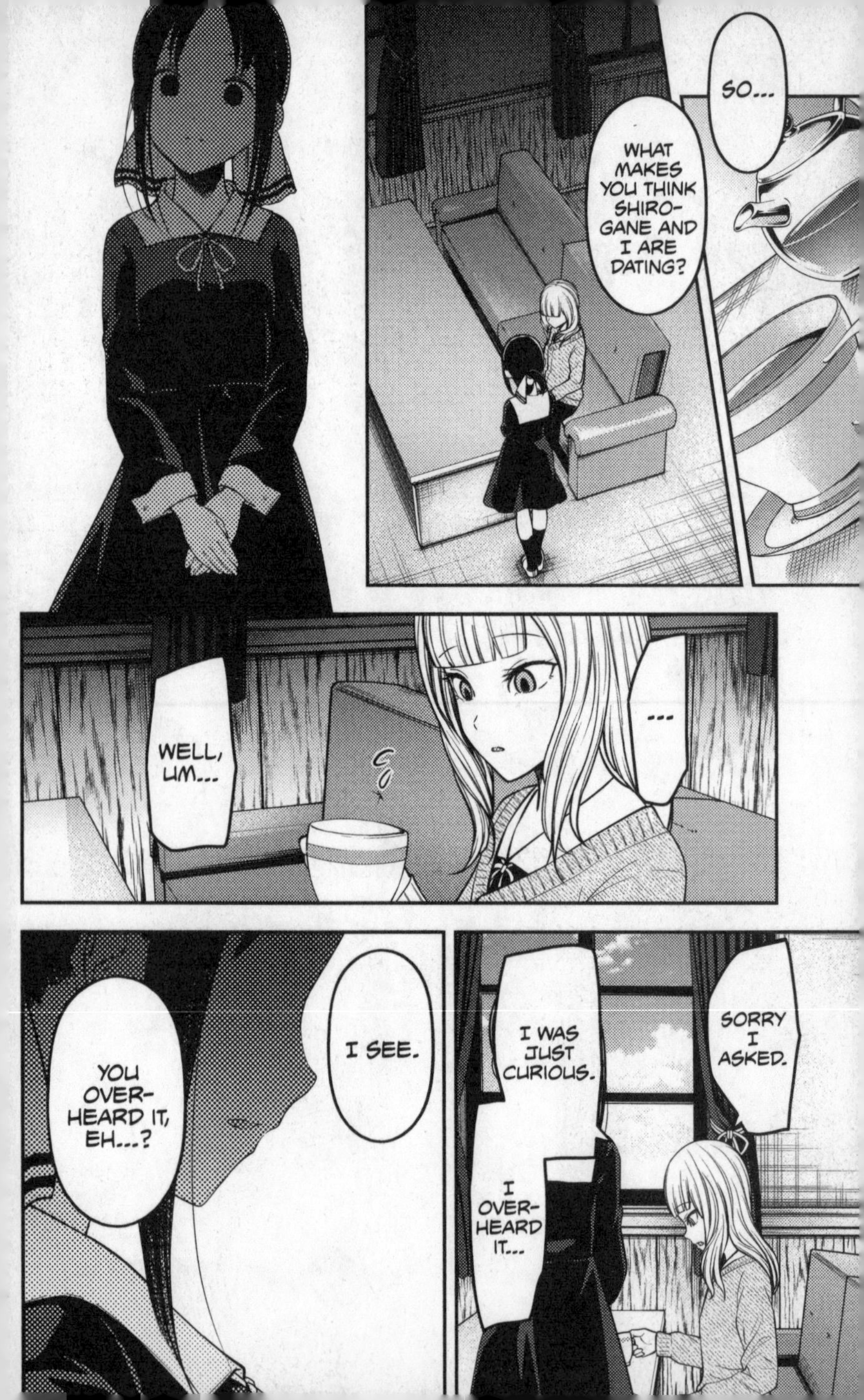
SO...
WHAT MAKES YOU THINK SHIRO-GANE AND I ARE DATING?
...
WELL, UM...
SORRY I ASKED.
I WAS JUST CURIOUS.
I OVER-HEARD IT...
I SEE.
YOU OVER-HEARD IT, EH...?

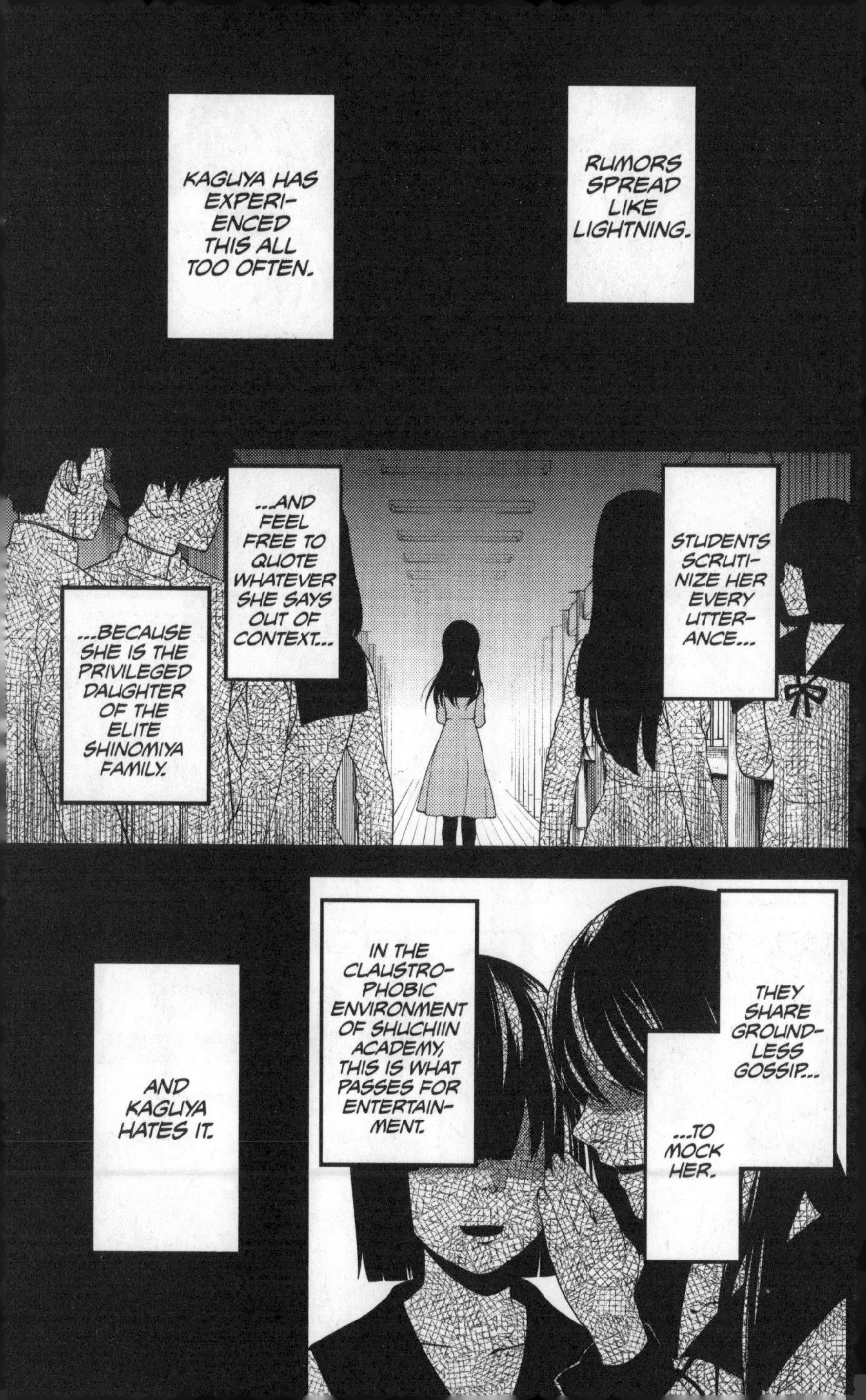
RUMORS SPREAD LIKE LIGHTNING.
KAGUYA HAS EXPERIENCED THIS ALL TOO OFTEN.
STUDENTS SCRUTINIZE HER EVERY UTTERANCE...
...AND FEEL FREE TO QUOTE WHATEVER SHE SAYS OUT OF CONTEXT...
...BECAUSE SHE IS THE PRIVILEGED DAUGHTER OF THE ELITE SHINOMIYA FAMILY.
THEY SHARE GROUNDLESS GOSSIP...
...TO MOCK HER.
IN THE CLAUSTROPHOBIC ENVIRONMENT OF SHUCHIIN ACADEMY, THIS IS WHAT PASSES FOR ENTERTAINMENT.
AND KAGUYA HATES IT.

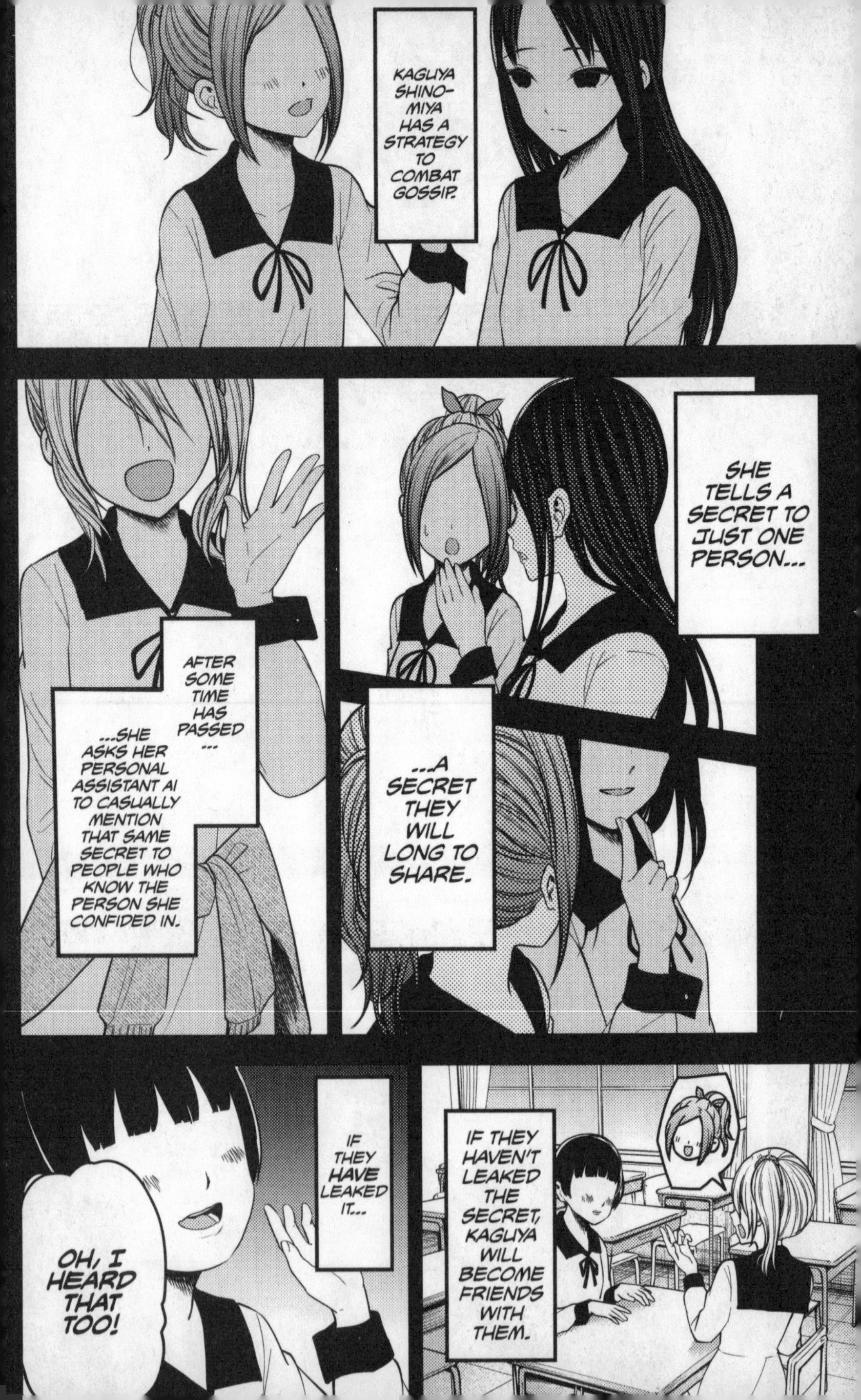
KAGUYA SHINOMIYA HAS A STRATEGY TO COMBAT GOSSIP.
SHE TELLS A SECRET TO JUST ONE PERSON...
...A SECRET THEY WILL LONG TO SHARE.
AFTER SOME TIME HAS PASSED...
...SHE ASKS HER PERSONAL ASSISTANT AI TO CASUALLY MENTION THAT SAME SECRET TO PEOPLE WHO KNOW THE PERSON SHE CONFIDED IN.
IF THEY HAVEN'T LEAKED THE SECRET, KAGUYA WILL BECOME FRIENDS WITH THEM.
IF THEY HAVE LEAKED IT...
OH, I HEARD THAT TOO!

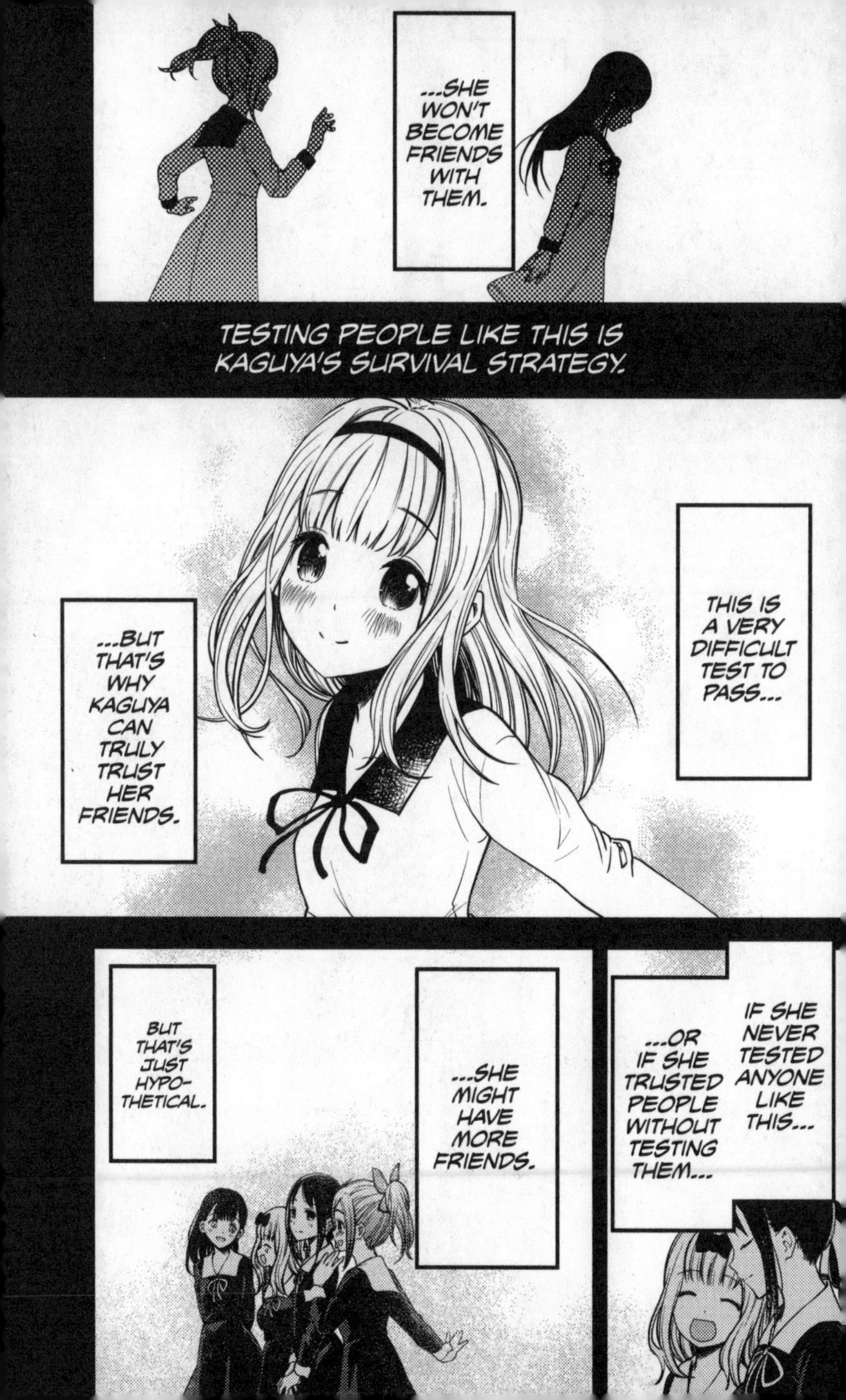
...SHE WON'T BECOME FRIENDS WITH THEM.
TESTING PEOPLE LIKE THIS IS KAGUYA'S SURVIVAL STRATEGY.
THIS IS A VERY DIFFICULT TEST TO PASS...
...BUT THAT'S WHY KAGUYA CAN TRULY TRUST HER FRIENDS.
IF SHE NEVER TESTED ANYONE LIKE THIS...
...OR IF SHE TRUSTED PEOPLE WITHOUT TESTING THEM...
...SHE MIGHT HAVE MORE FRIENDS.
BUT THAT'S JUST HYPO-THETICAL.

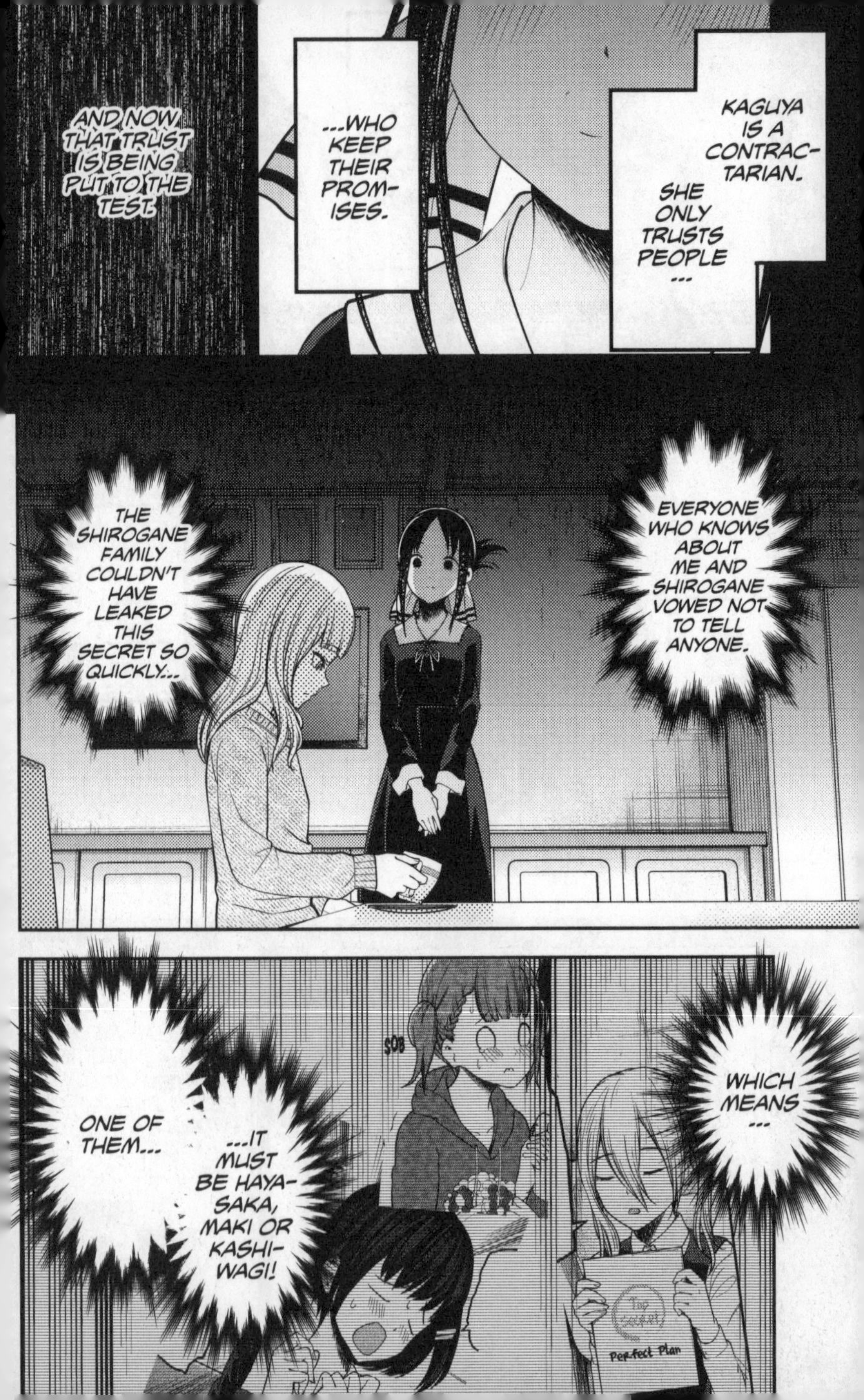
KAGUYA IS A CONTRACTARIAN.
SHE ONLY TRUSTS PEOPLE...
...WHO KEEP THEIR PROMISES.
AND NOW THAT TRUST IS BEING PUT TO THE TEST.
EVERYONE WHO KNOWS ABOUT ME AND SHIROGANE VOWED NOT TO TELL ANYONE.
THE SHIROGANE FAMILY COULDN'T HAVE LEAKED THIS SECRET SO QUICKLY...
WHICH MEANS...
SOB
...IT MUST BE HAYASAKA, MAKI OR KASHIWAGI!
ONE OF THEM...
Perfect Plan

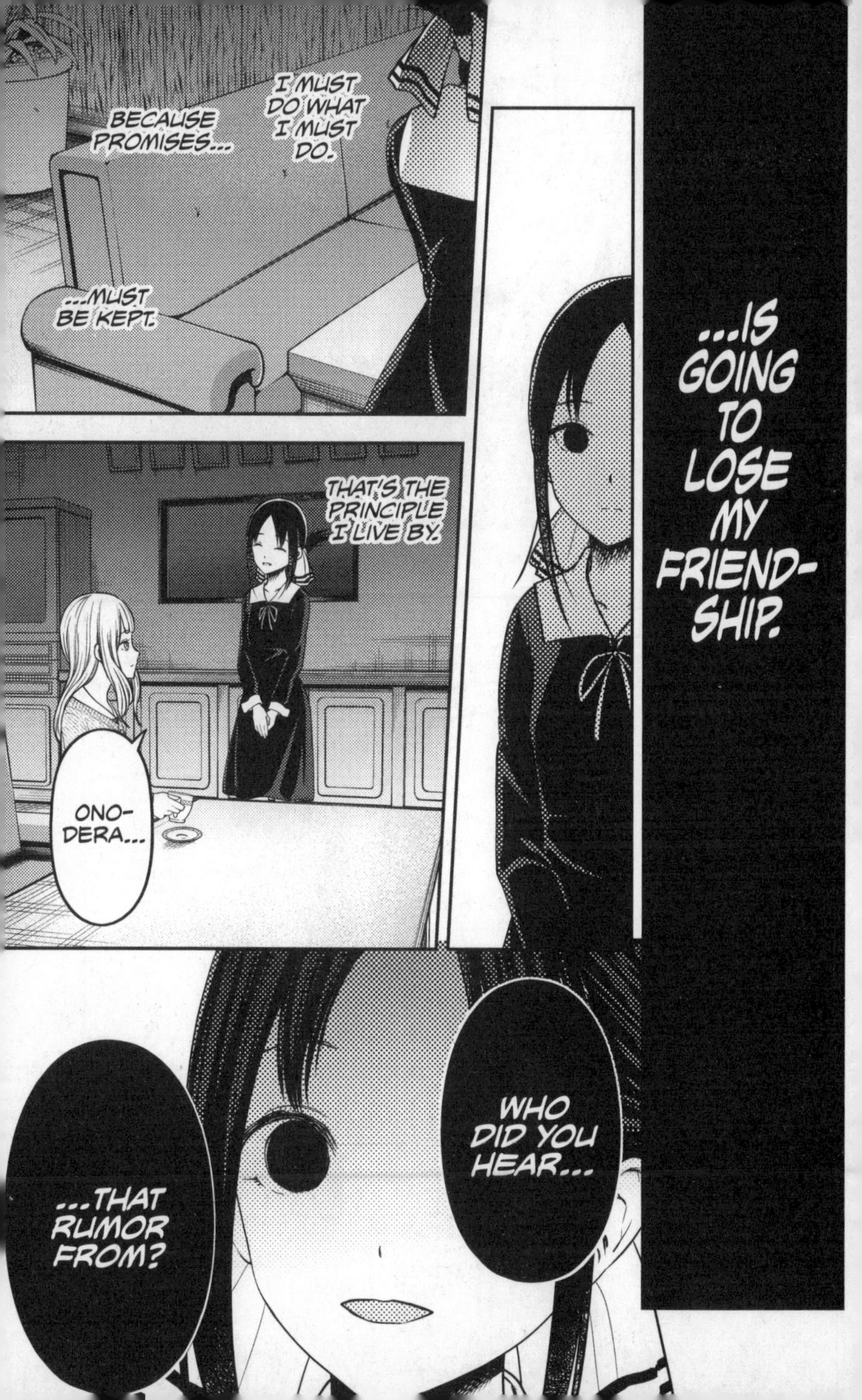
...IS GOING TO LOSE MY FRIEND-SHIP.
I MUST DO WHAT I MUST DO.
BECAUSE PROMISES...
...MUST BE KEPT.
THAT'S THE PRINCIPLE I LIVE BY.
ONO-DERA...
WHO DID YOU HEAR...
...THAT RUMOR FROM?

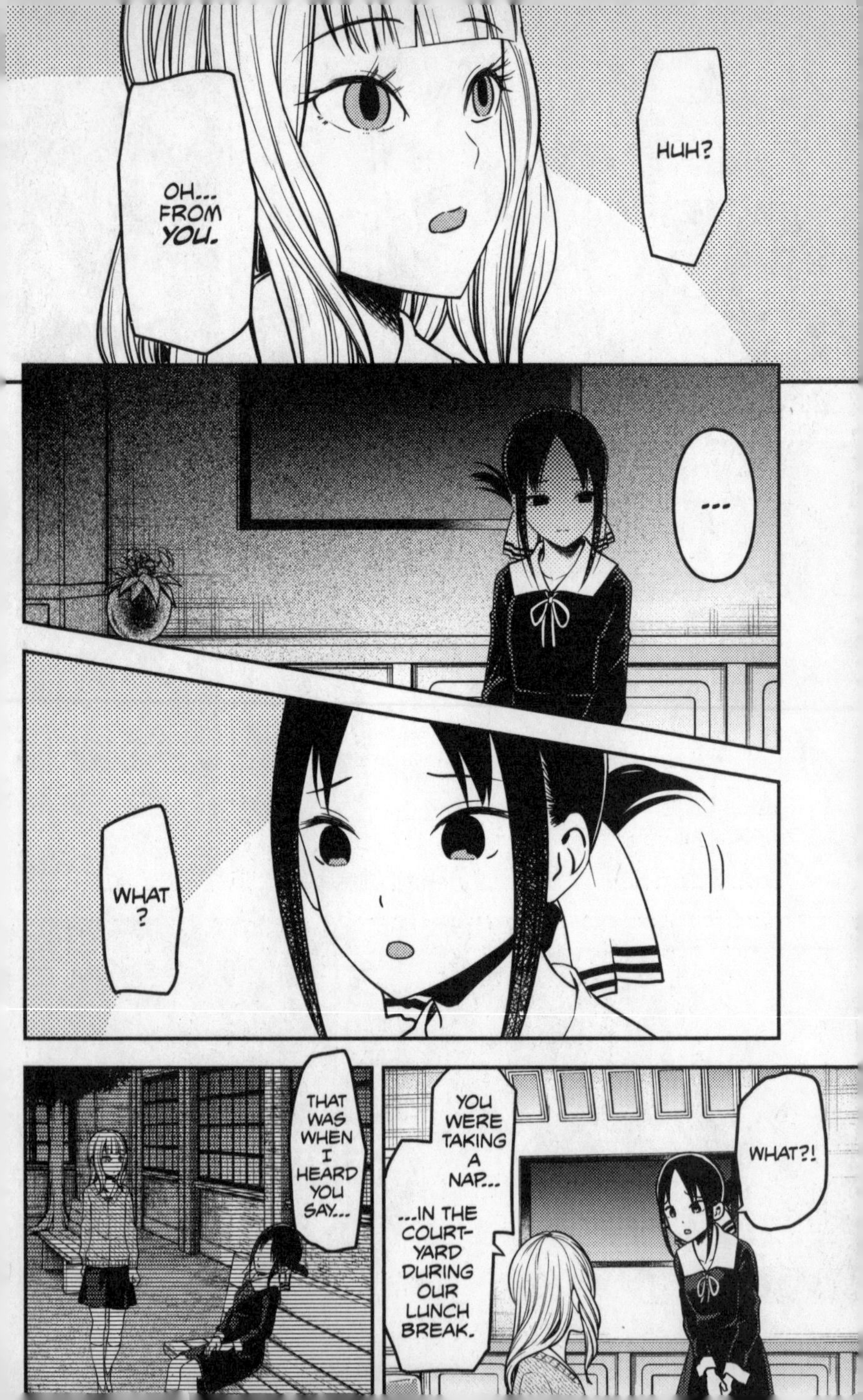
HUH?
OH... FROM YOU.
...
WHAT?
WHAT?!
YOU WERE TAKING A NAP...
...IN THE COURT-YARD DURING OUR LUNCH BREAK.
THAT WAS WHEN I HEARD YOU SAY...

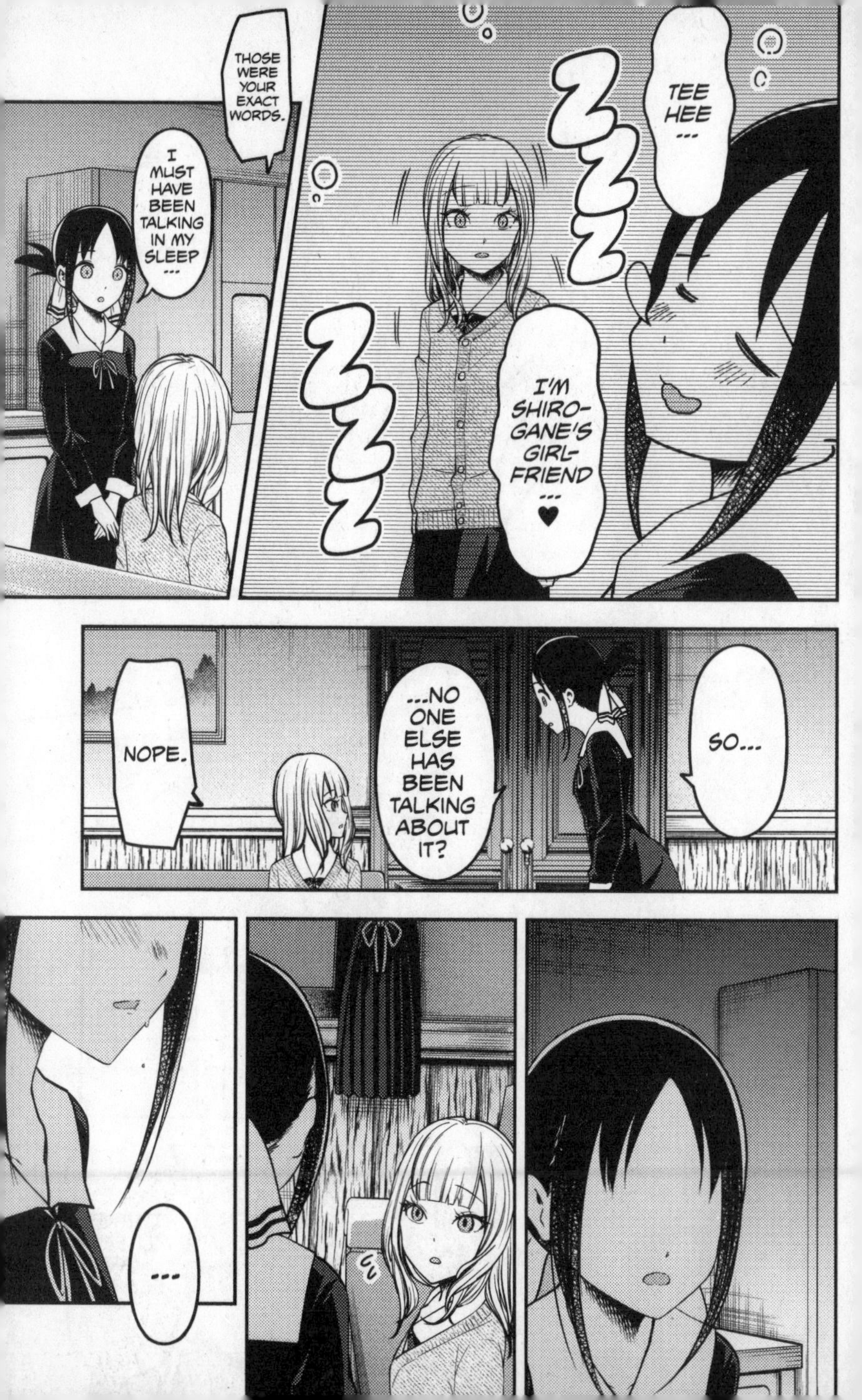
TEE HEE...
ZZZ
I'M SHIROGANE'S GIRLFRIEND... ♥
ZZZ
THOSE WERE YOUR EXACT WORDS.
I MUST HAVE BEEN TALKING IN MY SLEEP...
SO...
...NO ONE ELSE HAS BEEN TALKING ABOUT IT?
NOPE.
...

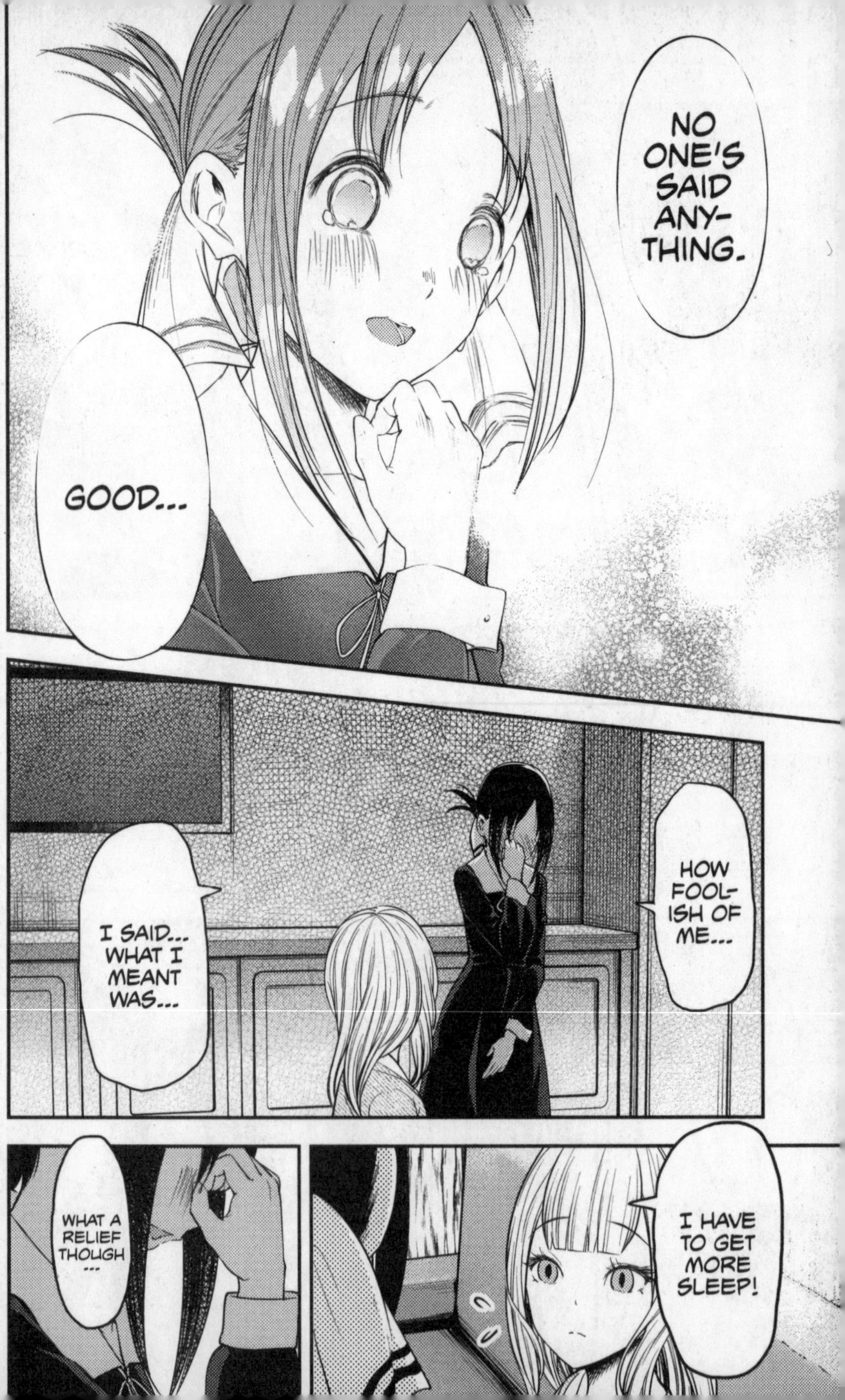
NO ONE'S SAID ANY-THING.
GOOD...
HOW FOOL-ISH OF ME...
I SAID... WHAT I MEANT WAS...
I HAVE TO GET MORE SLEEP!
WHAT A RELIEF THOUGH...

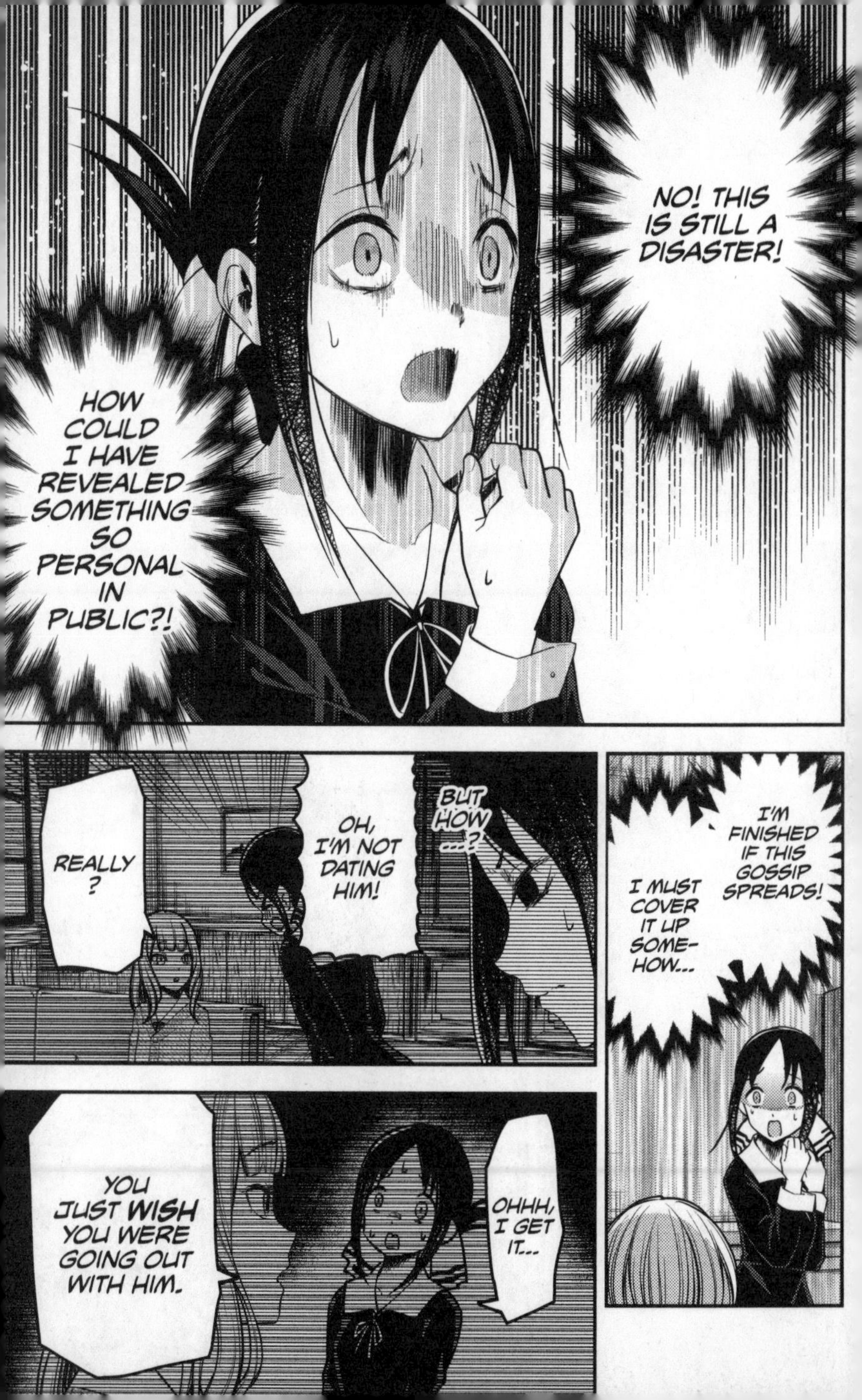
NO! THIS IS STILL A DISASTER!
HOW COULD I HAVE REVEALED SOMETHING SO PERSONAL IN PUBLIC?!
I'M FINISHED IF THIS GOSSIP SPREADS!
I MUST COVER IT UP SOME-HOW...
BUT HOW...?
OH, I'M NOT DATING HIM!
REALLY?
OHHH, I GET IT...
YOU JUST WISH YOU WERE GOING OUT WITH HIM.

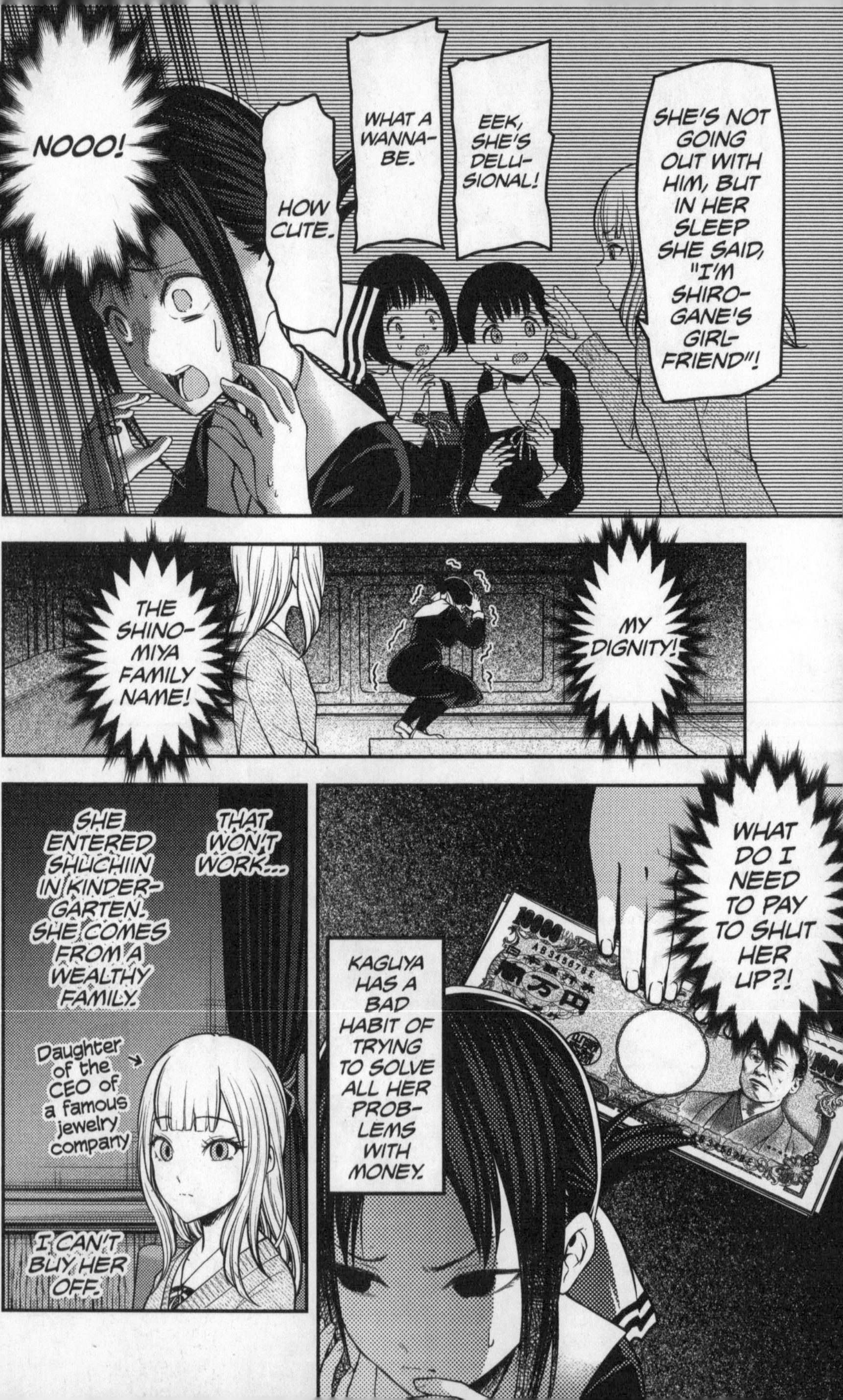

SHE'S NOT GOING OUT WITH HIM, BUT IN HER SLEEP SHE SAID, "I'M SHIROGANE'S GIRLFRIEND"!
EEK, SHE'S DELUSIONAL!
WHAT A WANNABE.
HOW CUTE.
NOOO!
MY DIGNITY!
THE SHINOMIYA FAMILY NAME!
WHAT DO I NEED TO PAY TO SHUT HER UP?!
KAGUYA HAS A BAD HABIT OF TRYING TO SOLVE ALL HER PROBLEMS WITH MONEY.
THAT WON'T WORK...
SHE ENTERED SHUCHIIN IN KINDERGARTEN. SHE COMES FROM A WEALTHY FAMILY.
Daughter of the CEO of a famous jewelry company
I CAN'T BUY HER OFF.

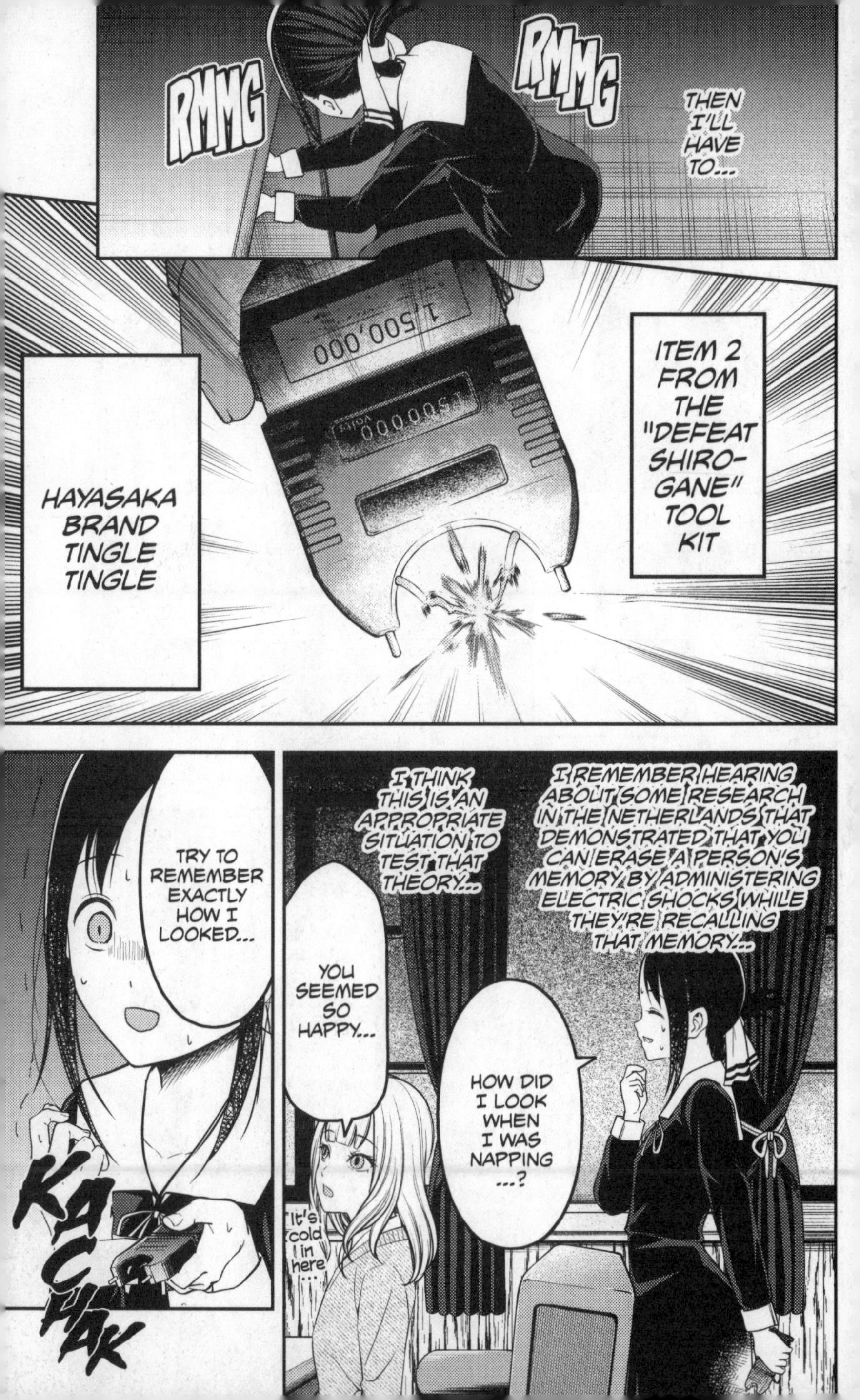
THEN I'LL HAVE TO...
RMMG
RMMG
ITEM 2 FROM THE "DEFEAT SHIRO-GANE" TOOL KIT
HAYASAKA BRAND TINGLE TINGLE
I REMEMBER HEARING ABOUT SOME RESEARCH IN THE NETHERLANDS THAT DEMONSTRATED THAT YOU CAN ERASE A PERSON'S MEMORY BY ADMINISTERING ELECTRIC SHOCKS WHILE THEY'RE RECALLING THAT MEMORY...
I THINK THIS IS AN APPROPRIATE SITUATION TO TEST THAT THEORY...
HOW DID I LOOK WHEN I WAS NAPPING ...?
YOU SEEMED SO HAPPY...
It's cold in here...
TRY TO REMEMBER EXACTLY HOW I LOOKED...
KACHAK

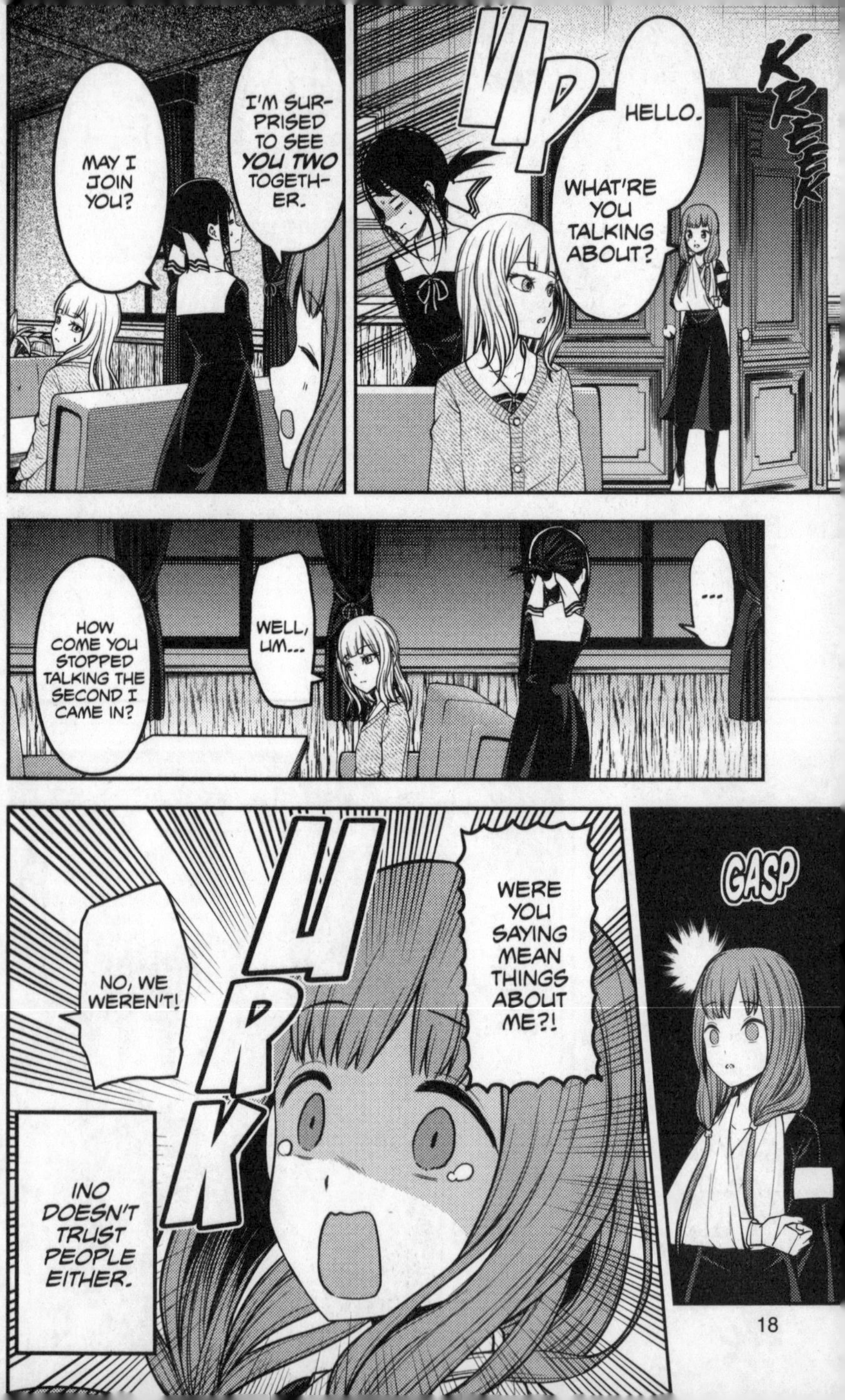
KREEK
HELLO.
WHAT'RE YOU TALKING ABOUT?
VIP
I'M SURPRISED TO SEE YOU TWO TOGETHER.
MAY I JOIN YOU?
...
WELL, UM...
HOW COME YOU STOPPED TALKING THE SECOND I CAME IN?
GASP
WERE YOU SAYING MEAN THINGS ABOUT ME?!
URK
NO, WE WEREN'T!
INO DOESN'T TRUST PEOPLE EITHER.

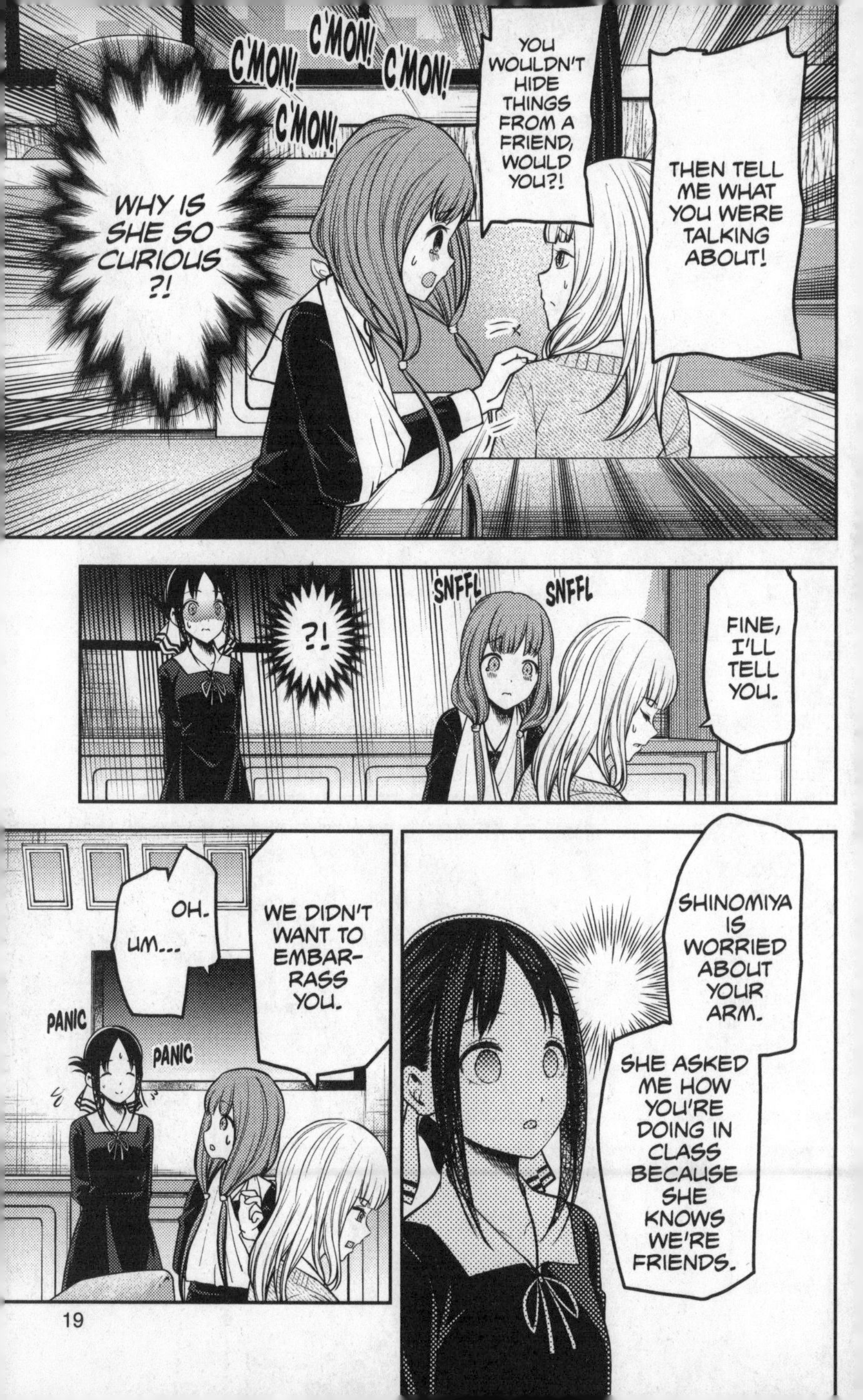
THEN TELL ME WHAT YOU WERE TALKING ABOUT!
YOU WOULDN'T HIDE THINGS FROM A FRIEND, WOULD YOU?!
C'MON! C'MON! C'MON! C'MON!
WHY IS SHE SO CURIOUS?!
FINE, I'LL TELL YOU.
SNFFL SNFFL
?!
SHINOMIYA IS WORRIED ABOUT YOUR ARM.
SHE ASKED ME HOW YOU'RE DOING IN CLASS BECAUSE SHE KNOWS WE'RE FRIENDS.
WE DIDN'T WANT TO EMBARRASS YOU.
OH. UM...
PANIC PANIC

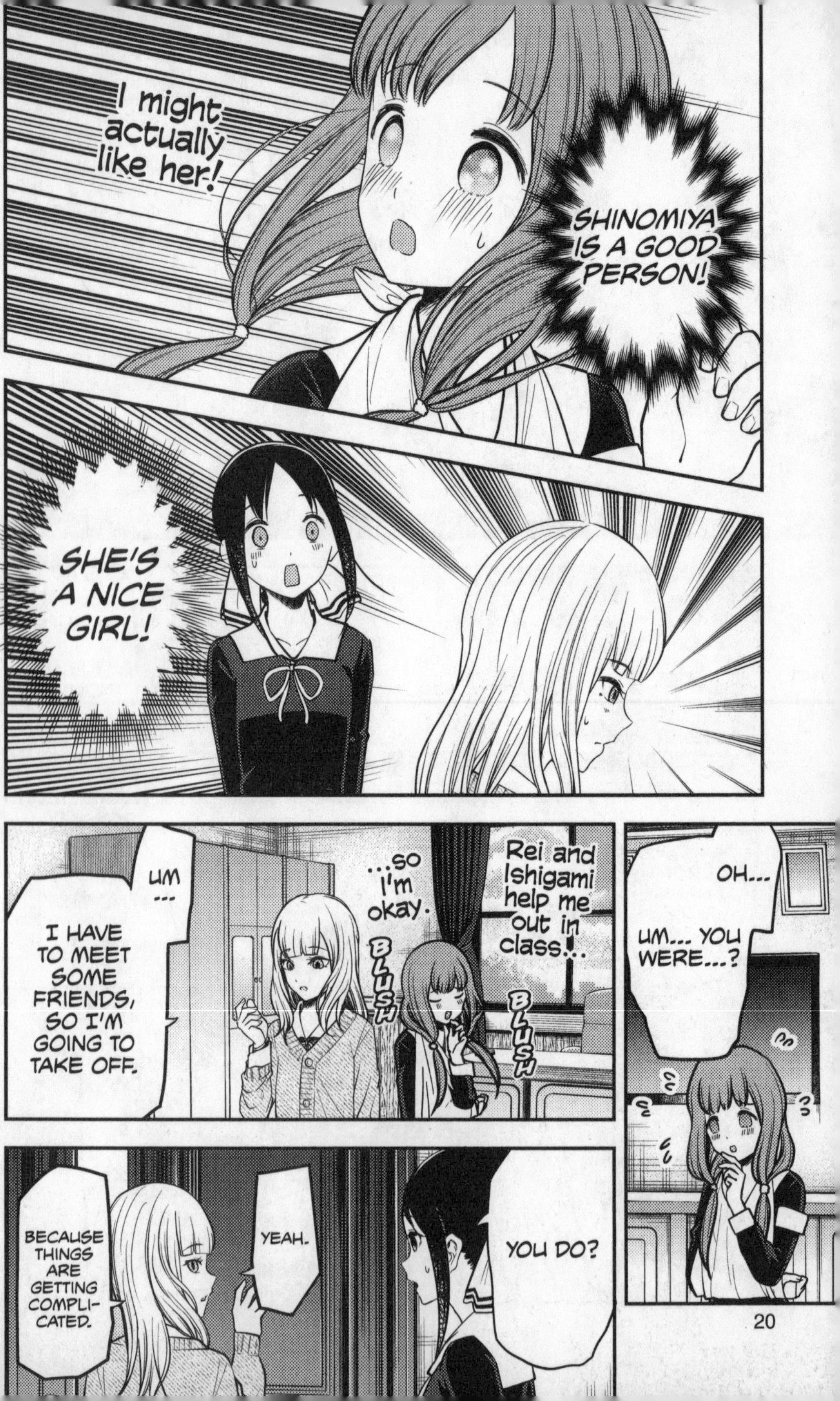
SHINOMIYA IS A GOOD PERSON!
I might actually like her!
SHE'S A NICE GIRL!
OH...
UM... YOU WERE...?
Rei and Ishigami help me out in class...
...so I'm okay.
BLUSH
BLUSH
um ---
I HAVE TO MEET SOME FRIENDS, SO I'M GOING TO TAKE OFF.
YOU DO?
YEAH.
BECAUSE THINGS ARE GETTING COMPLI-CATED.

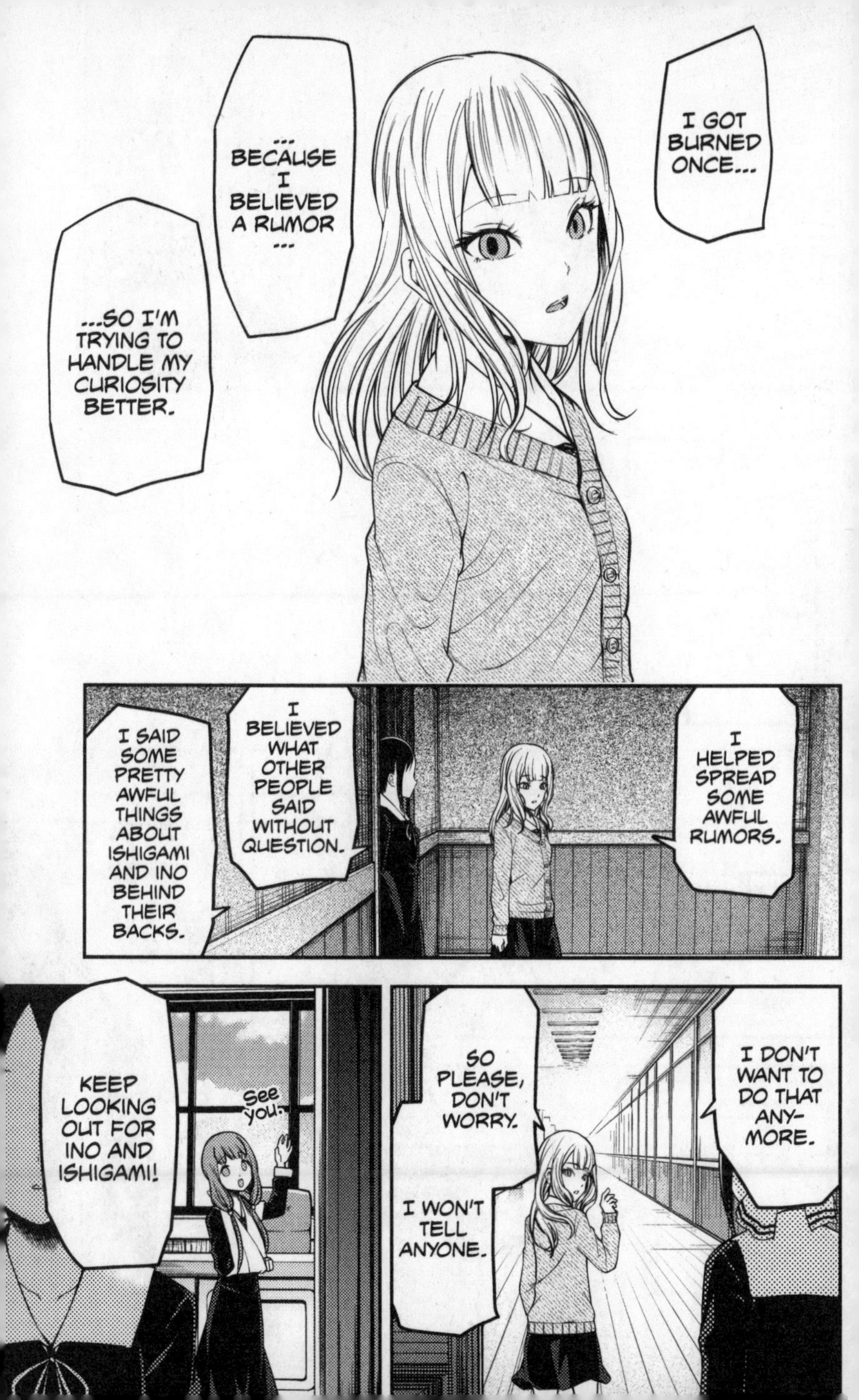
I GOT BURNED ONCE...
...BECAUSE I BELIEVED A RUMOR...
...SO I'M TRYING TO HANDLE MY CURIOSITY BETTER.
I HELPED SPREAD SOME AWFUL RUMORS.
I BELIEVED WHAT OTHER PEOPLE SAID WITHOUT QUESTION.
I SAID SOME PRETTY AWFUL THINGS ABOUT ISHIGAMI AND INO BEHIND THEIR BACKS.
I DON'T WANT TO DO THAT ANYMORE.
SO PLEASE, DON'T WORRY.
I WON'T TELL ANYONE.
KEEP LOOKING OUT FOR INO AND ISHIGAMI!
See you.

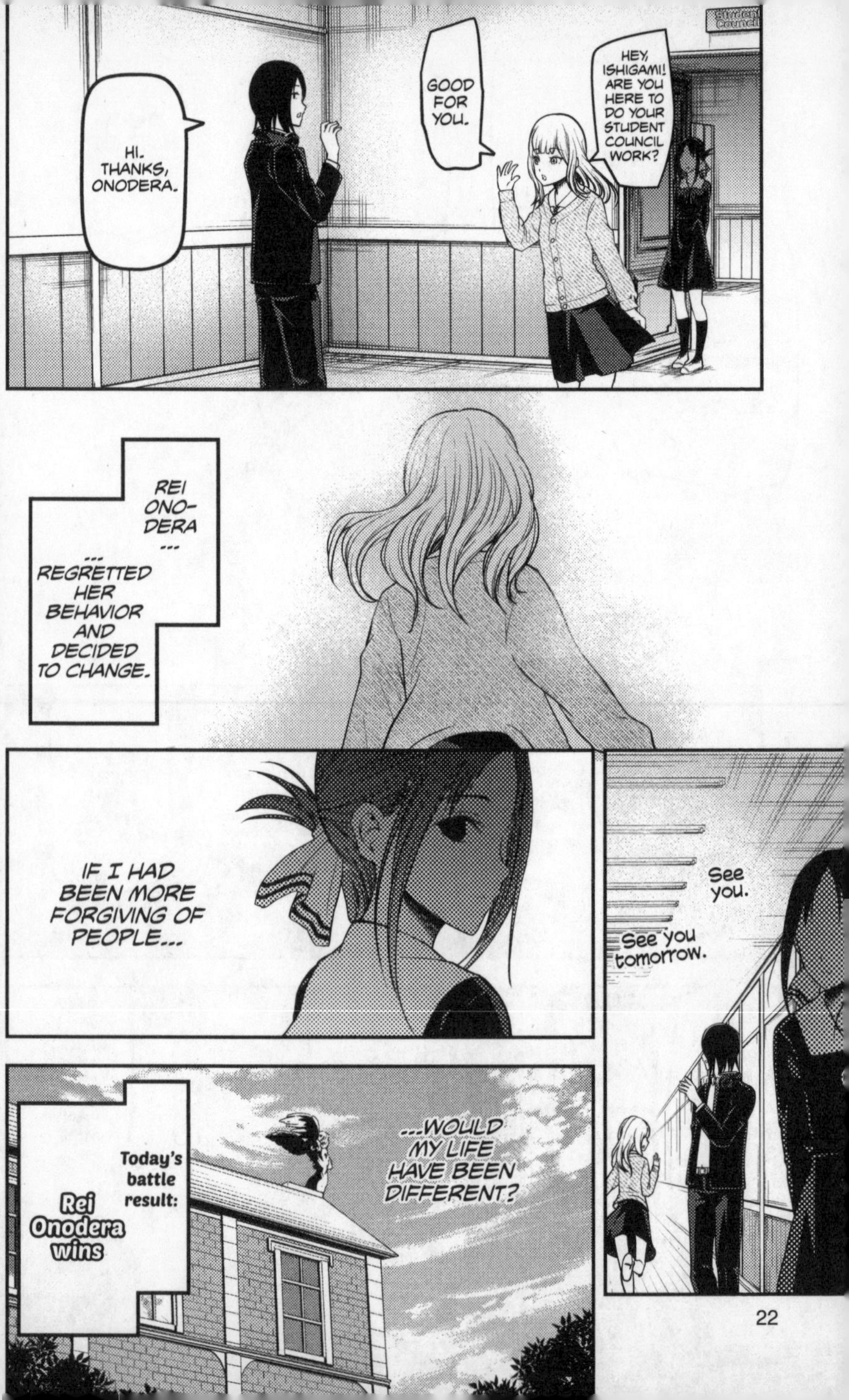
Student Council
HEY, ISHIGAMI! ARE YOU HERE TO DO YOUR STUDENT COUNCIL WORK?
GOOD FOR YOU.
HI. THANKS, ONODERA.
REI ONODERA ...
...REGRETTED HER BEHAVIOR AND DECIDED TO CHANGE.
See you.
See you tomorrow.
IF I HAD BEEN MORE FORGIVING OF PEOPLE...
...WOULD MY LIFE HAVE BEEN DIFFERENT?
Today's battle result:
Rei Onodera wins

Kaguya's Friendship Test

Maki Shijo: Pass
Chika Fujiwara: Pass
Nagisa Kashiwagi: Pass
Yu Ishigami: Pass, judging from his behavior
Miko Ino: Not tested yet
Miyuki Shirogane: Not tested yet
Ai Hayasaka: Not tested yet

KAGUYA-SAMA

LOVE IS WAR

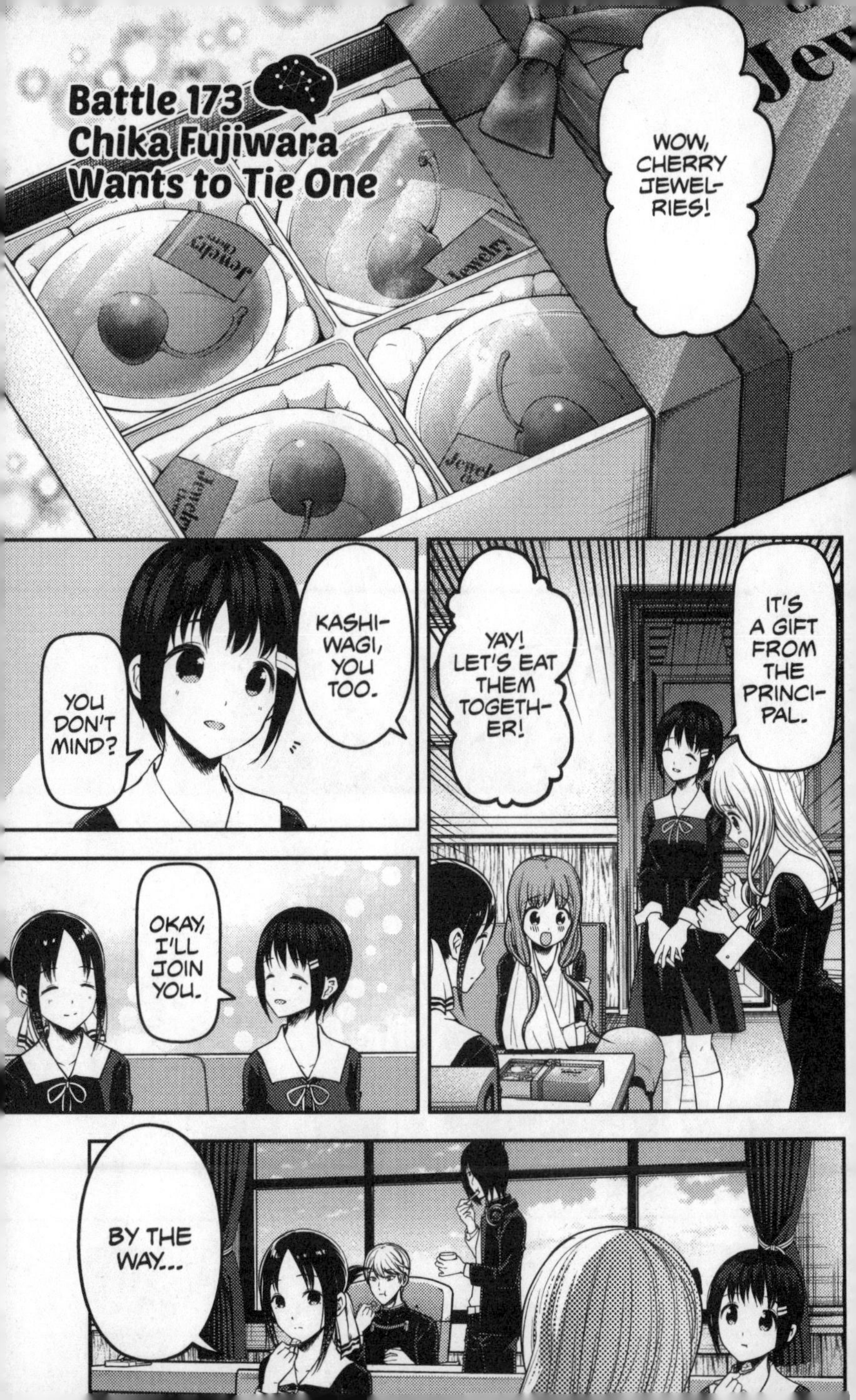
WOW, CHERRY JEWEL-RIES!
Battle 173 Chika Fujiwara Wants to Tie One
IT'S A GIFT FROM THE PRINCI-PAL.
YAY! LET'S EAT THEM TOGETH-ER!
KASHI-WAGI, YOU TOO.
YOU DON'T MIND?
OKAY, I'LL JOIN YOU.
BY THE WAY...

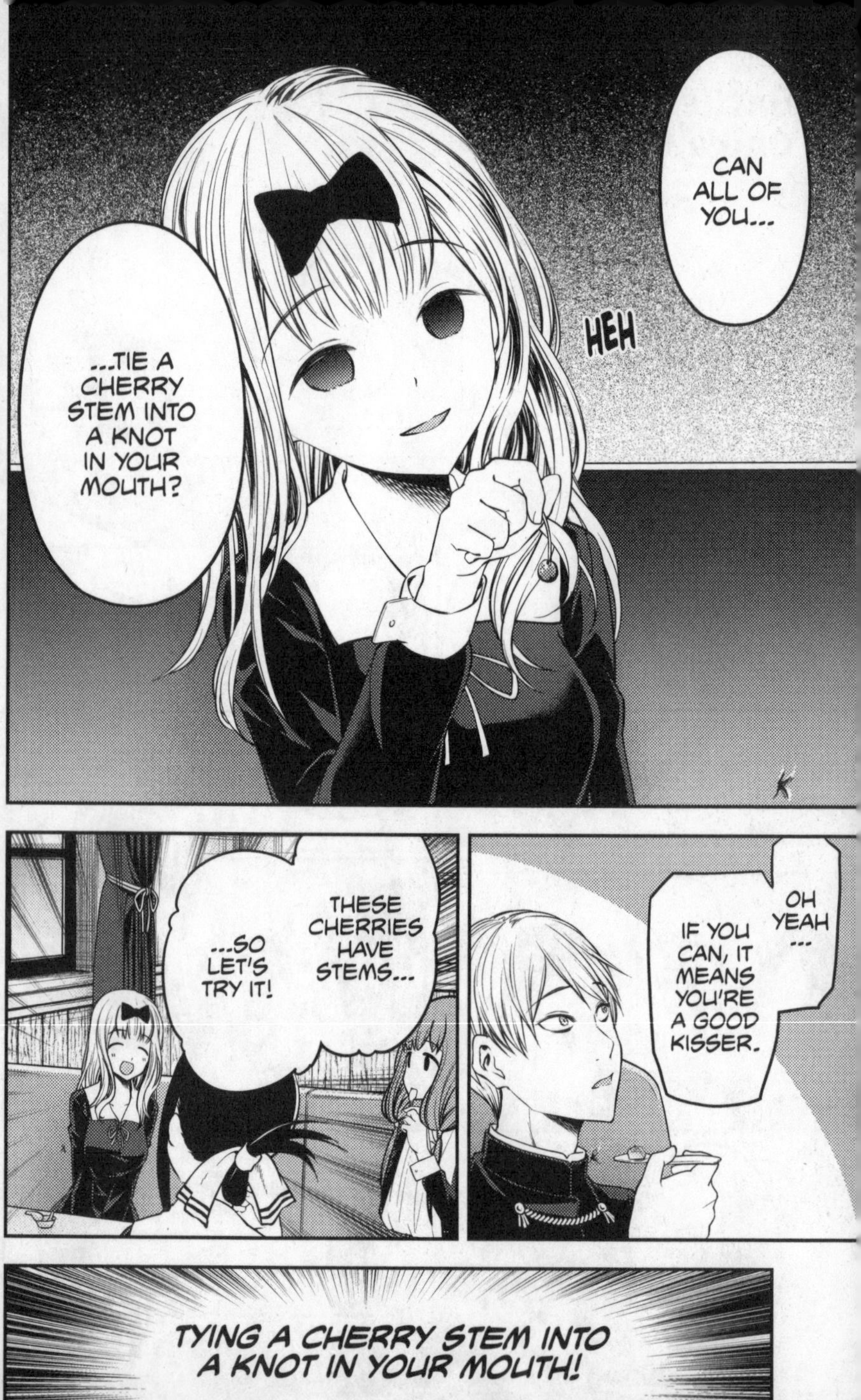
CAN ALL OF YOU...
HEH
...TIE A CHERRY STEM INTO A KNOT IN YOUR MOUTH?
OH YEAH...
IF YOU CAN, IT MEANS YOU'RE A GOOD KISSER.
THESE CHERRIES HAVE STEMS...
...SO LET'S TRY IT!
TYING A CHERRY STEM INTO A KNOT IN YOUR MOUTH!

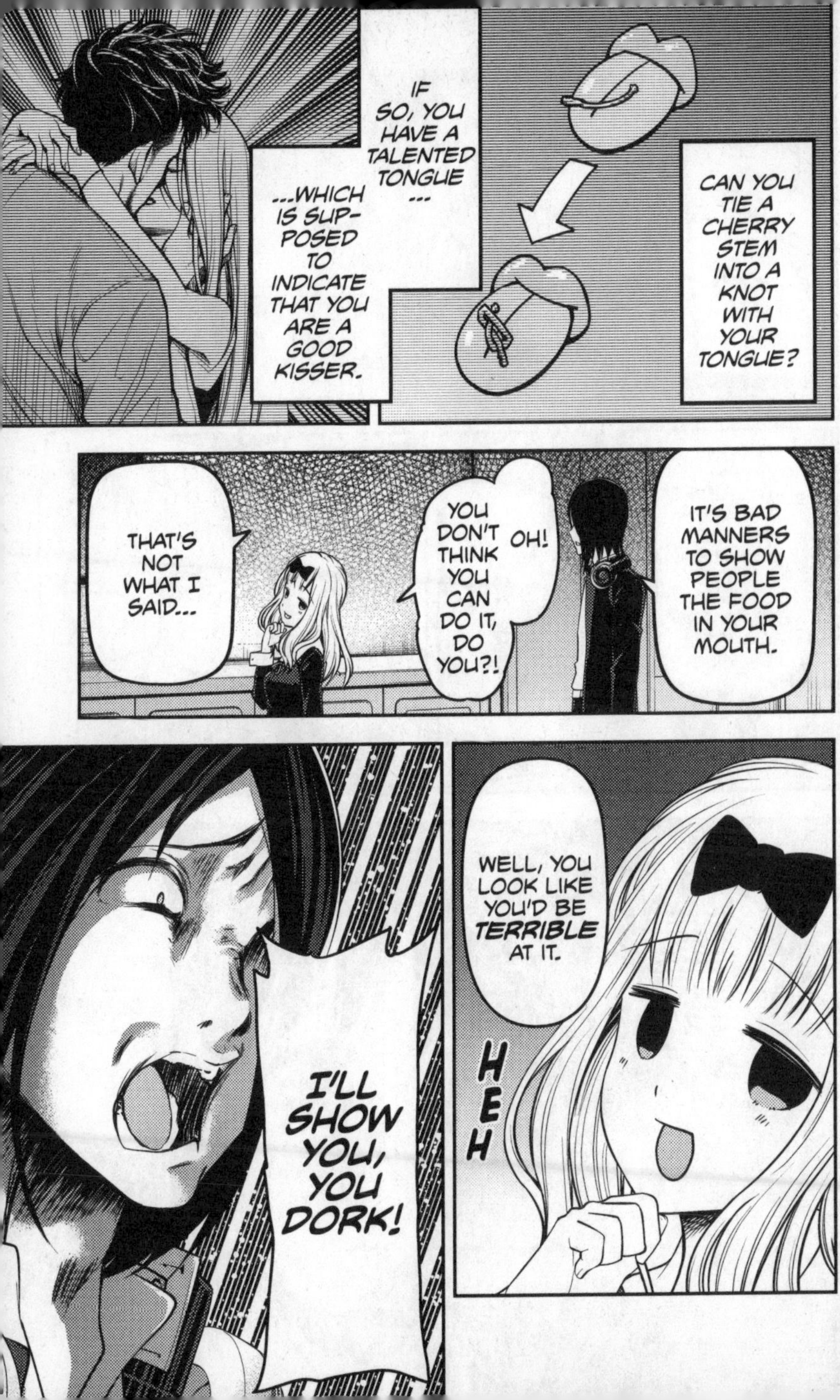
CAN YOU TIE A CHERRY STEM INTO A KNOT WITH YOUR TONGUE?
IF SO, YOU HAVE A TALENTED TONGUE ...
...WHICH IS SUP-POSED TO INDICATE THAT YOU ARE A GOOD KISSER.
IT'S BAD MANNERS TO SHOW PEOPLE THE FOOD IN YOUR MOUTH.
OH!
YOU DON'T THINK YOU CAN DO IT, DO YOU?!
THAT'S NOT WHAT I SAID...
WELL, YOU LOOK LIKE YOU'D BE TERRIBLE AT IT.
HEH
I'LL SHOW YOU, YOU DORK!

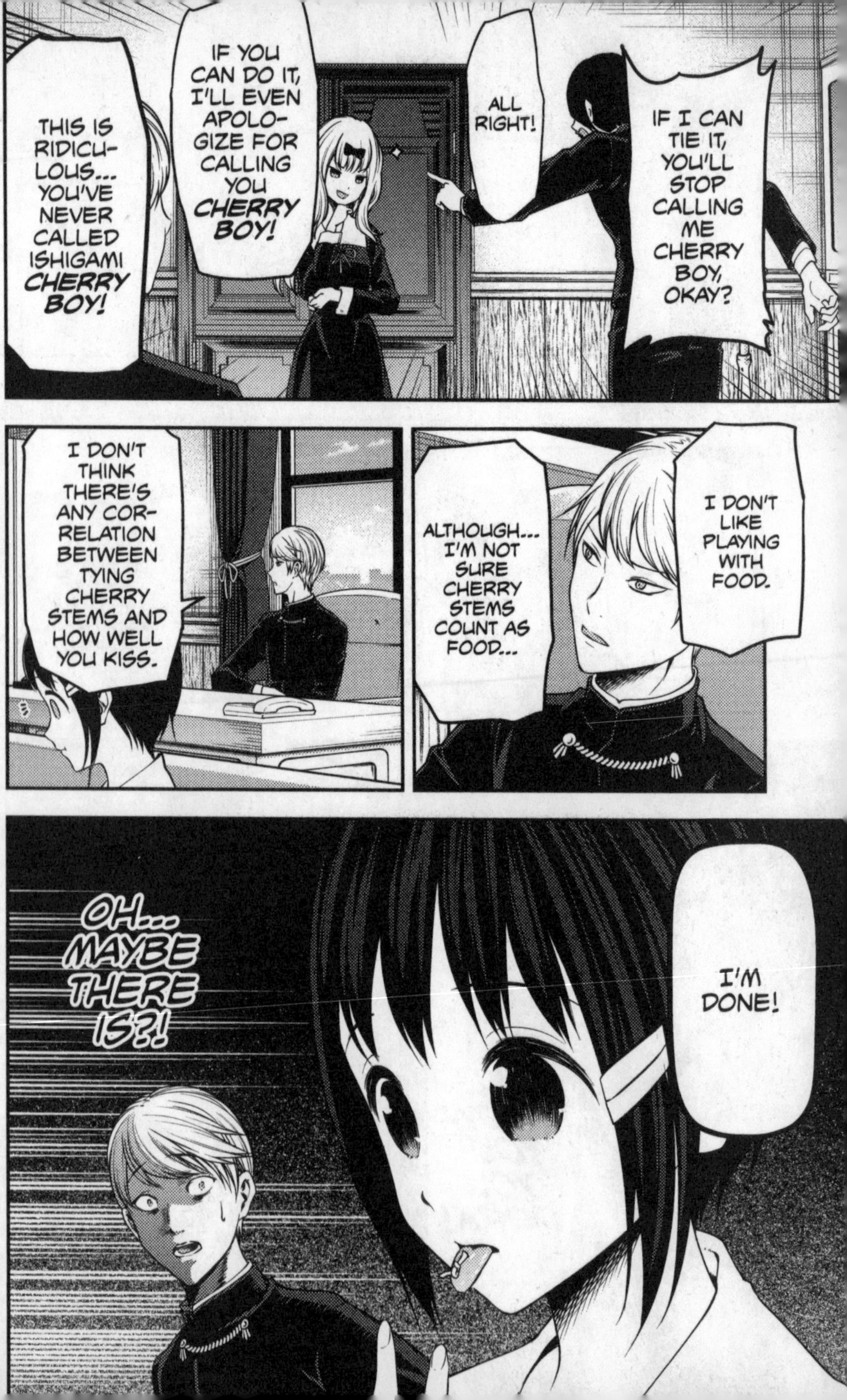
IF I CAN TIE IT, YOU'LL STOP CALLING ME CHERRY BOY, OKAY?
ALL RIGHT!
IF YOU CAN DO IT, I'LL EVEN APOLOGIZE FOR CALLING YOU *CHERRY BOY!*
THIS IS RIDICULOUS... YOU'VE NEVER CALLED ISHIGAMI *CHERRY BOY!*
I DON'T LIKE PLAYING WITH FOOD.
ALTHOUGH... I'M NOT SURE CHERRY STEMS COUNT AS FOOD...
I DON'T THINK THERE'S ANY CORRELATION BETWEEN TYING CHERRY STEMS AND HOW WELL YOU KISS.
I'M DONE!
OH... MAYBE THERE IS?!

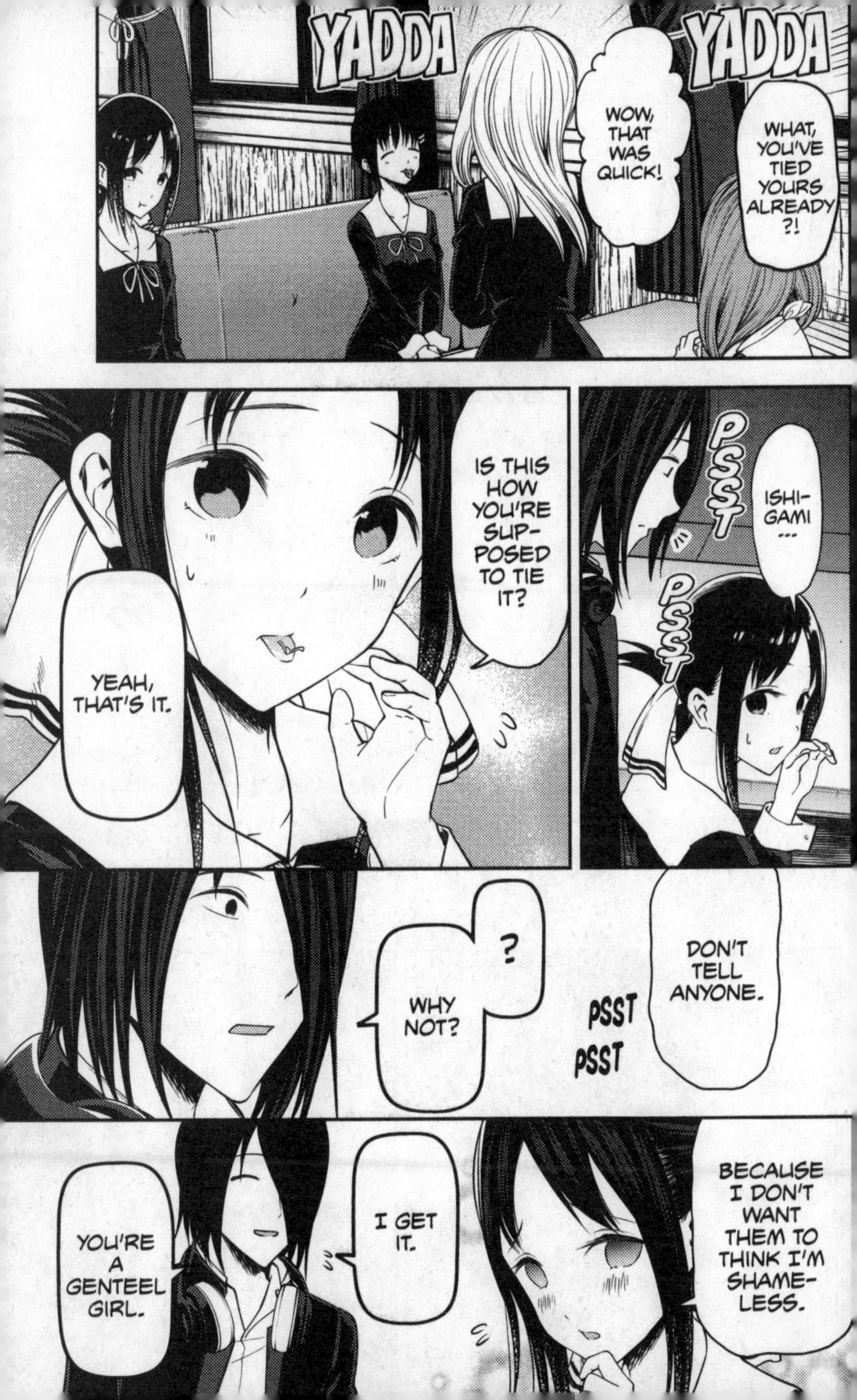
YADDA YADDA
WHAT, YOU'VE TIED YOURS ALREADY?!
WOW, THAT WAS QUICK!
PSST
ISHI-GAMI...
PSST
IS THIS HOW YOU'RE SUP-POSED TO TIE IT?
YEAH, THAT'S IT.
DON'T TELL ANYONE.
PSST
PSST
?
WHY NOT?
BECAUSE I DON'T WANT THEM TO THINK I'M SHAME-LESS.
I GET IT.
YOU'RE A GENTEEL GIRL.

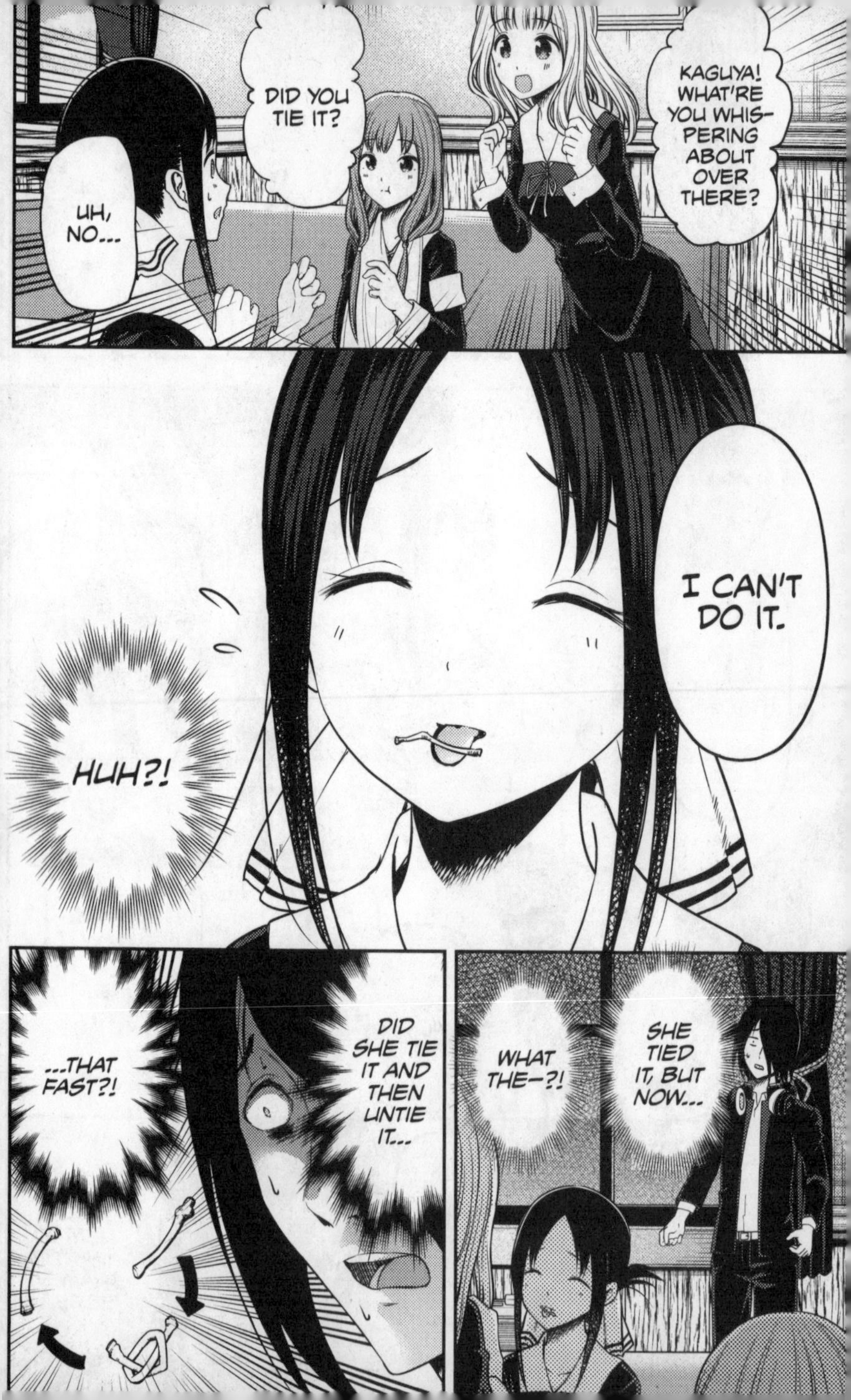
KAGUYA! WHAT'RE YOU WHISPERING ABOUT OVER THERE?
DID YOU TIE IT?
UH, NO...
I CAN'T DO IT.
HUH?!
SHE TIED IT, BUT NOW...
WHAT THE—?!
DID SHE TIE IT AND THEN UNTIE IT...
...THAT FAST?!

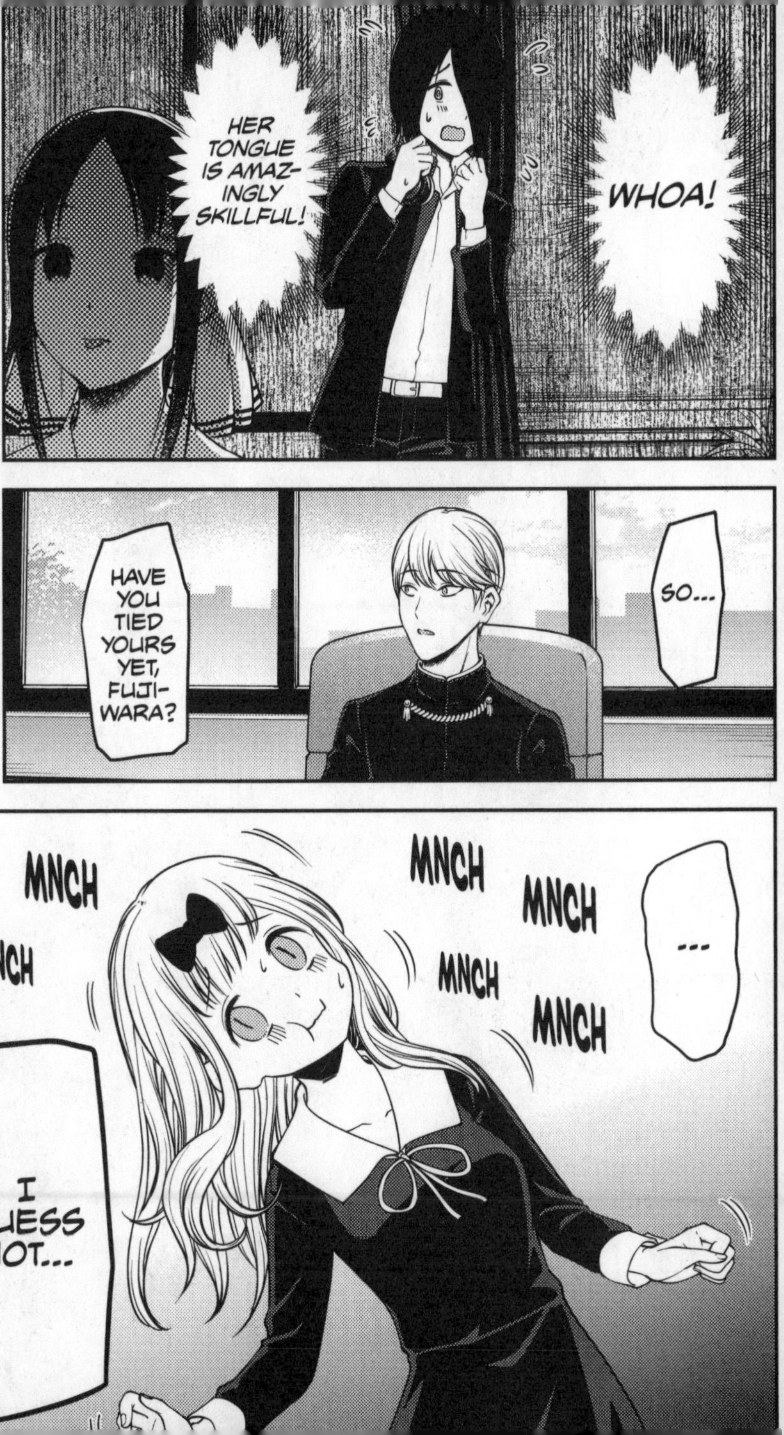
WHOA!
HER TONGUE IS AMAZINGLY SKILLFUL!
SO...
HAVE YOU TIED YOURS YET, FUJIWARA?
...
MNCH
MNCH
MNCH
MNCH
MNCH
MNCH
I GUESS NOT...

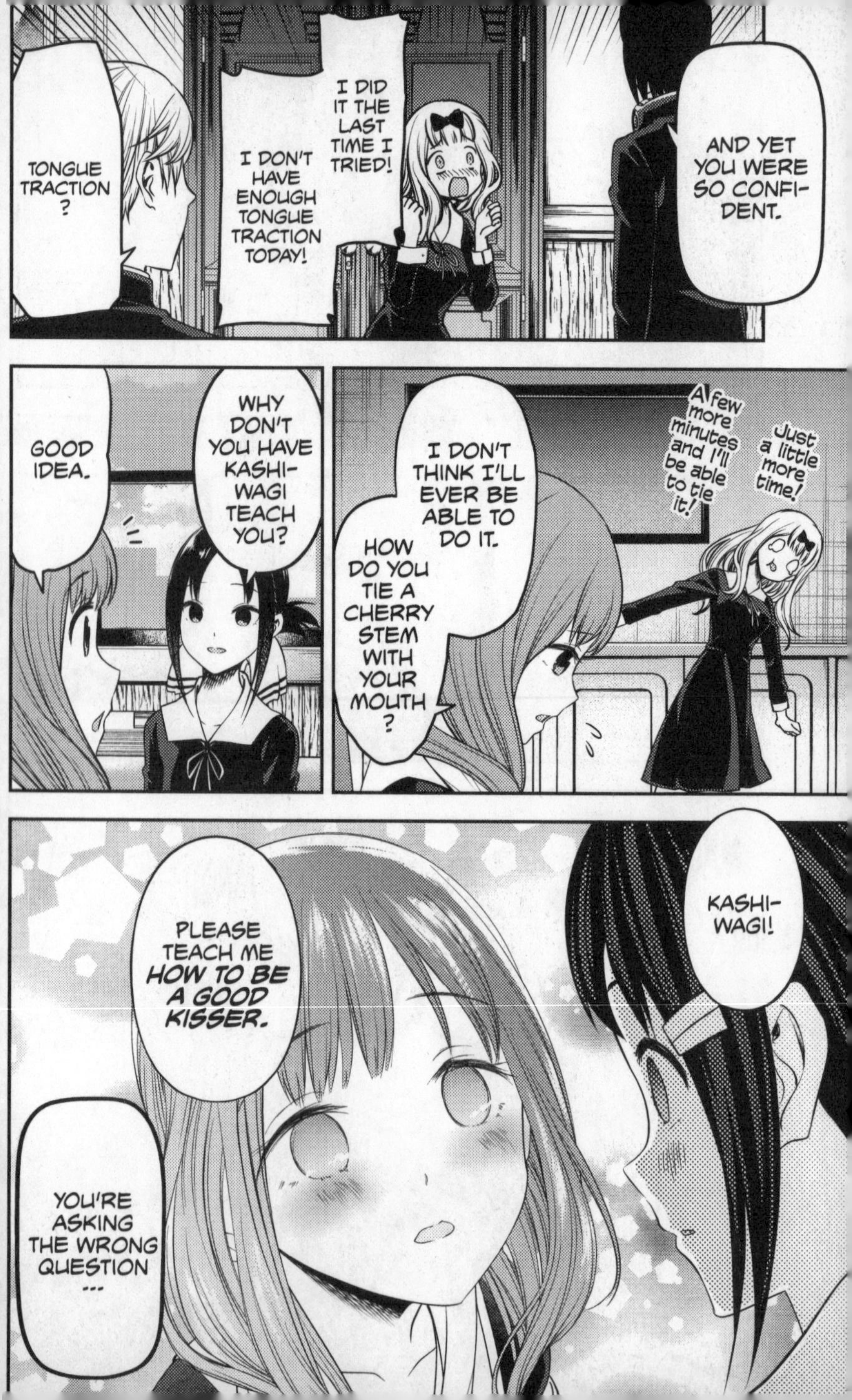
AND YET YOU WERE SO CONFIDENT.
I DID IT THE LAST TIME I TRIED!
I DON'T HAVE ENOUGH TONGUE TRACTION TODAY!
TONGUE TRACTION?
Just a little more time!
A few more minutes and I'll be able to tie it!
I DON'T THINK I'LL EVER BE ABLE TO DO IT.
HOW DO YOU TIE A CHERRY STEM WITH YOUR MOUTH?
WHY DON'T YOU HAVE KASHIWAGI TEACH YOU?
GOOD IDEA.
KASHIWAGI!
PLEASE TEACH ME *HOW TO BE A GOOD KISSER.*
YOU'RE ASKING THE WRONG QUESTION...

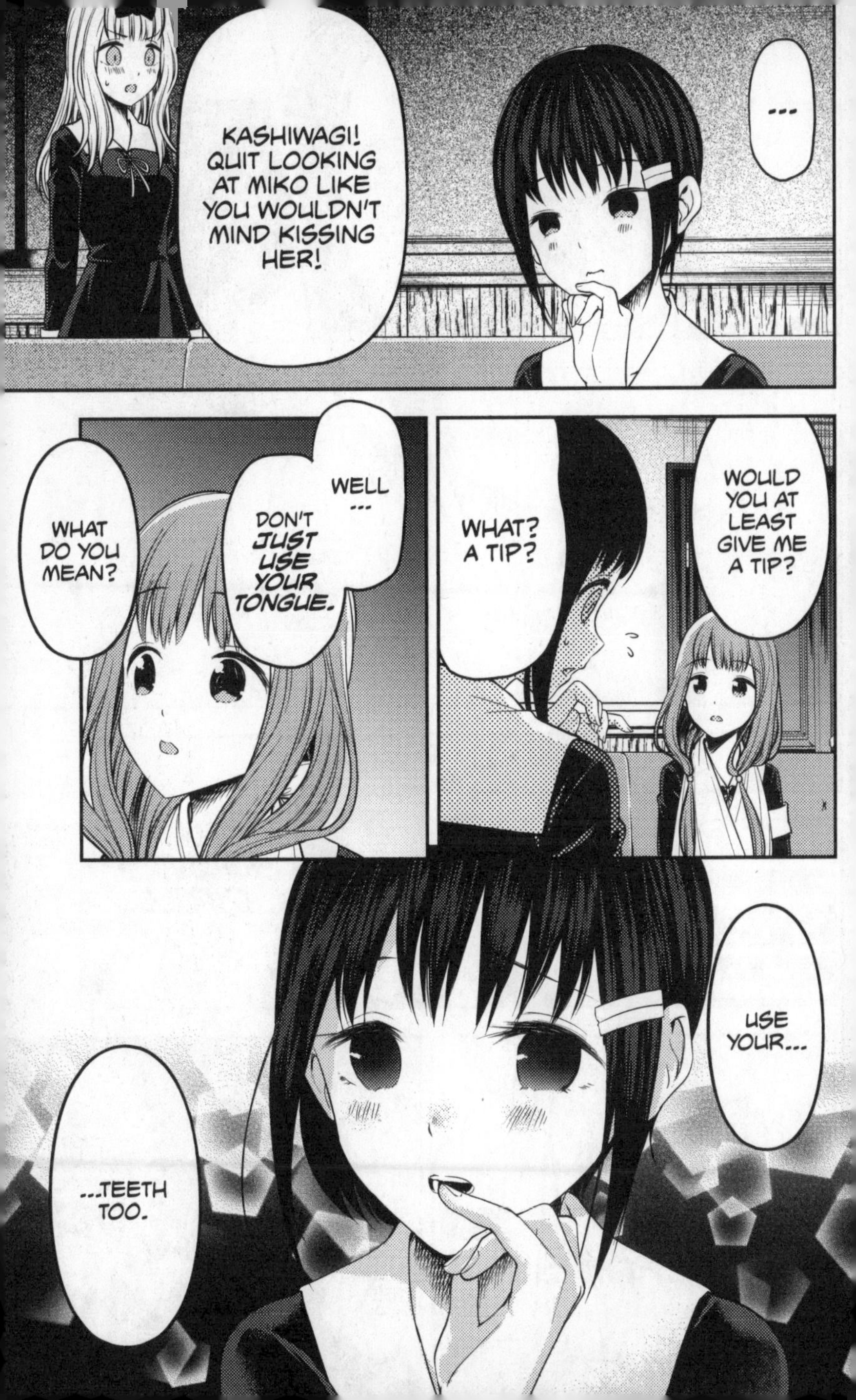
...
KASHIWAGI! QUIT LOOKING AT MIKO LIKE YOU WOULDN'T MIND KISSING HER!
WOULD YOU AT LEAST GIVE ME A TIP?
WHAT? A TIP?
WELL...
DON'T JUST USE YOUR TONGUE.
WHAT DO YOU MEAN?
USE YOUR...
...TEETH TOO.

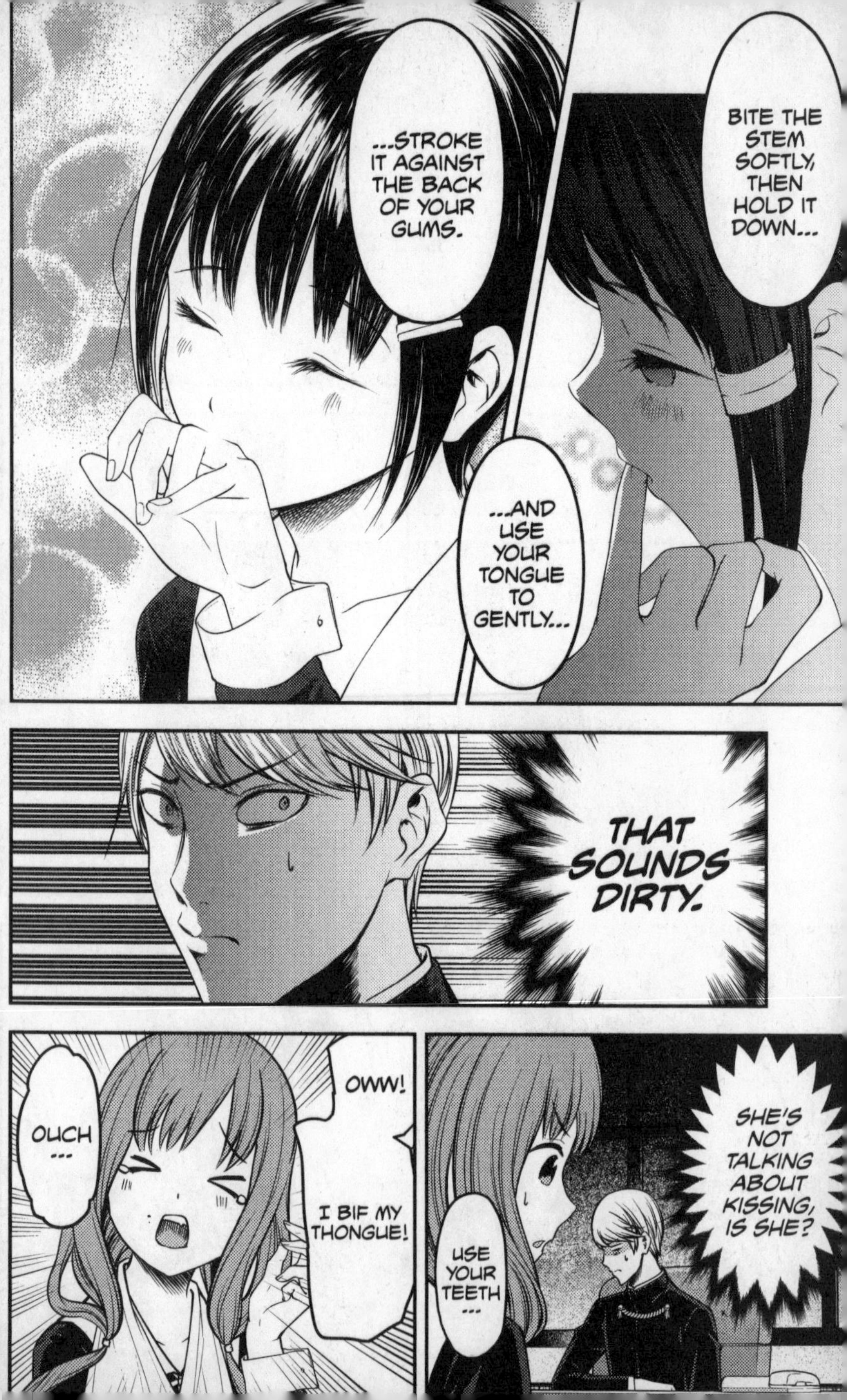
BITE THE STEM SOFTLY, THEN HOLD IT DOWN...
...AND USE YOUR TONGUE TO GENTLY...
...STROKE IT AGAINST THE BACK OF YOUR GUMS.
THAT SOUNDS DIRTY.
SHE'S NOT TALKING ABOUT KISSING, IS SHE?
USE YOUR TEETH...
OWW!
I BIF MY THONGUE!
OUCH...

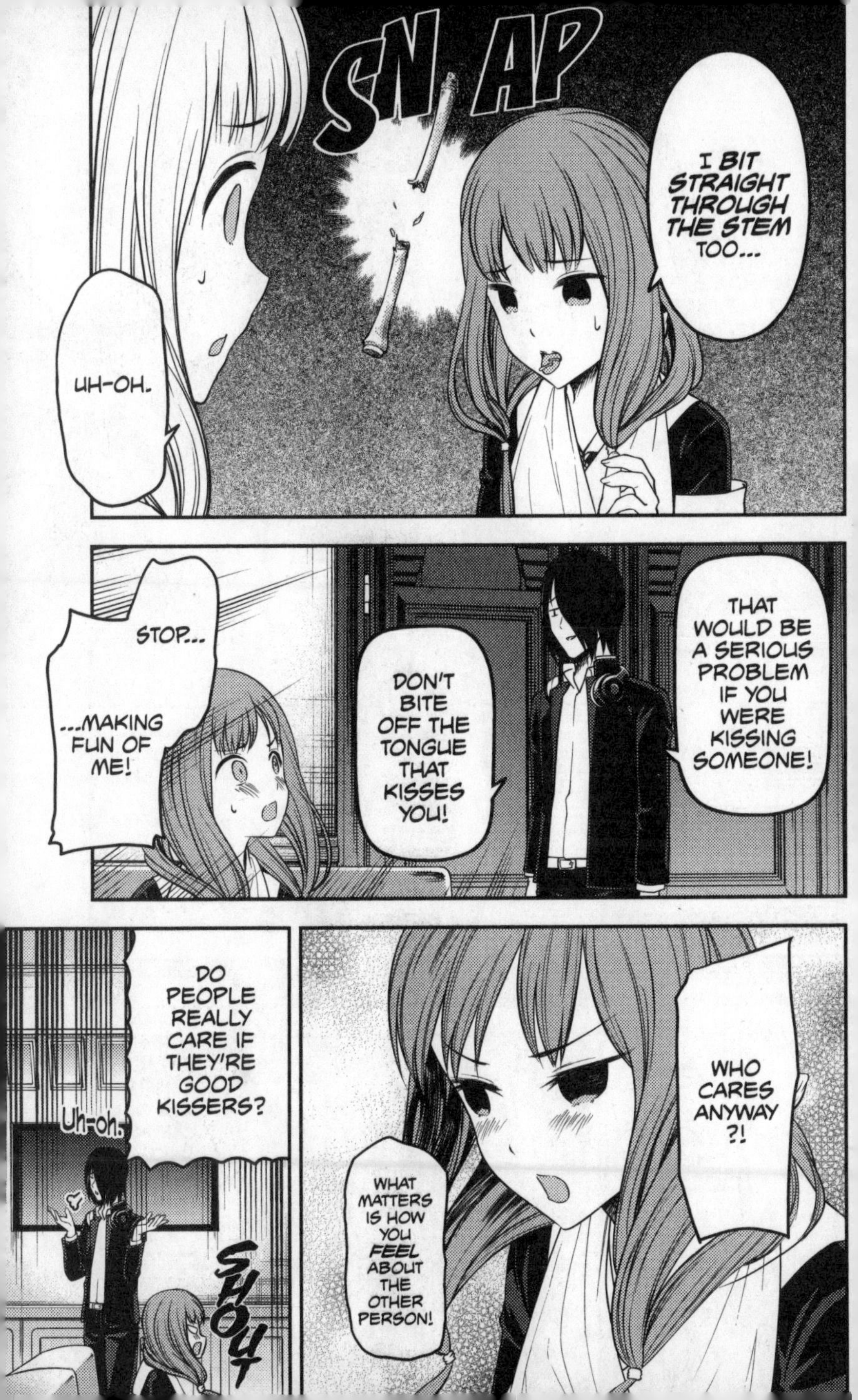
SNAP
I BIT STRAIGHT THROUGH THE STEM TOO...
UH-OH.
THAT WOULD BE A SERIOUS PROBLEM IF YOU WERE KISSING SOMEONE!
DON'T BITE OFF THE TONGUE THAT KISSES YOU!
STOP...
...MAKING FUN OF ME!
WHO CARES ANYWAY ?!
WHAT MATTERS IS HOW YOU FEEL ABOUT THE OTHER PERSON!
DO PEOPLE REALLY CARE IF THEY'RE GOOD KISSERS?
Uh-oh.
SHOUT

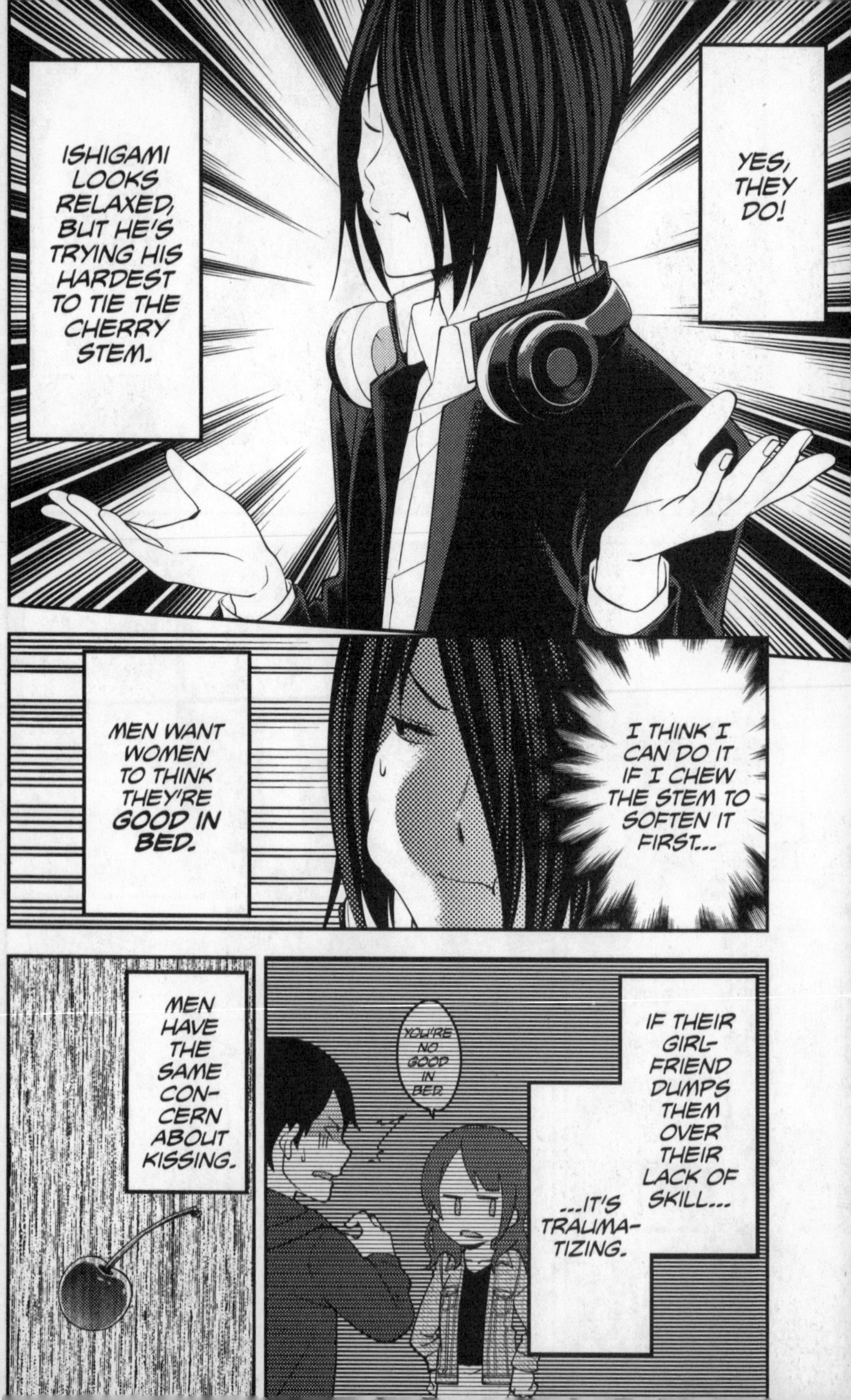
YES, THEY DO!
ISHIGAMI LOOKS RELAXED, BUT HE'S TRYING HIS HARDEST TO TIE THE CHERRY STEM.
I THINK I CAN DO IT IF I CHEW THE STEM TO SOFTEN IT FIRST...
MEN WANT WOMEN TO THINK THEY'RE GOOD IN BED.
IF THEIR GIRL-FRIEND DUMPS THEM OVER THEIR LACK OF SKILL...
YOU'RE NO GOOD IN BED.
...IT'S TRAUMA-TIZING.
MEN HAVE THE SAME CON-CERN ABOUT KISSING.

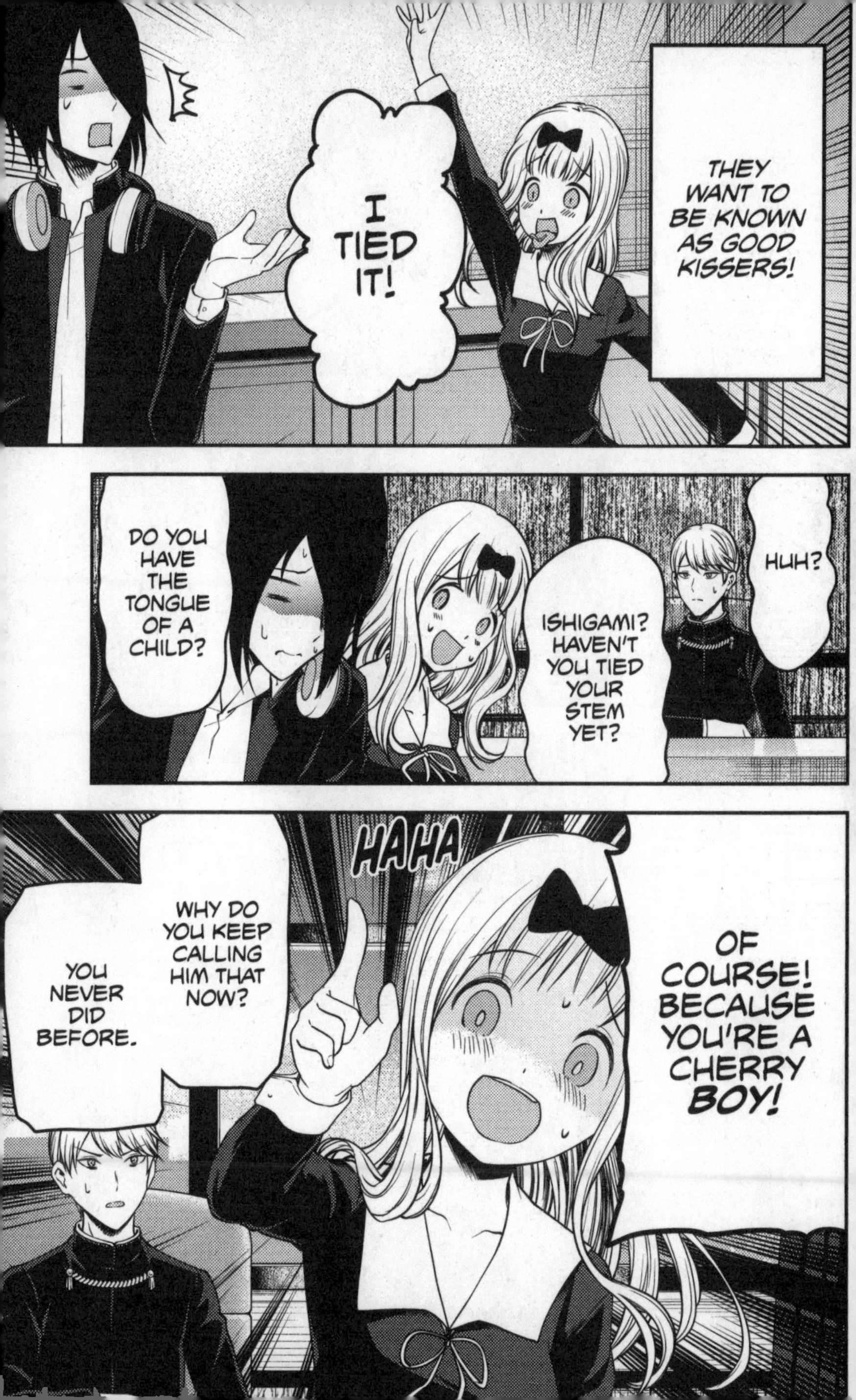
THEY WANT TO BE KNOWN AS GOOD KISSERS!
I TIED IT!
HUH?
ISHIGAMI? HAVEN'T YOU TIED YOUR STEM YET?
DO YOU HAVE THE TONGUE OF A CHILD?
HAHA
OF COURSE! BECAUSE YOU'RE A CHERRY BOY!
WHY DO YOU KEEP CALLING HIM THAT NOW?
YOU NEVER DID BEFORE.

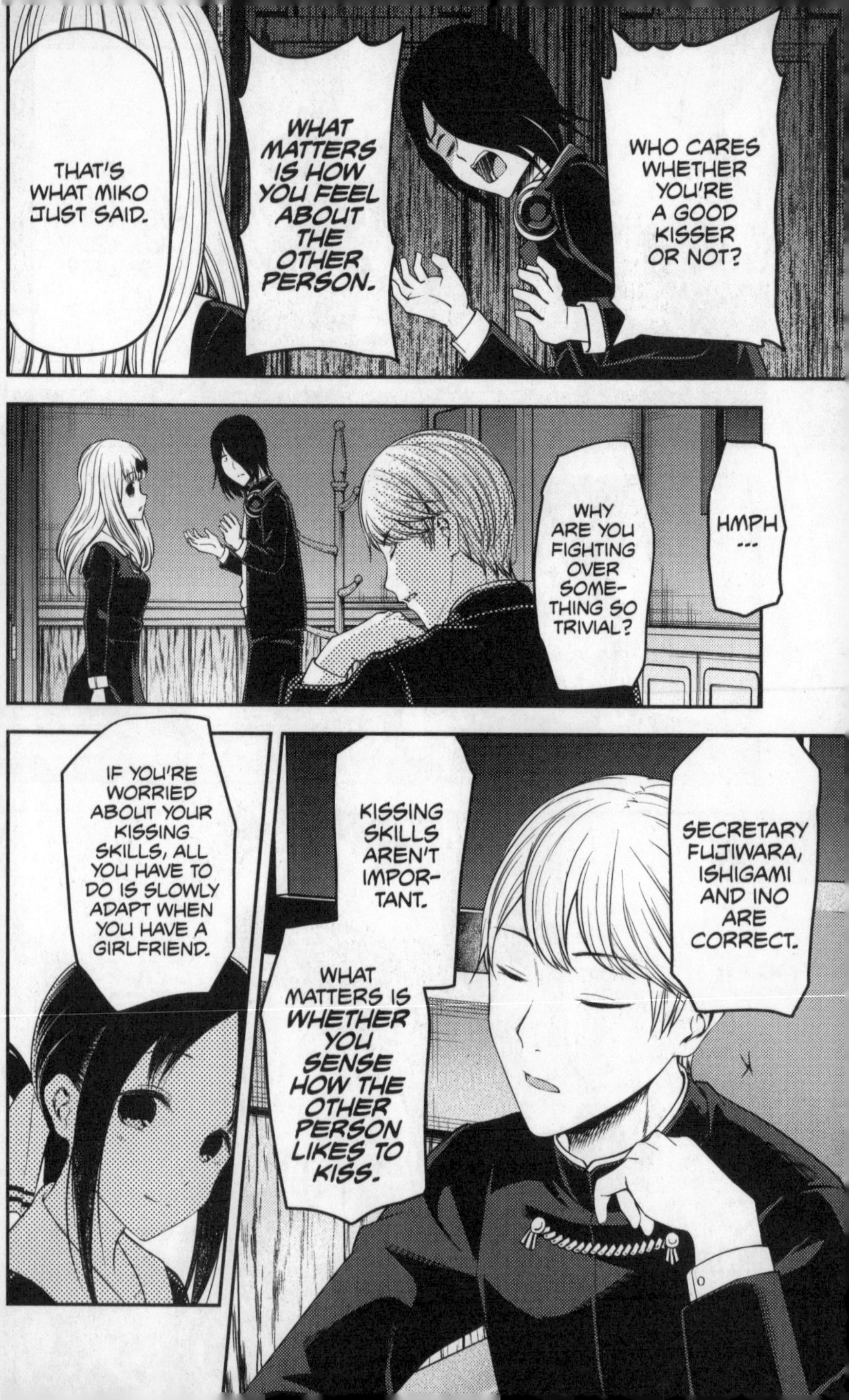
WHO CARES WHETHER YOU'RE A GOOD KISSER OR NOT?
WHAT MATTERS IS HOW YOU FEEL ABOUT THE OTHER PERSON.
THAT'S WHAT MIKO JUST SAID.
HMPH ---
WHY ARE YOU FIGHTING OVER SOME-THING SO TRIVIAL?
SECRETARY FUJIWARA, ISHIGAMI AND INO ARE CORRECT.
KISSING SKILLS AREN'T IMPOR-TANT.
WHAT MATTERS IS WHETHER YOU SENSE HOW THE OTHER PERSON LIKES TO KISS.
IF YOU'RE WORRIED ABOUT YOUR KISSING SKILLS, ALL YOU HAVE TO DO IS SLOWLY ADAPT WHEN YOU HAVE A GIRLFRIEND.

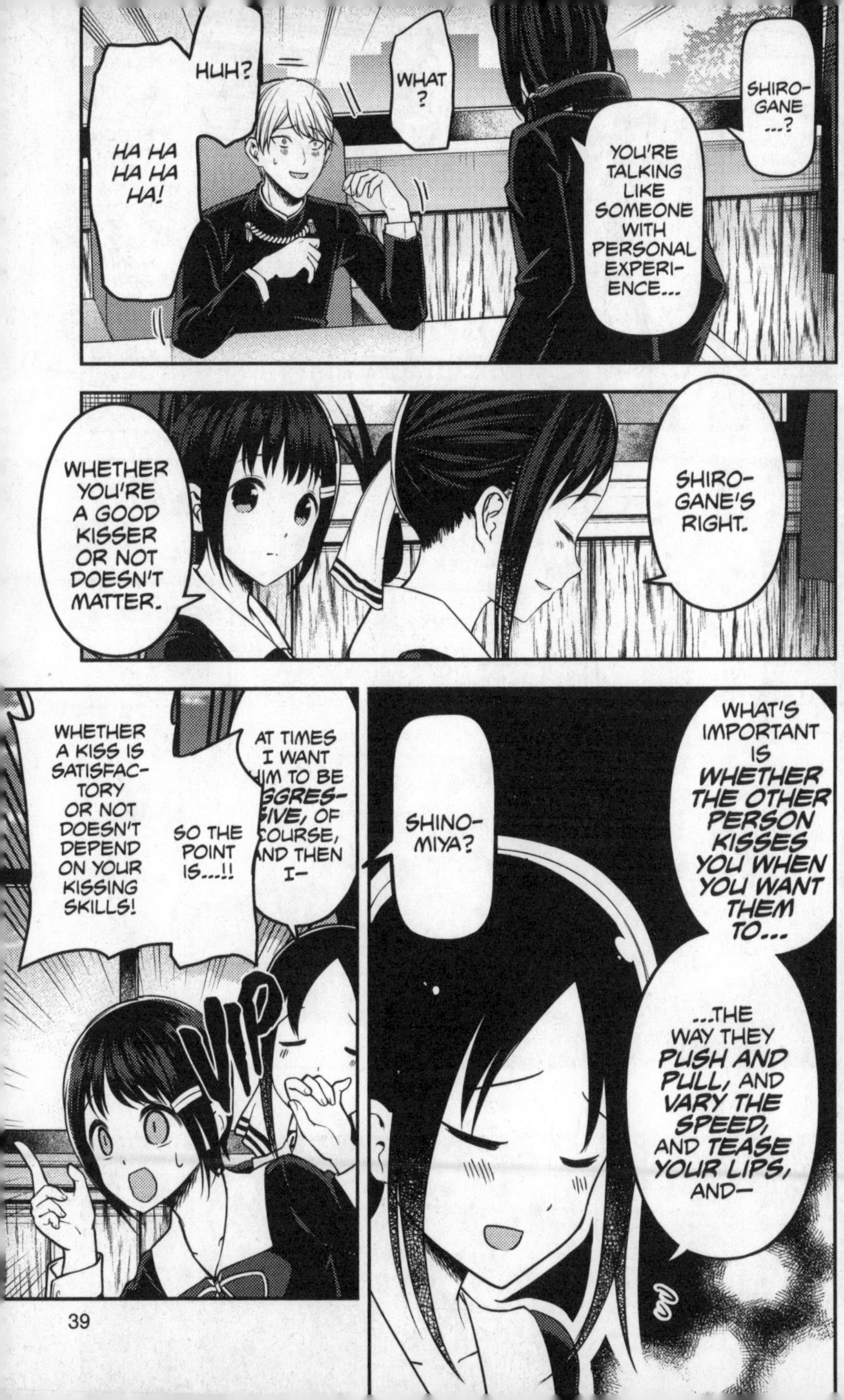
SHIRO-GANE ...?
YOU'RE TALKING LIKE SOMEONE WITH PERSONAL EXPERI-ENCE...
WHAT ?
HUH?
HA HA HA HA HA!
SHIRO-GANE'S RIGHT.
WHETHER YOU'RE A GOOD KISSER OR NOT DOESN'T MATTER.
WHAT'S IMPORTANT IS WHETHER THE OTHER PERSON KISSES YOU WHEN YOU WANT THEM TO...
...THE WAY THEY PUSH AND PULL, AND VARY THE SPEED, AND TEASE YOUR LIPS, AND—
SHINO-MIYA?
AT TIMES I WANT IM TO BE GGRES-IVE, OF COURSE, ND THEN I—
SO THE POINT IS...!!
WHETHER A KISS IS SATISFAC-TORY OR NOT DOESN'T DEPEND ON YOUR KISSING SKILLS!

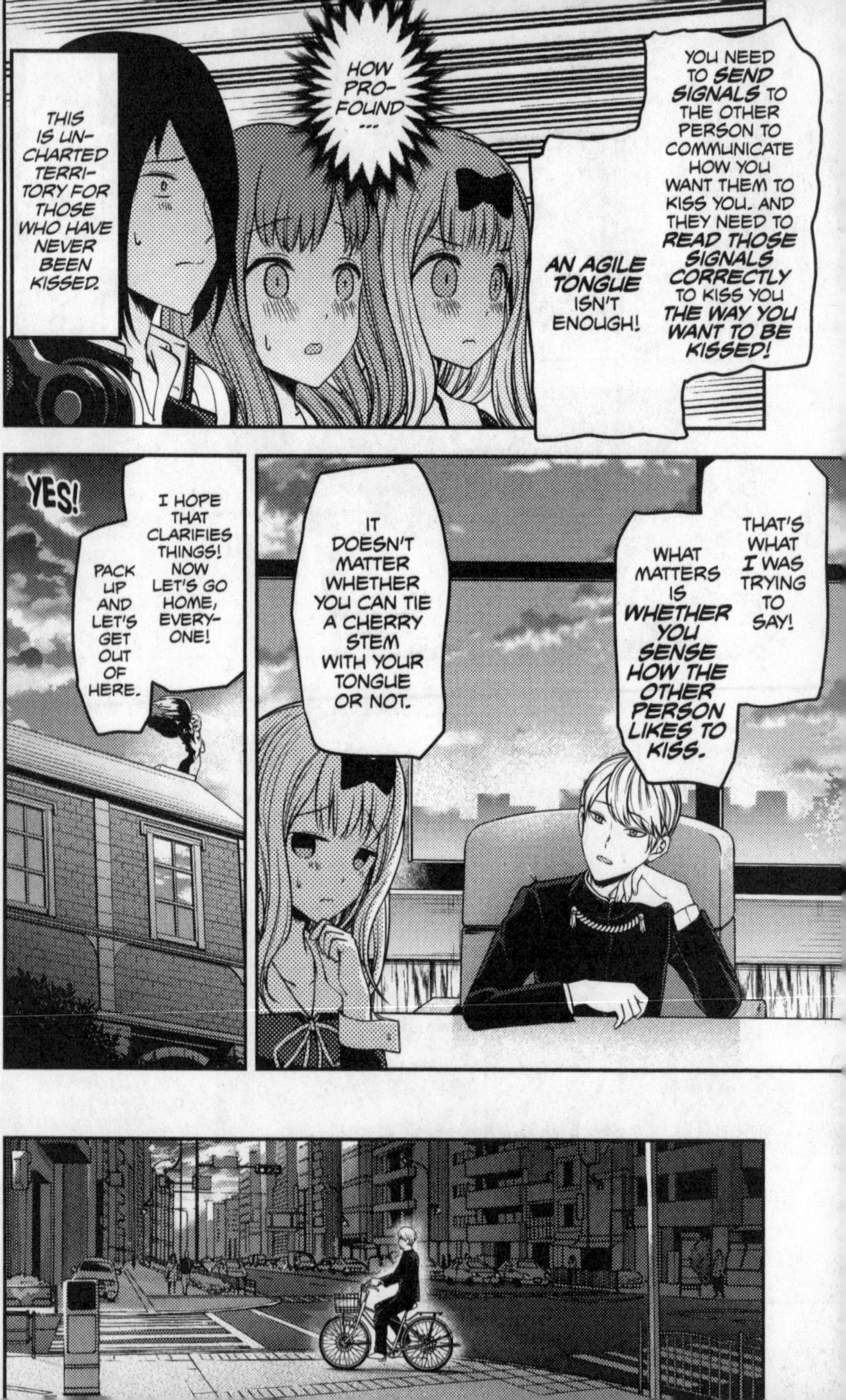
YOU NEED TO SEND SIGNALS TO THE OTHER PERSON TO COMMUNICATE HOW YOU WANT THEM TO KISS YOU. AND THEY NEED TO READ THOSE SIGNALS CORRECTLY TO KISS YOU THE WAY YOU WANT TO BE KISSED!
AN AGILE TONGUE ISN'T ENOUGH!
HOW PRO-FOUND...
THIS IS UN-CHARTED TERRI-TORY FOR THOSE WHO HAVE NEVER BEEN KISSED.
THAT'S WHAT I WAS TRYING TO SAY!
WHAT MATTERS IS WHETHER YOU SENSE HOW THE OTHER PERSON LIKES TO KISS.
IT DOESN'T MATTER WHETHER YOU CAN TIE A CHERRY STEM WITH YOUR TONGUE OR NOT.
I HOPE THAT CLARIFIES THINGS! NOW LET'S GO HOME, EVERY-ONE!
PACK UP AND LET'S GET OUT OF HERE.
YES!

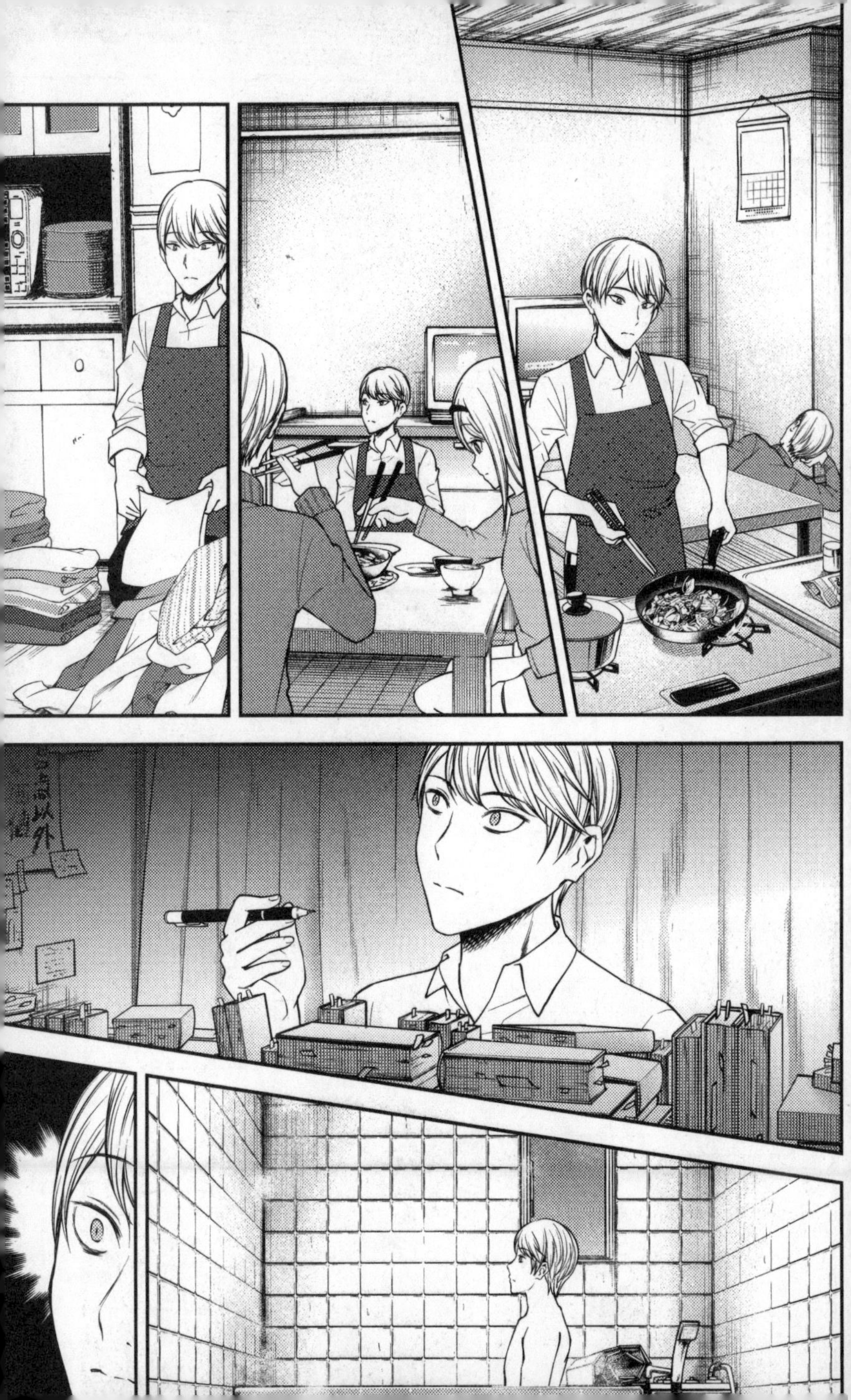

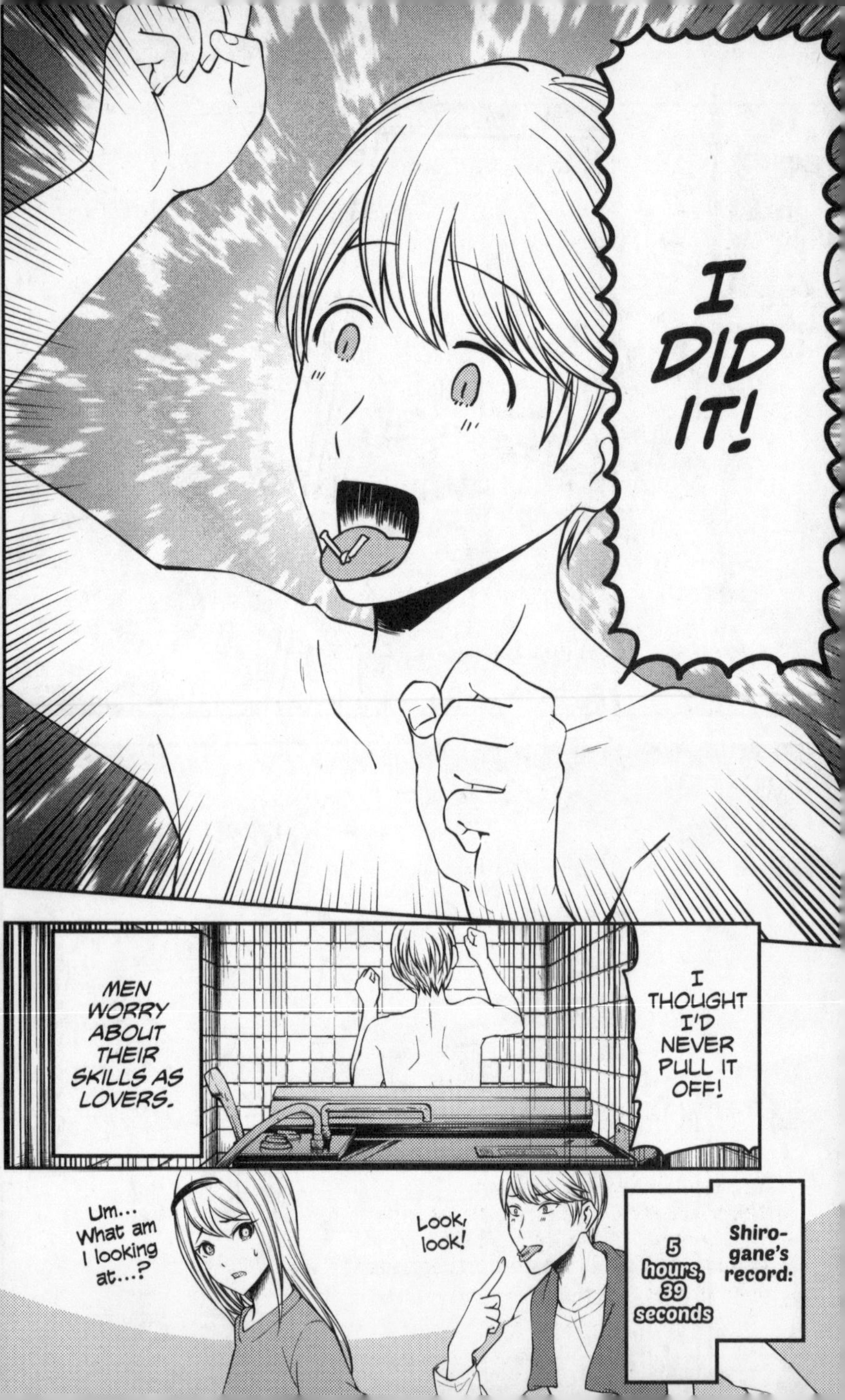
I DID IT!
I THOUGHT I'D NEVER PULL IT OFF!
MEN WORRY ABOUT THEIR SKILLS AS LOVERS.
Shirogane's record:
5 hours, 39 seconds
Look, look!
Um... What am I looking at...?

Cherry Tying Ranking

Kaguya Shinomiya: 16 seconds
Nagisa Kashiwagi: 41 seconds
Chika Fujiwara: 3 minutes, 33 seconds
Yu Ishigami: 47 minutes, 19 seconds
Miyuki Shirogane: 5 hours, 39 seconds
Miko Ino: dropped out

KAGUYA-SAMA
LOVE IS WAR

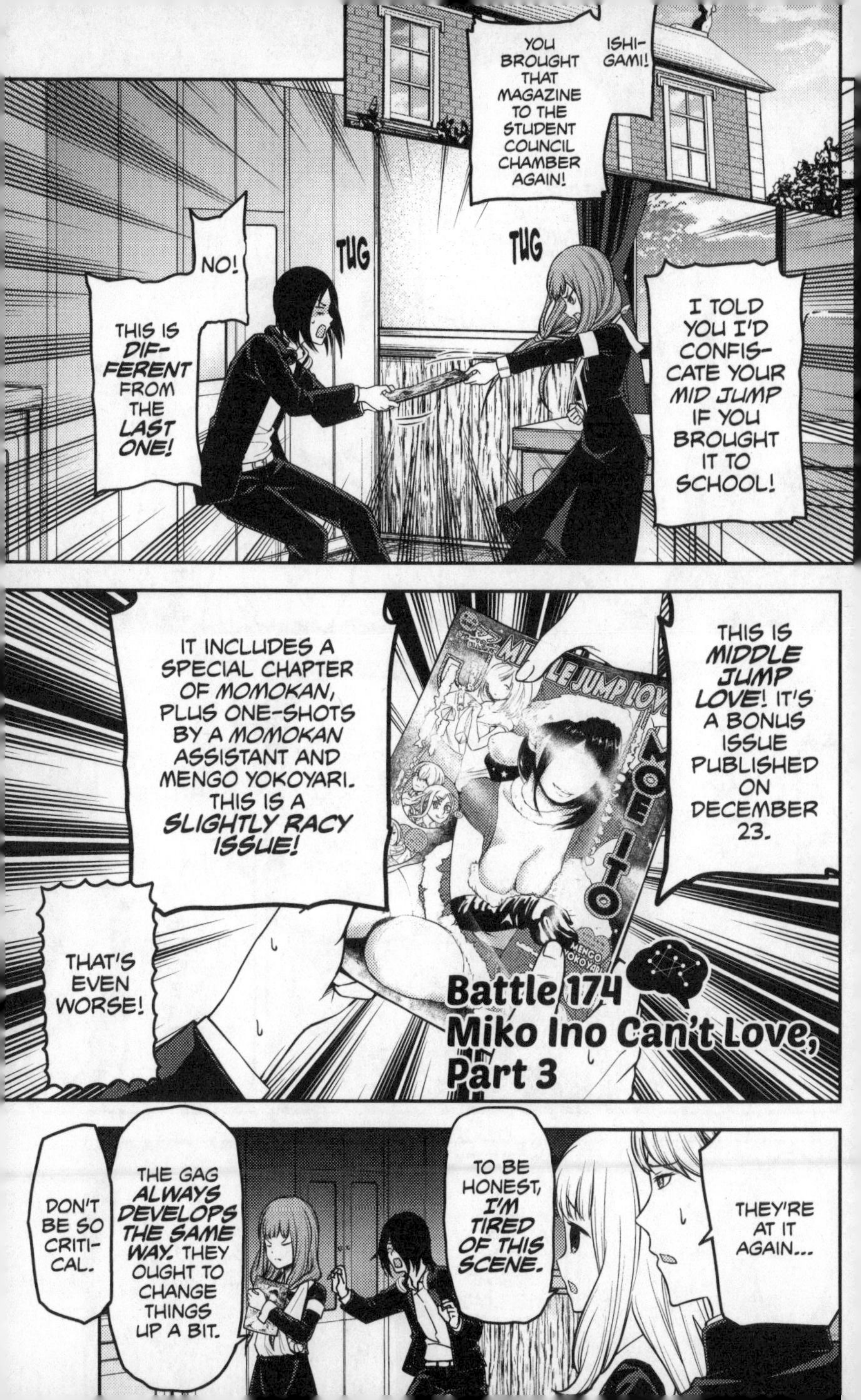
ISHI-GAMI!
YOU BROUGHT THAT MAGAZINE TO THE STUDENT COUNCIL CHAMBER AGAIN!
I TOLD YOU I'D CONFIS-CATE YOUR *MID JUMP* IF YOU BROUGHT IT TO SCHOOL!
TUG
TUG
NO!
THIS IS *DIF-FERENT* FROM THE *LAST ONE!*
THIS IS *MIDDLE JUMP LOVE*! IT'S A BONUS ISSUE PUBLISHED ON DECEMBER 23.
IT INCLUDES A SPECIAL CHAPTER OF *MOMOKAN*, PLUS ONE-SHOTS BY A *MOMOKAN* ASSISTANT AND MENGO YOKOYARI. THIS IS A *SLIGHTLY RACY ISSUE!*
MIDDLE JUMP LOVE
MOE ITO
THAT'S EVEN WORSE!
Battle 174
Miko Ino Can't Love, Part 3
THEY'RE AT IT AGAIN...
TO BE HONEST, *I'M TIRED OF THIS SCENE.*
THE GAG *ALWAYS DEVELOPS THE SAME WAY.* THEY OUGHT TO CHANGE THINGS UP A BIT.
DON'T BE SO CRITI-CAL.

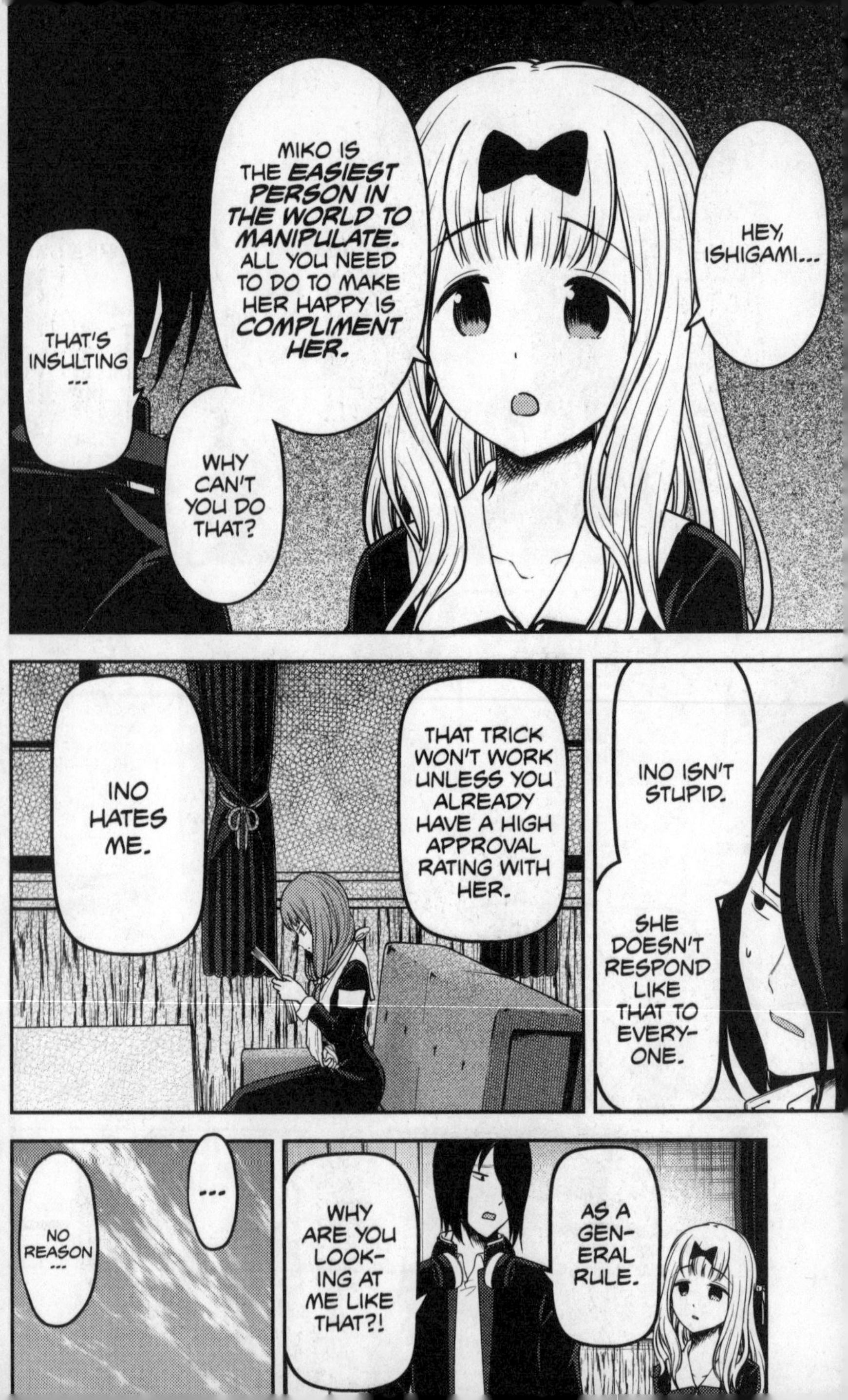
HEY, ISHIGAMI...
MIKO IS THE EASIEST PERSON IN THE WORLD TO MANIPULATE. ALL YOU NEED TO DO TO MAKE HER HAPPY IS COMPLIMENT HER.
WHY CAN'T YOU DO THAT?
THAT'S INSULTING ...
INO ISN'T STUPID.
SHE DOESN'T RESPOND LIKE THAT TO EVERY-ONE.
THAT TRICK WON'T WORK UNLESS YOU ALREADY HAVE A HIGH APPROVAL RATING WITH HER.
INO HATES ME.
AS A GEN-ERAL RULE.
WHY ARE YOU LOOK-ING AT ME LIKE THAT?!
...
NO REASON ...

The Next Day

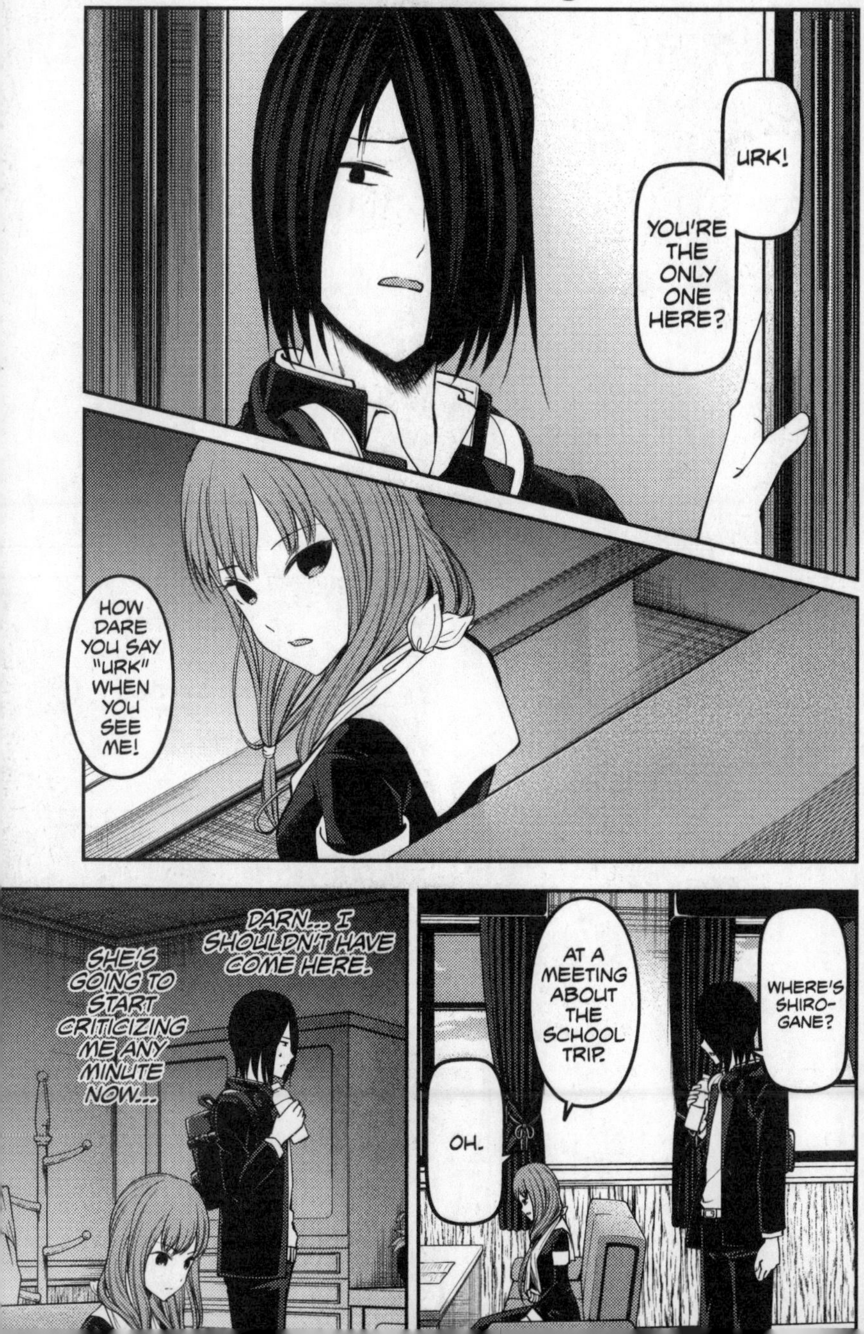
URK!
YOU'RE THE ONLY ONE HERE?
HOW DARE YOU SAY "URK" WHEN YOU SEE ME!
WHERE'S SHIRO-GANE?
AT A MEETING ABOUT THE SCHOOL TRIP.
OH.
DARN... I SHOULDN'T HAVE COME HERE.
SHE'S GOING TO START CRITICIZING ME ANY MINUTE NOW...

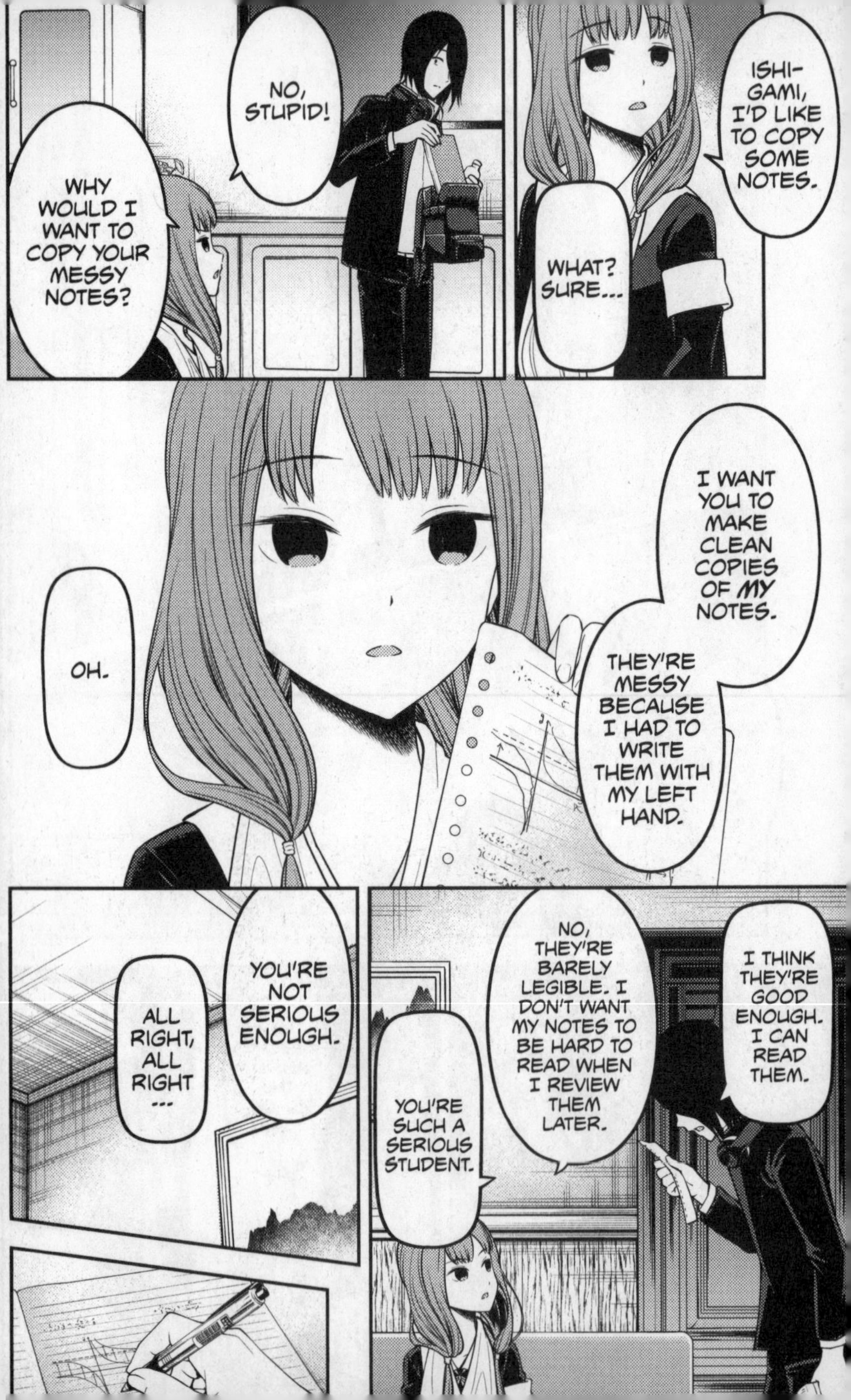
ISHI-GAMI, I'D LIKE TO COPY SOME NOTES.
WHAT? SURE...
NO, STUPID!
WHY WOULD I WANT TO COPY YOUR MESSY NOTES?
I WANT YOU TO MAKE CLEAN COPIES OF *MY* NOTES.
THEY'RE MESSY BECAUSE I HAD TO WRITE THEM WITH MY LEFT HAND.
OH.
I THINK THEY'RE GOOD ENOUGH. I CAN READ THEM.
NO, THEY'RE BARELY LEGIBLE. I DON'T WANT MY NOTES TO BE HARD TO READ WHEN I REVIEW THEM LATER.
YOU'RE SUCH A SERIOUS STUDENT.
YOU'RE NOT SERIOUS ENOUGH.
ALL RIGHT, ALL RIGHT...

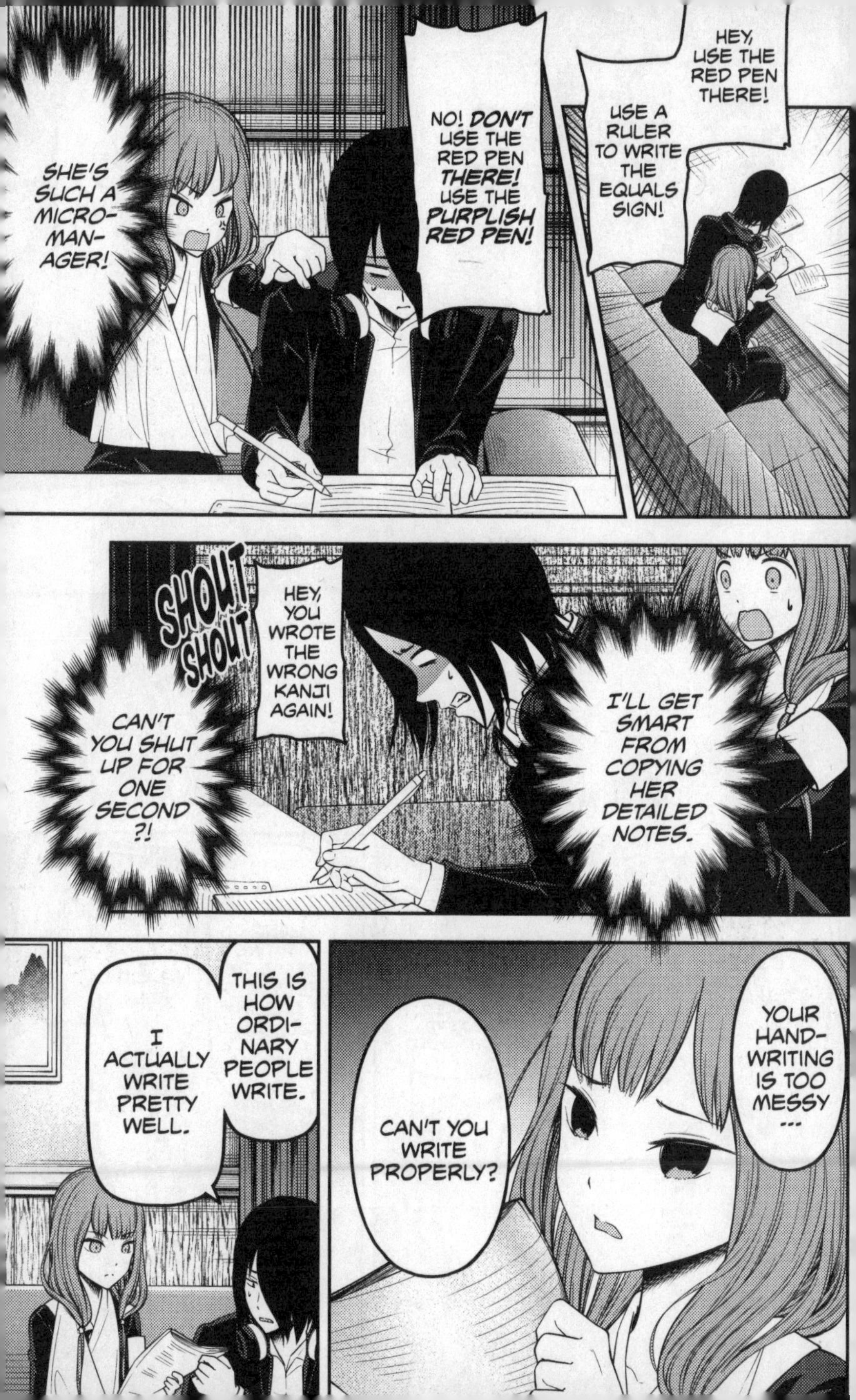
HEY, USE THE RED PEN THERE!
USE A RULER TO WRITE THE EQUALS SIGN!
NO! *DON'T* USE THE RED PEN *THERE!* USE THE *PURPLISH* RED PEN!
SHE'S SUCH A MICRO-MANAGER!
I'LL GET SMART FROM COPYING HER DETAILED NOTES.
HEY, YOU WROTE THE WRONG KANJI AGAIN!
SHOUT SHOUT
CAN'T YOU SHUT UP FOR ONE SECOND?!
YOUR HAND-WRITING IS TOO MESSY...
CAN'T YOU WRITE PROPERLY?
THIS IS HOW ORDI-NARY PEOPLE WRITE.
I ACTUALLY WRITE PRETTY WELL.

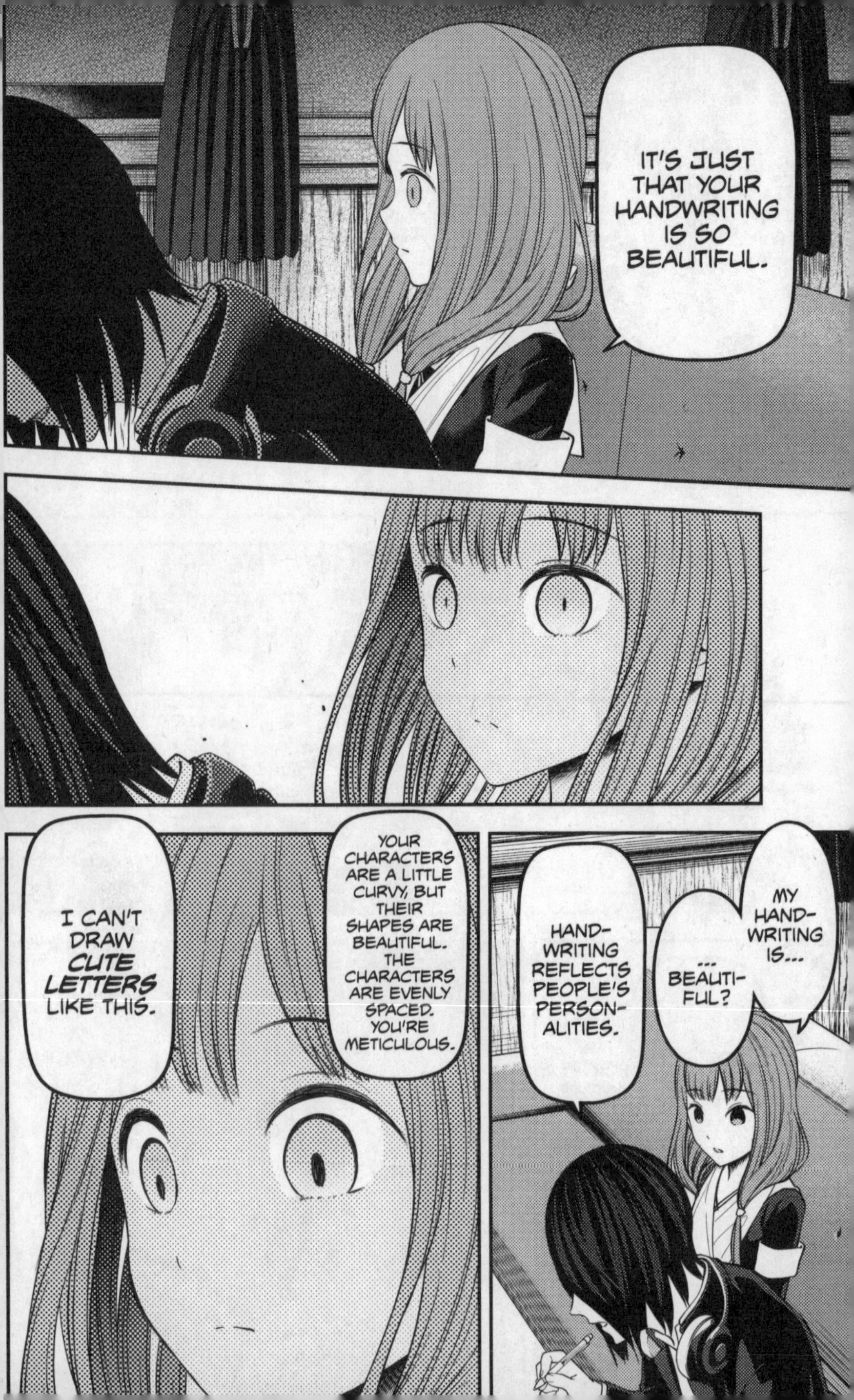
IT'S JUST THAT YOUR HANDWRITING IS SO BEAUTIFUL.
MY HAND-WRITING IS...
...BEAUTI-FUL?
HAND-WRITING REFLECTS PEOPLE'S PERSON-ALITIES.
YOUR CHARACTERS ARE A LITTLE CURVY, BUT THEIR SHAPES ARE BEAUTIFUL. THE CHARACTERS ARE EVENLY SPACED. YOU'RE METICULOUS.
I CAN'T DRAW *CUTE LETTERS* LIKE THIS.

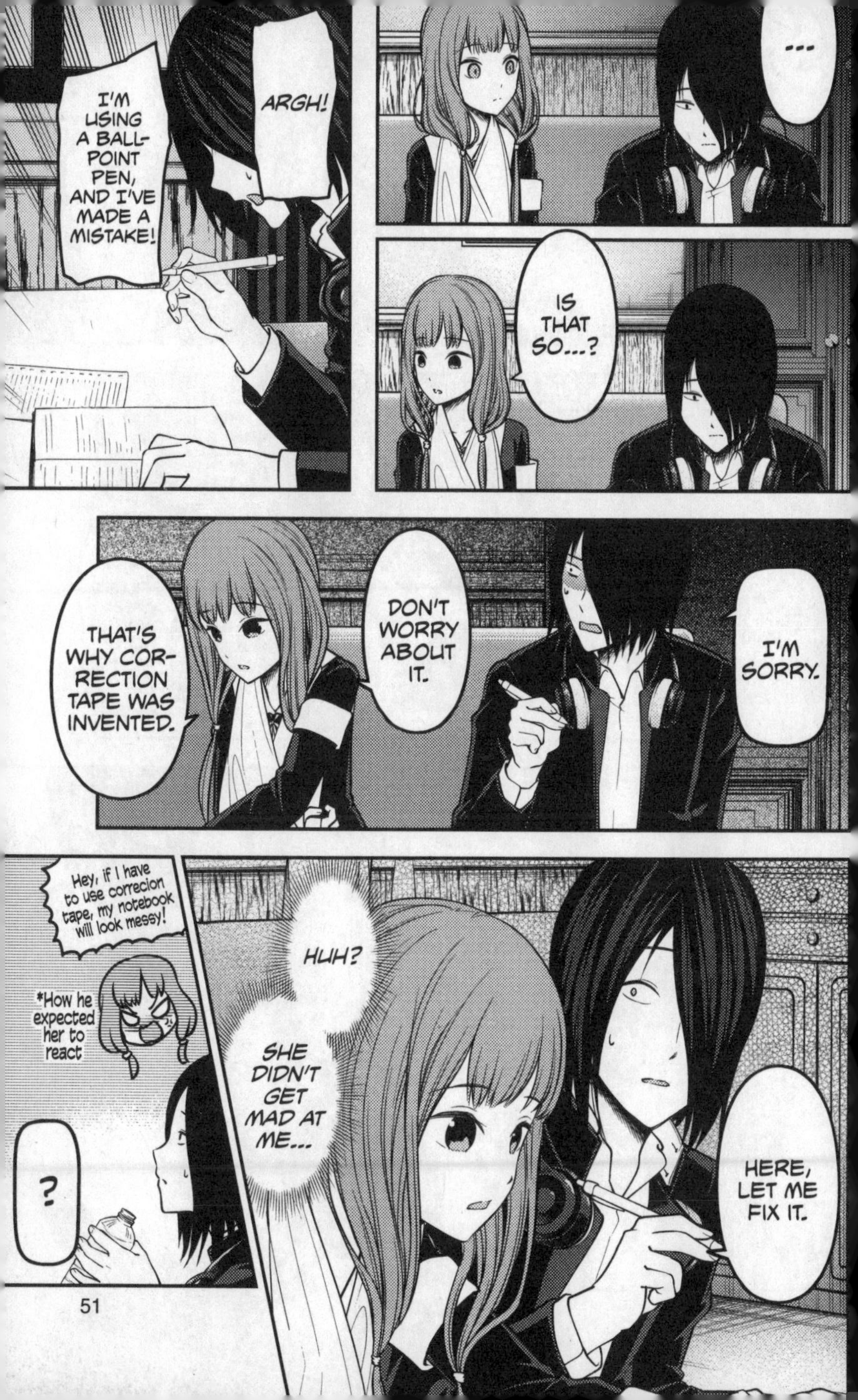
...
IS THAT SO...?
ARGH!
I'M USING A BALL-POINT PEN, AND I'VE MADE A MISTAKE!
I'M SORRY.
DON'T WORRY ABOUT IT.
THAT'S WHY COR-RECTION TAPE WAS INVENTED.
HERE, LET ME FIX IT.
HUH?
SHE DIDN'T GET MAD AT ME...
Hey, if I have to use correcion tape, my notebook will look messy!
*How he expected her to react
?

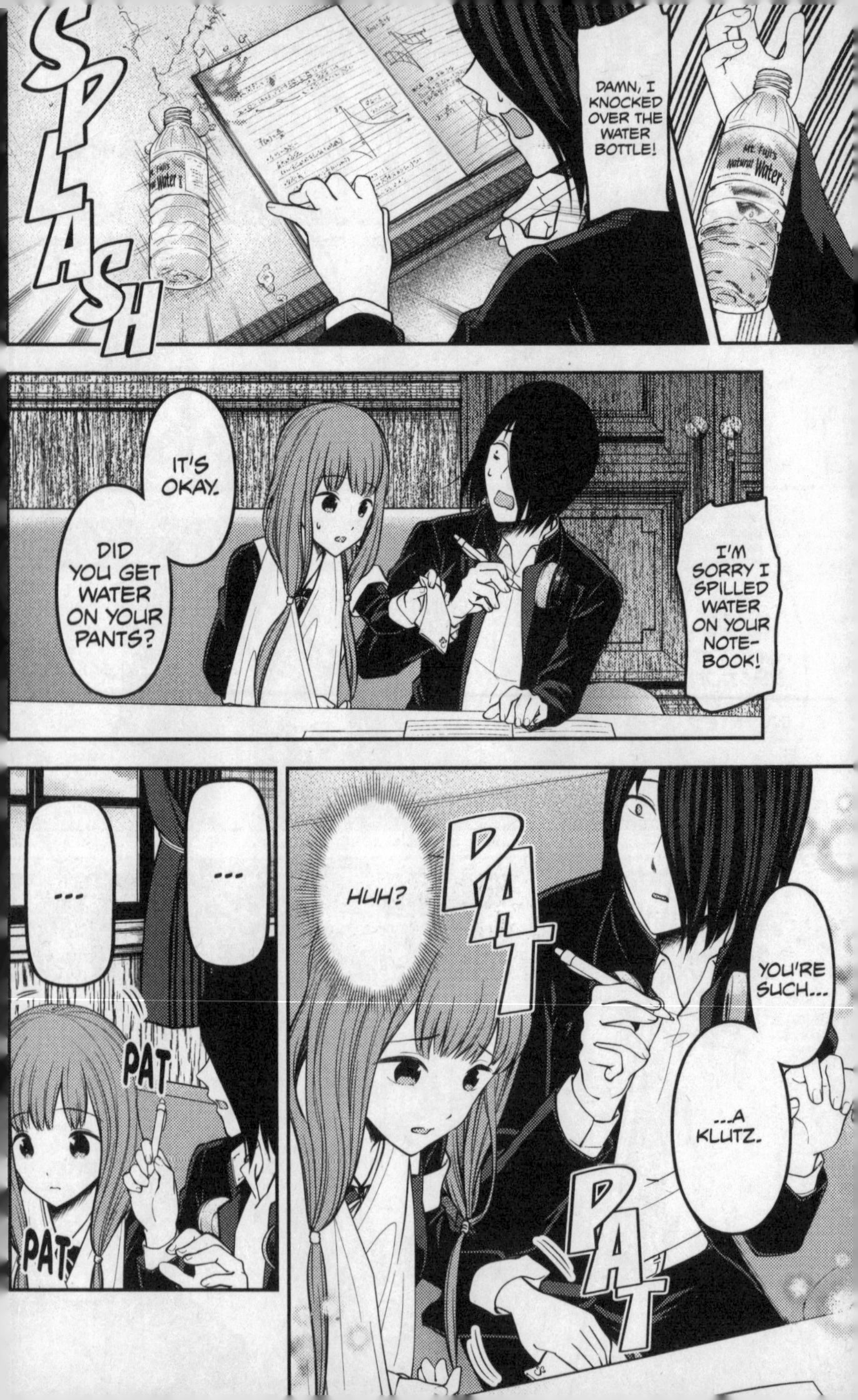
DAMN, I KNOCKED OVER THE WATER BOTTLE!
SPLASH
I'M SORRY I SPILLED WATER ON YOUR NOTE-BOOK!
IT'S OKAY.
DID YOU GET WATER ON YOUR PANTS?
YOU'RE SUCH...
PAT
HUH?
...A KLUTZ.
PAT

PAT
PAT

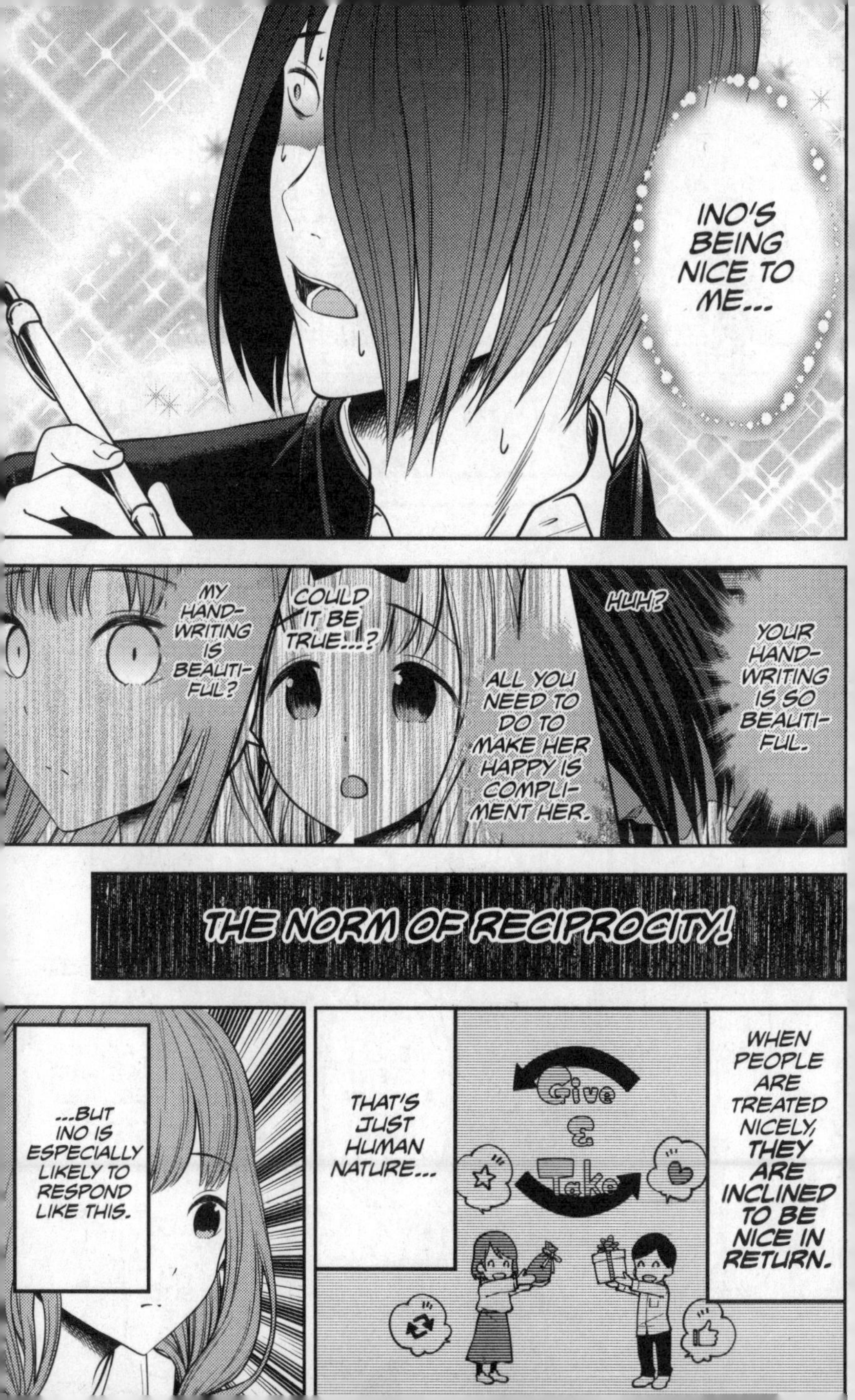
INO'S BEING NICE TO ME...
YOUR HAND-WRITING IS SO BEAUTI-FUL.
HUH?
ALL YOU NEED TO DO TO MAKE HER HAPPY IS COMPLI-MENT HER.
COULD IT BE TRUE...?
MY HAND-WRITING IS BEAUTI-FUL?
THE NORM OF RECIPROCITY!
WHEN PEOPLE ARE TREATED NICELY, THEY ARE INCLINED TO BE NICE IN RETURN.
Give & Take
THAT'S JUST HUMAN NATURE...
...BUT INO IS ESPECIALLY LIKELY TO RESPOND LIKE THIS.

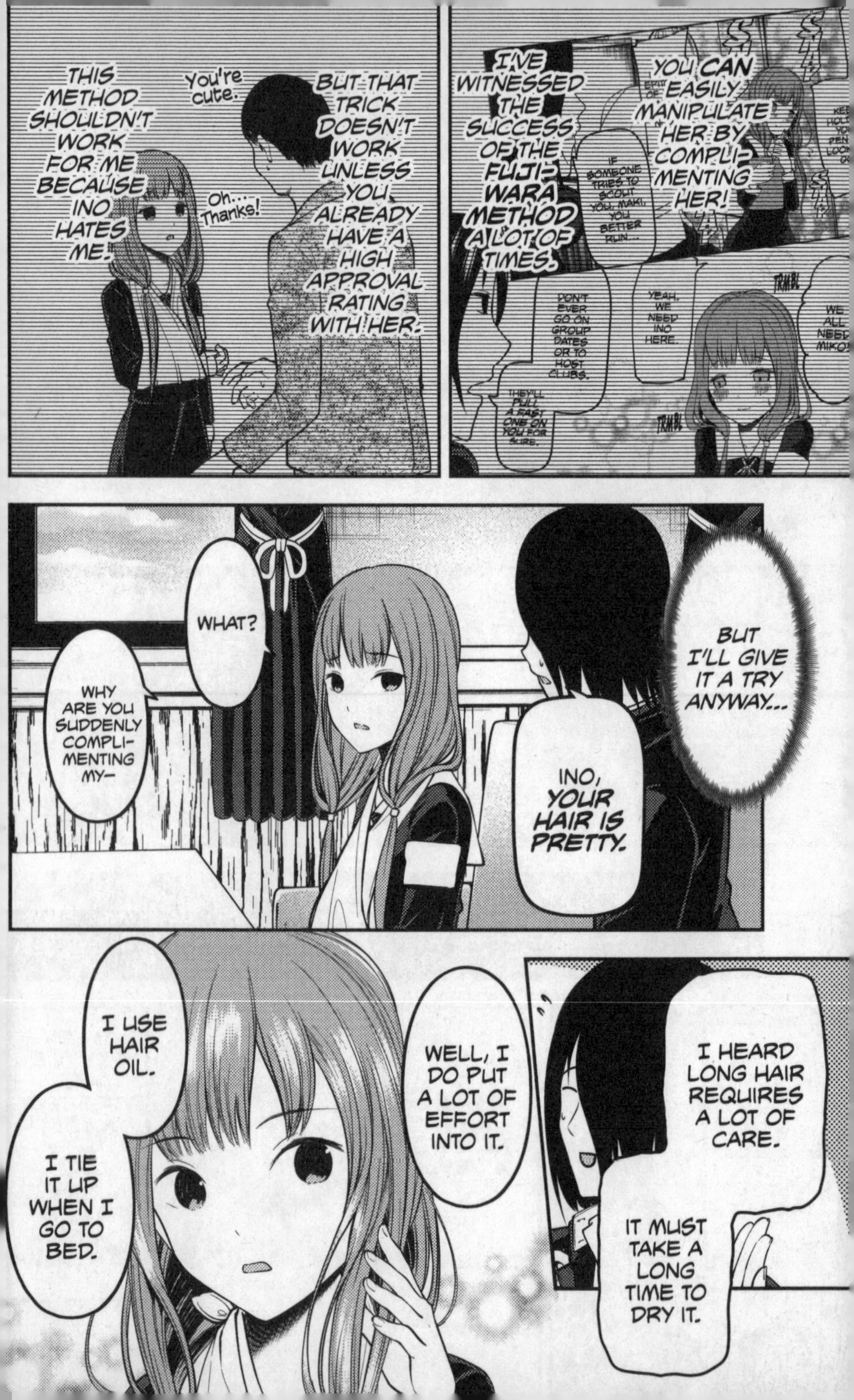
YOU CAN EASILY MANIPULATE HER BY COMPLIMENTING HER!
I'VE WITNESSED THE SUCCESS OF THE FUJIWARA METHOD A LOT OF TIMES.
IF SOMEONE TRIES TO SCOUT YOU, MAKI, YOU BETTER RUN...
TRMBL
WE ALL NEED MIKO!
YEAH, WE NEED INO HERE.
DON'T EVER GO ON GROUP DATES OR TO HOST CLUBS.
THEY'LL PULL A FAST ONE ON YOU FOR SURE.
TRMBL
BUT THAT TRICK DOESN'T WORK UNLESS YOU ALREADY HAVE A HIGH APPROVAL RATING WITH HER.
You're cute.
Oh... Thanks!
THIS METHOD SHOULDN'T WORK FOR ME BECAUSE INO HATES ME.
BUT I'LL GIVE IT A TRY ANYWAY...
INO, YOUR HAIR IS PRETTY.
WHAT?
WHY ARE YOU SUDDENLY COMPLIMENTING MY—
I HEARD LONG HAIR REQUIRES A LOT OF CARE.
IT MUST TAKE A LONG TIME TO DRY IT.
WELL, I DO PUT A LOT OF EFFORT INTO IT.
I USE HAIR OIL.
I TIE IT UP WHEN I GO TO BED.

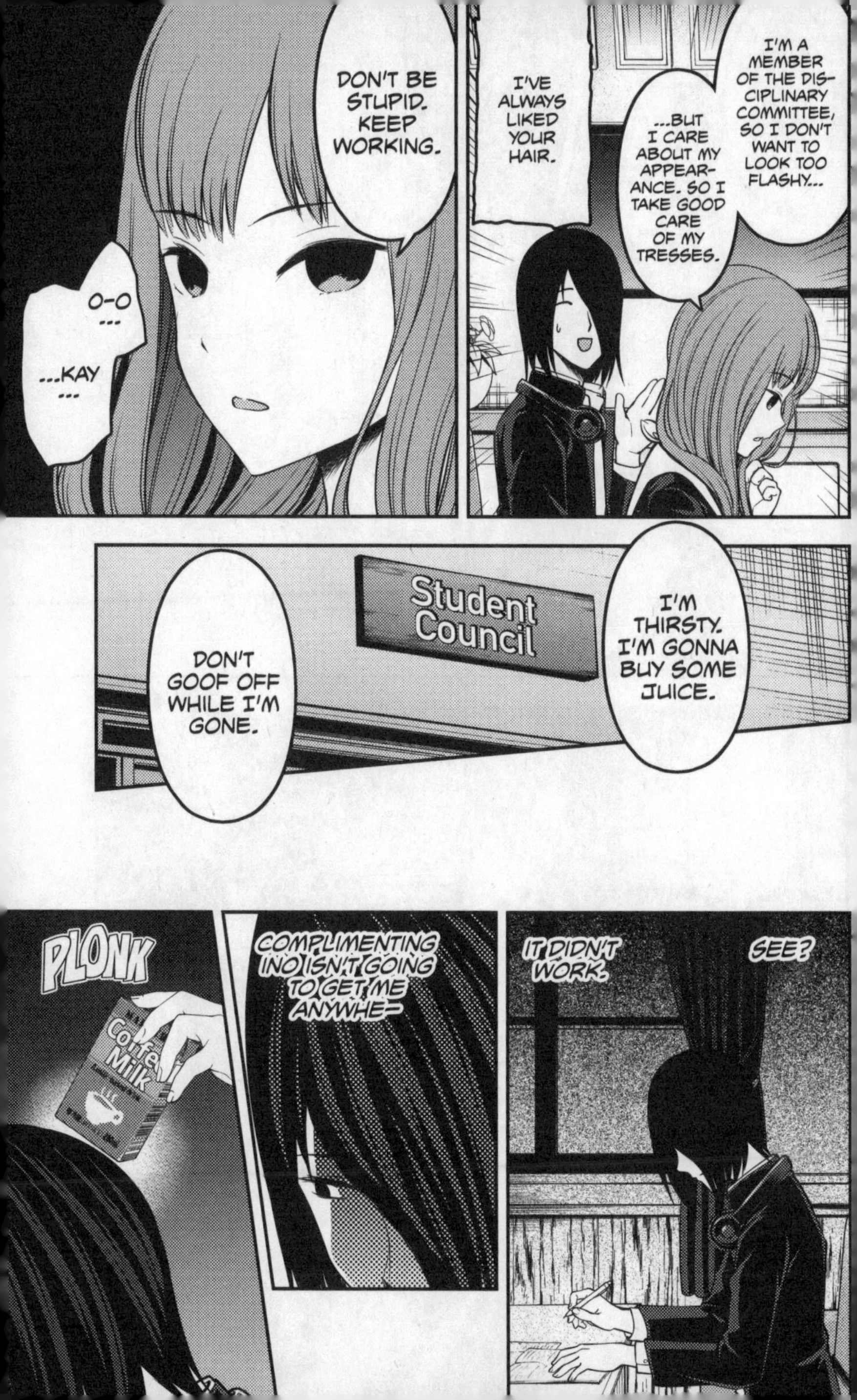
I'M A MEMBER OF THE DIS-CIPLINARY COMMITTEE, SO I DON'T WANT TO LOOK TOO FLASHY...
...BUT I CARE ABOUT MY APPEAR-ANCE. SO I TAKE GOOD CARE OF MY TRESSES.
I'VE ALWAYS LIKED YOUR HAIR.
DON'T BE STUPID. KEEP WORKING.
O-O...
...KAY...
I'M THIRSTY. I'M GONNA BUY SOME JUICE.
Student Council
DON'T GOOF OFF WHILE I'M GONE.
SEE?
IT DIDN'T WORK.
COMPLIMENTING INO ISN'T GOING TO GET ME ANYWHE—
PLONK
Coffe
Milk

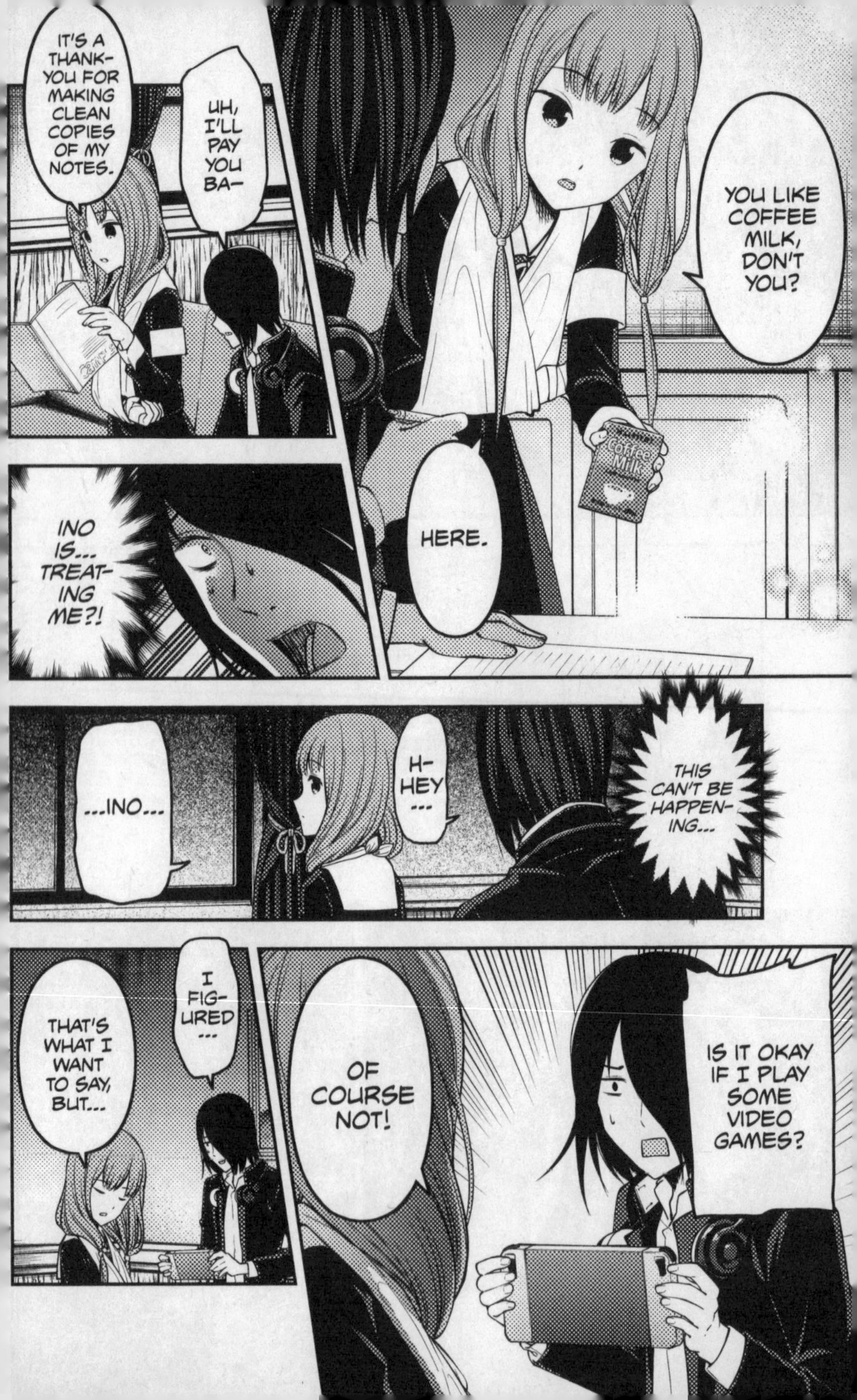
YOU LIKE COFFEE MILK, DON'T YOU?
Coffee Milk
HERE.
UH, I'LL PAY YOU BA-
IT'S A THANK-YOU FOR MAKING CLEAN COPIES OF MY NOTES.
INO IS... TREATING ME?!
THIS CAN'T BE HAPPENING...
H-HEY...
...INO...
IS IT OKAY IF I PLAY SOME VIDEO GAMES?
OF COURSE NOT!
I FIGURED...
THAT'S WHAT I WANT TO SAY, BUT...

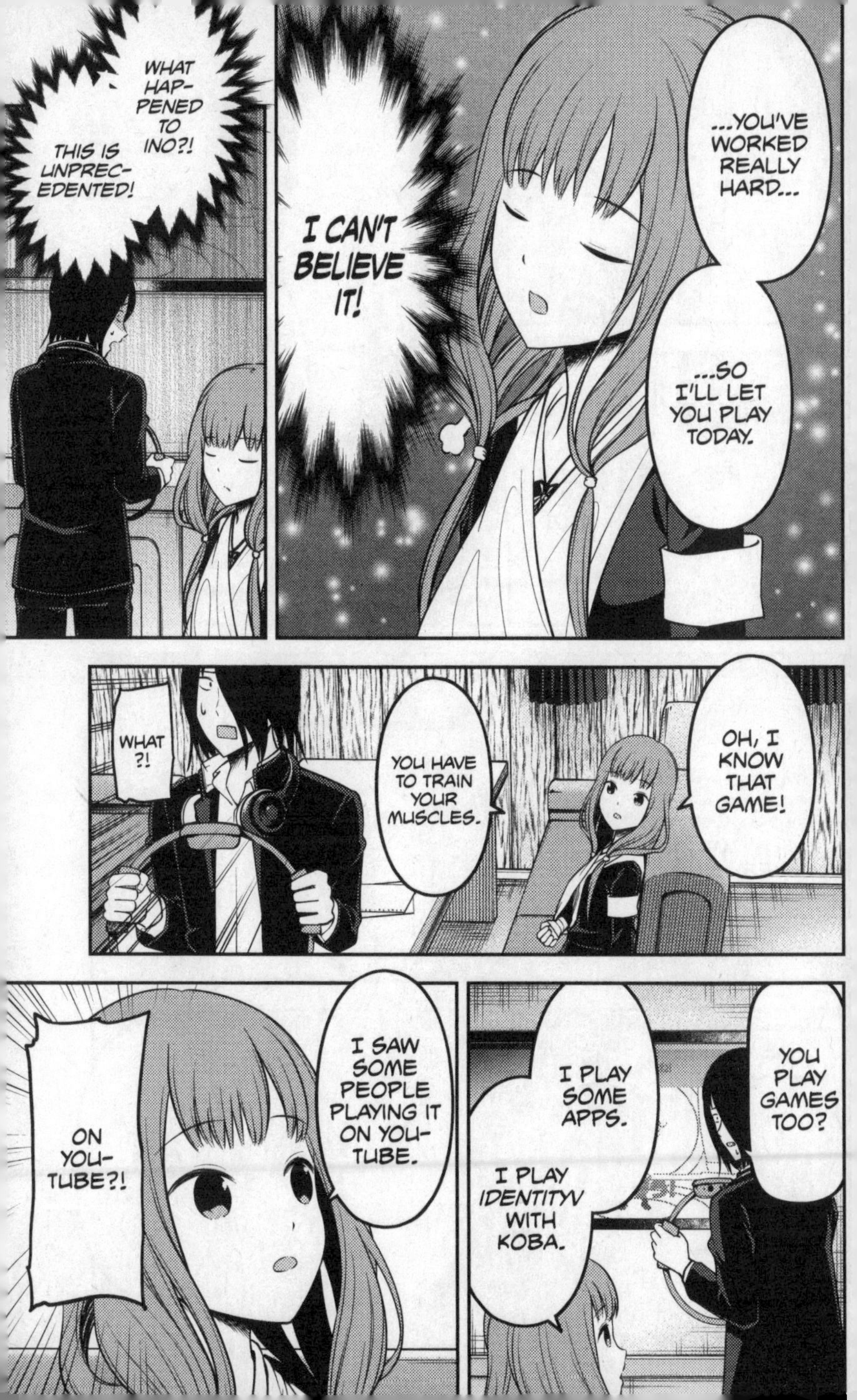
...YOU'VE WORKED REALLY HARD...
...SO I'LL LET YOU PLAY TODAY.
I CAN'T BELIEVE IT!
WHAT HAP-PENED TO INO?!
THIS IS UNPREC-EDENTED!
OH, I KNOW THAT GAME!
YOU HAVE TO TRAIN YOUR MUSCLES.
WHAT?!
YOU PLAY GAMES TOO?
I PLAY SOME APPS.
I PLAY IDENTITYV WITH KOBA.
I SAW SOME PEOPLE PLAYING IT ON YOU-TUBE.
ON YOU-TUBE?!

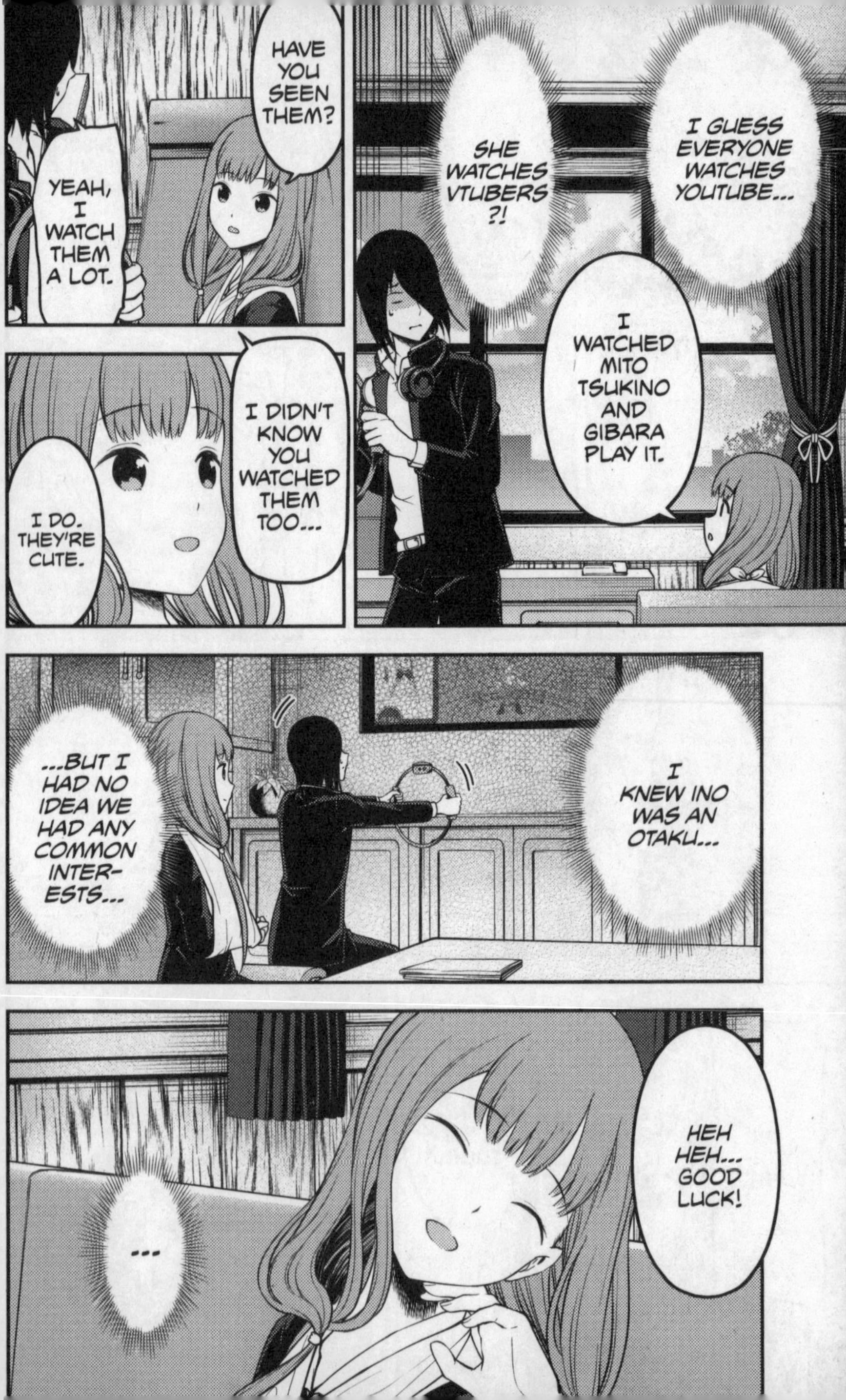
I GUESS EVERYONE WATCHES YOUTUBE...
SHE WATCHES VTUBERS?!
I WATCHED MITO TSUKINO AND GIBARA PLAY IT.
HAVE YOU SEEN THEM?
YEAH, I WATCH THEM A LOT.
I DIDN'T KNOW YOU WATCHED THEM TOO...
I DO. THEY'RE CUTE.
I KNEW INO WAS AN OTAKU...
...BUT I HAD NO IDEA WE HAD ANY COMMON INTER-ESTS...
HEH HEH... GOOD LUCK!
...

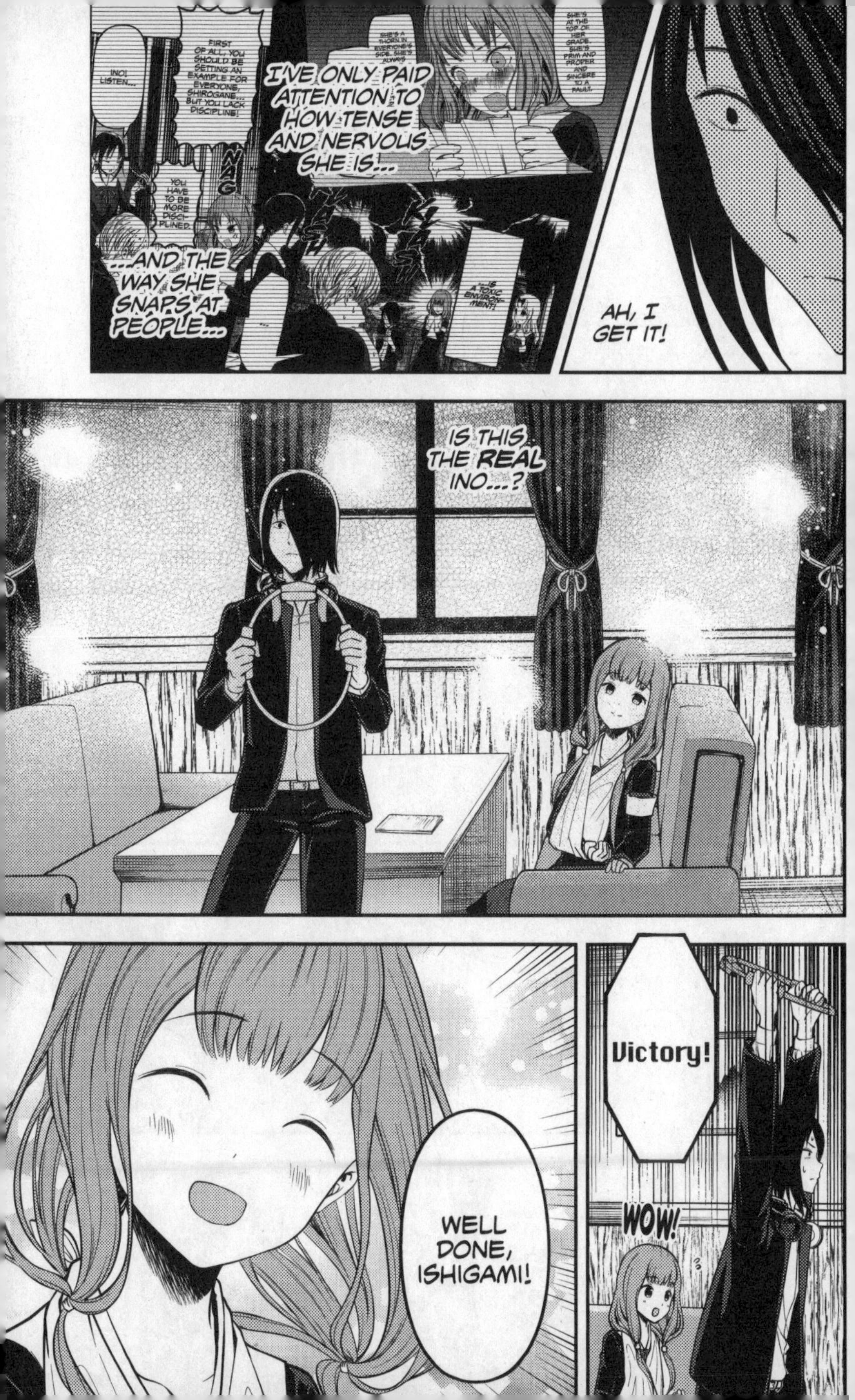
AH, I GET IT!
SHE'S AT THE TOP OF HER GRADE. SHE'S PRIM AND PROPER AND SINCERE TO A FAULT.
SHE'S A THORN IN EVERYONE'S SIDE. SHE'S ALWAYS
I'VE ONLY PAID ATTENTION TO HOW TENSE AND NERVOUS SHE IS...
FIRST OF ALL, YOU SHOULD BE SETTING AN EXAMPLE FOR EVERYONE, SHIROGANE... BUT YOU LACK DISCIPLINE!
INO! LISTEN...
NAG
YOU HAVE TO BE MORE DISCI-PLINED.
...IS A TOXIC ENVIRON-MENT!
...AND THE WAY SHE SNAPS AT PEOPLE...
IS THIS THE REAL INO...?
Victory!
WOW!
WELL DONE, ISHIGAMI!

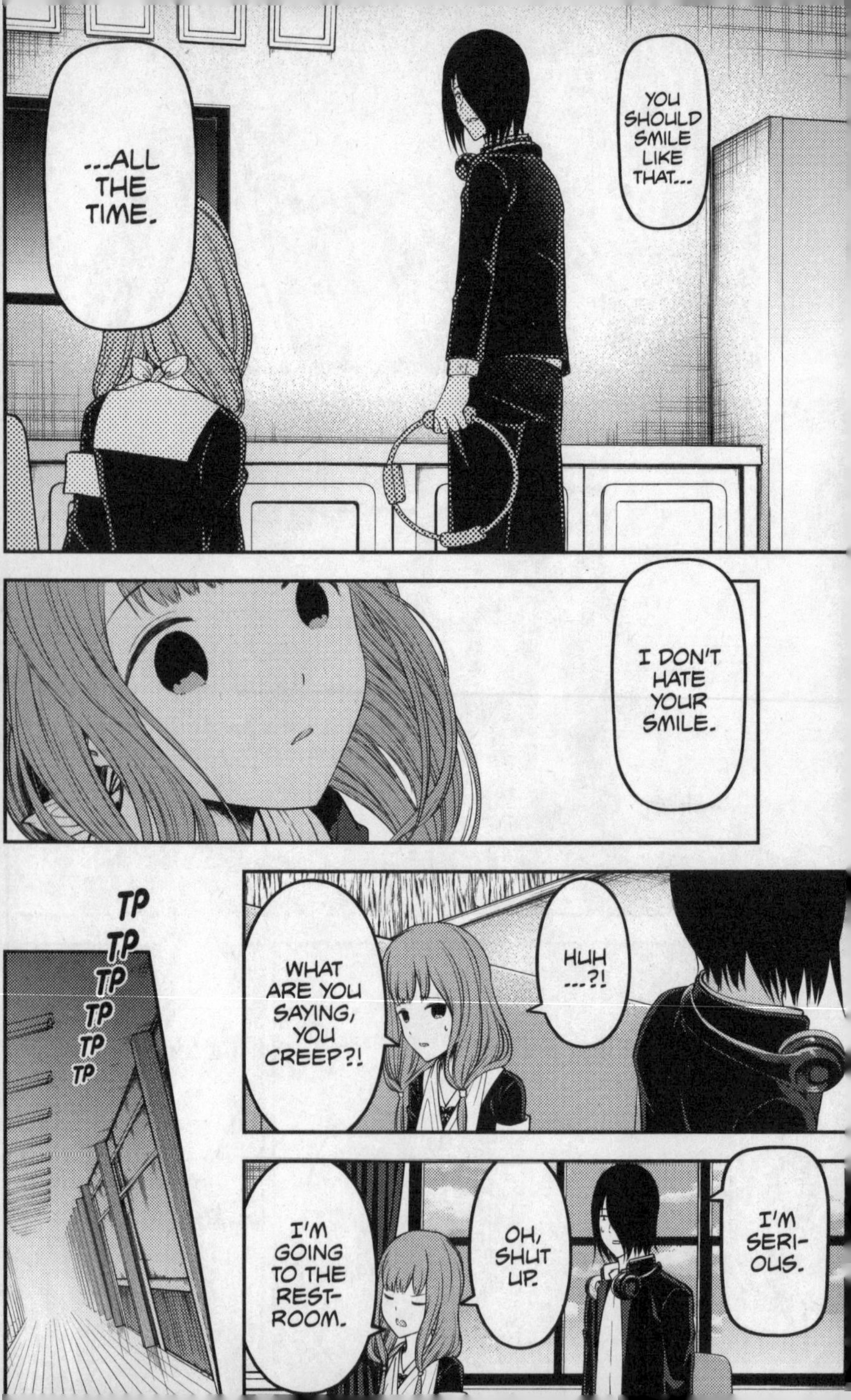
YOU SHOULD SMILE LIKE THAT...
...ALL THE TIME.
I DON'T HATE YOUR SMILE.
HUH...?!
WHAT ARE YOU SAYING, YOU CREEP?!
I'M SERIOUS.
OH, SHUT UP.
I'M GOING TO THE REST-ROOM.
TP TP TP TP TP TP

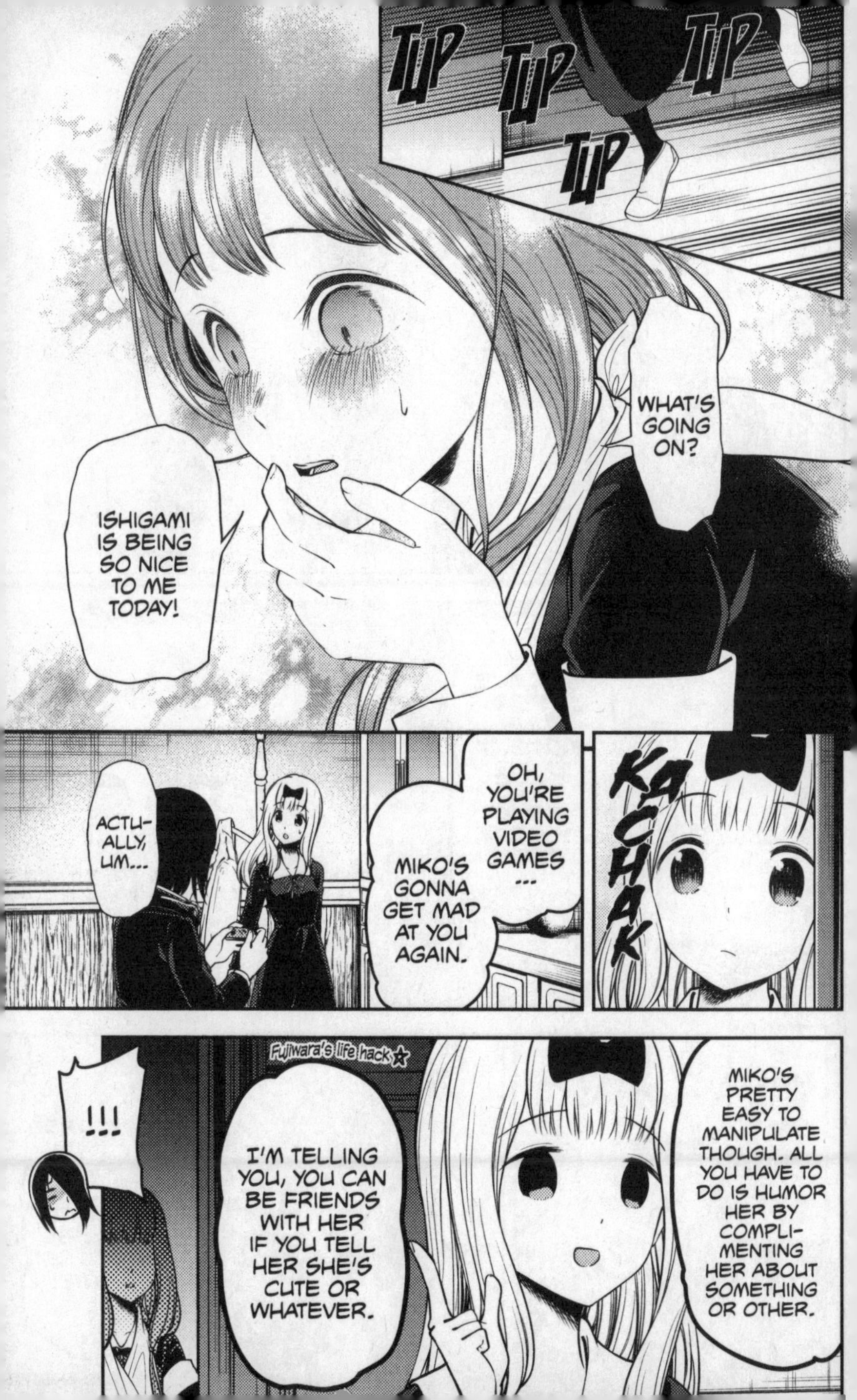
TUP
TUP
TUP
TUP
WHAT'S GOING ON?
ISHIGAMI IS BEING SO NICE TO ME TODAY!
KA CHAK
OH, YOU'RE PLAYING VIDEO GAMES...
MIKO'S GONNA GET MAD AT YOU AGAIN.
ACTU-ALLY, UM...
Fujiwara's life hack☆
MIKO'S PRETTY EASY TO MANIPULATE THOUGH. ALL YOU HAVE TO DO IS HUMOR HER BY COMPLI-MENTING HER ABOUT SOMETHING OR OTHER.
I'M TELLING YOU, YOU CAN BE FRIENDS WITH HER IF YOU TELL HER SHE'S CUTE OR WHATEVER.
!!!

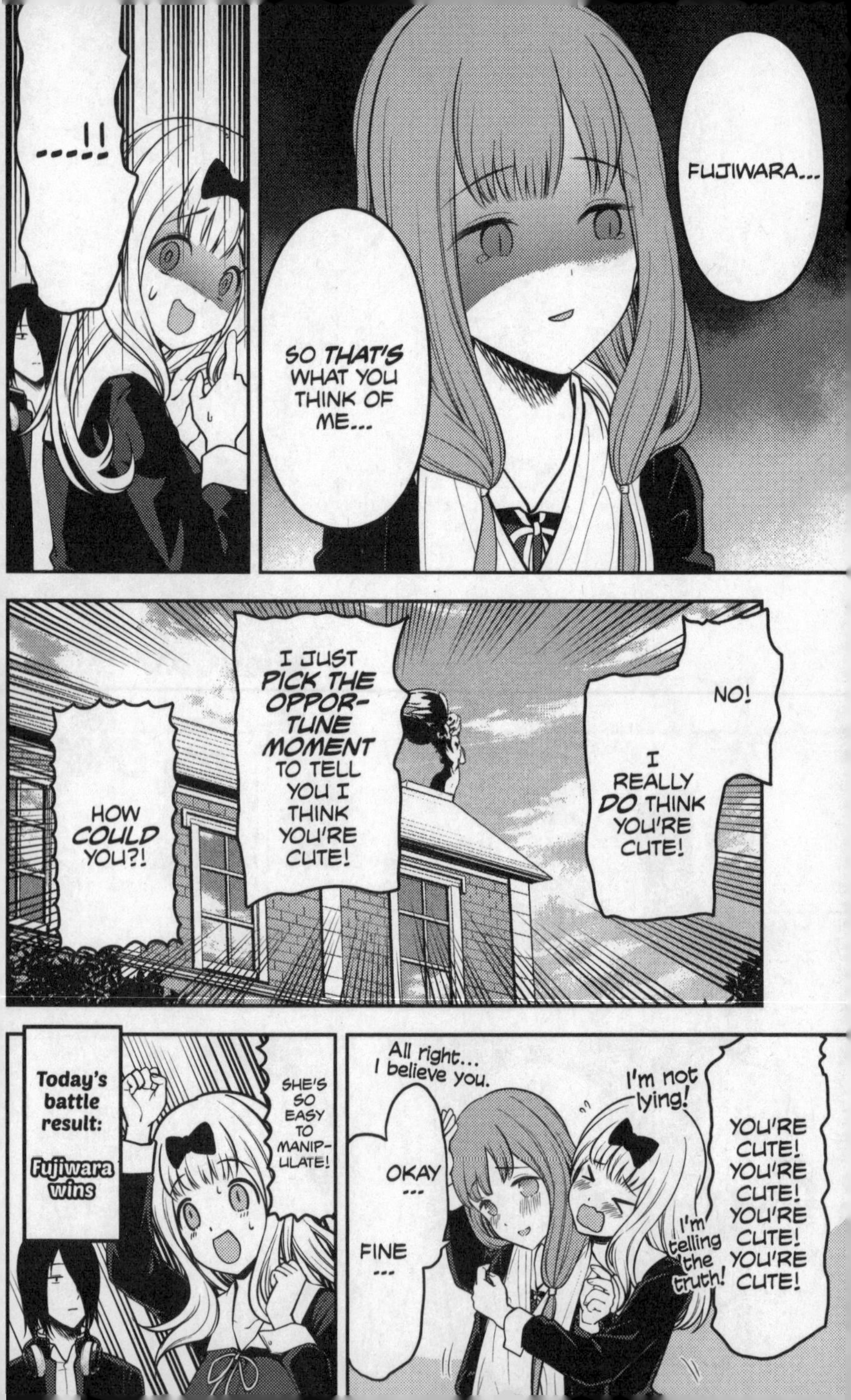
FUJIWARA...
SO THAT'S WHAT YOU THINK OF ME...
...!!
NO!
I REALLY DO THINK YOU'RE CUTE!
I JUST PICK THE OPPOR-TUNE MOMENT TO TELL YOU I THINK YOU'RE CUTE!
HOW COULD YOU?!
I'm not lying!
YOU'RE CUTE! YOU'RE CUTE! YOU'RE CUTE! YOU'RE CUTE!
I'm telling the truth!
All right... I believe you.
OKAY...
FINE...
SHE'S SO EASY TO MANIP-ULATE!
Today's battle result:
Fujiwara wins

I study while playing videos in the background as study BGM.
Really...?
If I hear words, I can't concentrate.
MULTI-TASKER
SINGLE-TASKER

Battle 175 Kaguya Wants Attention

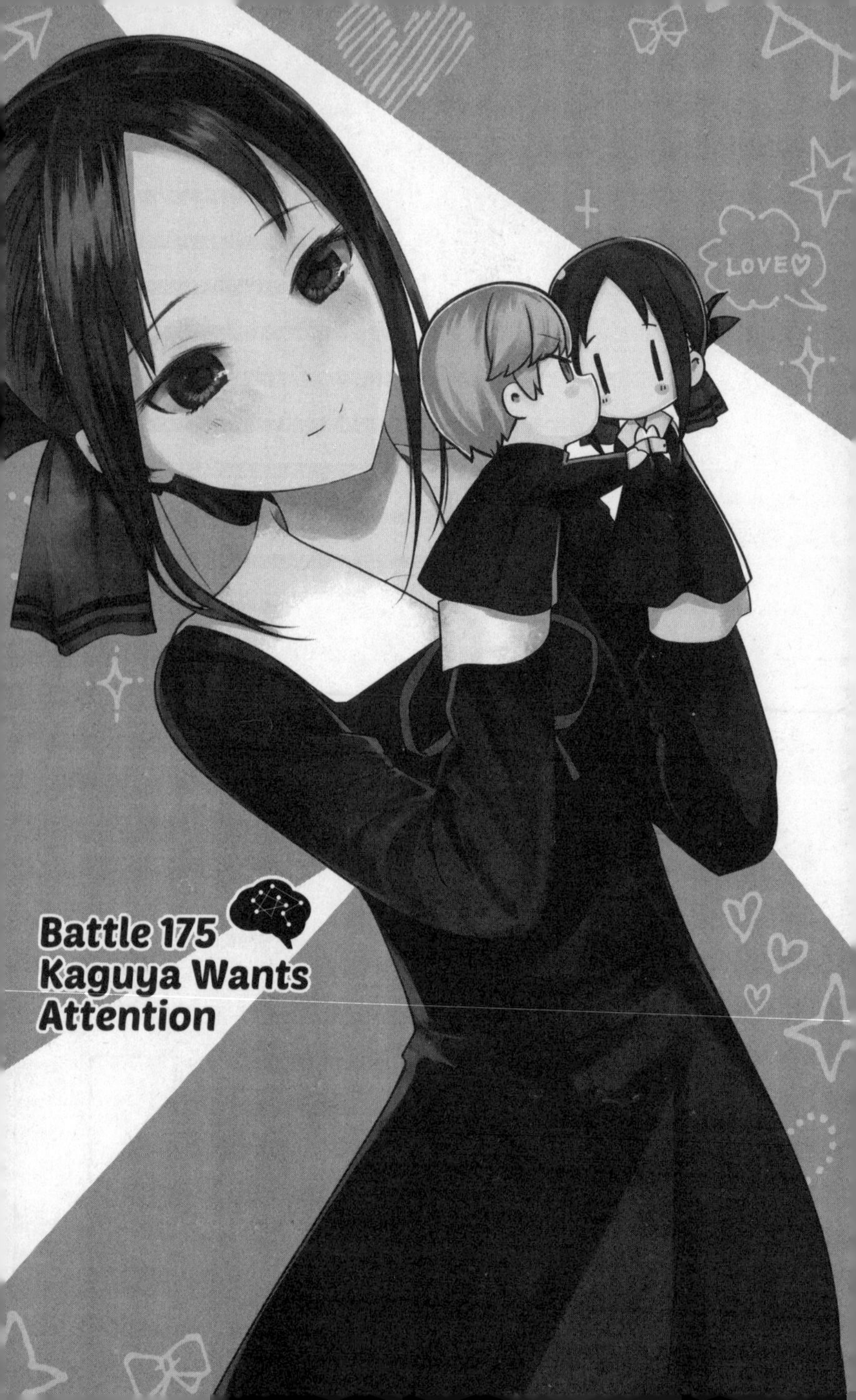
LOVE

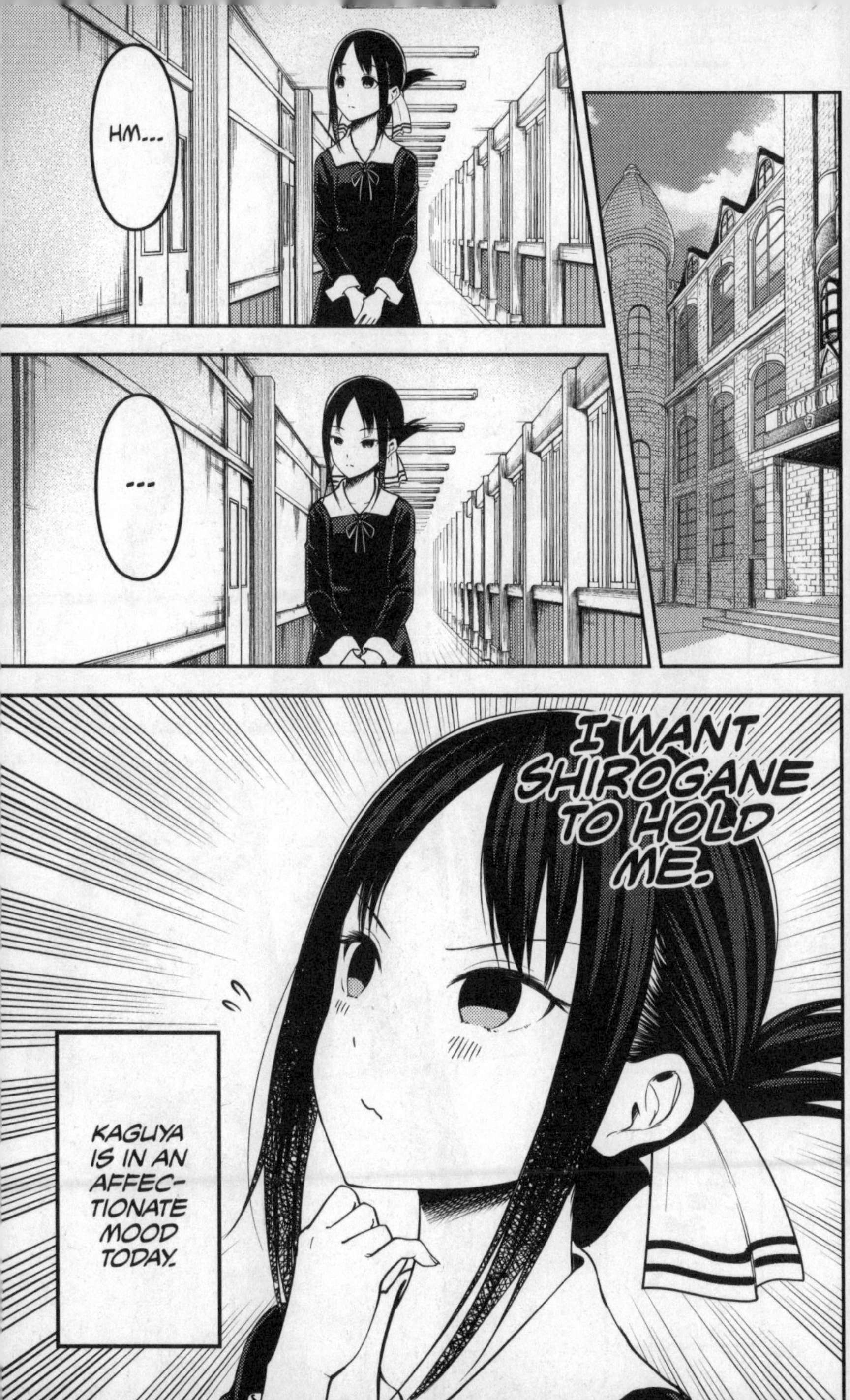
HM...
...
I WANT SHIROGANE TO HOLD ME.
KAGUYA IS IN AN AFFECTIONATE MOOD TODAY.

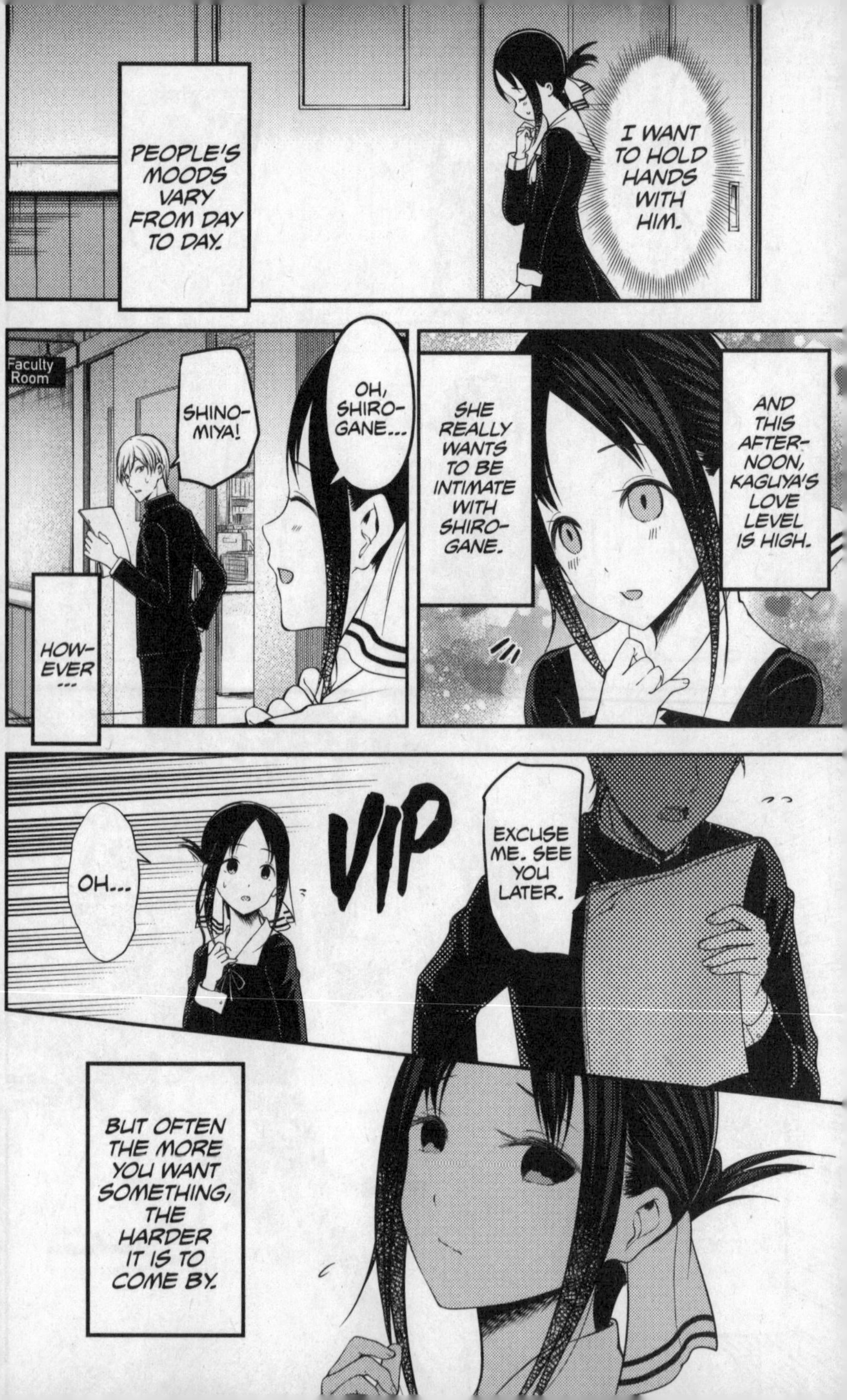
I WANT TO HOLD HANDS WITH HIM.
PEOPLE'S MOODS VARY FROM DAY TO DAY.
AND THIS AFTERNOON, KAGUYA'S LOVE LEVEL IS HIGH.
SHE REALLY WANTS TO BE INTIMATE WITH SHIROGANE.
OH, SHIROGANE...
SHINOMIYA!
Faculty Room
HOWEVER...
EXCUSE ME. SEE YOU LATER.
VIP
OH...
BUT OFTEN THE MORE YOU WANT SOMETHING, THE HARDER IT IS TO COME BY.

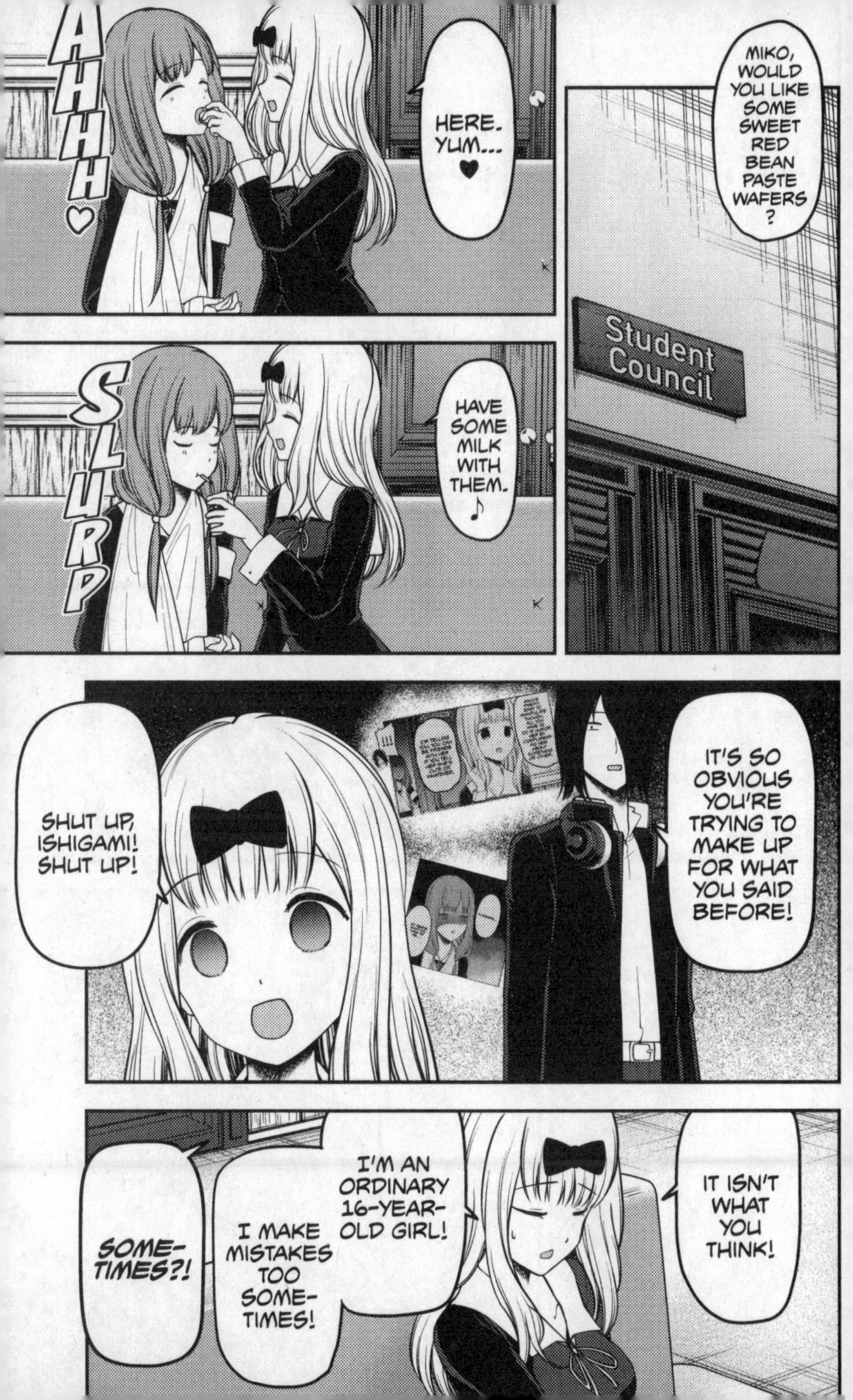
MIKO, WOULD YOU LIKE SOME SWEET RED BEAN PASTE WAFERS?
Student Council
HERE. YUM... ♥
AHHHH ♥
HAVE SOME MILK WITH THEM. ♪
SLURP
IT'S SO OBVIOUS YOU'RE TRYING TO MAKE UP FOR WHAT YOU SAID BEFORE!
SHUT UP, ISHIGAMI! SHUT UP!
IT ISN'T WHAT YOU THINK!
I'M AN ORDINARY 16-YEAR-OLD GIRL!
I MAKE MISTAKES TOO SOMETIMES!
SOMETIMES?!

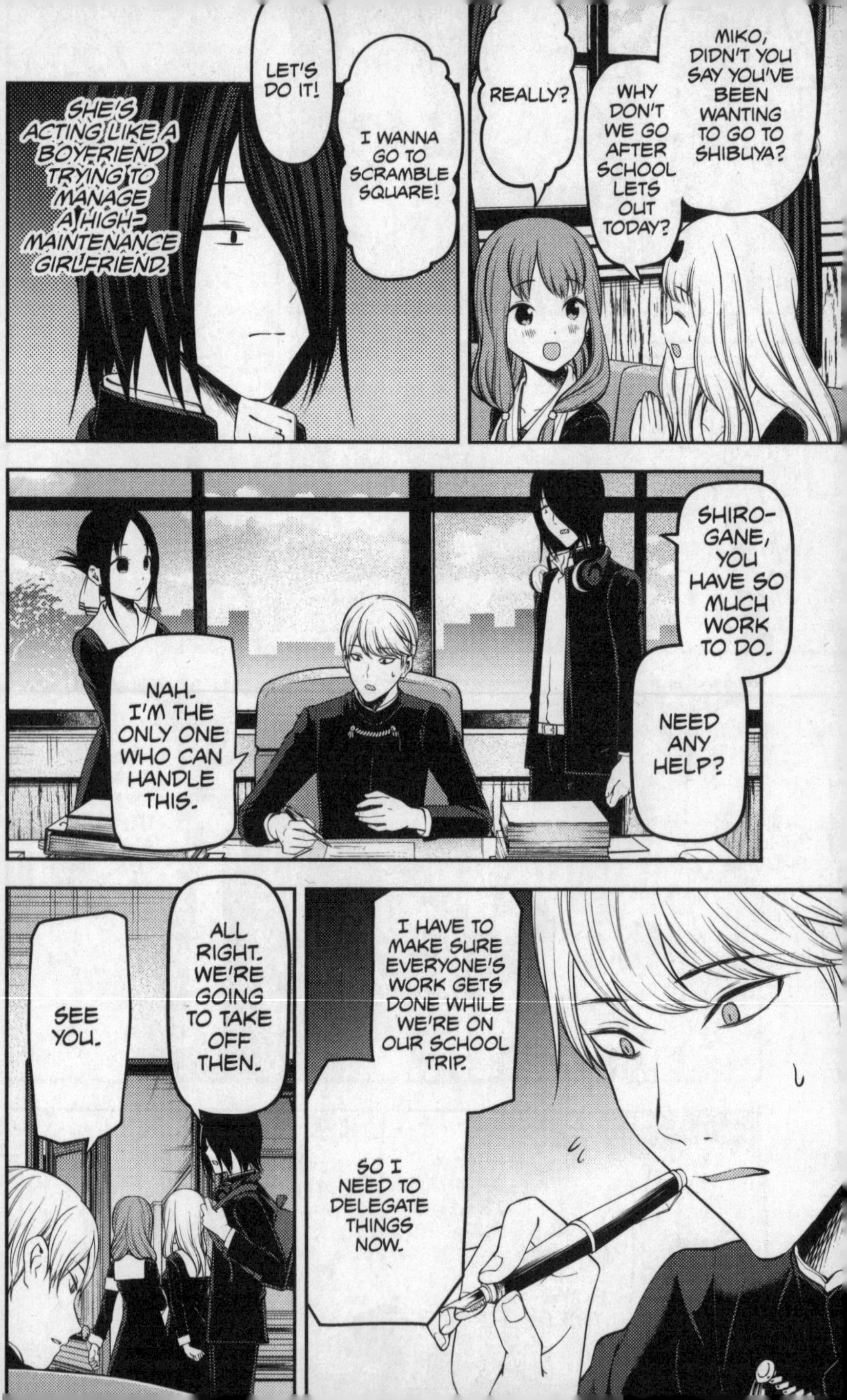
MIKO, DIDN'T YOU SAY YOU'VE BEEN WANTING TO GO TO SHIBUYA?
WHY DON'T WE GO AFTER SCHOOL LETS OUT TODAY?
REALLY?
I WANNA GO TO SCRAMBLE SQUARE!
LET'S DO IT!
SHE'S ACTING LIKE A BOYFRIEND TRYING TO MANAGE A HIGH-MAINTENANCE GIRLFRIEND.
SHIRO-GANE, YOU HAVE SO MUCH WORK TO DO.
NEED ANY HELP?
NAH. I'M THE ONLY ONE WHO CAN HANDLE THIS.
I HAVE TO MAKE SURE EVERYONE'S WORK GETS DONE WHILE WE'RE ON OUR SCHOOL TRIP.
SO I NEED TO DELEGATE THINGS NOW.
ALL RIGHT. WE'RE GOING TO TAKE OFF THEN.
SEE YOU.

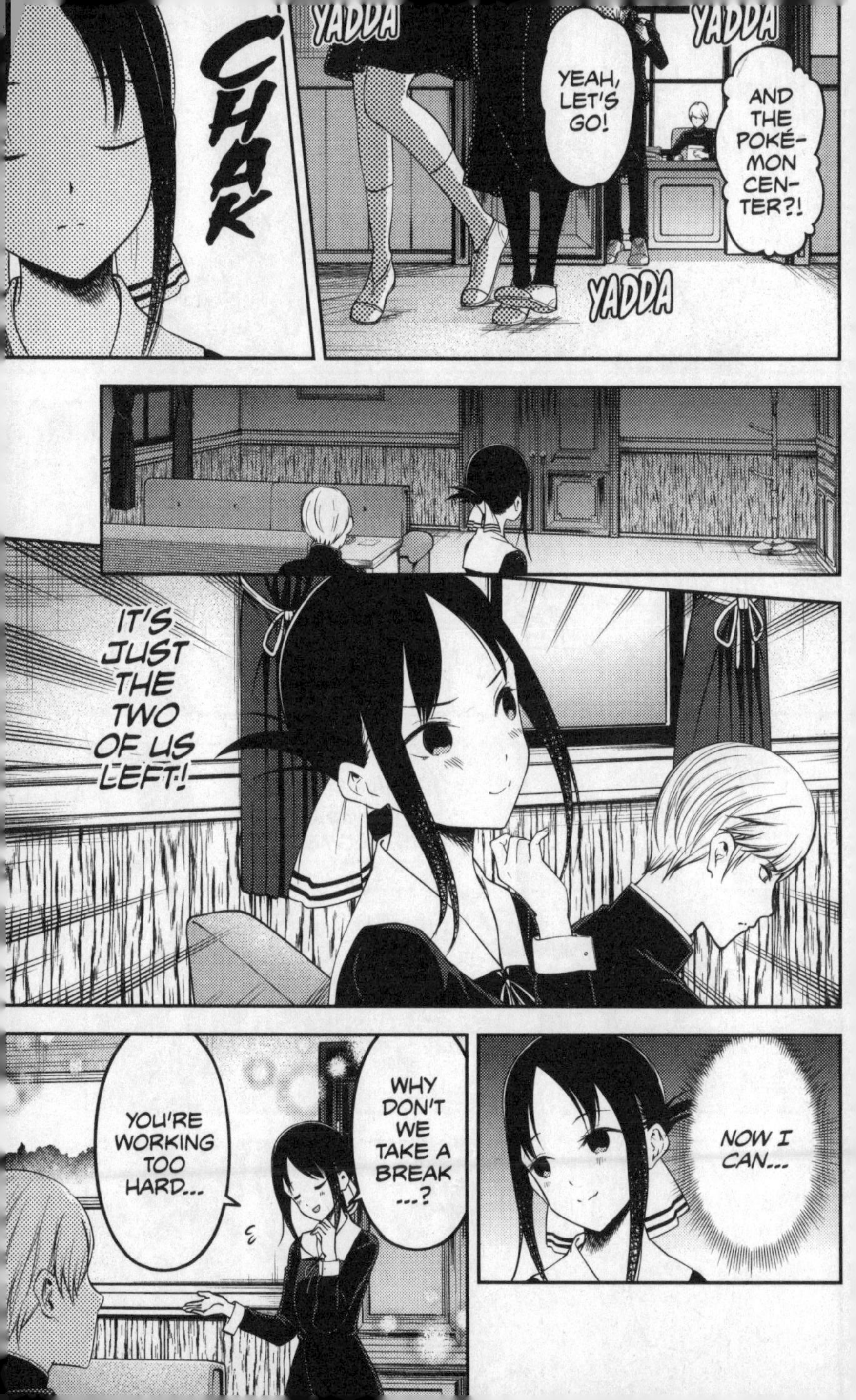
YADDA
AND THE POKÉMON CENTER?!
YEAH, LET'S GO!
YADDA
YADDA
CHAK
IT'S JUST THE TWO OF US LEFT!
NOW I CAN...
WHY DON'T WE TAKE A BREAK...?
YOU'RE WORKING TOO HARD...

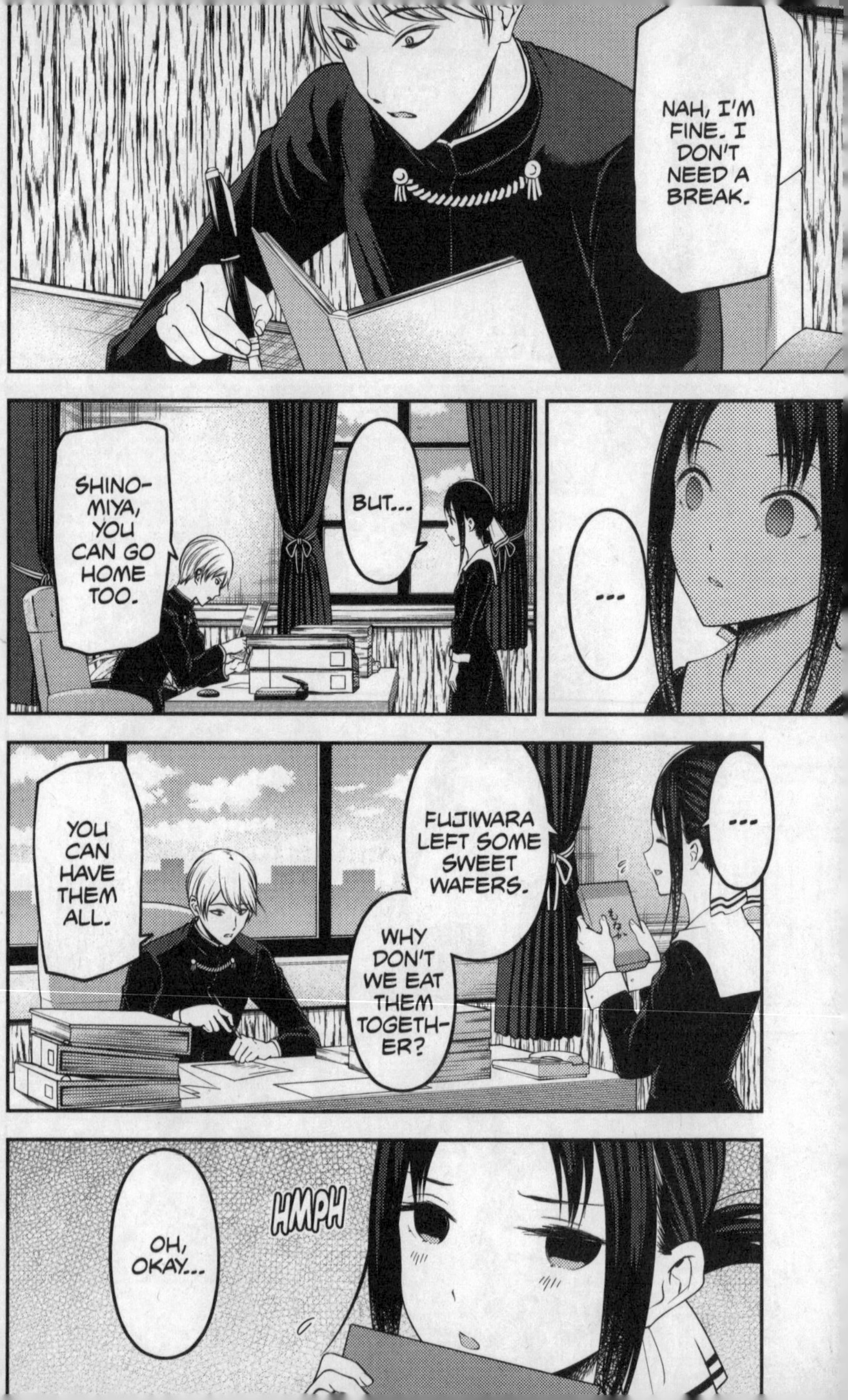
NAH, I'M FINE. I DON'T NEED A BREAK.
...
BUT...
SHINO-MIYA, YOU CAN GO HOME TOO.
...
FUJIWARA LEFT SOME SWEET WAFERS.
WHY DON'T WE EAT THEM TOGETH-ER?
YOU CAN HAVE THEM ALL.
HMPH
OH, OKAY...

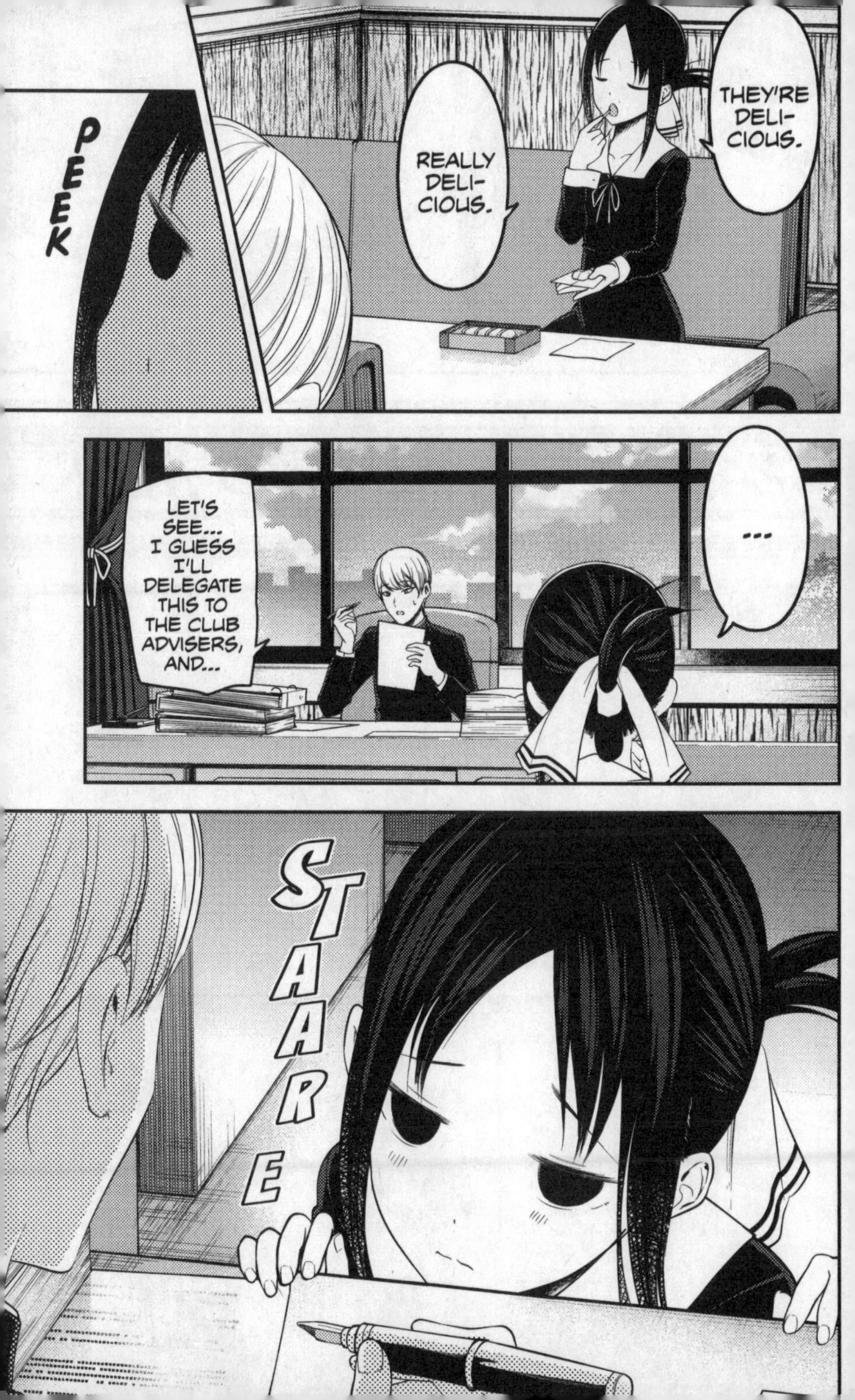
THEY'RE DELI-CIOUS.
REALLY DELI-CIOUS.
PEEK
...
LET'S SEE... I GUESS I'LL DELEGATE THIS TO THE CLUB ADVISERS, AND...
STAARE

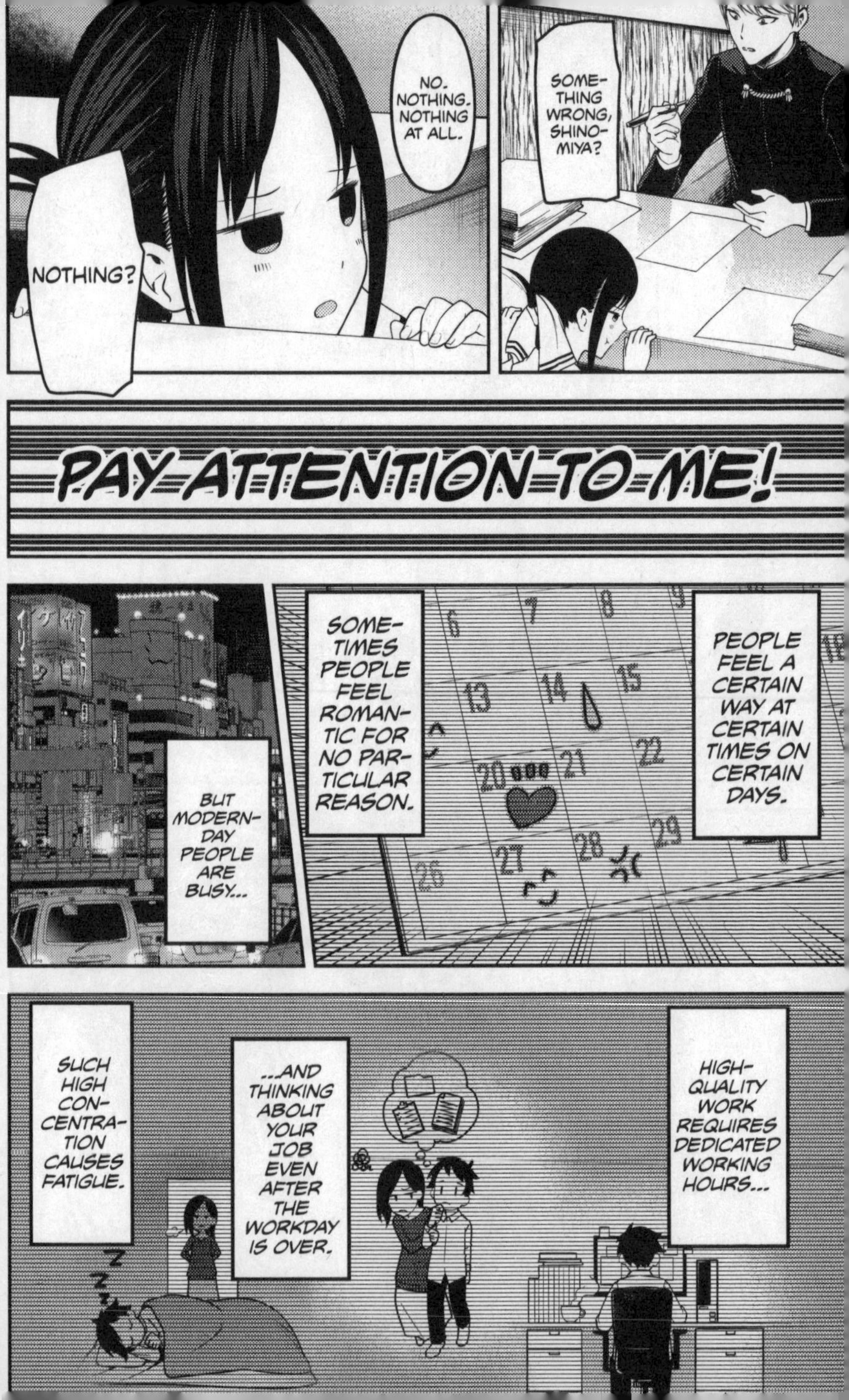

SOMETHING WRONG, SHINOMIYA?
NO. NOTHING. NOTHING AT ALL.
NOTHING?
PAY ATTENTION TO ME!
PEOPLE FEEL A CERTAIN WAY AT CERTAIN TIMES ON CERTAIN DAYS.
SOMETIMES PEOPLE FEEL ROMANTIC FOR NO PARTICULAR REASON.
BUT MODERN-DAY PEOPLE ARE BUSY...
HIGH-QUALITY WORK REQUIRES DEDICATED WORKING HOURS...
...AND THINKING ABOUT YOUR JOB EVEN AFTER THE WORKDAY IS OVER.
SUCH HIGH CONCENTRATION CAUSES FATIGUE.

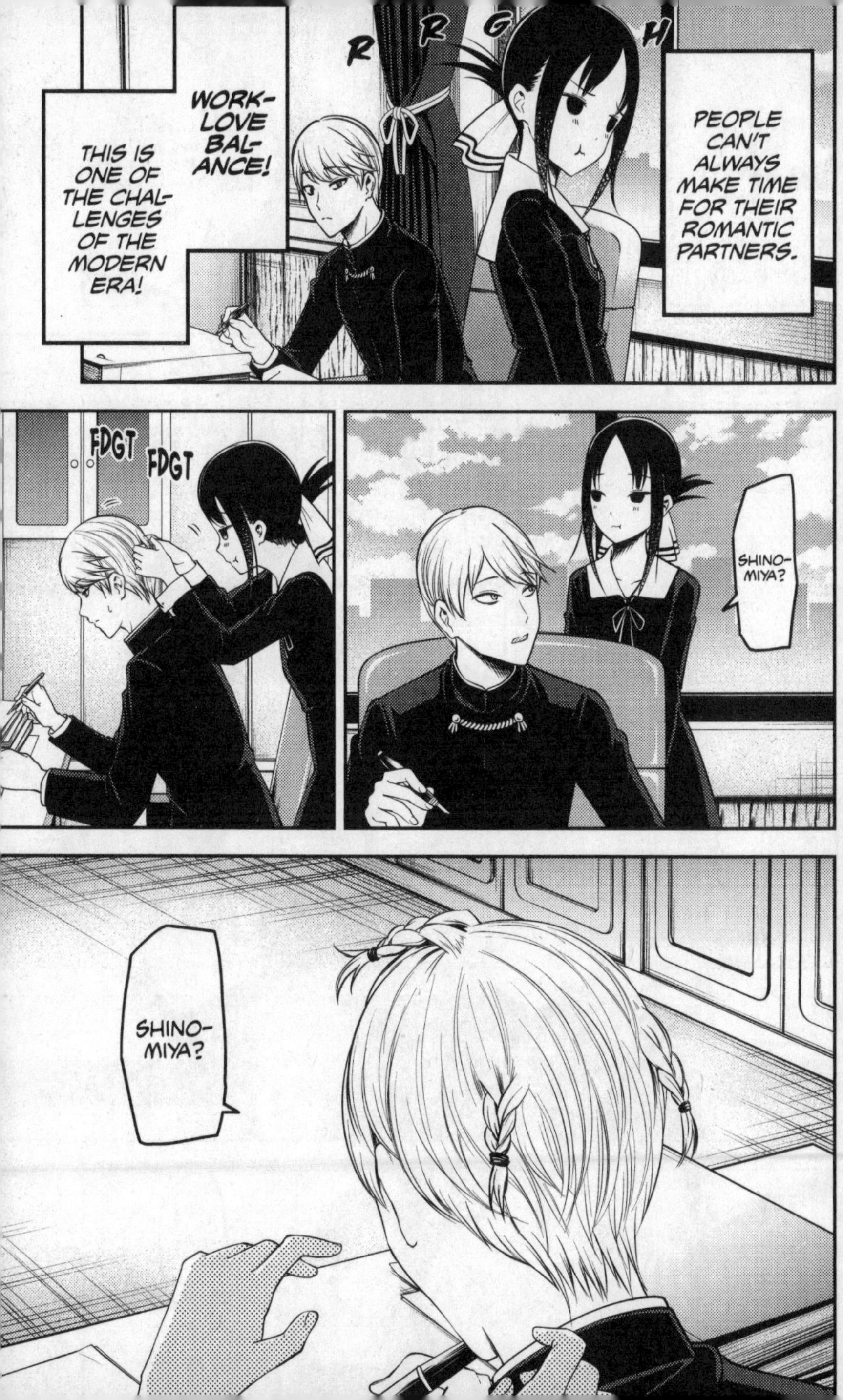
PEOPLE CAN'T ALWAYS MAKE TIME FOR THEIR ROMANTIC PARTNERS.
RRGH
WORK-LOVE BALANCE!
THIS IS ONE OF THE CHALLENGES OF THE MODERN ERA!
SHINOMIYA?
FDGT FDGT
SHINOMIYA?

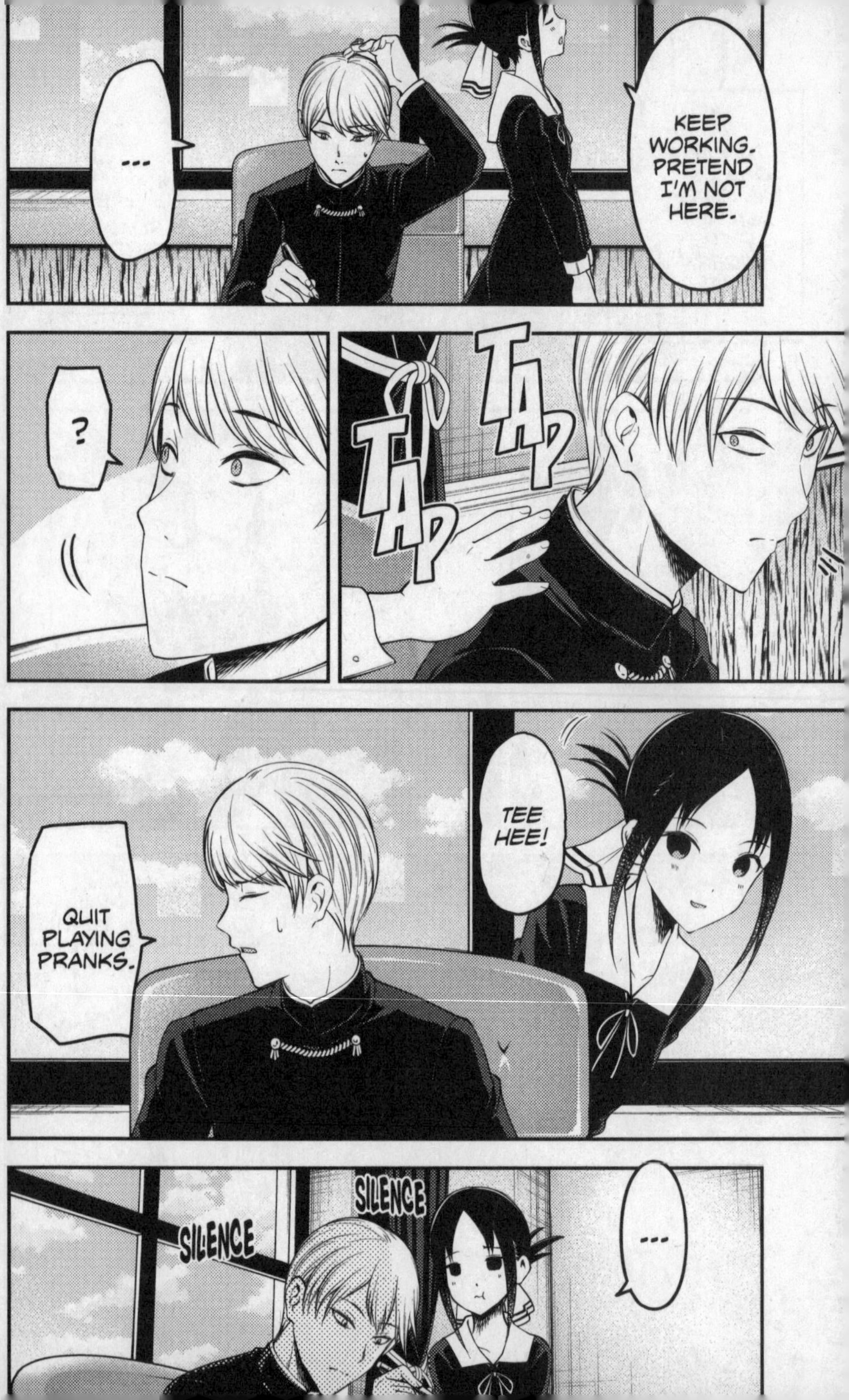
KEEP WORKING. PRETEND I'M NOT HERE.
...
TAP
TAP
?
TEE HEE!
QUIT PLAYING PRANKS.
...
SILENCE
SILENCE

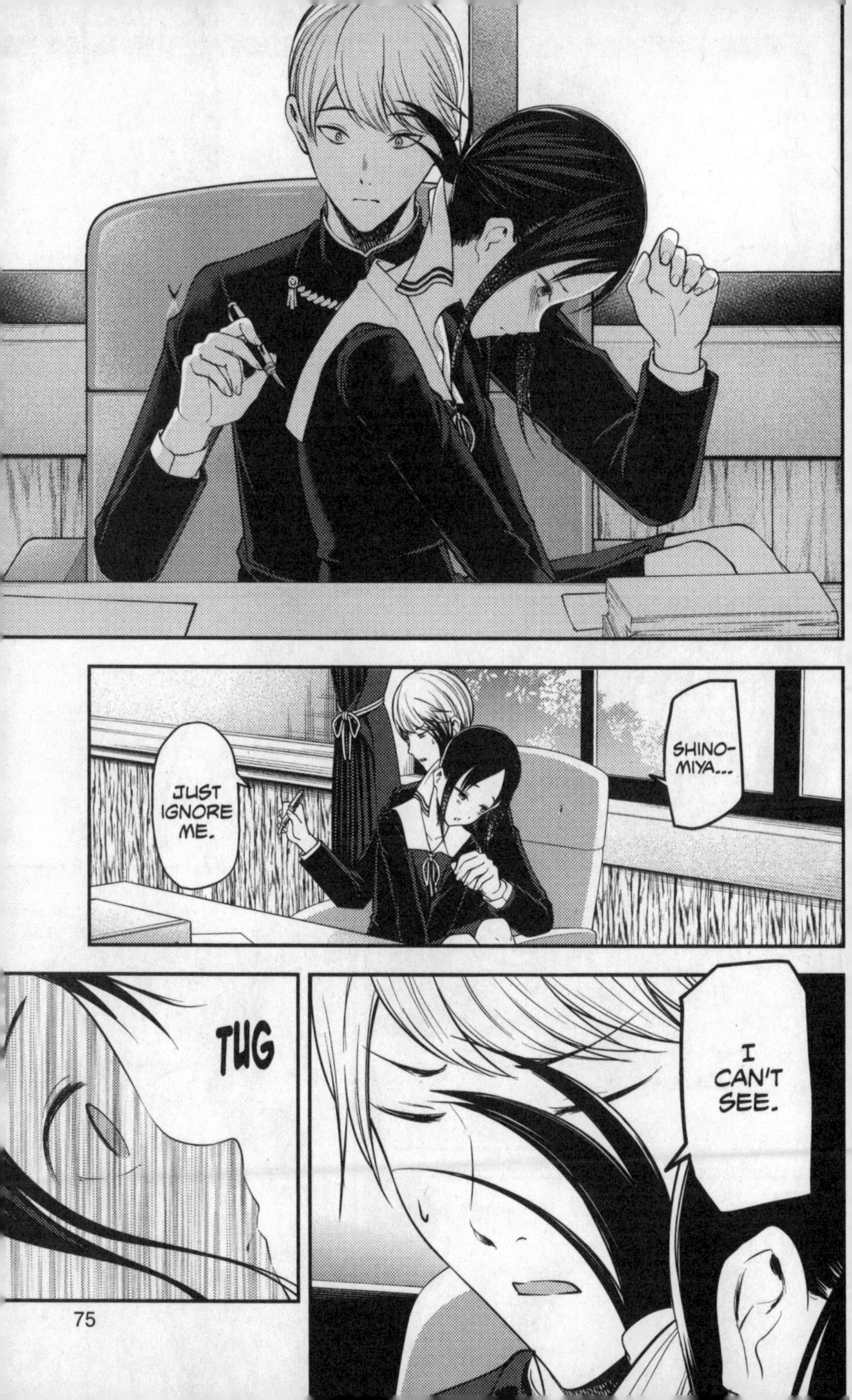
SHINO-MIYA...
JUST IGNORE ME.
I CAN'T SEE.
TUG

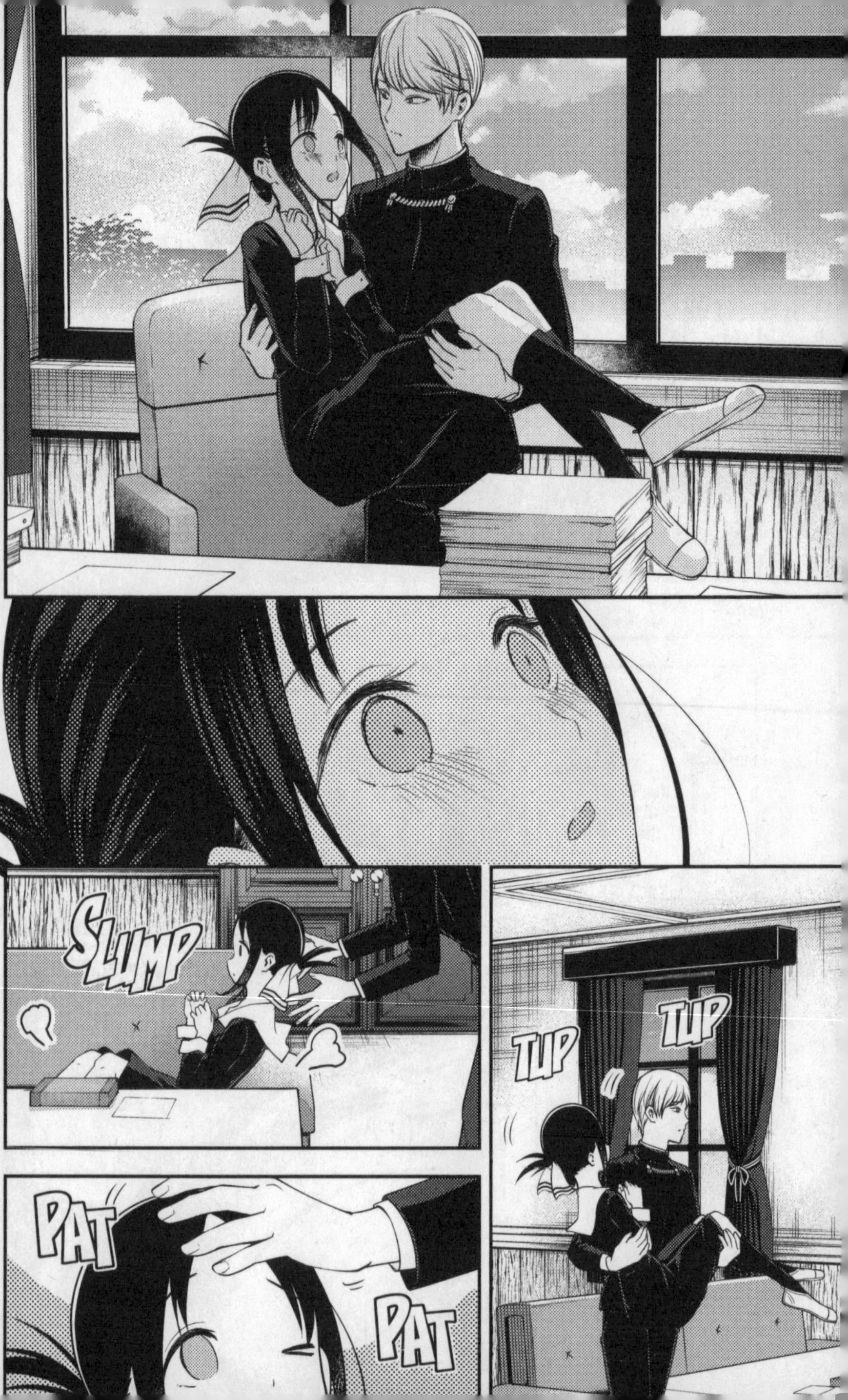
TUP
TUP
SLUMP
PAT
PAT

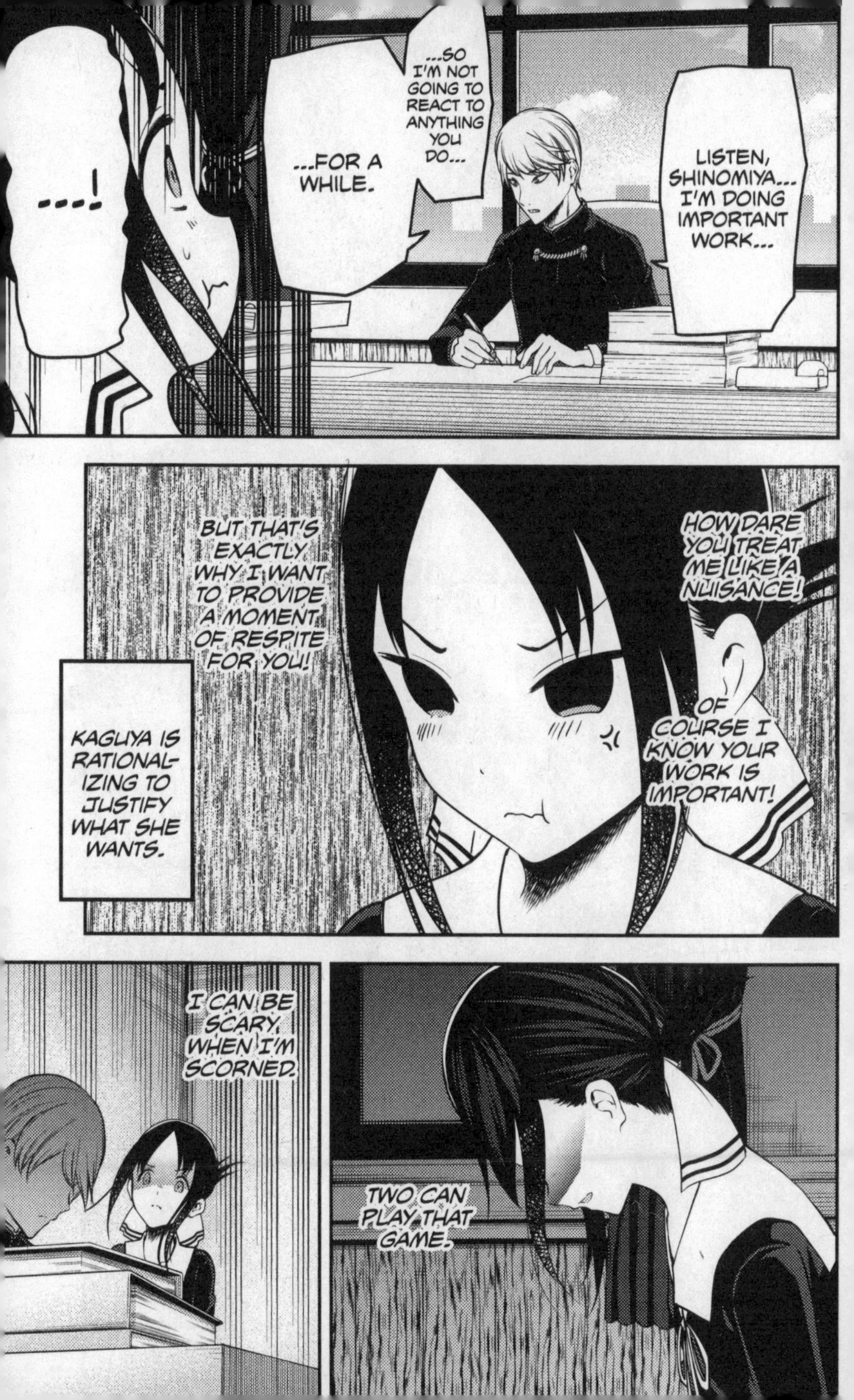
LISTEN, SHINOMIYA... I'M DOING IMPORTANT WORK...
...SO I'M NOT GOING TO REACT TO ANYTHING YOU DO...
...FOR A WHILE.
...!
HOW DARE YOU TREAT ME LIKE A NUISANCE!
OF COURSE I KNOW YOUR WORK IS IMPORTANT!
BUT THAT'S EXACTLY WHY I WANT TO PROVIDE A MOMENT OF RESPITE FOR YOU!
KAGUYA IS RATIONALIZING TO JUSTIFY WHAT SHE WANTS.
TWO CAN PLAY THAT GAME.
I CAN BE SCARY WHEN I'M SCORNED.

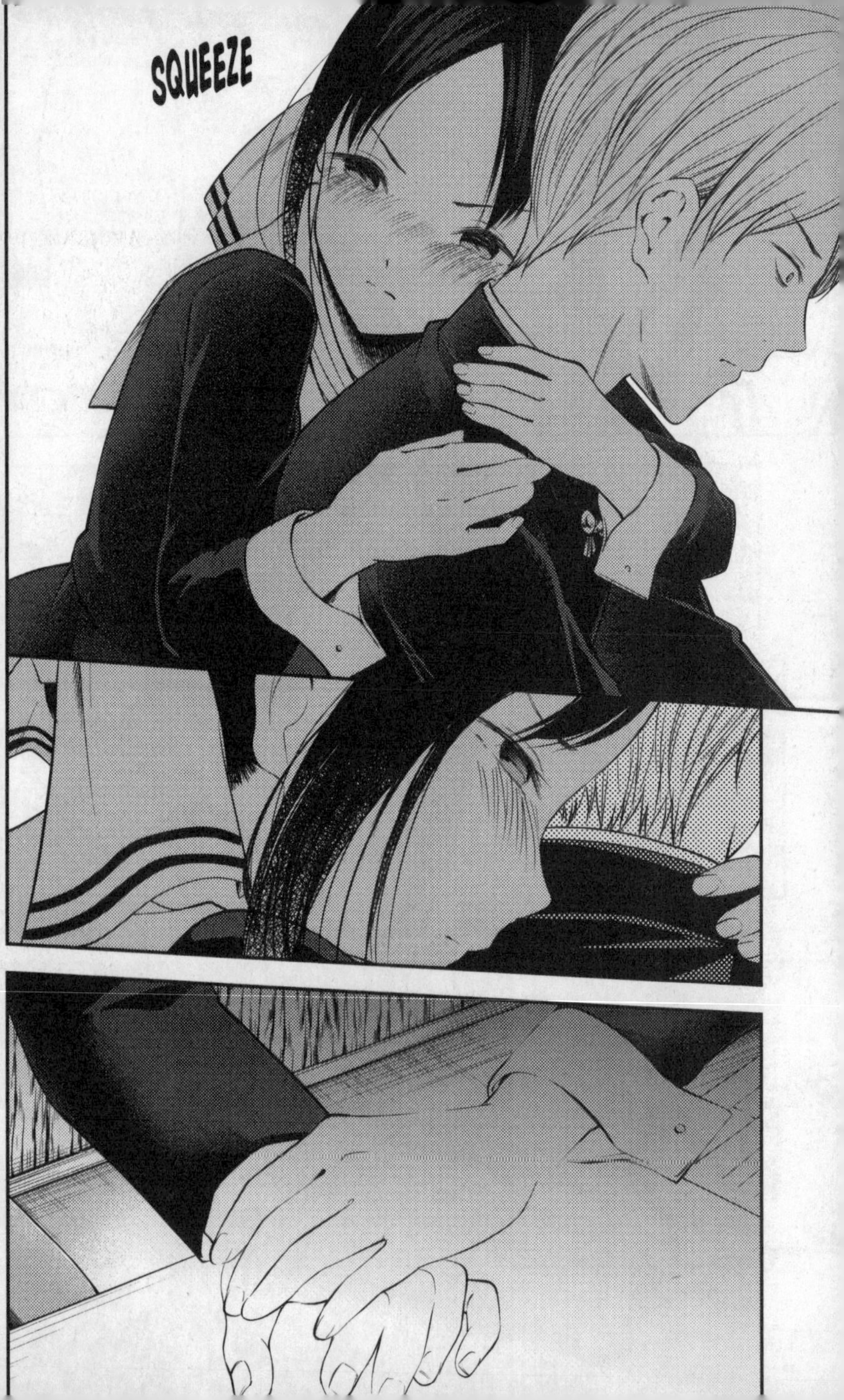
SQUEEZE

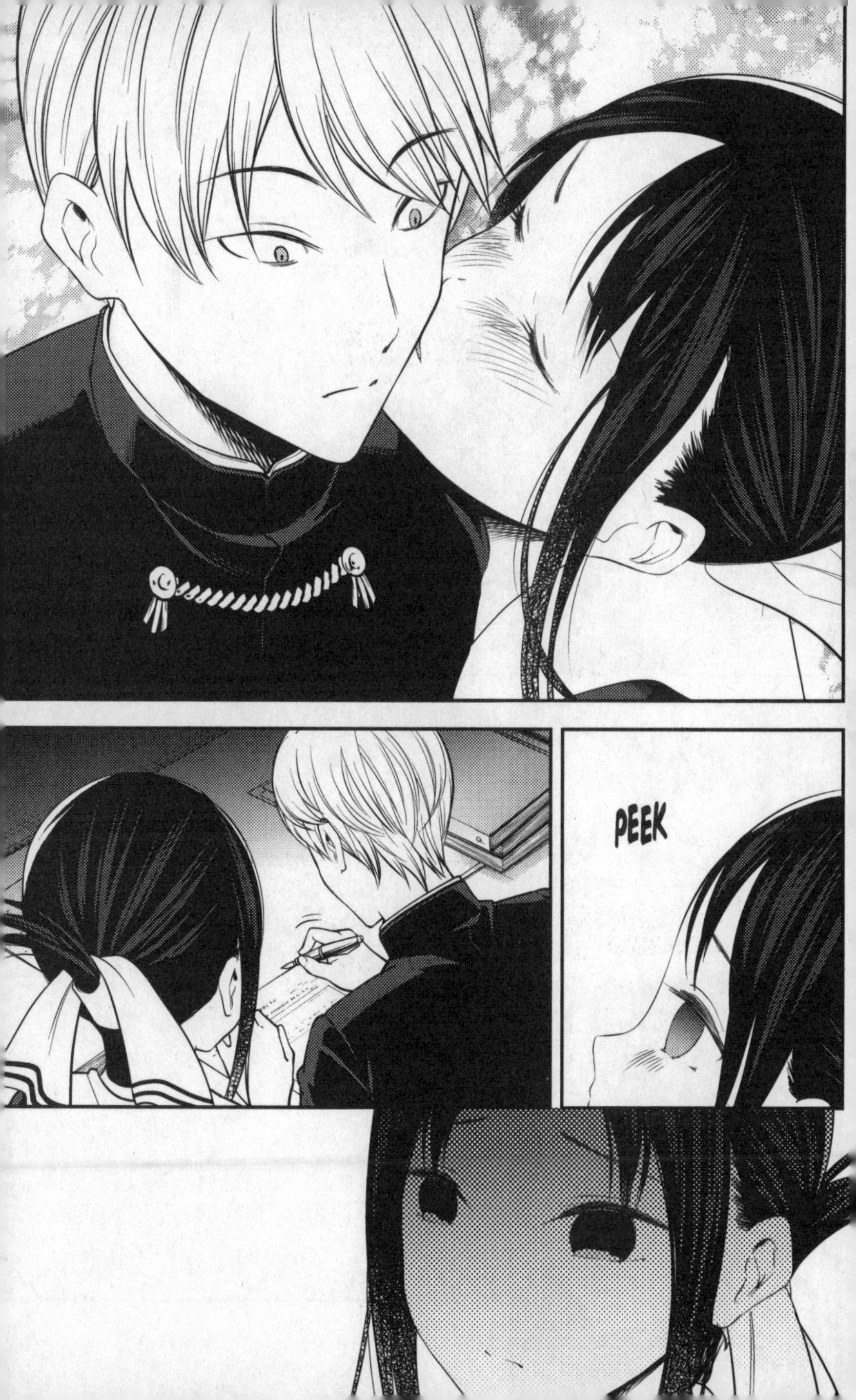
PEEK

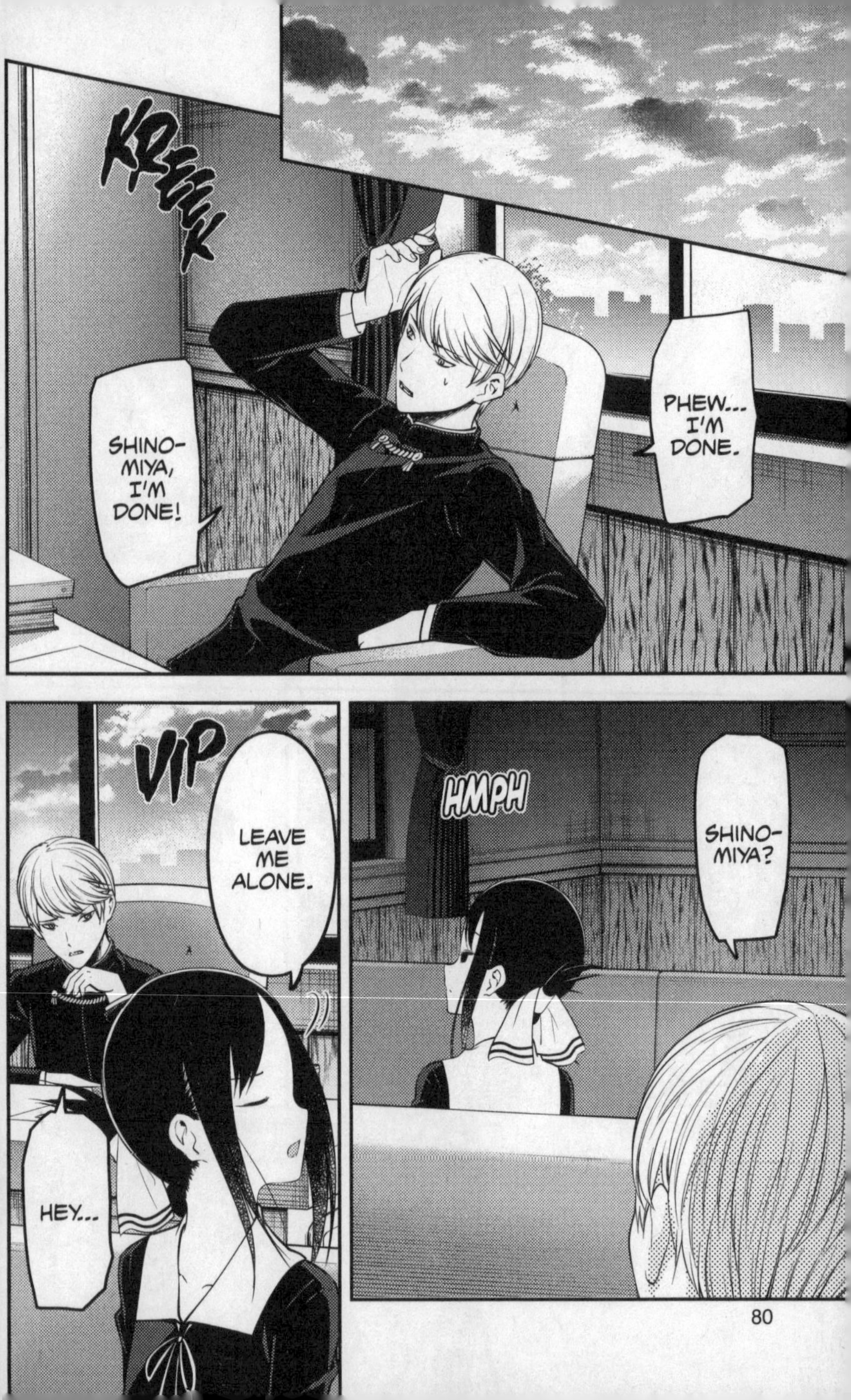
KREEEK
PHEW... I'M DONE.
SHINO-MIYA, I'M DONE!
SHINO-MIYA?
HMPH
VIP
LEAVE ME ALONE.
HEY...

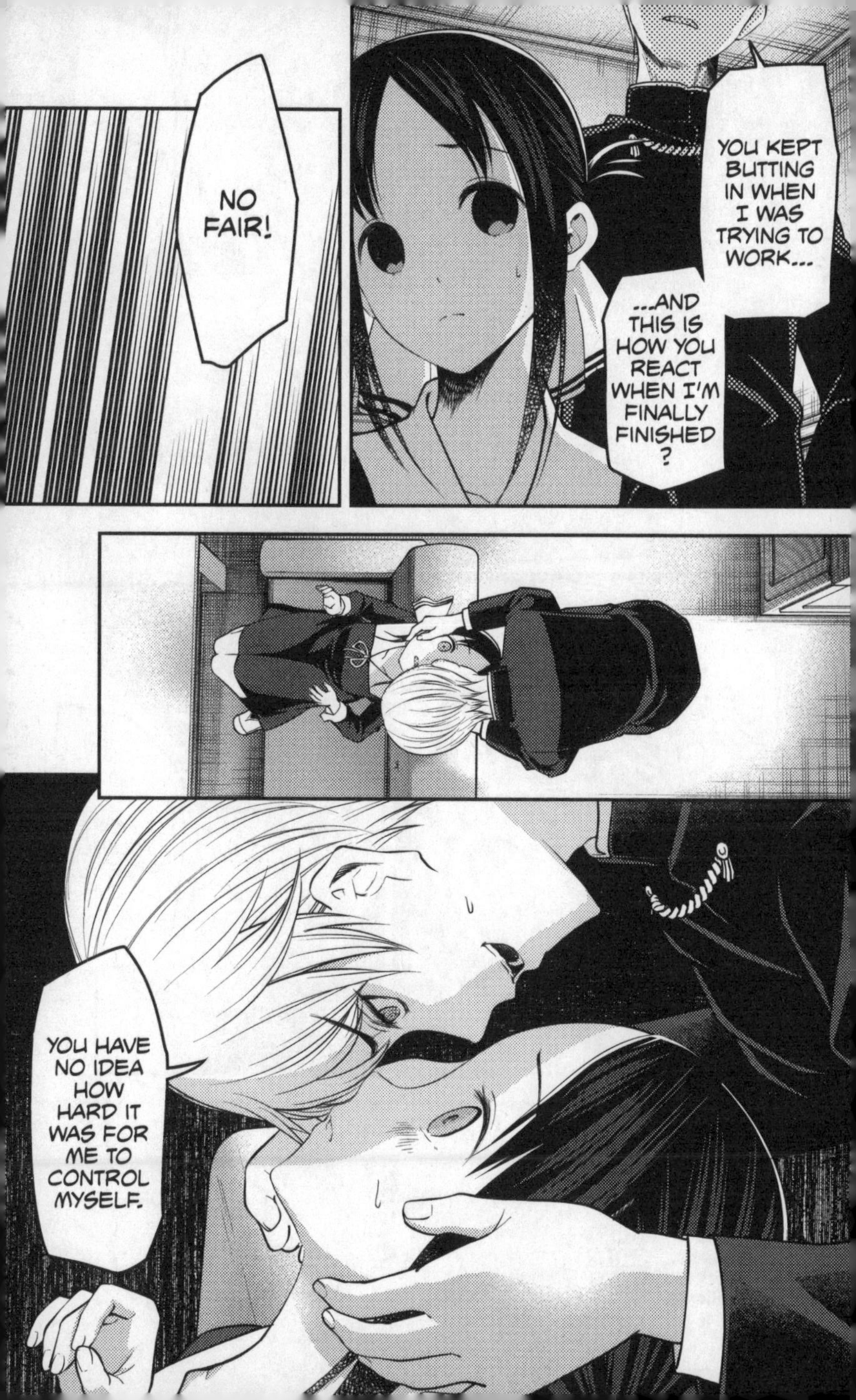
YOU KEPT BUTTING IN WHEN I WAS TRYING TO WORK...
...AND THIS IS HOW YOU REACT WHEN I'M FINALLY FINISHED?
NO FAIR!
YOU HAVE NO IDEA HOW HARD IT WAS FOR ME TO CONTROL MYSELF.

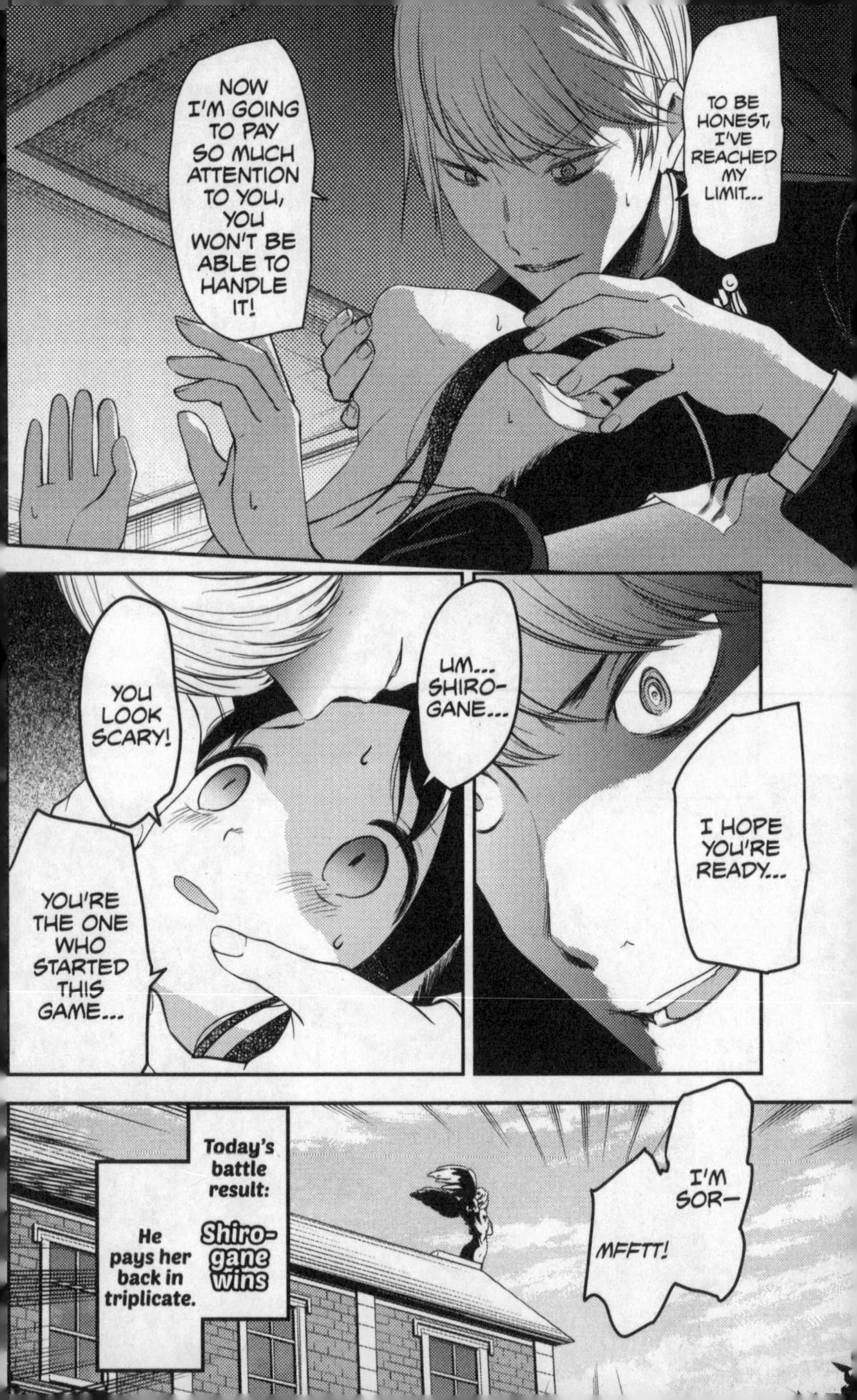
TO BE HONEST, I'VE REACHED MY LIMIT...
NOW I'M GOING TO PAY SO MUCH ATTENTION TO YOU, YOU WON'T BE ABLE TO HANDLE IT!
I HOPE YOU'RE READY...
UM... SHIRO-GANE...
YOU LOOK SCARY!
YOU'RE THE ONE WHO STARTED THIS GAME...
I'M SOR—
MFFTT!
Today's battle result:
Shiro-gane wins
He pays her back in triplicate.

PANIC
PANIC

← Came
to
visit

KAGUYA-SAMA

LOVE IS WAR

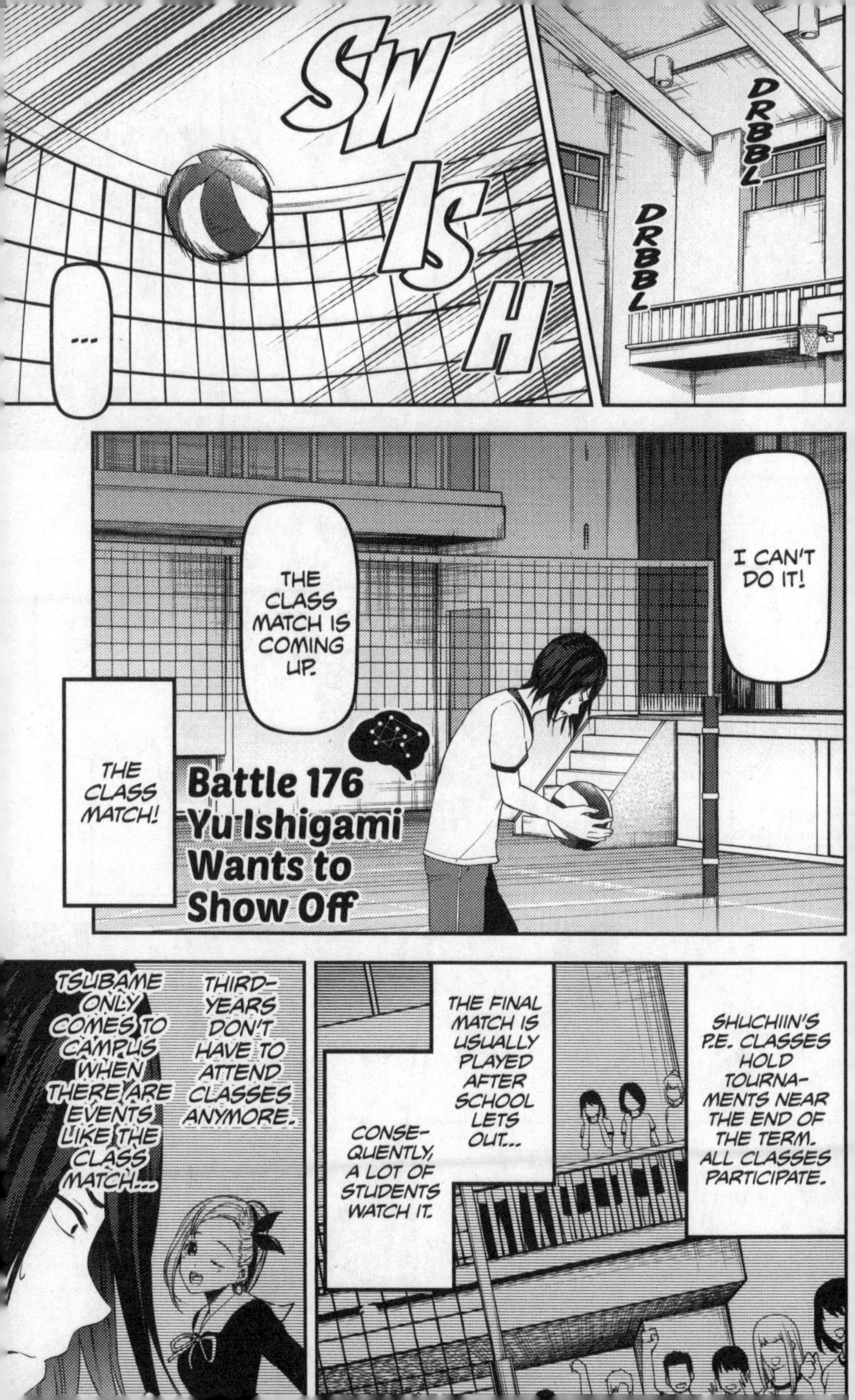
DRBBL
DRBBL
SWISH
...
I CAN'T DO IT!
THE CLASS MATCH IS COMING UP.
Battle 176 Yu Ishigami Wants to Show Off
THE CLASS MATCH!
SHUCHIIN'S P.E. CLASSES HOLD TOURNAMENTS NEAR THE END OF THE TERM. ALL CLASSES PARTICIPATE.
THE FINAL MATCH IS USUALLY PLAYED AFTER SCHOOL LETS OUT...
CONSEQUENTLY, A LOT OF STUDENTS WATCH IT.
THIRD-YEARS DON'T HAVE TO ATTEND CLASSES ANYMORE.
TSUBAME ONLY COMES TO CAMPUS WHEN THERE ARE EVENTS LIKE THE CLASS MATCH...

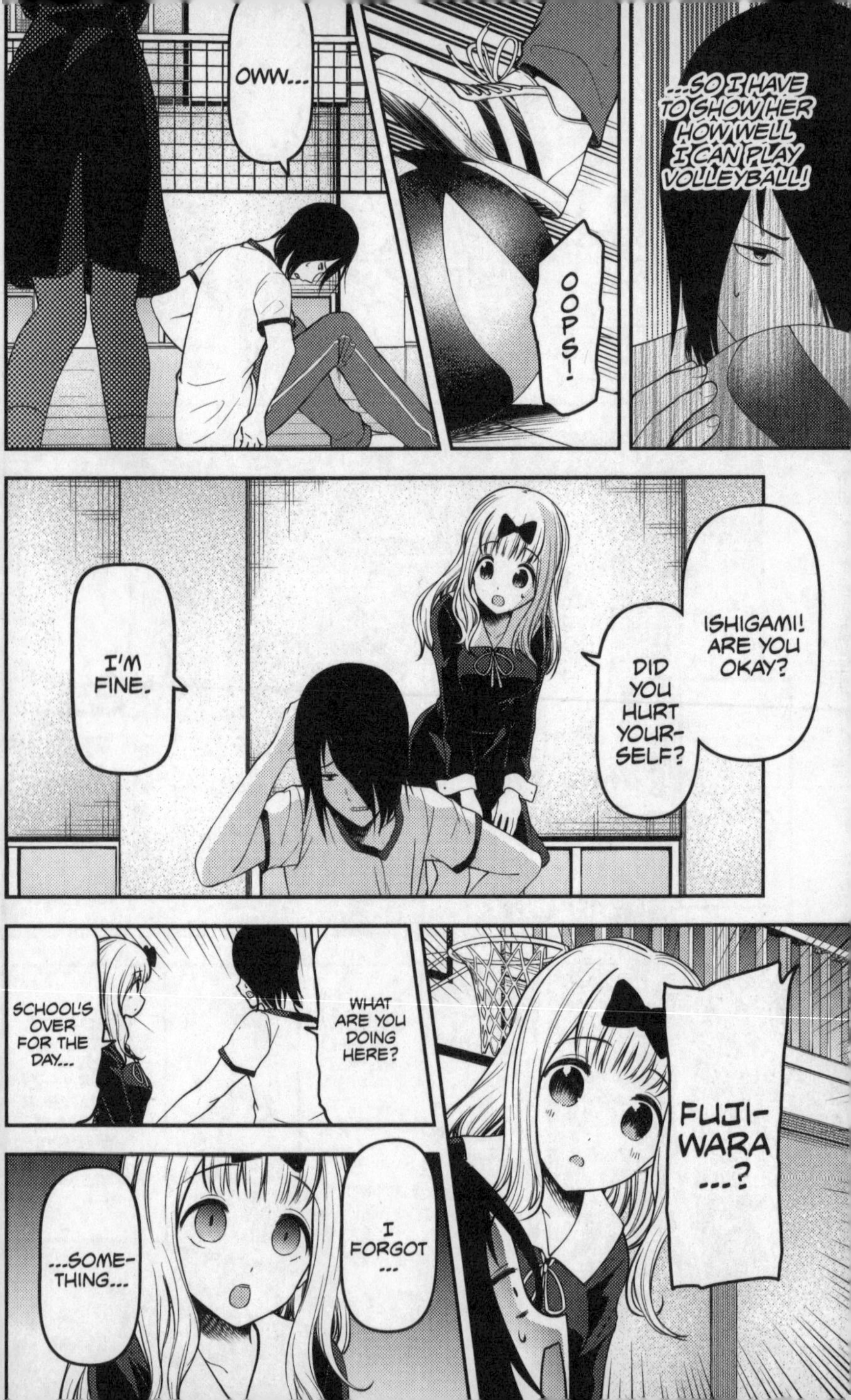
...SO I HAVE TO SHOW HER HOW WELL I CAN PLAY VOLLEYBALL!
OOPS!
OWW...
ISHIGAMI! ARE YOU OKAY?
DID YOU HURT YOURSELF?
I'M FINE.
FUJIWARA...?
WHAT ARE YOU DOING HERE?
SCHOOL'S OVER FOR THE DAY...
I FORGOT...
...SOMETHING...

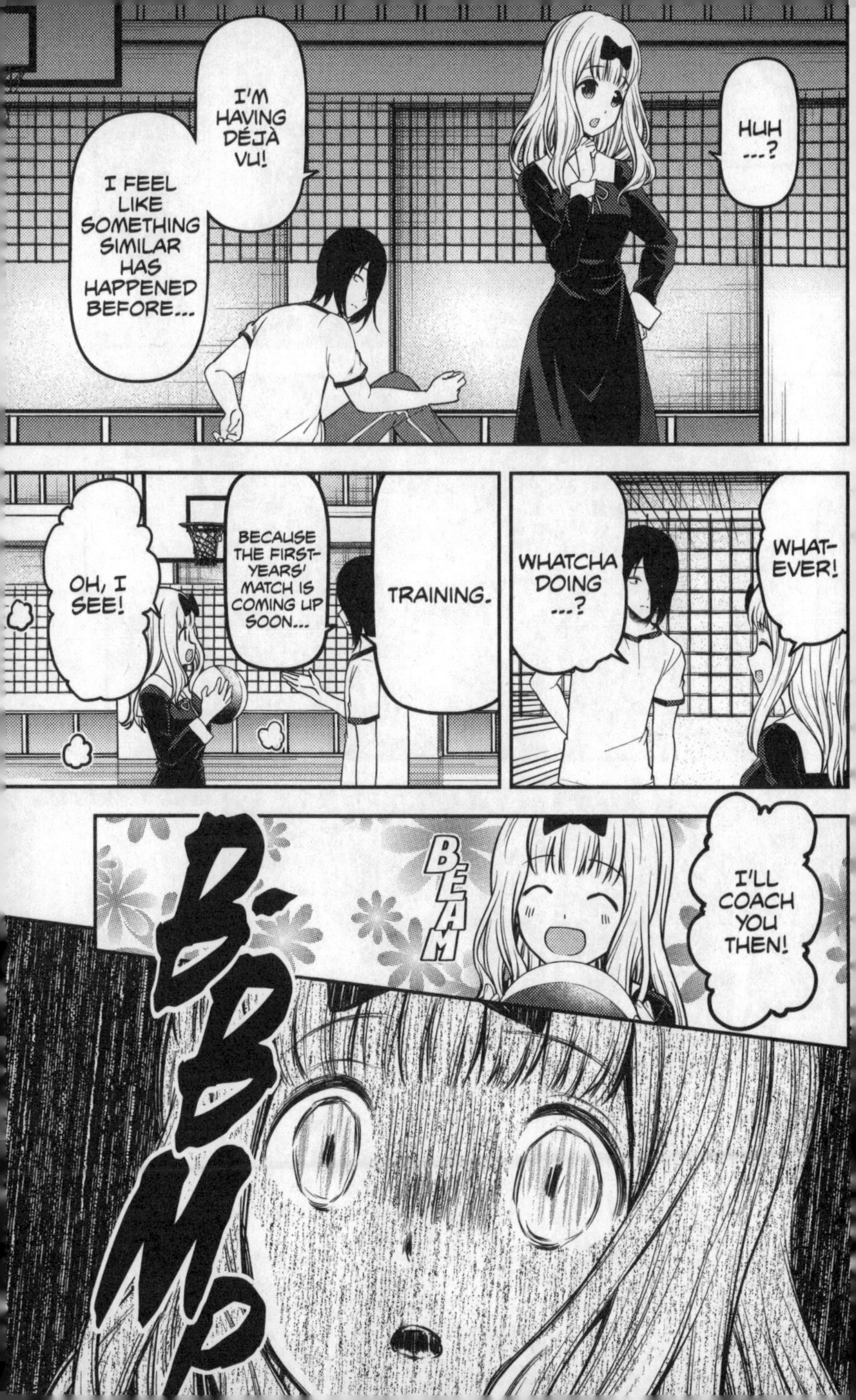
HUH ...?
I'M HAVING DÉJÀ VU!
I FEEL LIKE SOMETHING SIMILAR HAS HAPPENED BEFORE...
WHAT-EVER!
WHATCHA DOING ...?
TRAINING.
BECAUSE THE FIRST-YEARS' MATCH IS COMING UP SOON...
OH, I SEE!
I'LL COACH YOU THEN!
BEAM

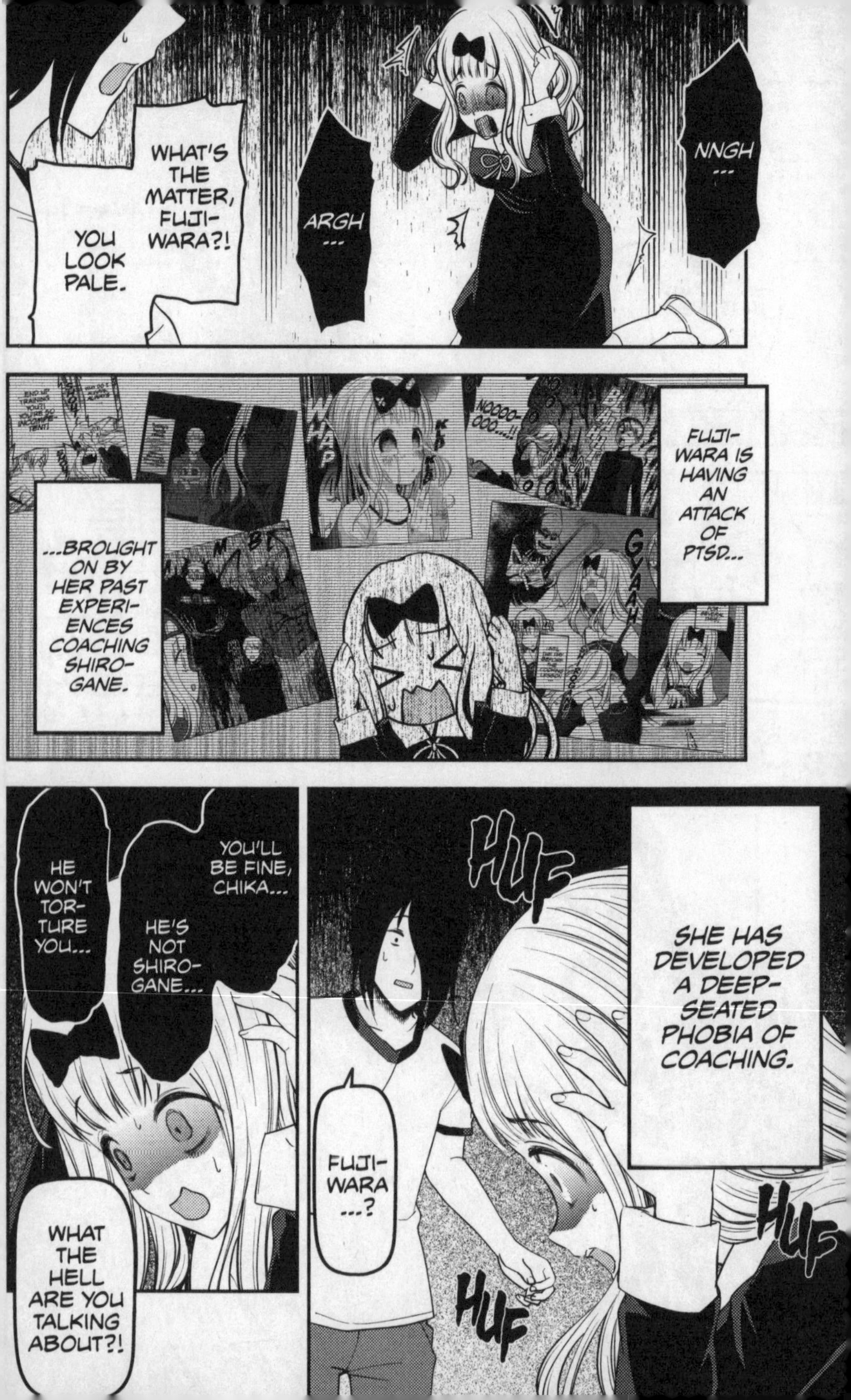
NNGH...
ARGH...
WHAT'S THE MATTER, FUJIWARA?!
YOU LOOK PALE.
FUJIWARA IS HAVING AN ATTACK OF PTSD...
NOOOO-OOO...!!
...BROUGHT ON BY HER PAST EXPERIENCES COACHING SHIROGANE.
HUF
SHE HAS DEVELOPED A DEEP-SEATED PHOBIA OF COACHING.
HUF
FUJIWARA...?
HUF
YOU'LL BE FINE, CHIKA...
HE'S NOT SHIROGANE...
HE WON'T TORTURE YOU...
WHAT THE HELL ARE YOU TALKING ABOUT?!

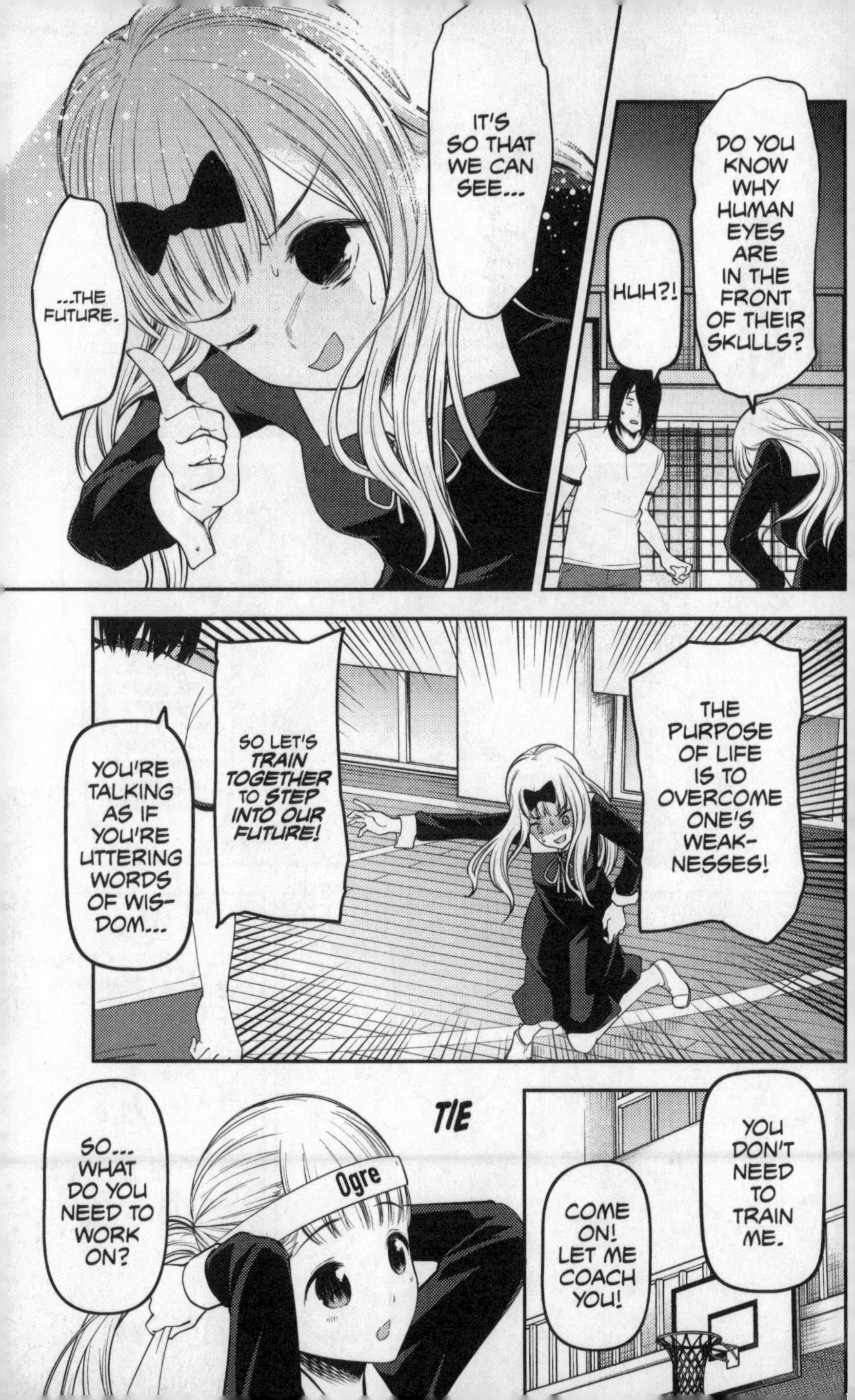
DO YOU KNOW WHY HUMAN EYES ARE IN THE FRONT OF THEIR SKULLS?
HUH?!
IT'S SO THAT WE CAN SEE...
...THE FUTURE.
THE PURPOSE OF LIFE IS TO OVERCOME ONE'S WEAK-NESSES!
SO LET'S *TRAIN TOGETHER* TO *STEP INTO OUR FUTURE!*
YOU'RE TALKING AS IF YOU'RE UTTERING WORDS OF WIS-DOM...
YOU DON'T NEED TO TRAIN ME.
COME ON! LET ME COACH YOU!
TIE
Ogre
SO... WHAT DO YOU NEED TO WORK ON?

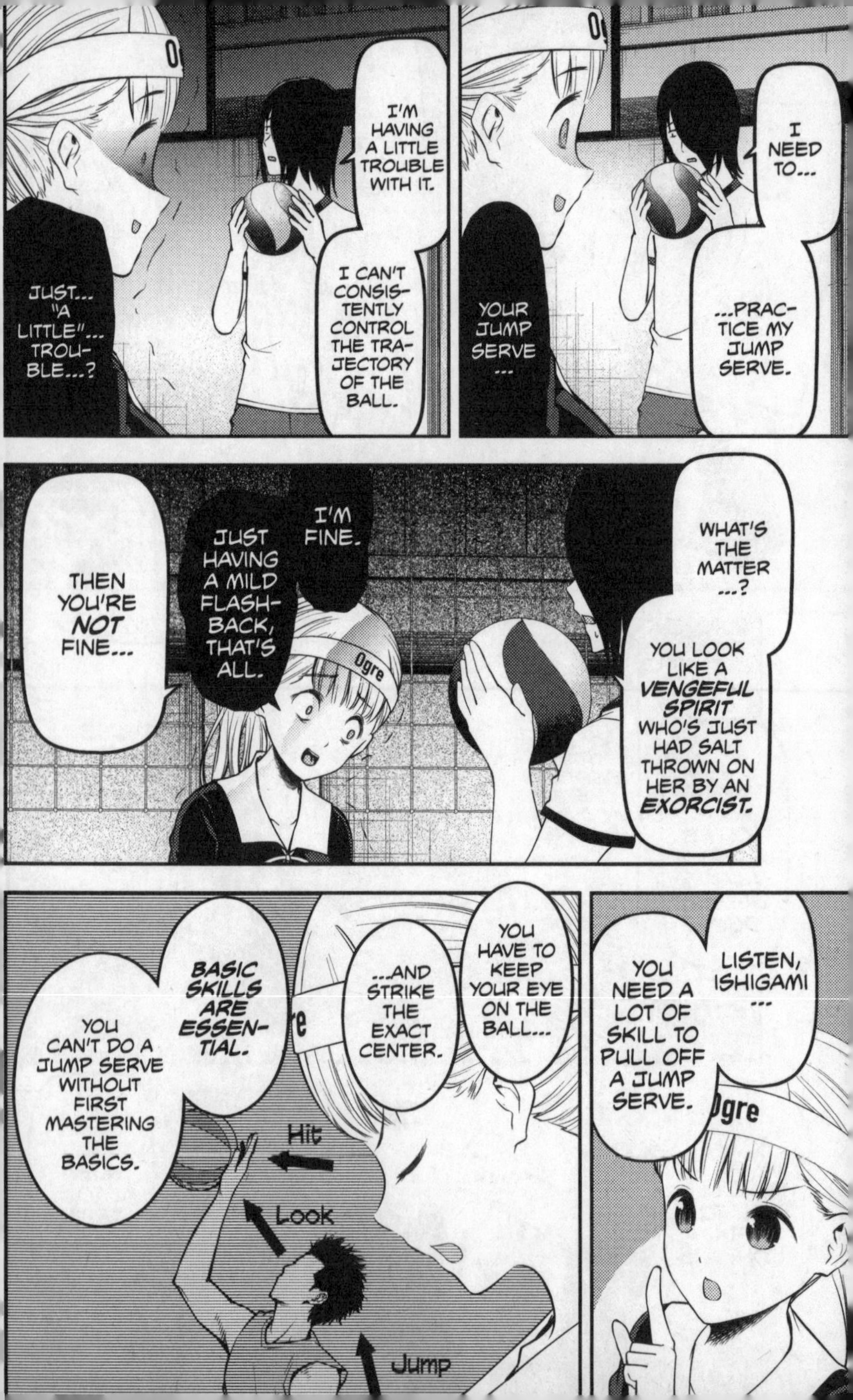
Ogre
I NEED TO...
...PRACTICE MY JUMP SERVE.
YOUR JUMP SERVE...
Og
I'M HAVING A LITTLE TROUBLE WITH IT.
I CAN'T CONSISTENTLY CONTROL THE TRAJECTORY OF THE BALL.
JUST... "A LITTLE"... TROUBLE...?
WHAT'S THE MATTER...?
YOU LOOK LIKE A VENGEFUL SPIRIT WHO'S JUST HAD SALT THROWN ON HER BY AN EXORCIST.
I'M FINE.
JUST HAVING A MILD FLASHBACK, THAT'S ALL.
Ogre
THEN YOU'RE NOT FINE...
LISTEN, ISHIGAMI...
YOU NEED A LOT OF SKILL TO PULL OFF A JUMP SERVE.
Ogre
YOU HAVE TO KEEP YOUR EYE ON THE BALL...
...AND STRIKE THE EXACT CENTER.
BASIC SKILLS ARE ESSENTIAL.
YOU CAN'T DO A JUMP SERVE WITHOUT FIRST MASTERING THE BASICS.
Hit
Look
Jump

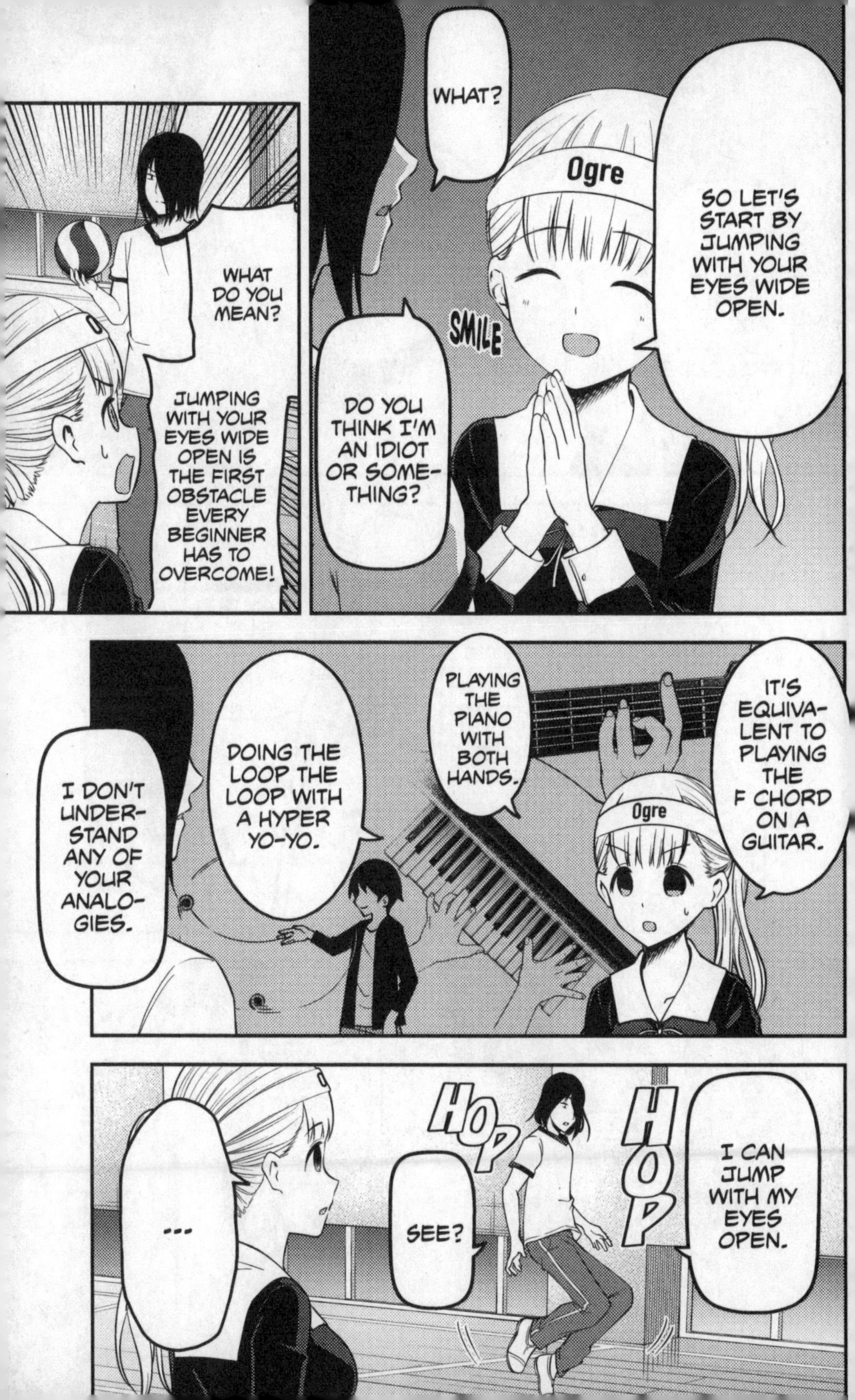

SO LET'S START BY JUMPING WITH YOUR EYES WIDE OPEN.
Ogre
WHAT?
SMILE
DO YOU THINK I'M AN IDIOT OR SOME-THING?
WHAT DO YOU MEAN?
JUMPING WITH YOUR EYES WIDE OPEN IS THE FIRST OBSTACLE EVERY BEGINNER HAS TO OVERCOME!
IT'S EQUIVA-LENT TO PLAYING THE F CHORD ON A GUITAR.
Ogre
PLAYING THE PIANO WITH BOTH HANDS.
DOING THE LOOP THE LOOP WITH A HYPER YO-YO.
I DON'T UNDER-STAND ANY OF YOUR ANALO-GIES.
I CAN JUMP WITH MY EYES OPEN.
HOP
HOP
SEE?
...

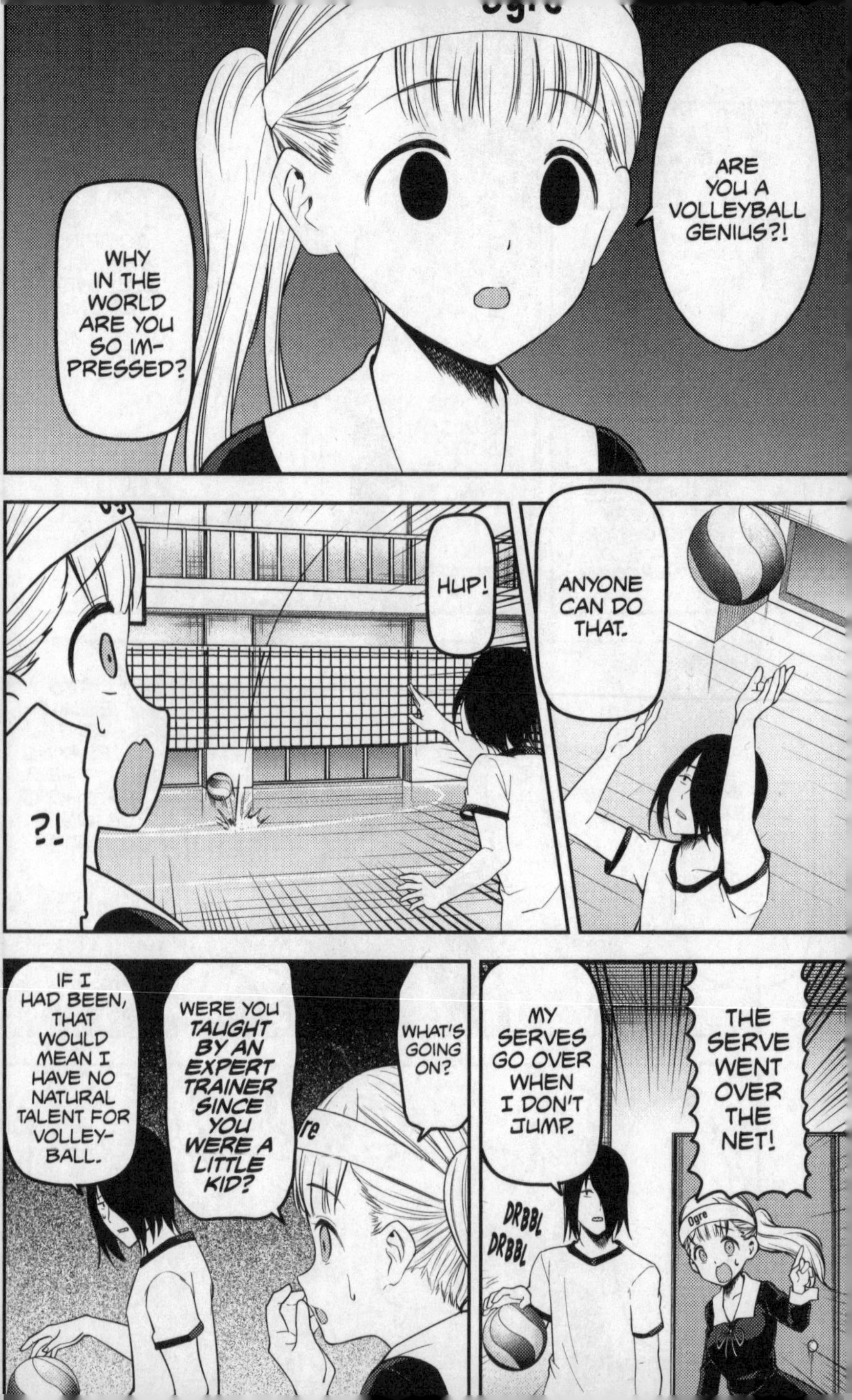
ARE YOU A VOLLEYBALL GENIUS?!
WHY IN THE WORLD ARE YOU SO IMPRESSED?
ANYONE CAN DO THAT.
HUP!
?!
THE SERVE WENT OVER THE NET!
Ogre
MY SERVES GO OVER WHEN I DON'T JUMP.
DRBBL DRBBL
WHAT'S GOING ON?
WERE YOU *TAUGHT BY AN EXPERT TRAINER SINCE YOU WERE A LITTLE KID?*
IF I HAD BEEN, THAT WOULD MEAN I HAVE NO NATURAL TALENT FOR VOLLEYBALL.

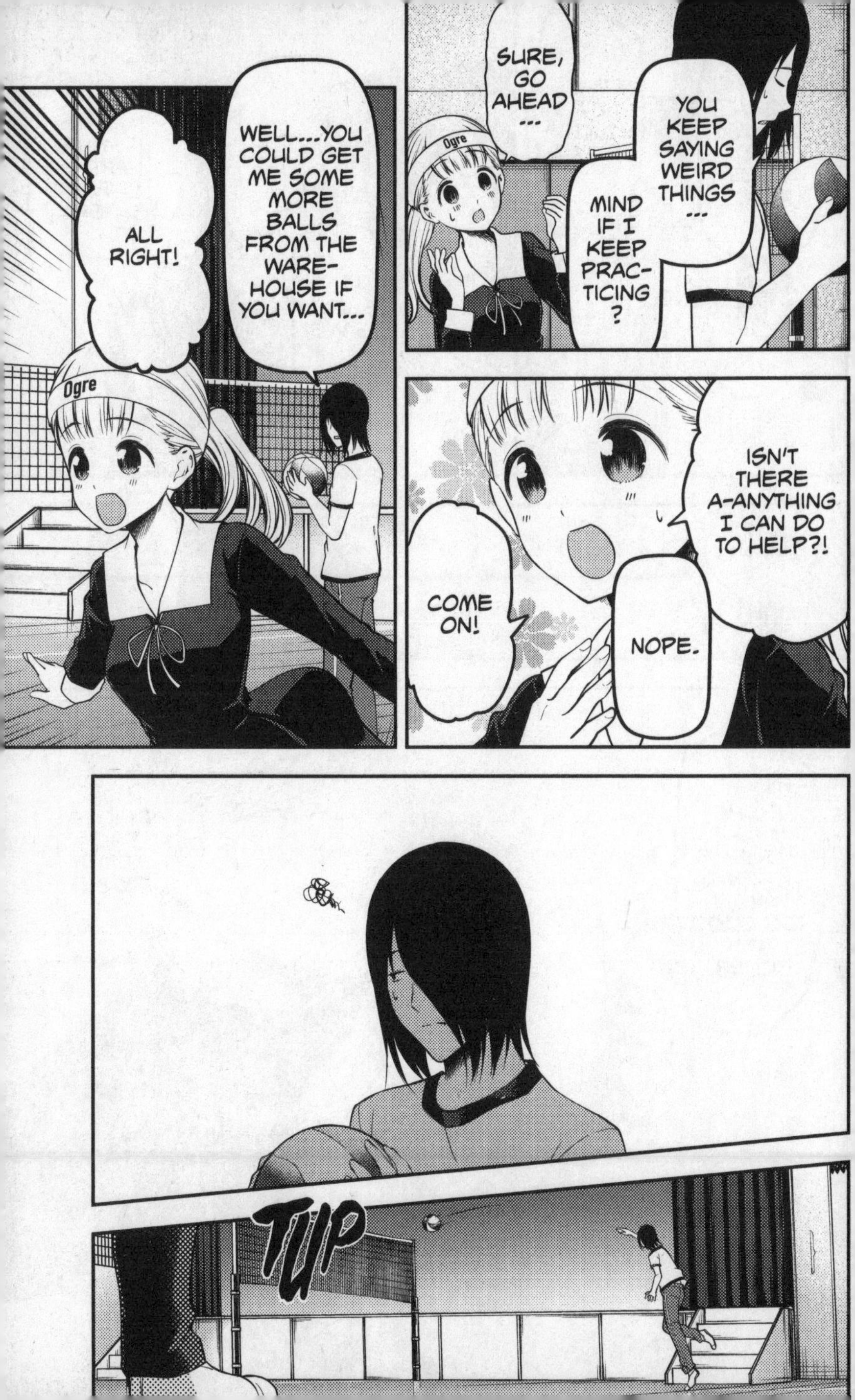
YOU KEEP SAYING WEIRD THINGS...
MIND IF I KEEP PRACTICING?
SURE, GO AHEAD...
Ogre
ISN'T THERE A-ANYTHING I CAN DO TO HELP?!
NOPE.
COME ON!
WELL...YOU COULD GET ME SOME MORE BALLS FROM THE WAREHOUSE IF YOU WANT...
ALL RIGHT!
Ogre
TUP

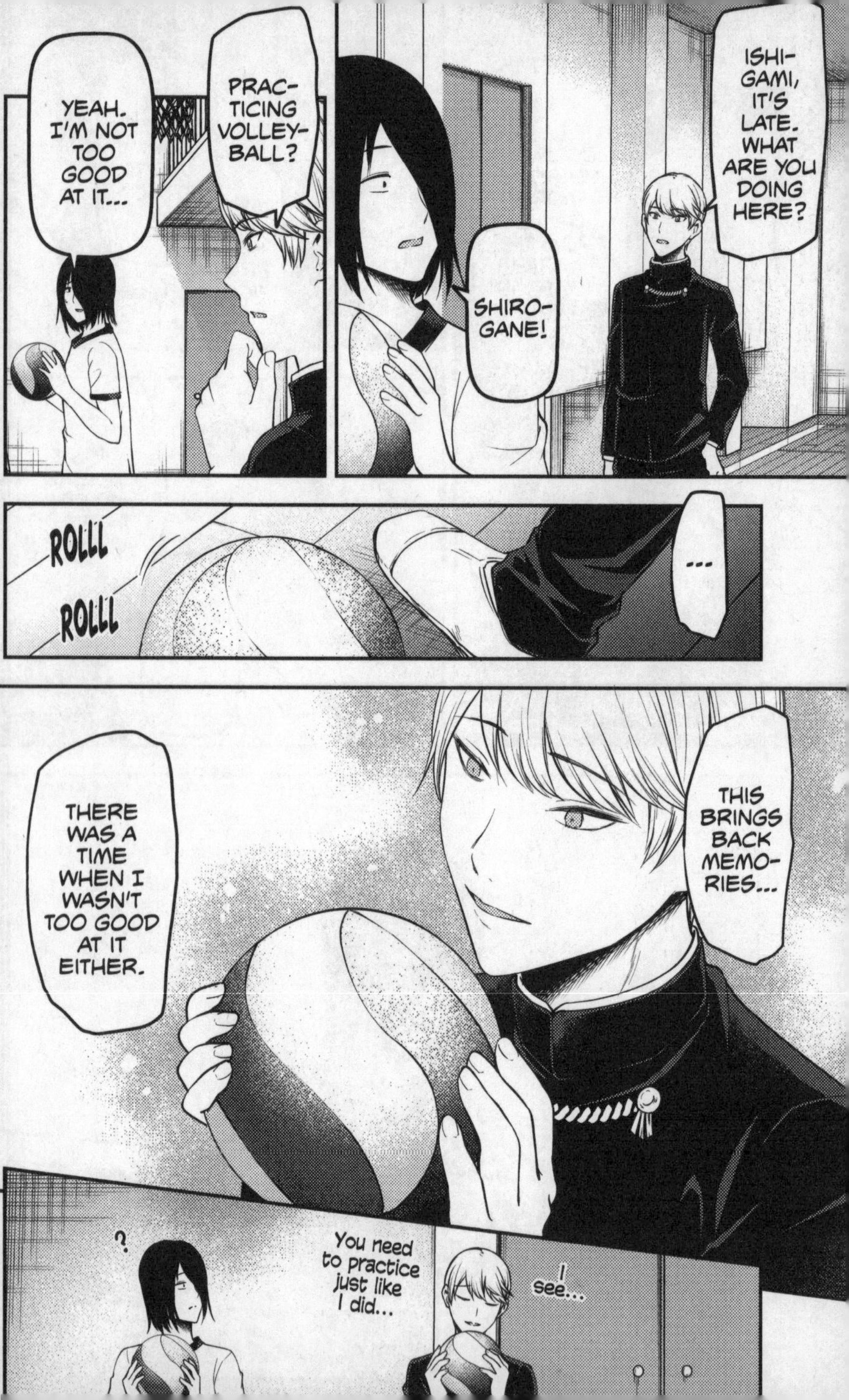
ISHIGAMI, IT'S LATE. WHAT ARE YOU DOING HERE?
SHIROGANE!
PRACTICING VOLLEYBALL?
YEAH. I'M NOT TOO GOOD AT IT...
...
ROLLL
ROLLL
THIS BRINGS BACK MEMORIES...
THERE WAS A TIME WHEN I WASN'T TOO GOOD AT IT EITHER.
I see...
You need to practice just like I did...
?

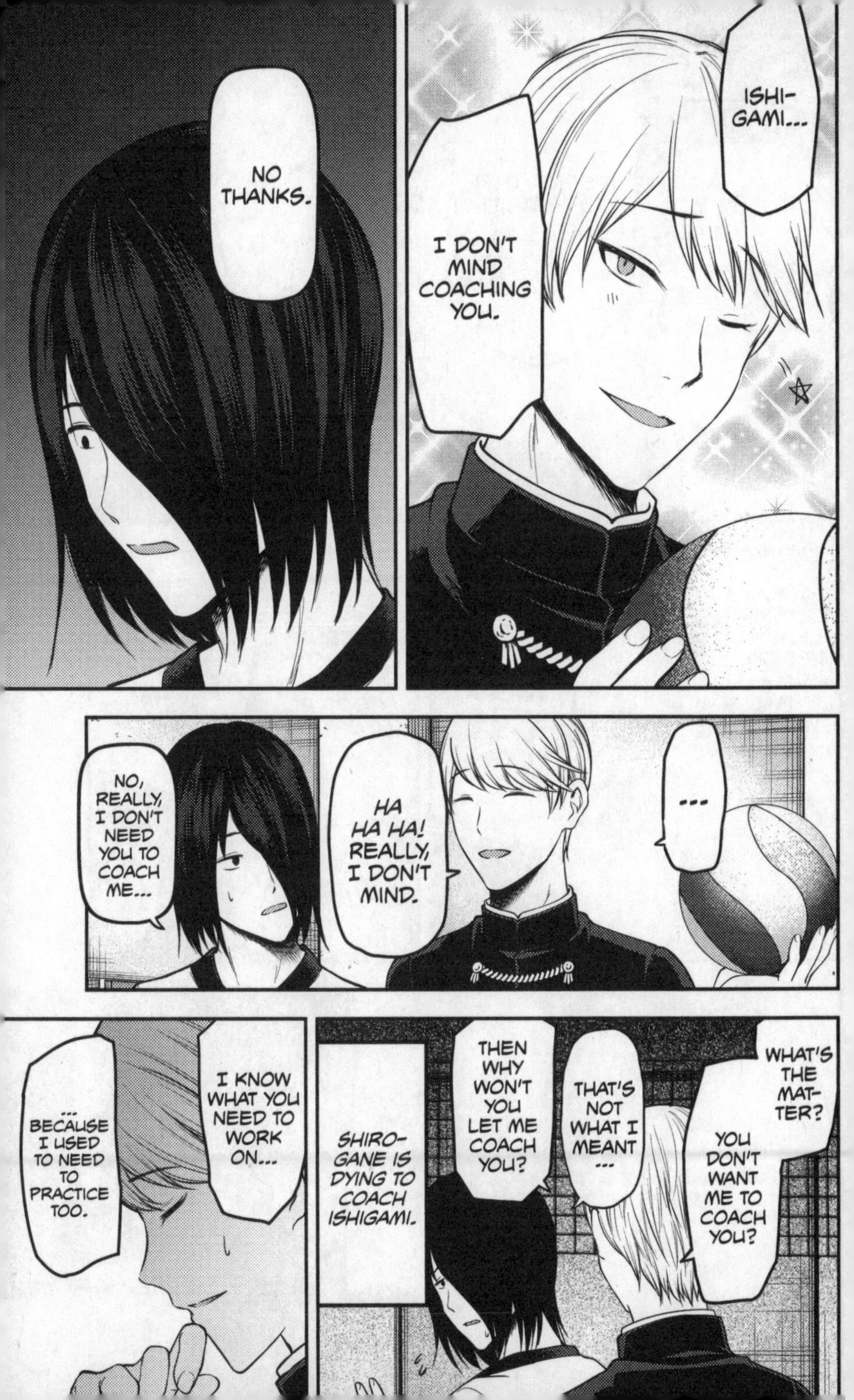
ISHI-GAMI...
I DON'T MIND COACHING YOU.
NO THANKS.
...
HA HA HA! REALLY, I DON'T MIND.
NO, REALLY, I DON'T NEED YOU TO COACH ME...
WHAT'S THE MAT-TER?
YOU DON'T WANT ME TO COACH YOU?
THAT'S NOT WHAT I MEANT...
THEN WHY WON'T YOU LET ME COACH YOU?
SHIRO-GANE IS DYING TO COACH ISHIGAMI.
I KNOW WHAT YOU NEED TO WORK ON...
...BECAUSE I USED TO NEED TO PRACTICE TOO.

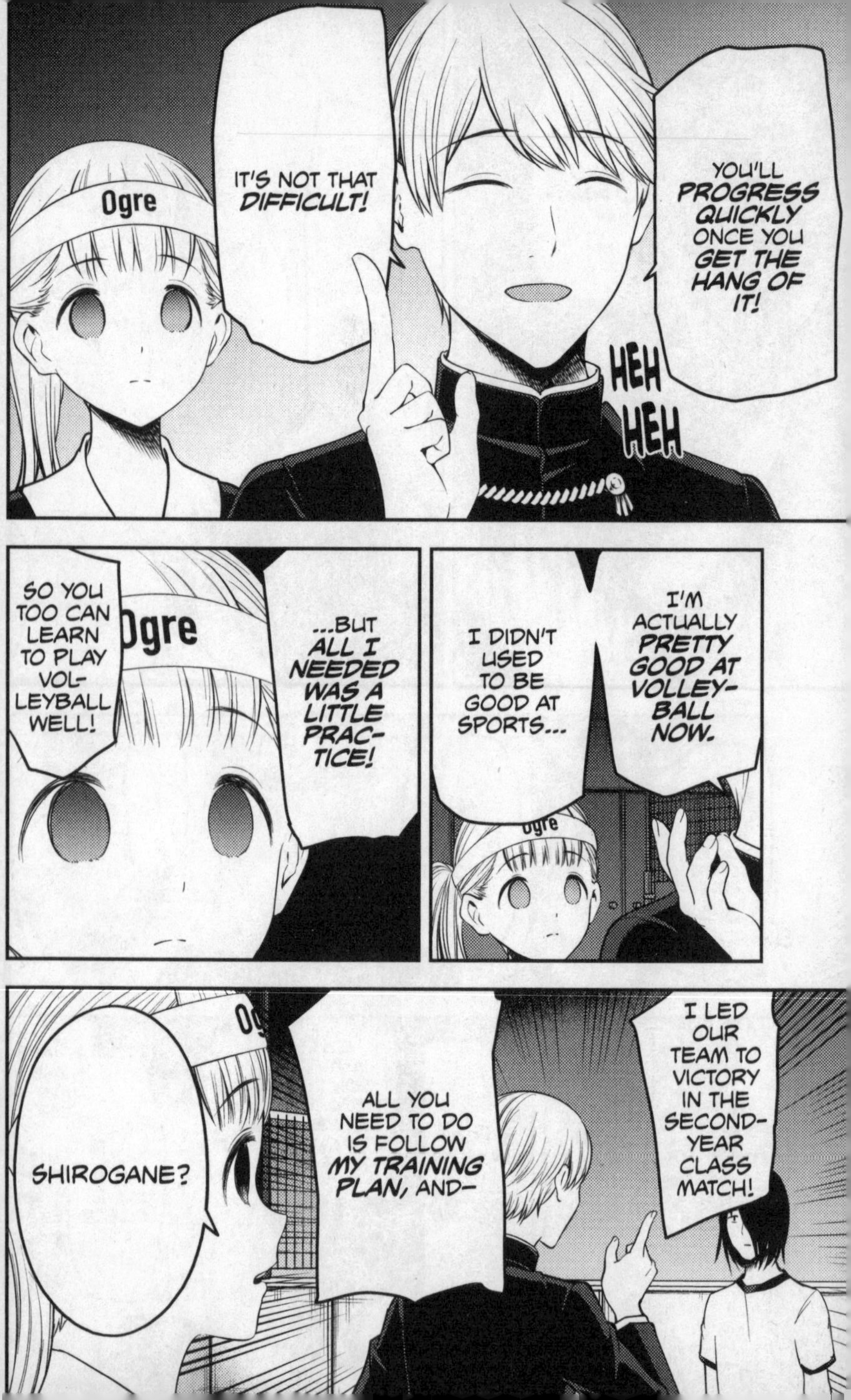
YOU'LL PROGRESS QUICKLY ONCE YOU GET THE HANG OF IT!
HEH HEH
IT'S NOT THAT DIFFICULT!
Ogre
I'M ACTUALLY PRETTY GOOD AT VOLLEY-BALL NOW.
I DIDN'T USED TO BE GOOD AT SPORTS...
Ogre
...BUT ALL I NEEDED WAS A LITTLE PRAC-TICE!
SO YOU TOO CAN LEARN TO PLAY VOL-LEYBALL WELL!
Ogre
I LED OUR TEAM TO VICTORY IN THE SECOND-YEAR CLASS MATCH!
ALL YOU NEED TO DO IS FOLLOW MY TRAINING PLAN, AND-
SHIROGANE?

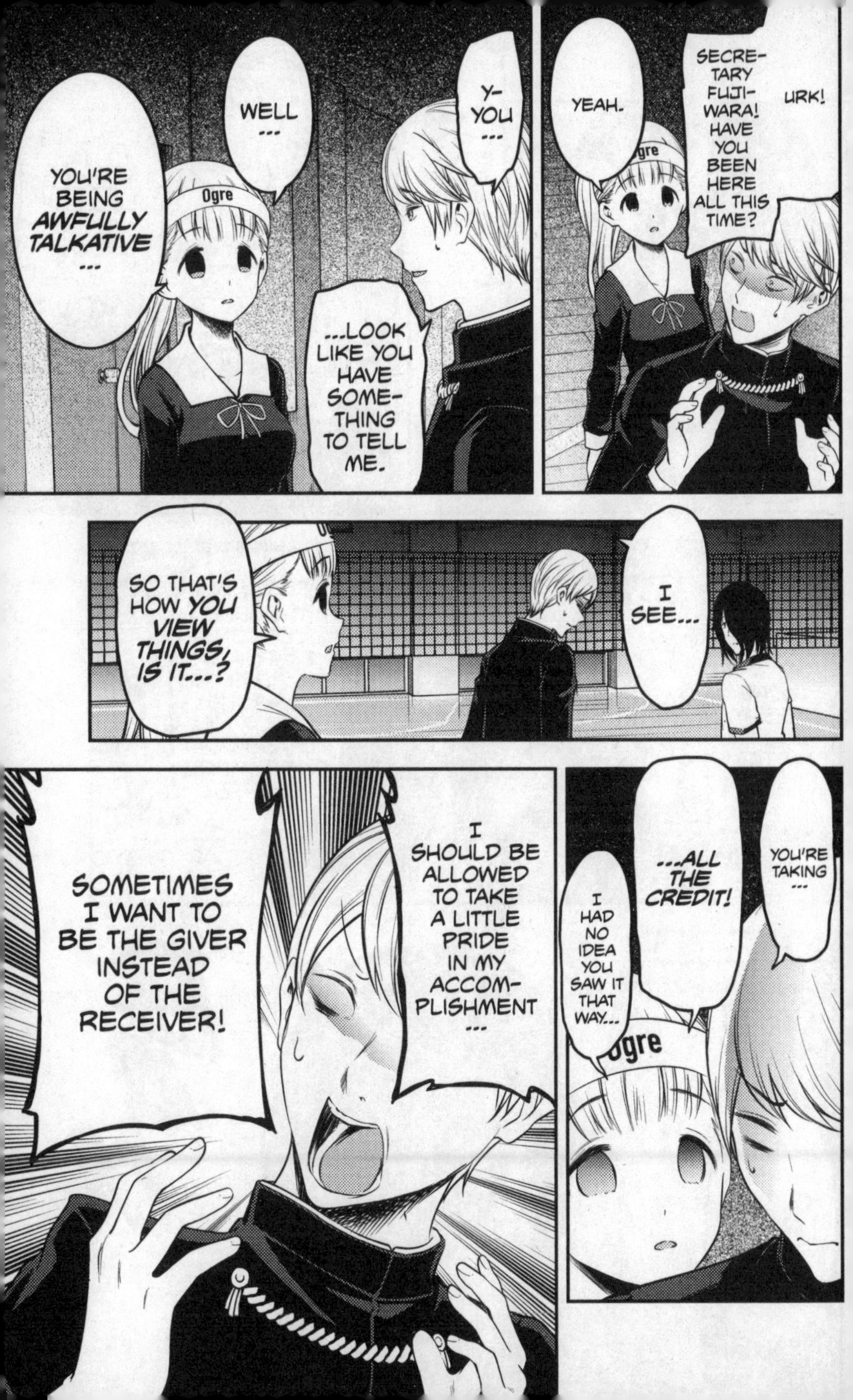
URK!
SECRETARY FUJIWARA! HAVE YOU BEEN HERE ALL THIS TIME?
YEAH.
Ogre
Y-YOU...
WELL...
YOU'RE BEING AWFULLY TALKATIVE...
Ogre
...LOOK LIKE YOU HAVE SOMETHING TO TELL ME.
I SEE...
SO THAT'S HOW YOU VIEW THINGS, IS IT...?
YOU'RE TAKING...
...ALL THE CREDIT!
I HAD NO IDEA YOU SAW IT THAT WAY...
Ogre
I SHOULD BE ALLOWED TO TAKE A LITTLE PRIDE IN MY ACCOMPLISHMENT...
SOMETIMES I WANT TO BE THE GIVER INSTEAD OF THE RECEIVER!

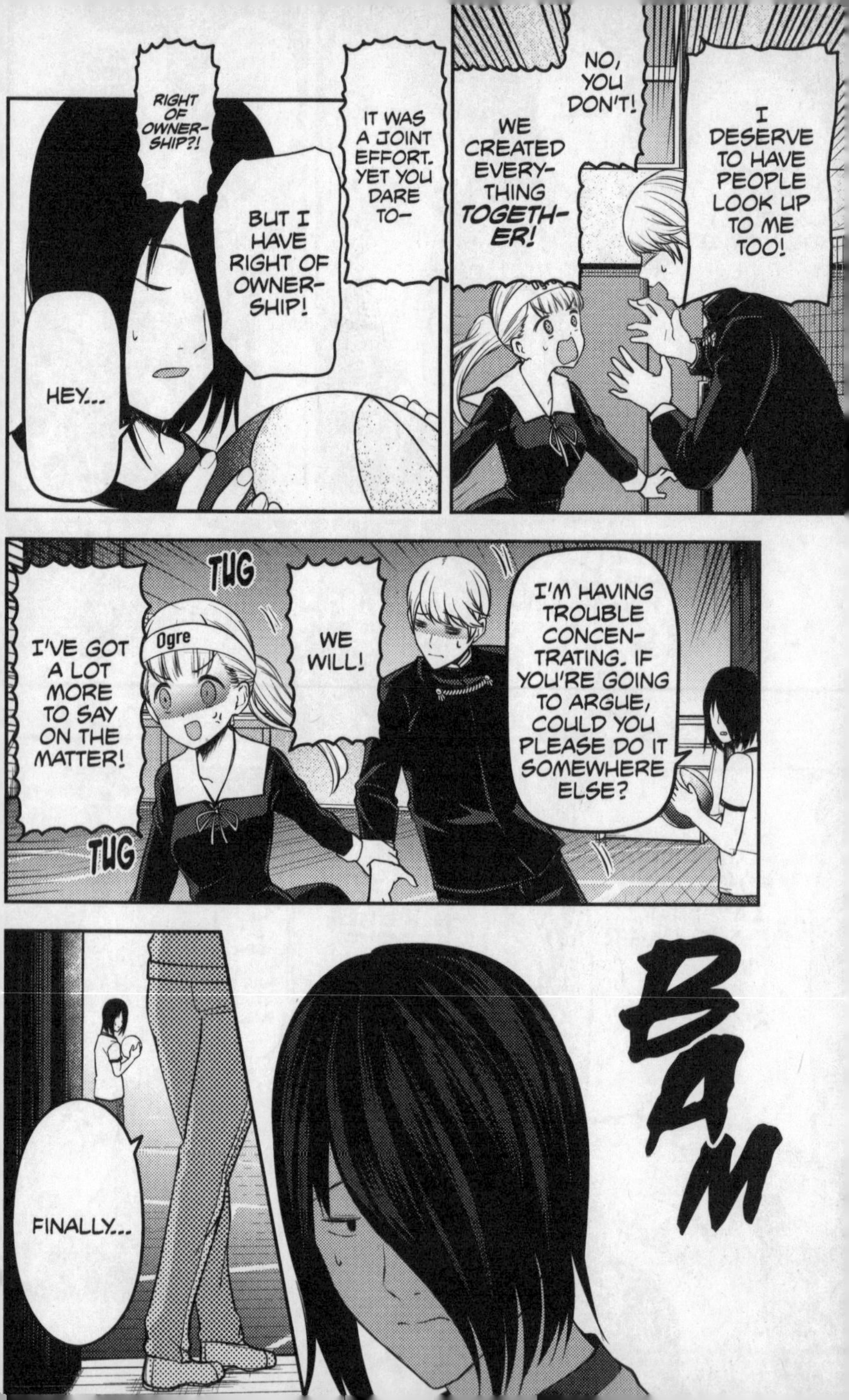
I DESERVE TO HAVE PEOPLE LOOK UP TO ME TOO!
NO, YOU DON'T!
WE CREATED EVERYTHING *TOGETHER!*
IT WAS A JOINT EFFORT. YET YOU DARE TO—
RIGHT OF OWNERSHIP?!
BUT I HAVE RIGHT OF OWNERSHIP!
HEY...
I'M HAVING TROUBLE CONCENTRATING. IF YOU'RE GOING TO ARGUE, COULD YOU PLEASE DO IT SOMEWHERE ELSE?
WE WILL!
TUG
Ogre
I'VE GOT A LOT MORE TO SAY ON THE MATTER!
TUG
BAM
FINALLY...

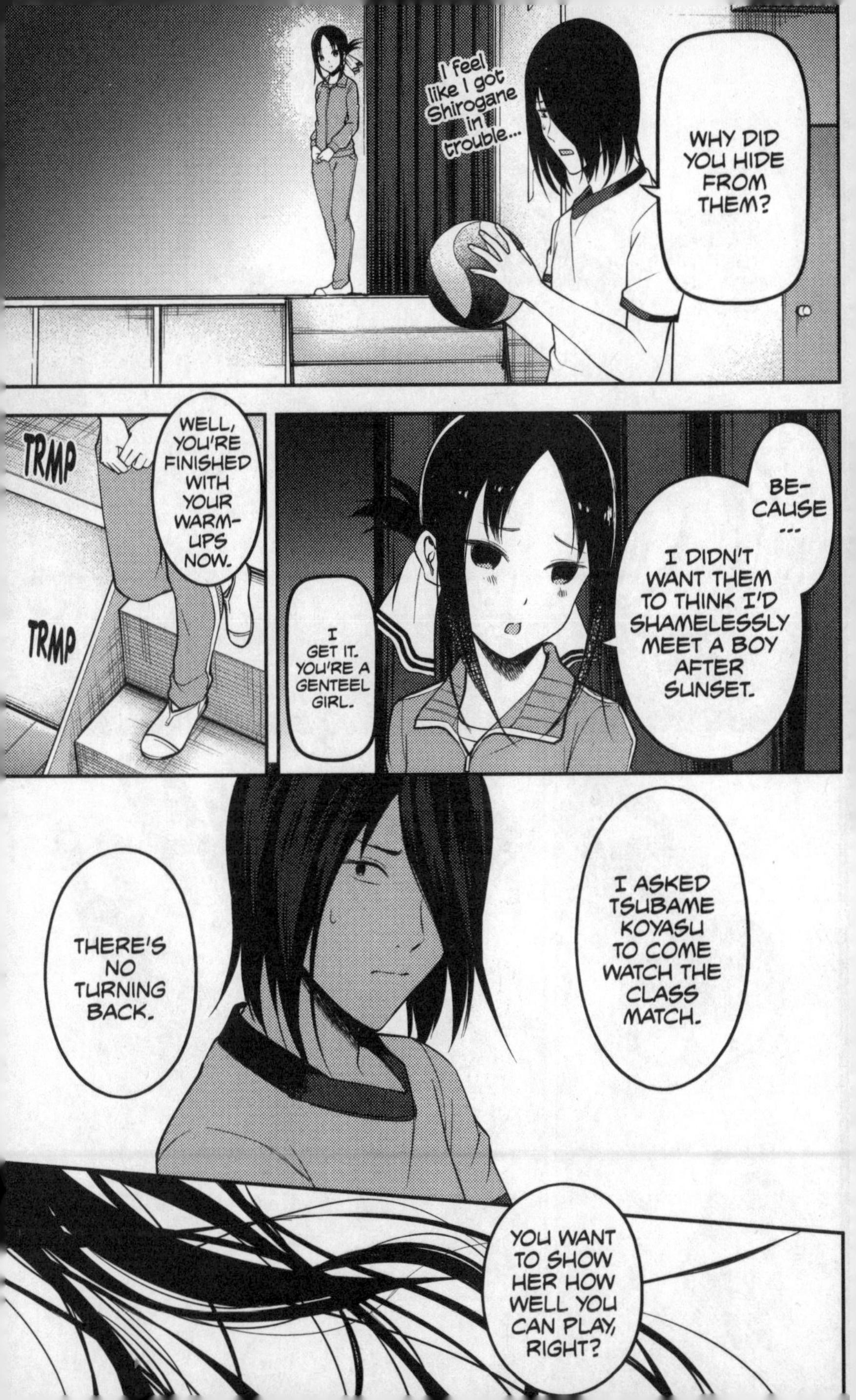
WHY DID YOU HIDE FROM THEM?
I feel like I got Shirogane in trouble...
BE-CAUSE...
I DIDN'T WANT THEM TO THINK I'D SHAMELESSLY MEET A BOY AFTER SUNSET.
I GET IT. YOU'RE A GENTEEL GIRL.
TRMP
WELL, YOU'RE FINISHED WITH YOUR WARM-UPS NOW.
TRMP
I ASKED TSUBAME KOYASU TO COME WATCH THE CLASS MATCH.
THERE'S NO TURNING BACK.
YOU WANT TO SHOW HER HOW WELL YOU CAN PLAY, RIGHT?

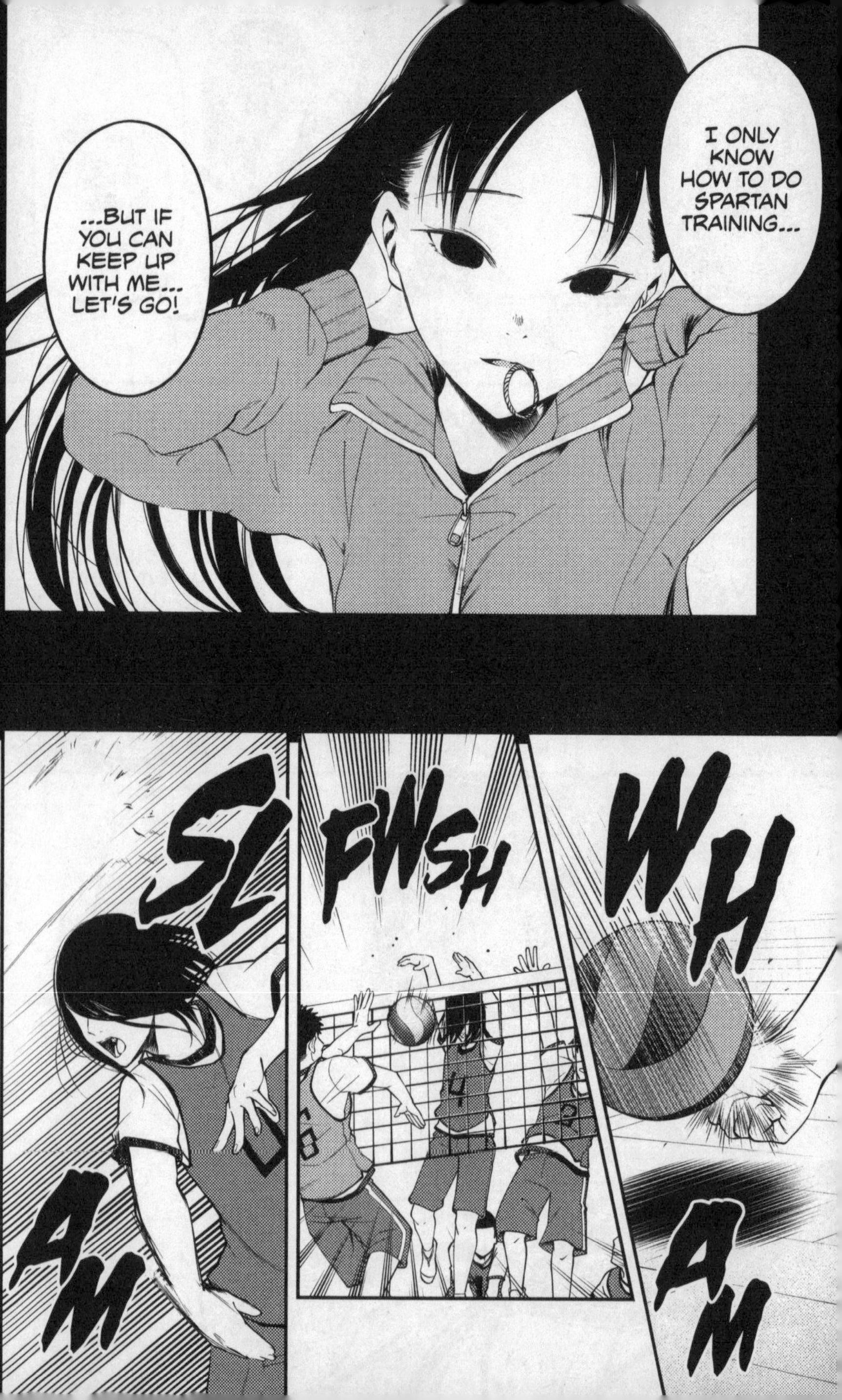
I ONLY KNOW HOW TO DO SPARTAN TRAINING...
...BUT IF YOU CAN KEEP UP WITH ME... LET'S GO!
WH
AM
FWSH
SL
AM

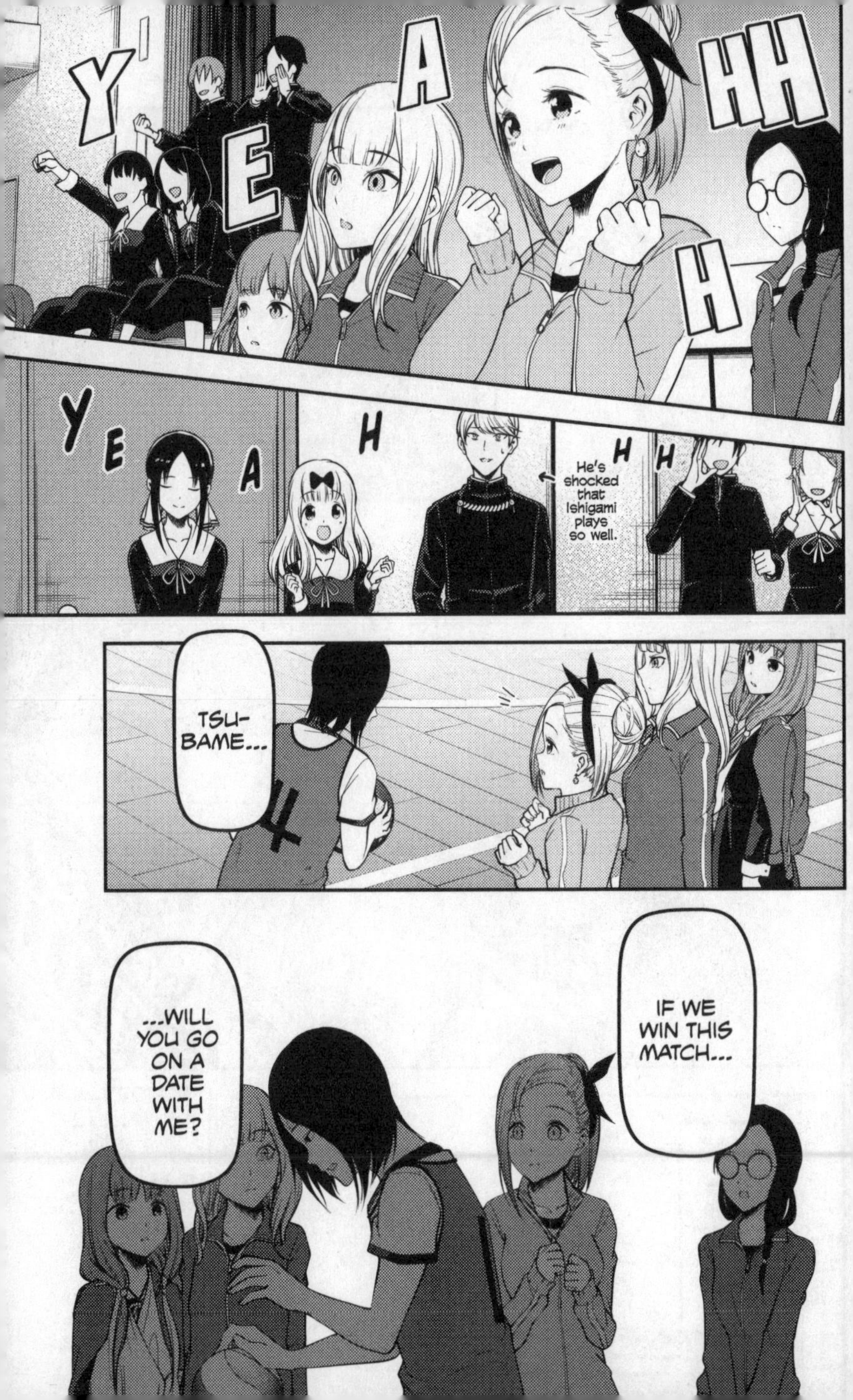
YEAHHH
YEAHHH
He's shocked that Ishigami plays so well.
TSU-BAME...
IF WE WIN THIS MATCH...
...WILL YOU GO ON A DATE WITH ME?

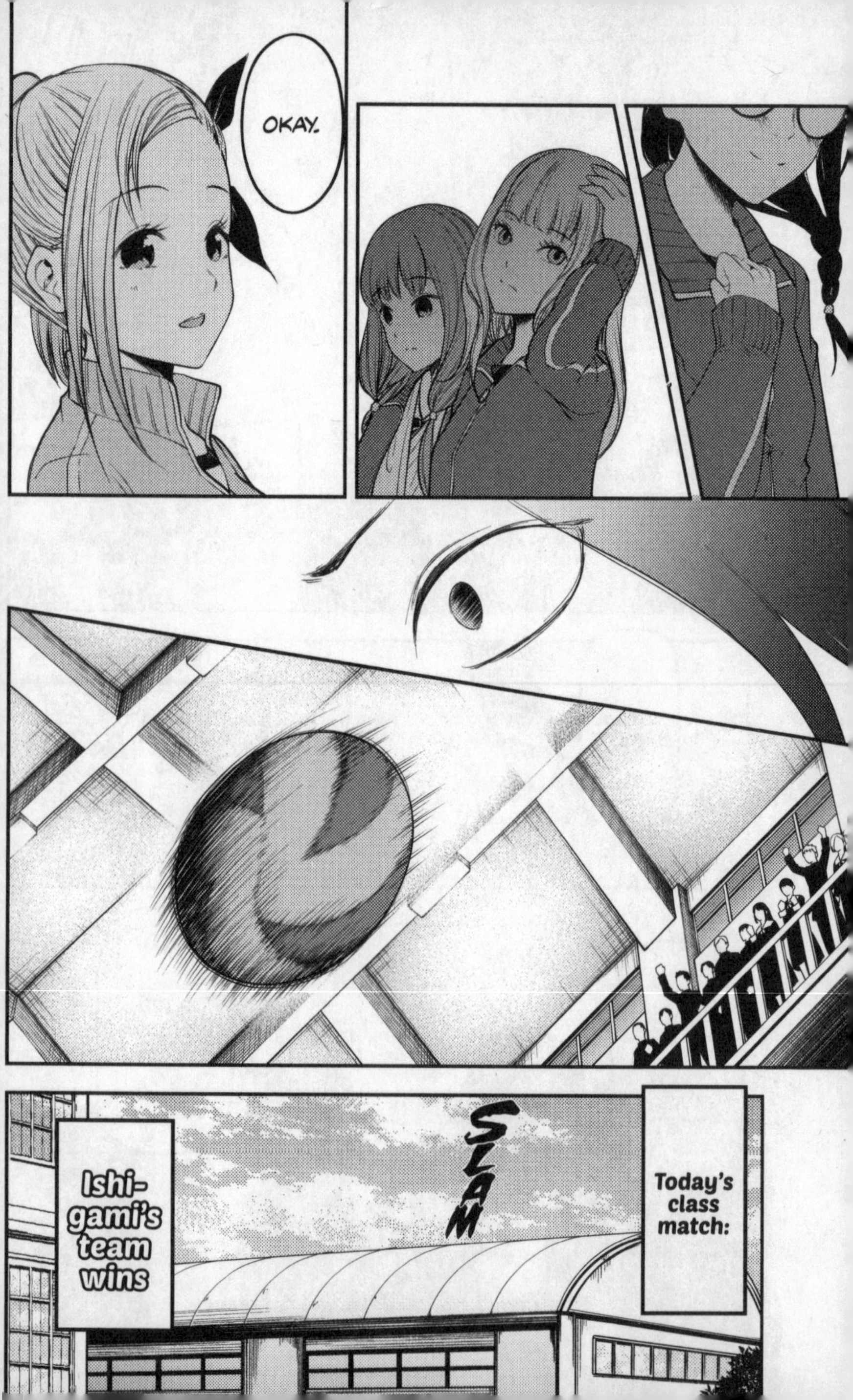
OKAY.
Today's class match:
SLAM
Ishi-gami's team wins

SHIROGANE
THINKS THE
FIRST
OBSTACLE
FOR HYPER
YO-YO
BEGINNERS
IS THE
MOONSAULT
MOVE.

KAGUYA-SAMA
LOVE IS WAR

BAM

SHINOMIYA, I DID IT!

I ASKED TSUBAME OUT ON A DATE!

Battle 177 Kaguya Shinomiya's Impossible Demand: "A Cowrie a Swallow Gave Birth To," Part 4

CONGRATU-LATIONS ON WINNING THE CLASS VOLLEYBALL MATCH.

WELL DONE, ISHIGAMI.

THANKS!

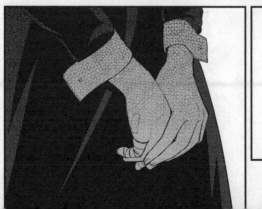

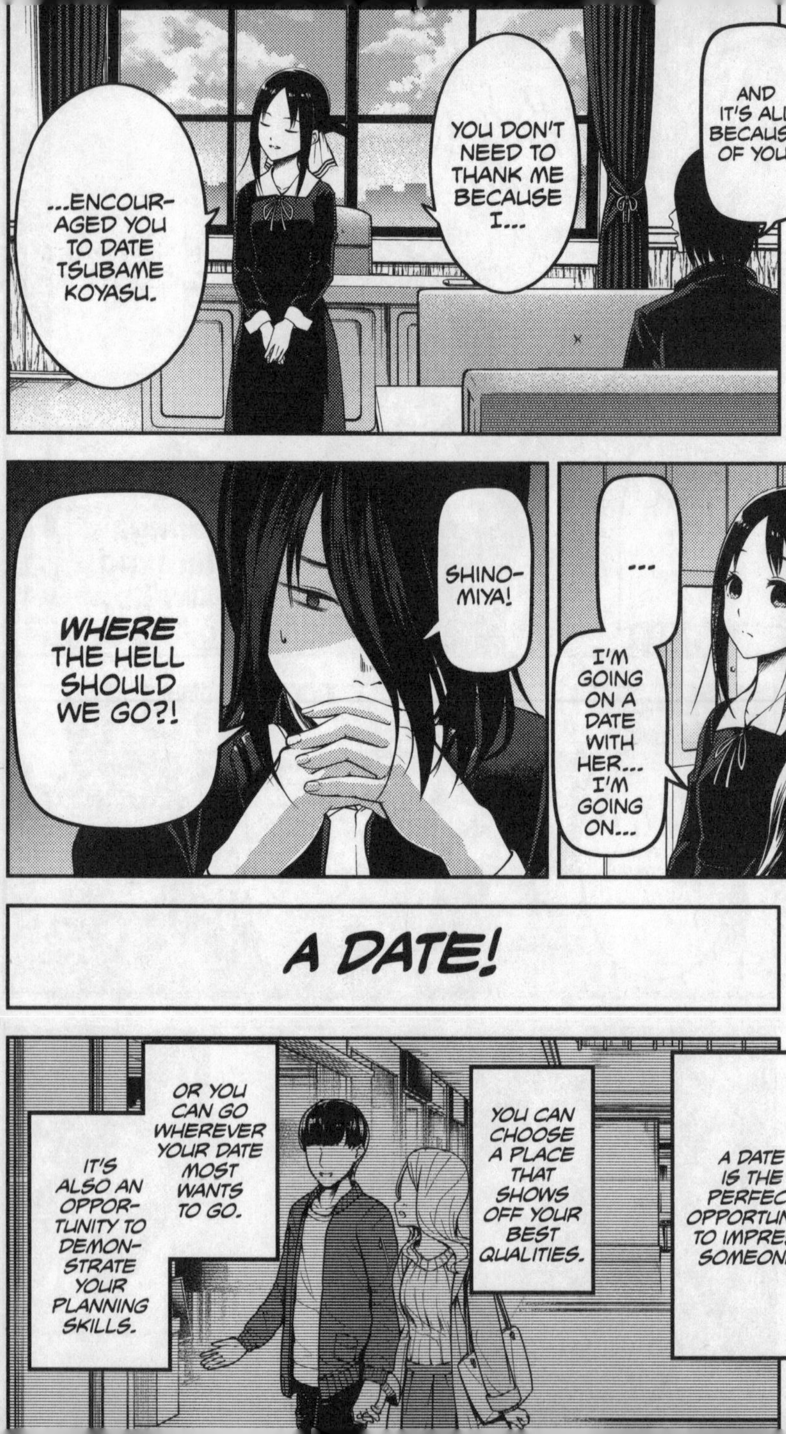
AND IT'S ALL BECAUSE OF YOU!
YOU DON'T NEED TO THANK ME BECAUSE I...
...ENCOURAGED YOU TO DATE TSUBAME KOYASU.
...
I'M GOING ON A DATE WITH HER... I'M GOING ON...
SHINOMIYA!
WHERE THE HELL SHOULD WE GO?!
A DATE!
A DATE IS THE PERFECT OPPORTUNITY TO IMPRESS SOMEONE.
YOU CAN CHOOSE A PLACE THAT SHOWS OFF YOUR BEST QUALITIES.
OR YOU CAN GO WHEREVER YOUR DATE MOST WANTS TO GO.
IT'S ALSO AN OPPORTUNITY TO DEMONSTRATE YOUR PLANNING SKILLS.

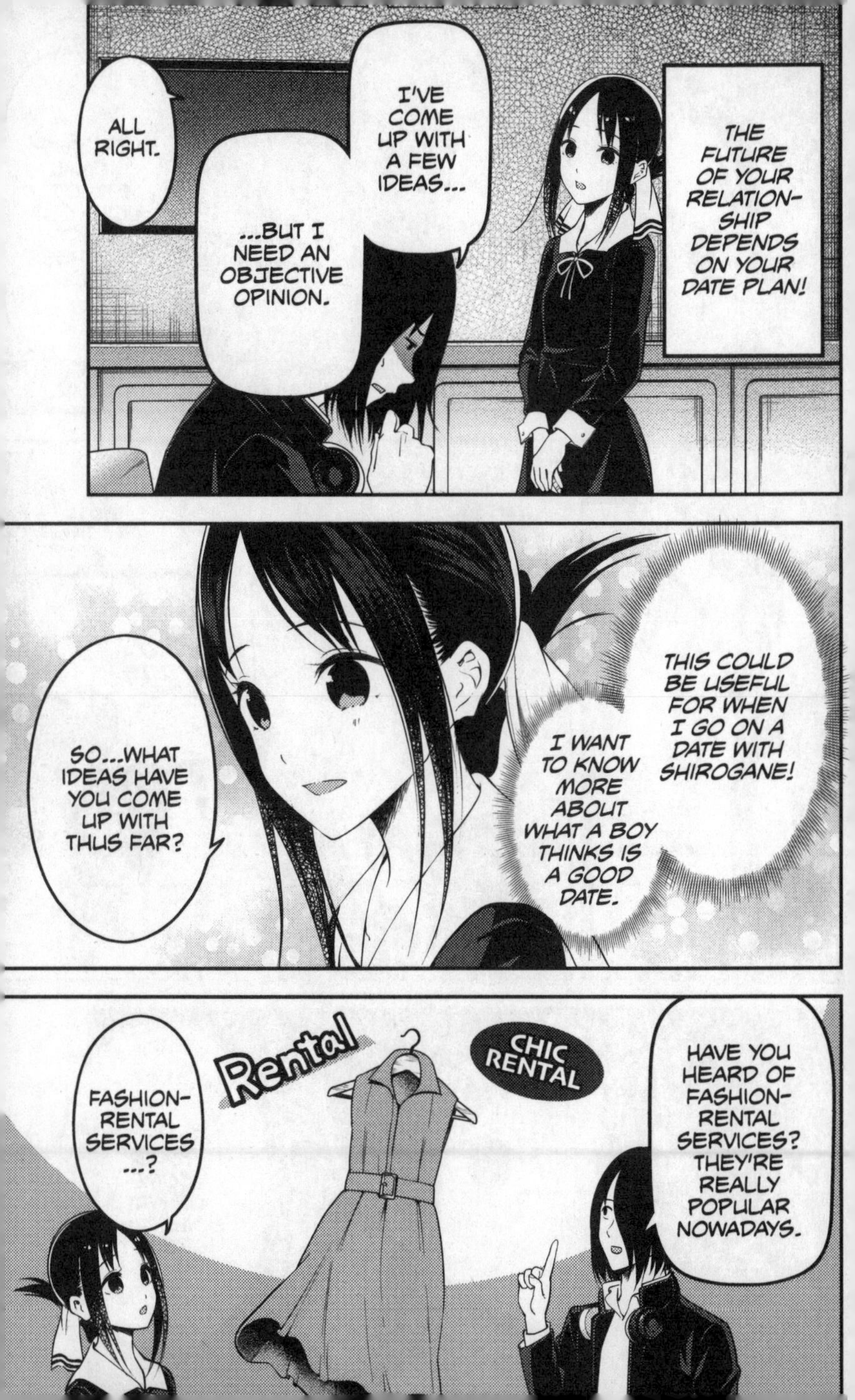
THE FUTURE OF YOUR RELATION-SHIP DEPENDS ON YOUR DATE PLAN!
I'VE COME UP WITH A FEW IDEAS...
...BUT I NEED AN OBJECTIVE OPINION.
ALL RIGHT.
THIS COULD BE USEFUL FOR WHEN I GO ON A DATE WITH SHIROGANE!
I WANT TO KNOW MORE ABOUT WHAT A BOY THINKS IS A GOOD DATE.
SO...WHAT IDEAS HAVE YOU COME UP WITH THUS FAR?
HAVE YOU HEARD OF FASHION-RENTAL SERVICES? THEY'RE REALLY POPULAR NOWADAYS.
CHIC RENTAL
Rental
FASHION-RENTAL SERVICES ...?

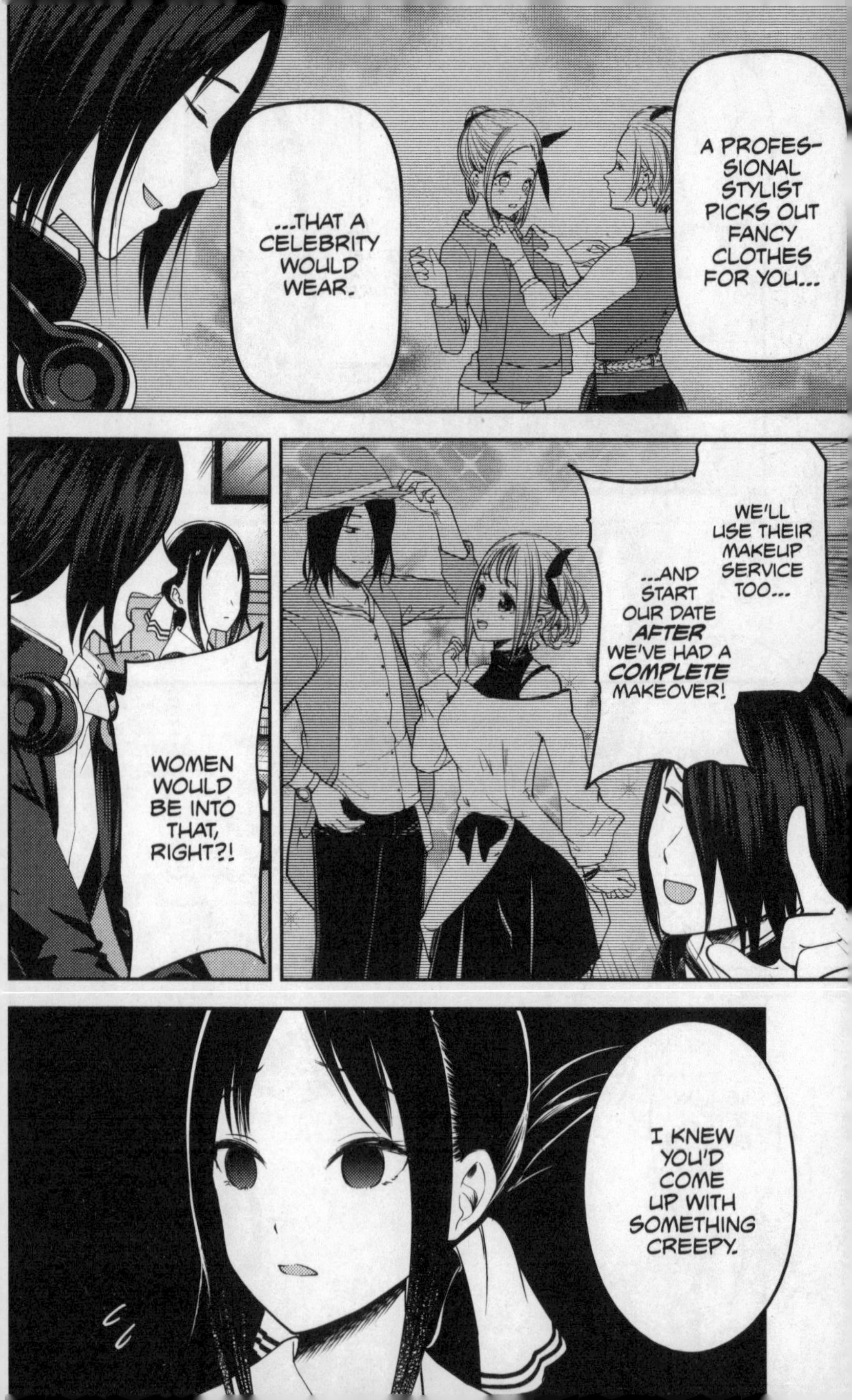
A PROFES-SIONAL STYLIST PICKS OUT FANCY CLOTHES FOR YOU...
...THAT A CELEBRITY WOULD WEAR.
WE'LL USE THEIR MAKEUP SERVICE TOO...
...AND START OUR DATE *AFTER* WE'VE HAD A *COMPLETE* MAKEOVER!
WOMEN WOULD BE INTO THAT, RIGHT?!
I KNEW YOU'D COME UP WITH SOMETHING CREEPY.

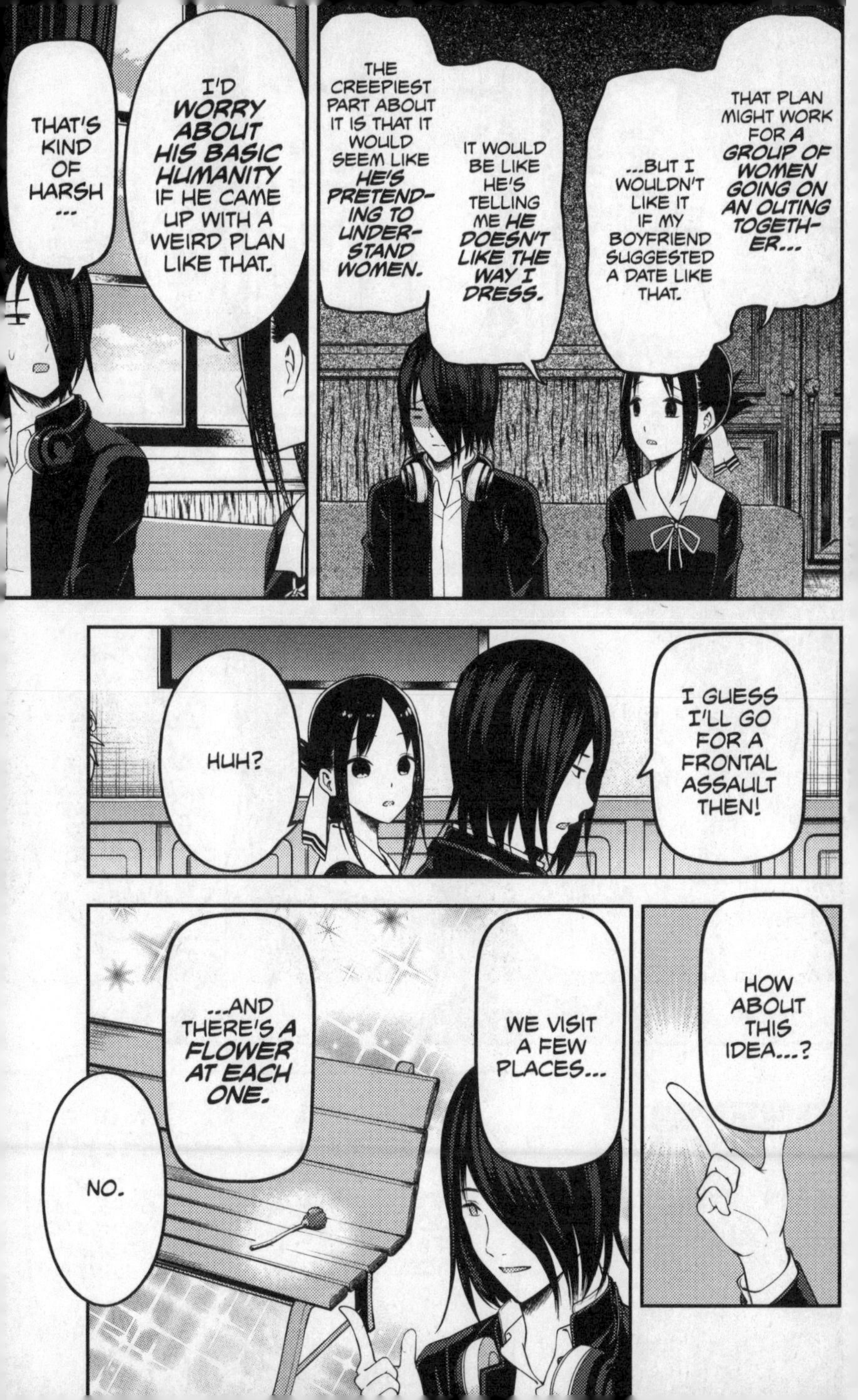
THAT PLAN MIGHT WORK FOR A GROUP OF WOMEN GOING ON AN OUTING TOGETH-ER...
...BUT I WOULDN'T LIKE IT IF MY BOYFRIEND SUGGESTED A DATE LIKE THAT.
IT WOULD BE LIKE HE'S TELLING ME HE DOESN'T LIKE THE WAY I DRESS.
THE CREEPIEST PART ABOUT IT IS THAT IT WOULD SEEM LIKE HE'S PRETEND-ING TO UNDER-STAND WOMEN.
I'D WORRY ABOUT HIS BASIC HUMANITY IF HE CAME UP WITH A WEIRD PLAN LIKE THAT.
THAT'S KIND OF HARSH...
I GUESS I'LL GO FOR A FRONTAL ASSAULT THEN!
HUH?
HOW ABOUT THIS IDEA...?
WE VISIT A FEW PLACES...
...AND THERE'S A FLOWER AT EACH ONE.
NO.

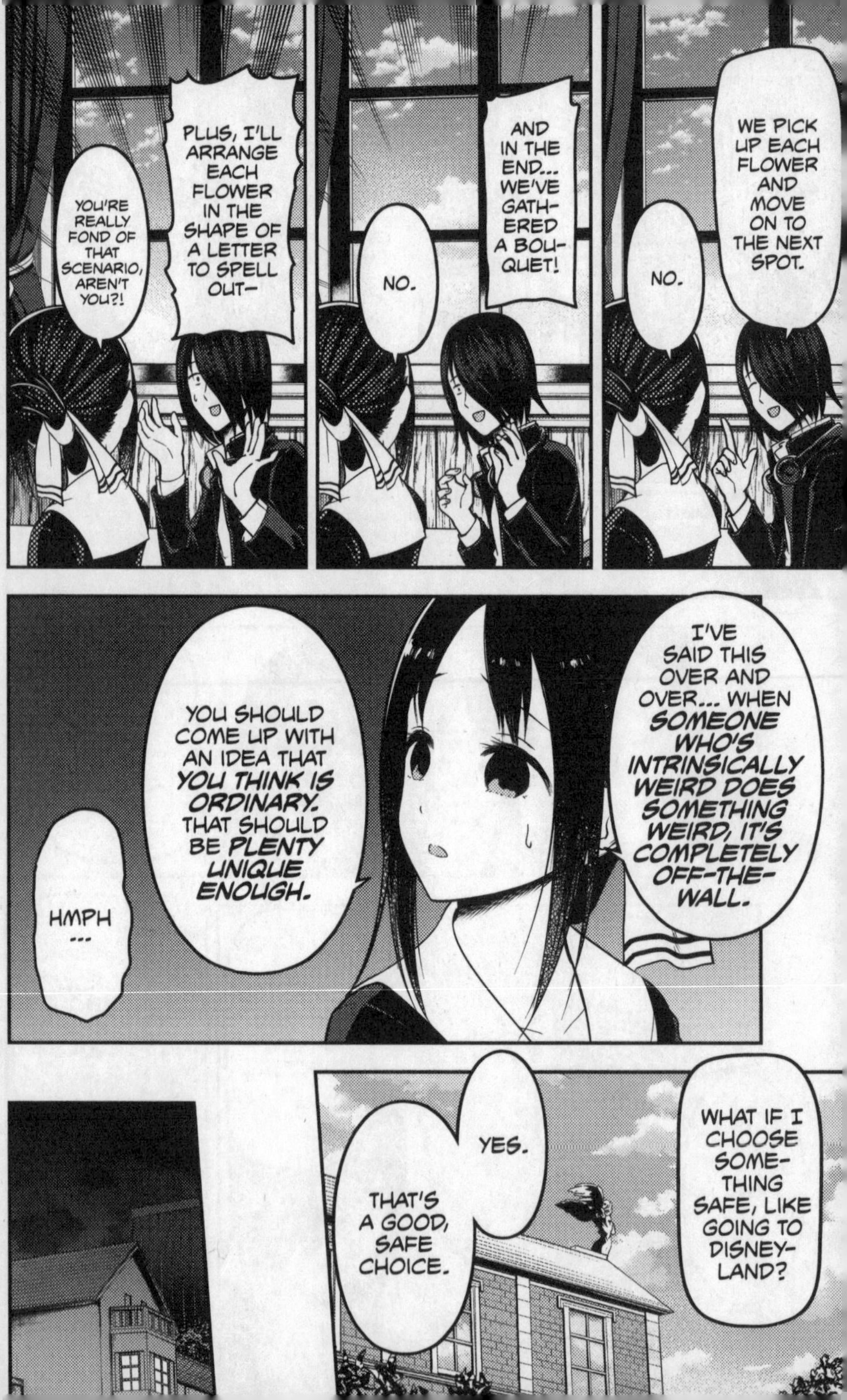
WE PICK UP EACH FLOWER AND MOVE ON TO THE NEXT SPOT.
NO.
AND IN THE END... WE'VE GATH-ERED A BOU-QUET!
NO.
PLUS, I'LL ARRANGE EACH FLOWER IN THE SHAPE OF A LETTER TO SPELL OUT—
YOU'RE REALLY FOND OF THAT SCENARIO, AREN'T YOU?!
I'VE SAID THIS OVER AND OVER... WHEN SOMEONE WHO'S INTRINSICALLY WEIRD DOES SOMETHING WEIRD, IT'S COMPLETELY OFF-THE-WALL.
YOU SHOULD COME UP WITH AN IDEA THAT YOU THINK IS ORDINARY. THAT SHOULD BE PLENTY UNIQUE ENOUGH.
HMPH...
WHAT IF I CHOOSE SOME-THING SAFE, LIKE GOING TO DISNEY-LAND?
YES.
THAT'S A GOOD, SAFE CHOICE.

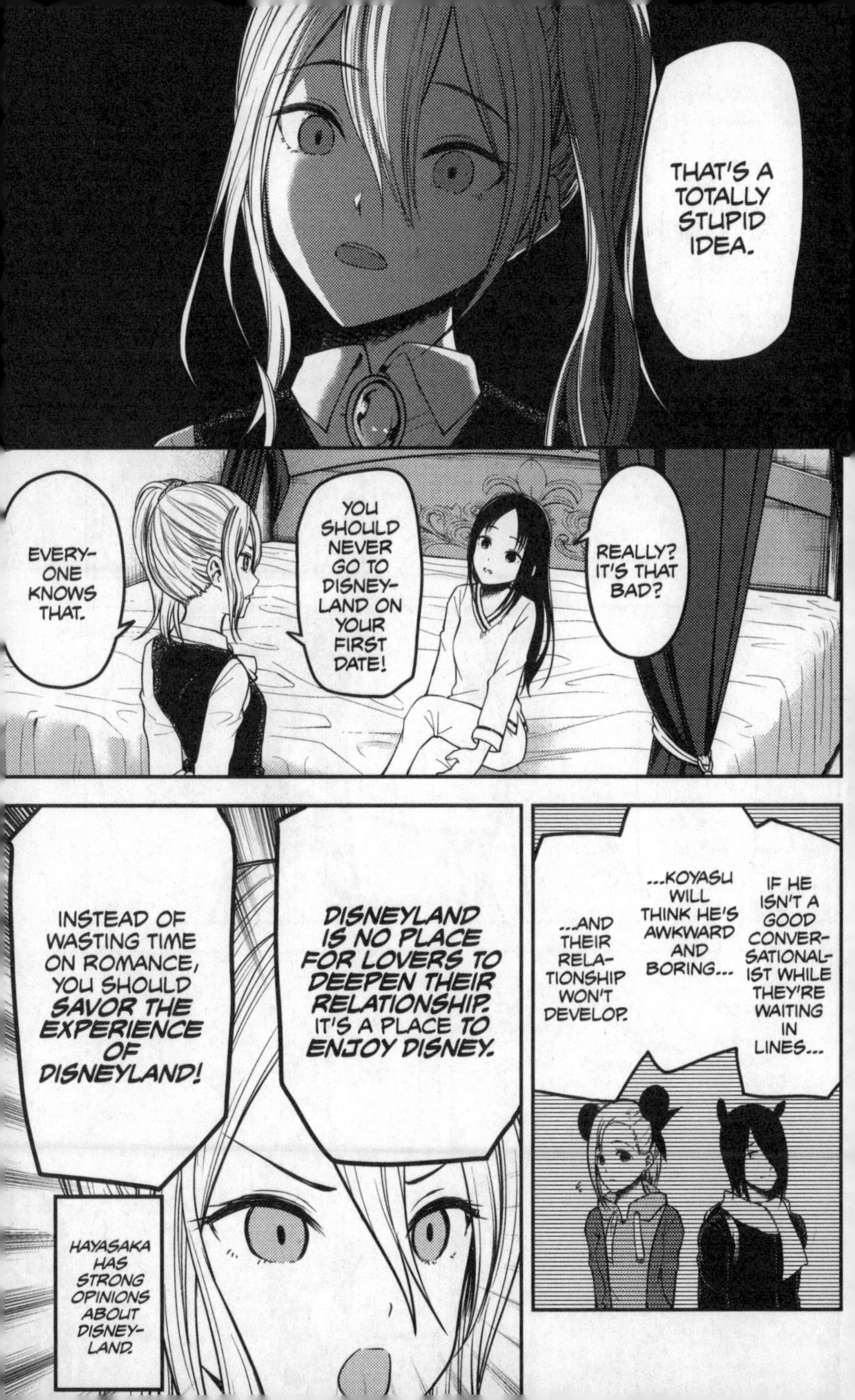
THAT'S A TOTALLY STUPID IDEA.
REALLY? IT'S THAT BAD?
YOU SHOULD NEVER GO TO DISNEYLAND ON YOUR FIRST DATE!
EVERYONE KNOWS THAT.
IF HE ISN'T A GOOD CONVERSATIONALIST WHILE THEY'RE WAITING IN LINES...
...KOYASU WILL THINK HE'S AWKWARD AND BORING...
...AND THEIR RELATIONSHIP WON'T DEVELOP.
DISNEYLAND IS NO PLACE FOR LOVERS TO DEEPEN THEIR RELATIONSHIP. IT'S A PLACE TO ENJOY DISNEY.
INSTEAD OF WASTING TIME ON ROMANCE, YOU SHOULD SAVOR THE EXPERIENCE OF DISNEYLAND!
HAYASAKA HAS STRONG OPINIONS ABOUT DISNEYLAND.

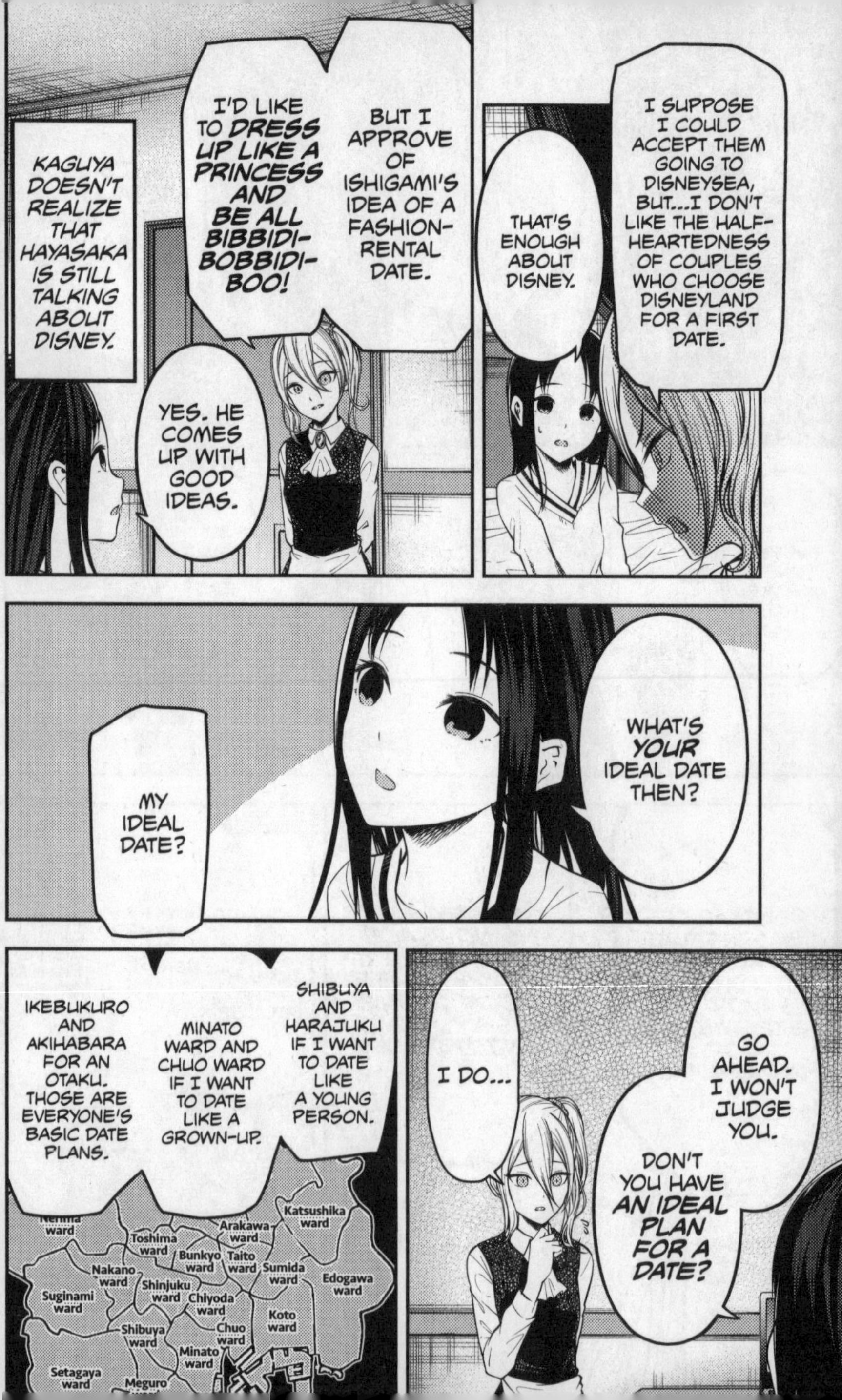
I SUPPOSE I COULD ACCEPT THEM GOING TO DISNEYSEA, BUT...I DON'T LIKE THE HALF-HEARTEDNESS OF COUPLES WHO CHOOSE DISNEYLAND FOR A FIRST DATE.
THAT'S ENOUGH ABOUT DISNEY.
BUT I APPROVE OF ISHIGAMI'S IDEA OF A FASHION-RENTAL DATE.
I'D LIKE TO *DRESS UP LIKE A PRINCESS AND BE ALL BIBBIDI-BOBBIDI-BOO!*
KAGUYA DOESN'T REALIZE THAT HAYASAKA IS STILL TALKING ABOUT DISNEY.
YES. HE COMES UP WITH GOOD IDEAS.
WHAT'S *YOUR* IDEAL DATE THEN?
MY IDEAL DATE?
GO AHEAD. I WON'T JUDGE YOU.
DON'T YOU HAVE *AN IDEAL PLAN FOR A DATE?*
I DO...
SHIBUYA AND HARAJUKU IF I WANT TO DATE LIKE A YOUNG PERSON.
MINATO WARD AND CHUO WARD IF I WANT TO DATE LIKE A GROWN-UP.
IKEBUKURO AND AKIHABARA FOR AN OTAKU. THOSE ARE EVERYONE'S BASIC DATE PLANS.
Katsushika ward
Arakawa ward
Toshima ward
Bunkyo ward
Taito ward
Nakano ward
Sumida ward
Edogawa ward
Shinjuku ward
Chiyoda ward
Suginami ward
Koto ward
Shibuya ward
Chuo ward
Minato ward
Setagaya ward
Meguro

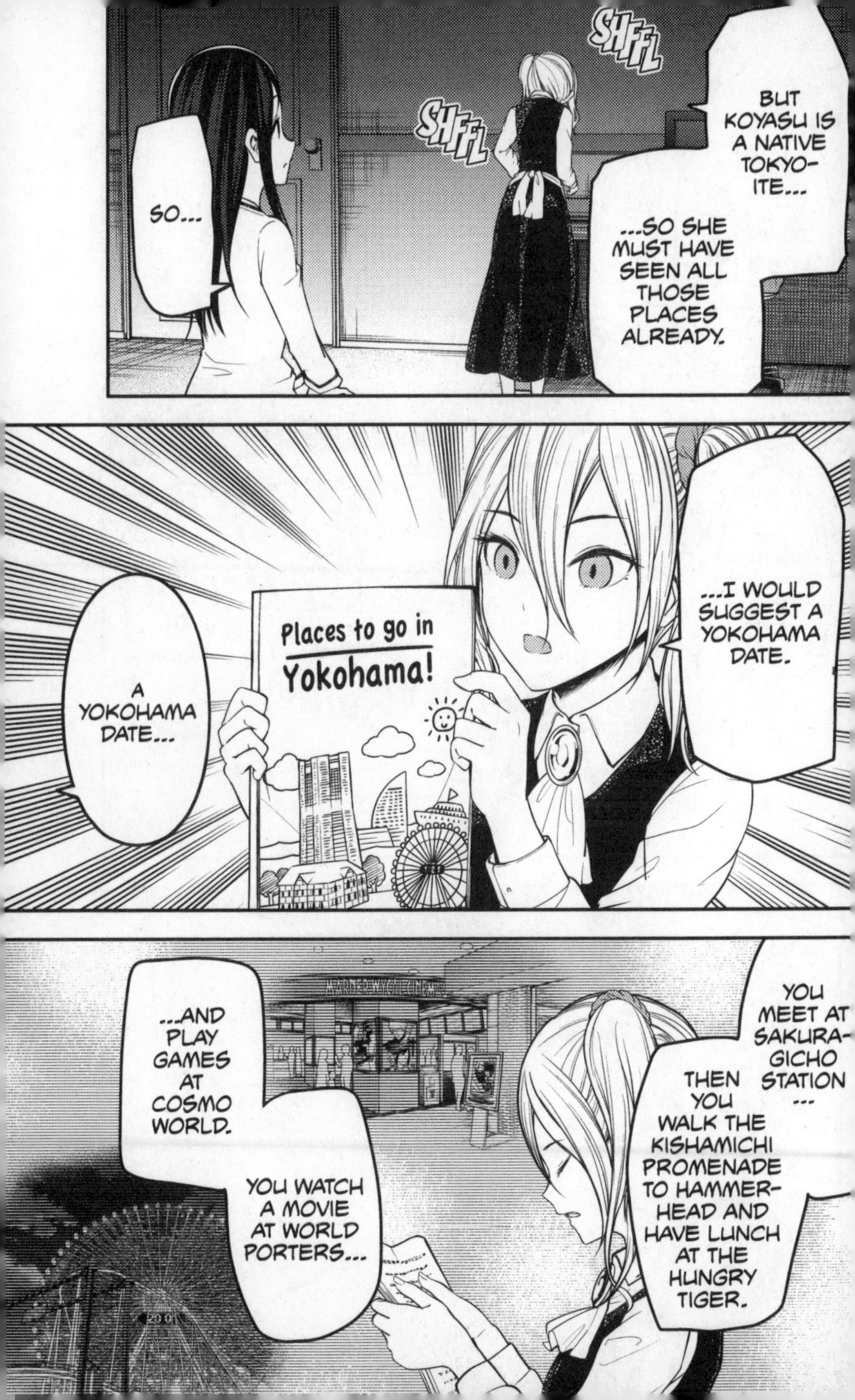
SHFFL
SHFFL
BUT KOYASU IS A NATIVE TOKYO-ITE...
...SO SHE MUST HAVE SEEN ALL THOSE PLACES ALREADY.
SO...
...I WOULD SUGGEST A YOKOHAMA DATE.
Places to go in Yokohama!
A YOKOHAMA DATE...
YOU MEET AT SAKURA-GICHO STATION...
THEN YOU WALK THE KISHAMICHI PROMENADE TO HAMMER-HEAD AND HAVE LUNCH AT THE HUNGRY TIGER.
YOU WATCH A MOVIE AT WORLD PORTERS...
...AND PLAY GAMES AT COSMO WORLD.

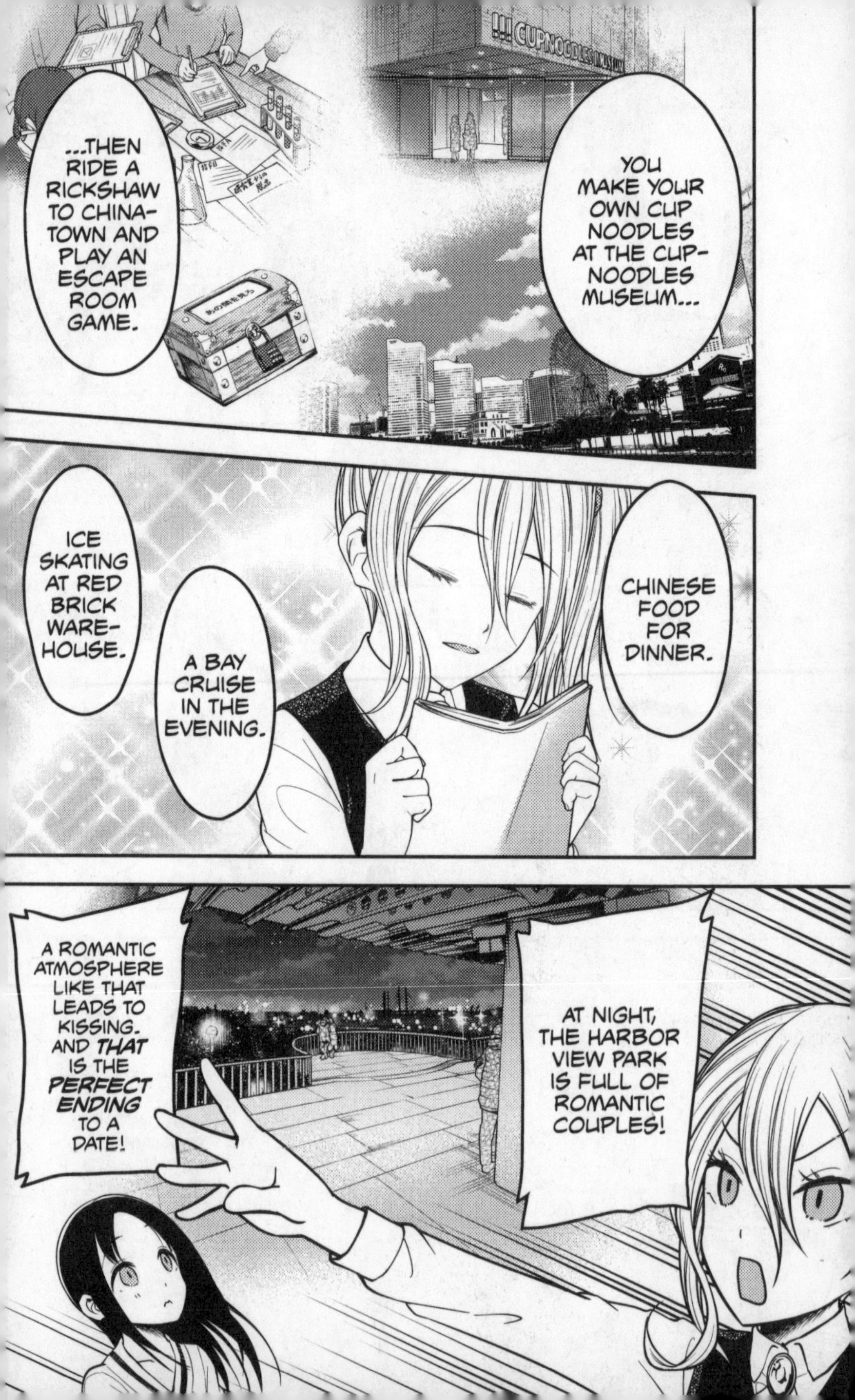
CUPNOODLES MUSEUM
YOU MAKE YOUR OWN CUP NOODLES AT THE CUP-NOODLES MUSEUM...
...THEN RIDE A RICKSHAW TO CHINA-TOWN AND PLAY AN ESCAPE ROOM GAME.
CHINESE FOOD FOR DINNER.
A BAY CRUISE IN THE EVENING.
ICE SKATING AT RED BRICK WARE-HOUSE.
AT NIGHT, THE HARBOR VIEW PARK IS FULL OF ROMANTIC COUPLES!
A ROMANTIC ATMOSPHERE LIKE THAT LEADS TO KISSING. AND *THAT* IS THE ***PERFECT ENDING*** TO A DATE!

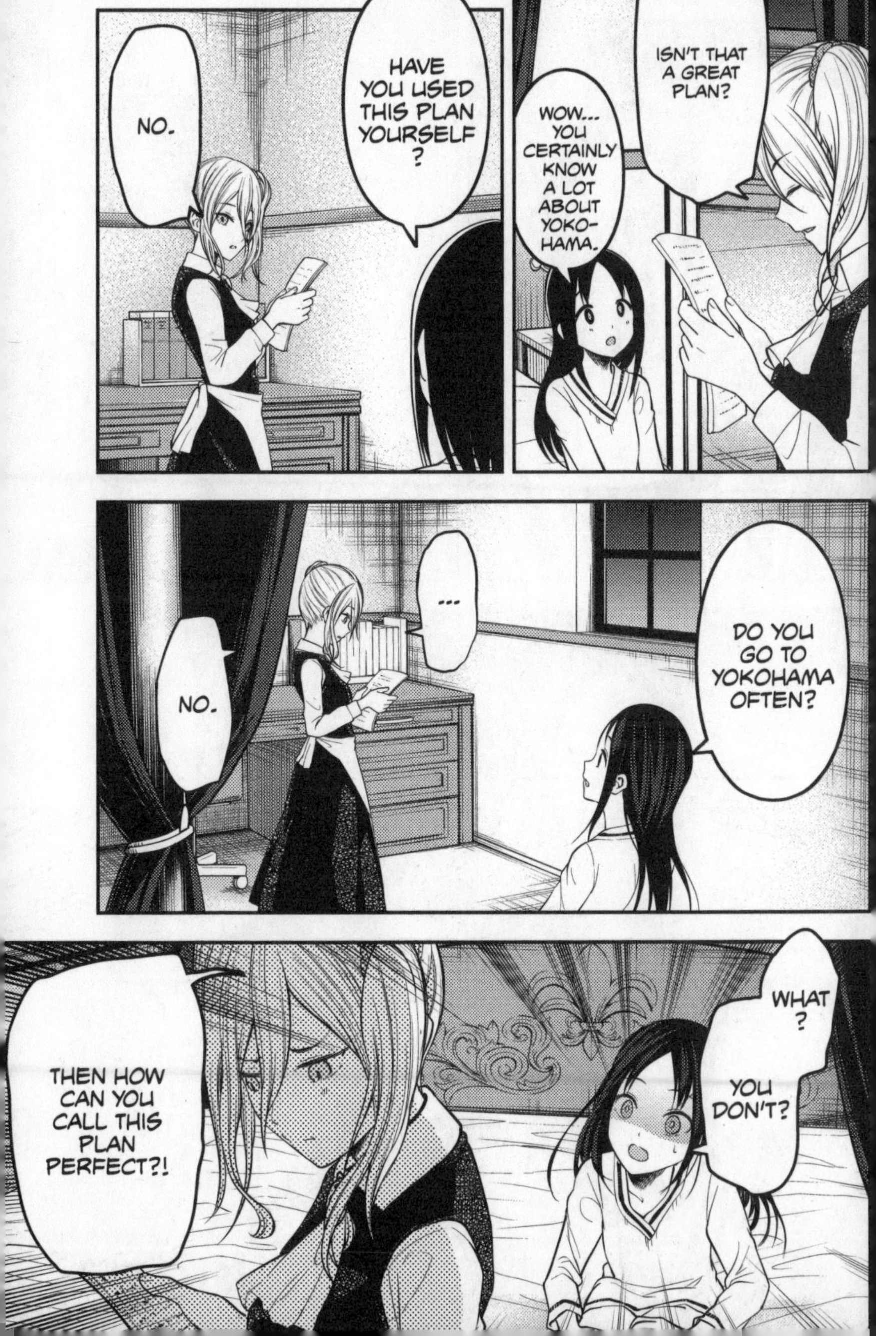
ISN'T THAT A GREAT PLAN?
WOW... YOU CERTAINLY KNOW A LOT ABOUT YOKO-HAMA.
HAVE YOU USED THIS PLAN YOURSELF?
NO.
DO YOU GO TO YOKOHAMA OFTEN?
...
NO.
WHAT? YOU DON'T?
THEN HOW CAN YOU CALL THIS PLAN PERFECT?!

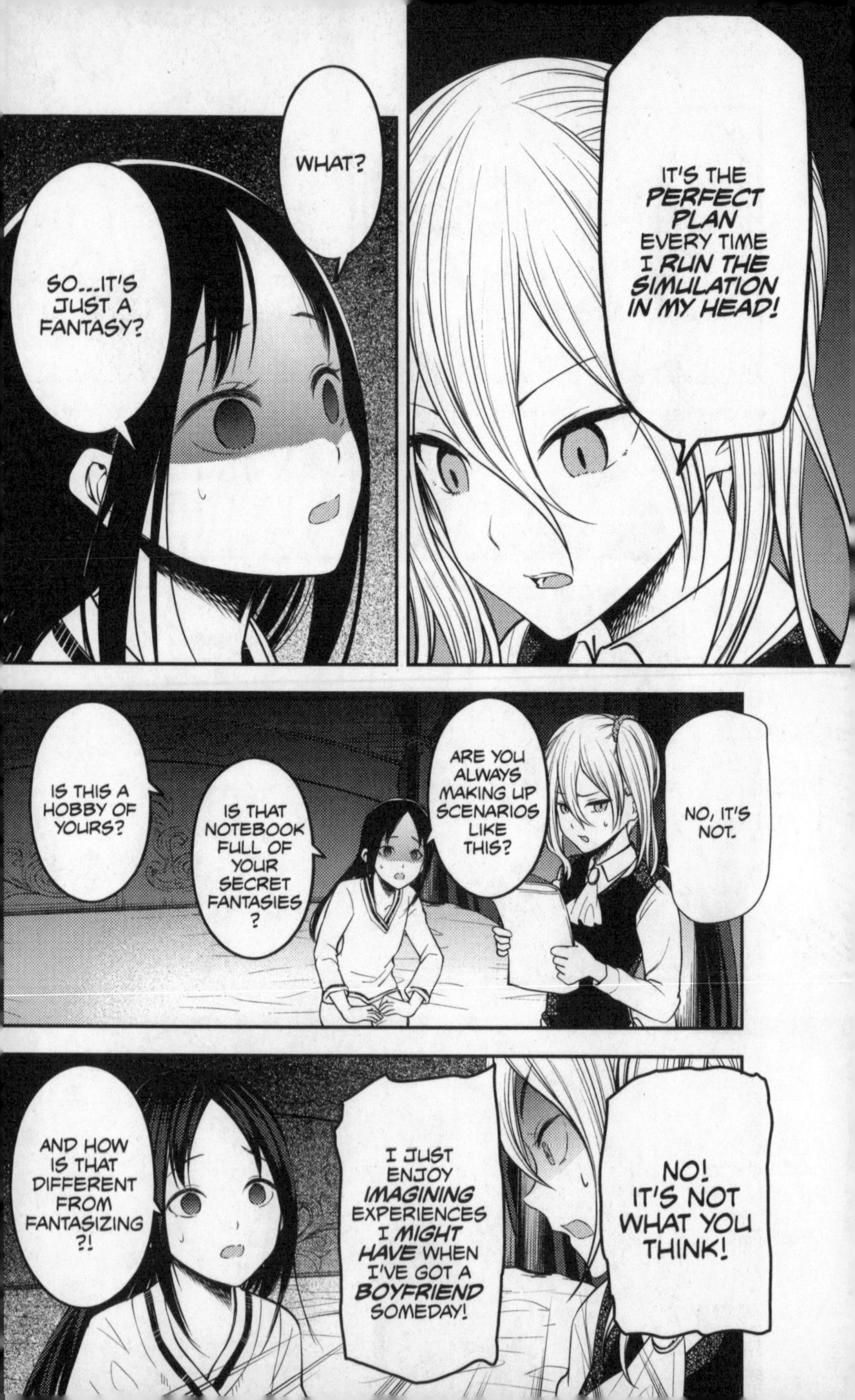
IT'S THE PERFECT PLAN EVERY TIME I RUN THE SIMULATION IN MY HEAD!
WHAT?
SO...IT'S JUST A FANTASY?
NO, IT'S NOT.
ARE YOU ALWAYS MAKING UP SCENARIOS LIKE THIS?
IS THAT NOTEBOOK FULL OF YOUR SECRET FANTASIES?
IS THIS A HOBBY OF YOURS?
NO! IT'S NOT WHAT YOU THINK!
I JUST ENJOY IMAGINING EXPERIENCES I MIGHT HAVE WHEN I'VE GOT A BOYFRIEND SOMEDAY!
AND HOW IS THAT DIFFERENT FROM FANTASIZING?!

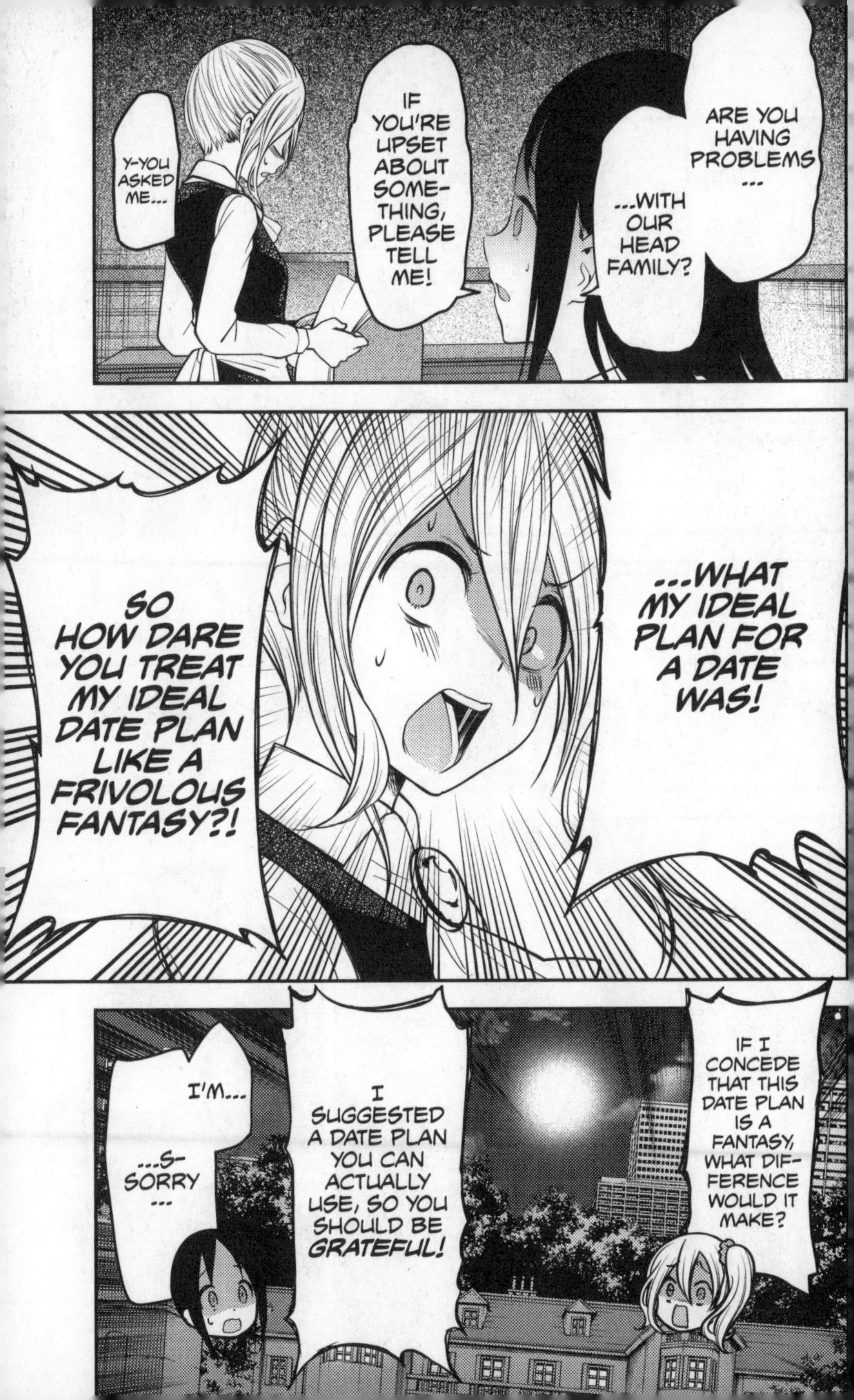
ARE YOU HAVING PROBLEMS ...
...WITH OUR HEAD FAMILY?
IF YOU'RE UPSET ABOUT SOME-THING, PLEASE TELL ME!
Y-YOU ASKED ME...
...WHAT MY IDEAL PLAN FOR A DATE WAS!
SO HOW DARE YOU TREAT MY IDEAL DATE PLAN LIKE A FRIVOLOUS FANTASY?!
IF I CONCEDE THAT THIS DATE PLAN IS A FANTASY, WHAT DIF-FERENCE WOULD IT MAKE?
I SUGGESTED A DATE PLAN YOU CAN ACTUALLY USE, SO YOU SHOULD BE ***GRATEFUL!***
I'M...
...S-SORRY ...

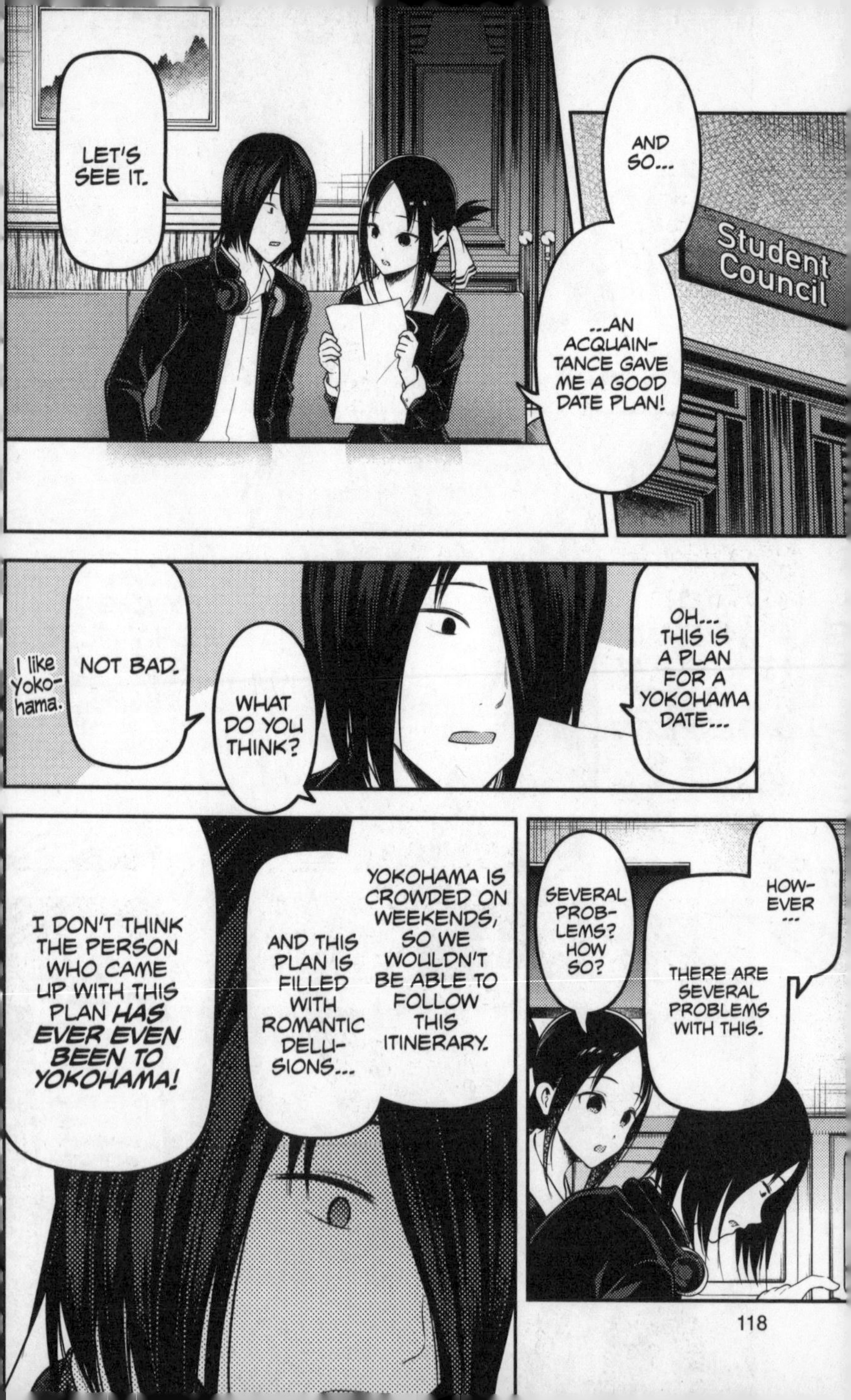
AND SO...
...AN ACQUAINTANCE GAVE ME A GOOD DATE PLAN!
Student Council
LET'S SEE IT.
OH... THIS IS A PLAN FOR A YOKOHAMA DATE...
WHAT DO YOU THINK?
NOT BAD.
I like Yokohama.
HOWEVER...
THERE ARE SEVERAL PROBLEMS WITH THIS.
SEVERAL PROBLEMS? HOW SO?
YOKOHAMA IS CROWDED ON WEEKENDS, SO WE WOULDN'T BE ABLE TO FOLLOW THIS ITINERARY.
AND THIS PLAN IS FILLED WITH ROMANTIC DELUSIONS...
I DON'T THINK THE PERSON WHO CAME UP WITH THIS PLAN ***HAS EVER EVEN BEEN TO YOKOHAMA!***

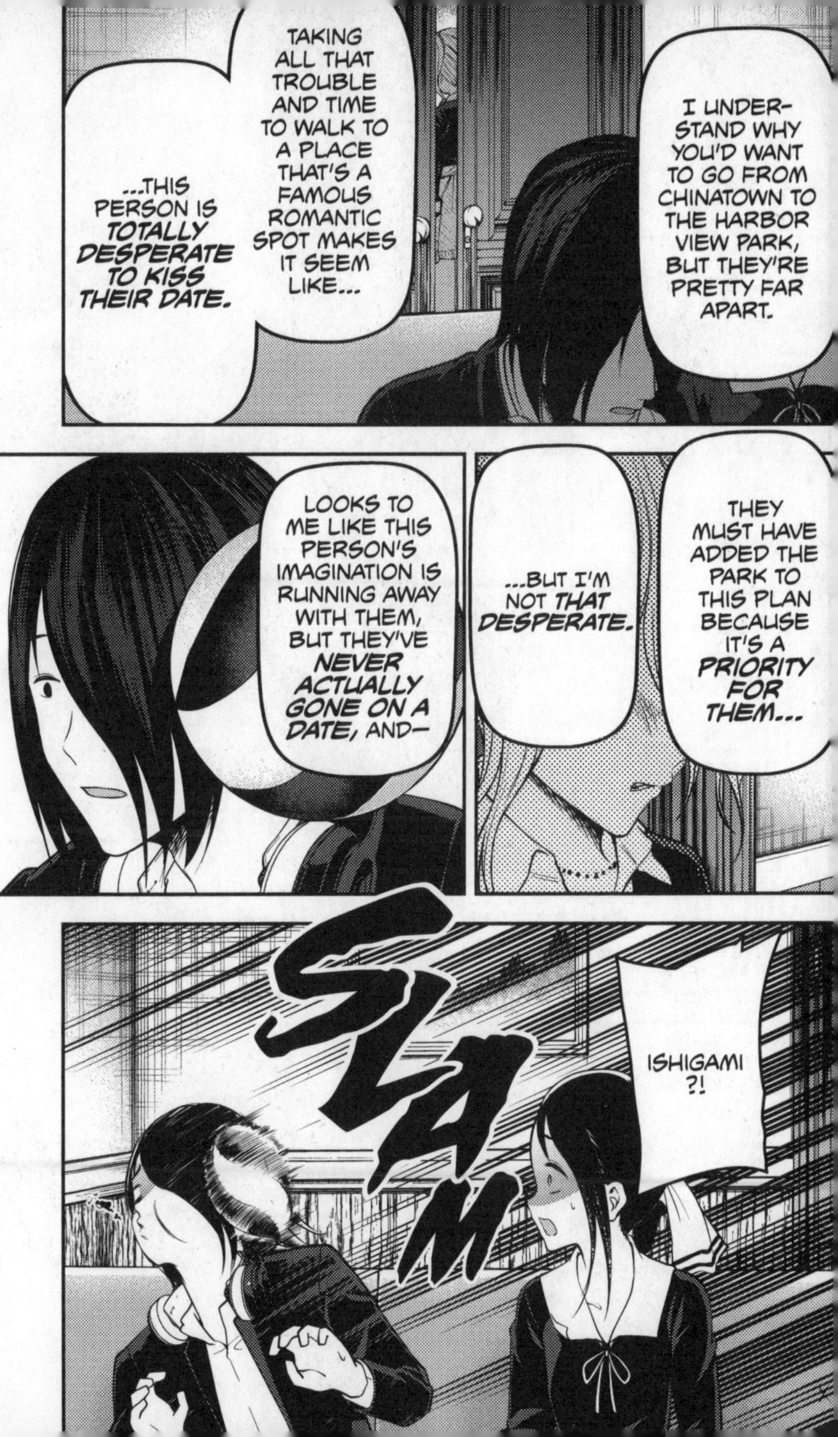
I UNDER-STAND WHY YOU'D WANT TO GO FROM CHINATOWN TO THE HARBOR VIEW PARK, BUT THEY'RE PRETTY FAR APART.
TAKING ALL THAT TROUBLE AND TIME TO WALK TO A PLACE THAT'S A FAMOUS ROMANTIC SPOT MAKES IT SEEM LIKE...
...THIS PERSON IS *TOTALLY DESPERATE TO KISS THEIR DATE.*
THEY MUST HAVE ADDED THE PARK TO THIS PLAN BECAUSE IT'S A *PRIORITY FOR THEM...*
...BUT I'M NOT *THAT DESPERATE.*
LOOKS TO ME LIKE THIS PERSON'S IMAGINATION IS RUNNING AWAY WITH THEM, BUT THEY'VE *NEVER ACTUALLY GONE ON A DATE,* AND—
ISHIGAMI ?!
SLAM

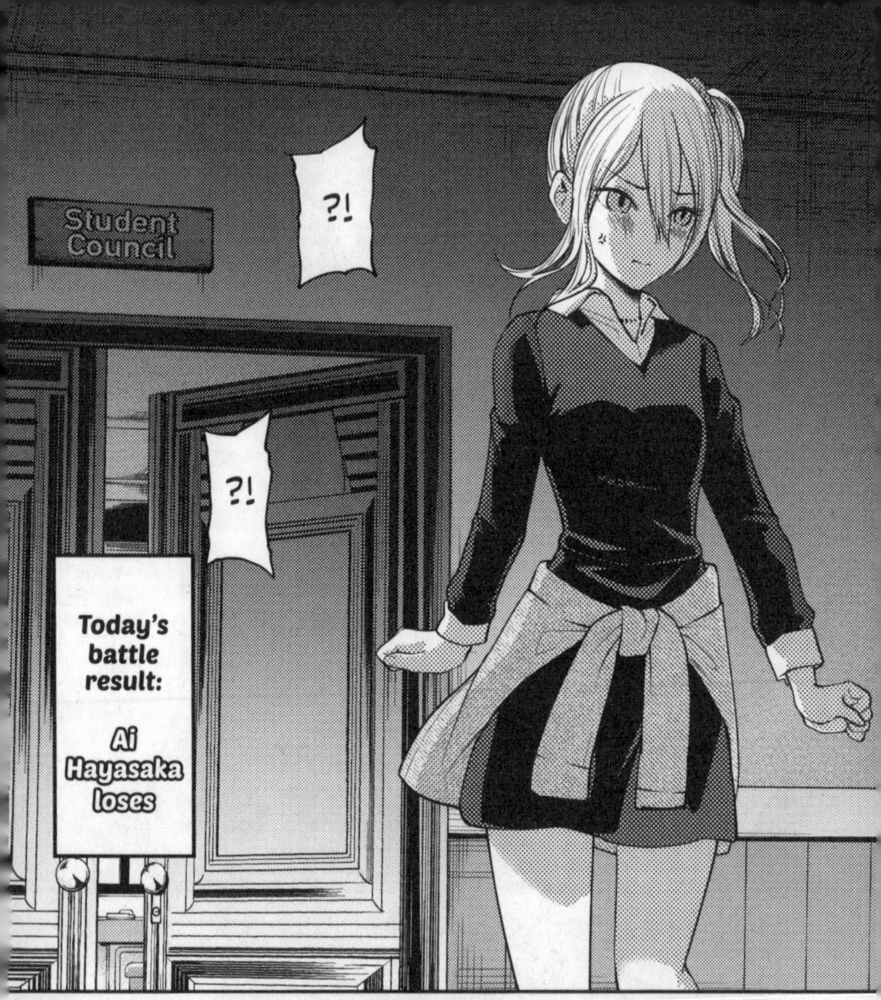
?!
Student Council
?!
Today's battle result:
Ai Hayasaka loses

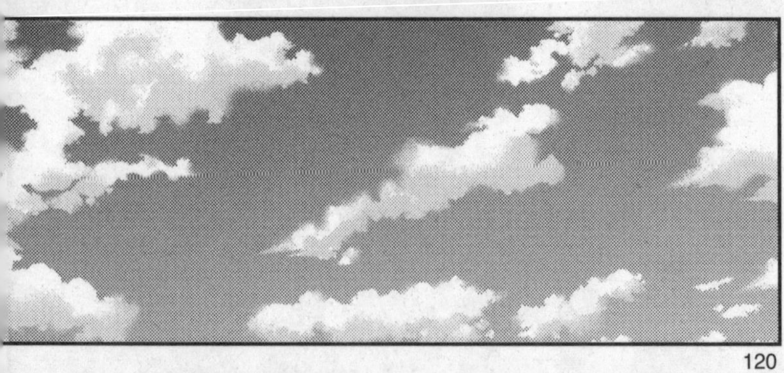

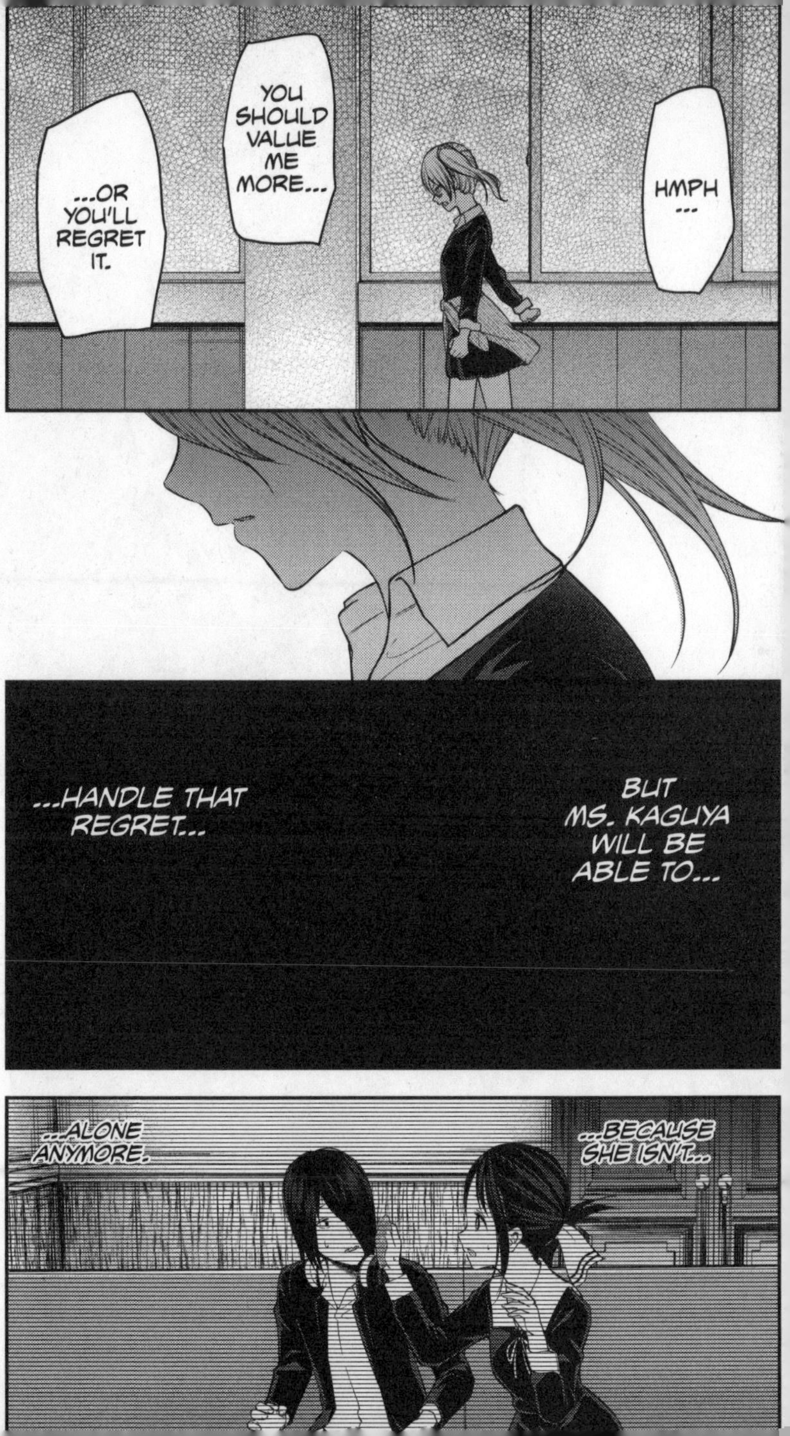
HMPH...
YOU SHOULD VALUE ME MORE...
...OR YOU'LL REGRET IT.
BUT MS. KAGUYA WILL BE ABLE TO...
...HANDLE THAT REGRET...
...BECAUSE SHE ISN'T...
...ALONE ANYMORE.

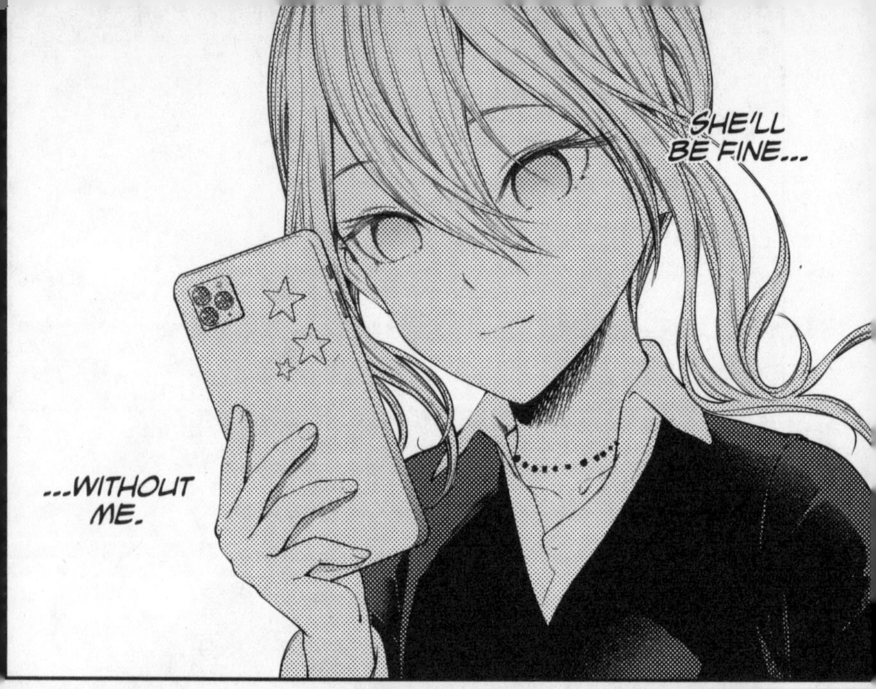
SHE'LL BE FINE...
...WITHOUT ME.

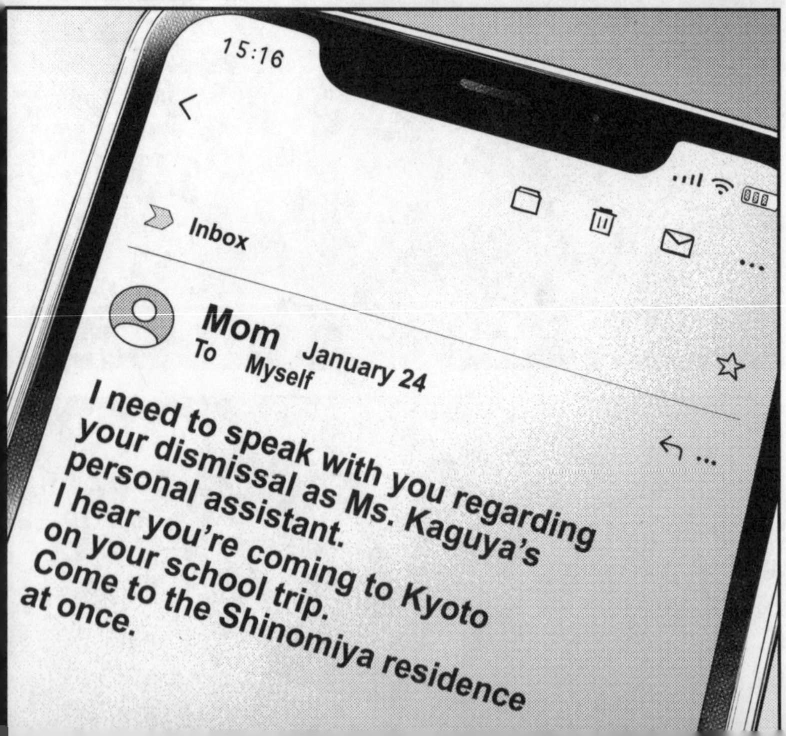
15:16
Inbox
Mom
To Myself
January 24
I need to speak with you regarding your dismissal as Ms. Kaguya's personal assistant.
I hear you're coming to Kyoto on your school trip.
Come to the Shinomiya residence at once.

COMING
SOON:
THEIR
YOKO-
HAMA
DATE!

KAGUYA-SAMA

LOVE IS WAR

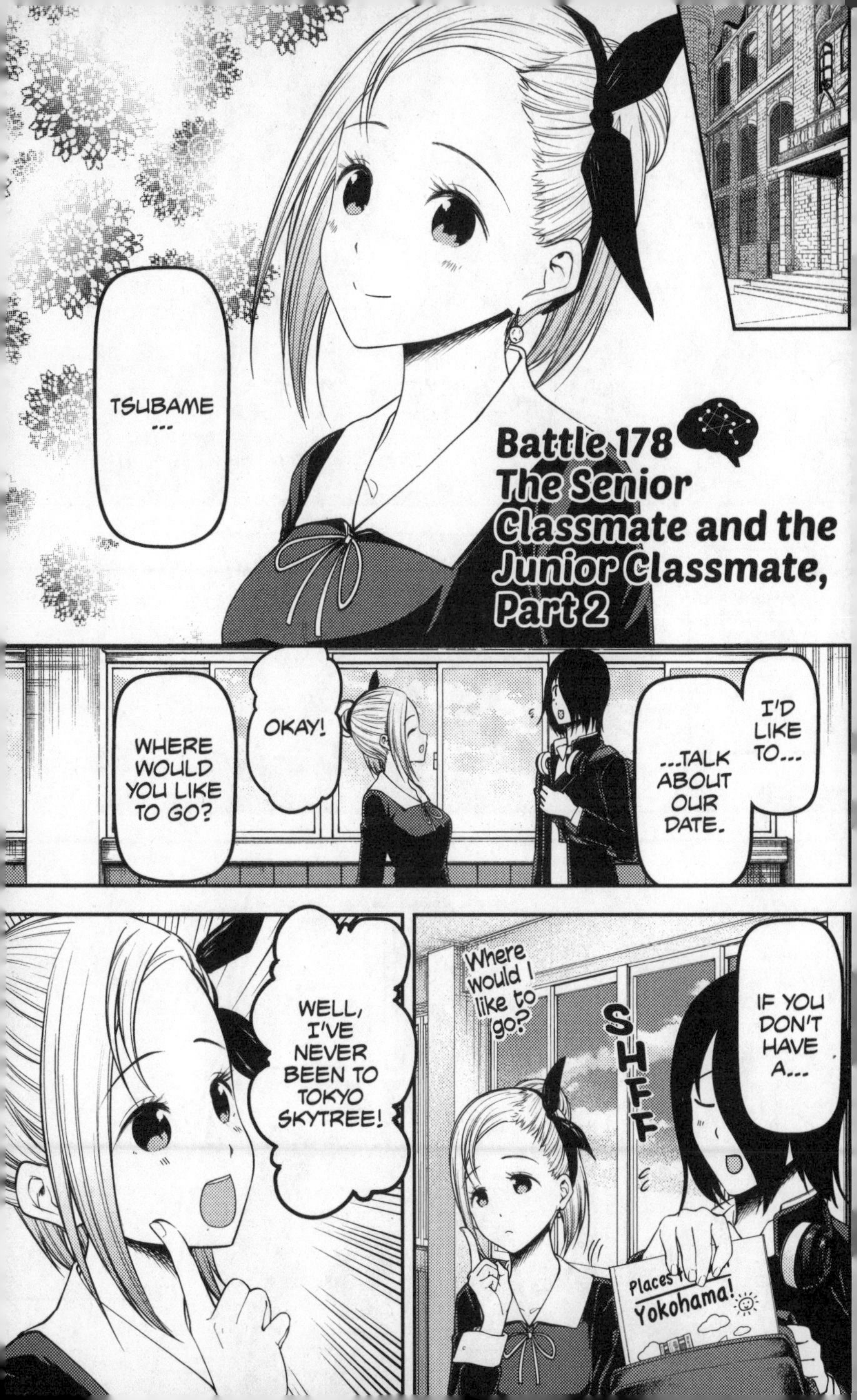
TSUBAME...
Battle 178 The Senior Classmate and the Junior Classmate, Part 2
I'D LIKE TO...
...TALK ABOUT OUR DATE.
OKAY!
WHERE WOULD YOU LIKE TO GO?
IF YOU DON'T HAVE A...
SHFF
Where would I like to go?
Places t
Yokohama!
WELL, I'VE NEVER BEEN TO TOKYO SKYTREE!

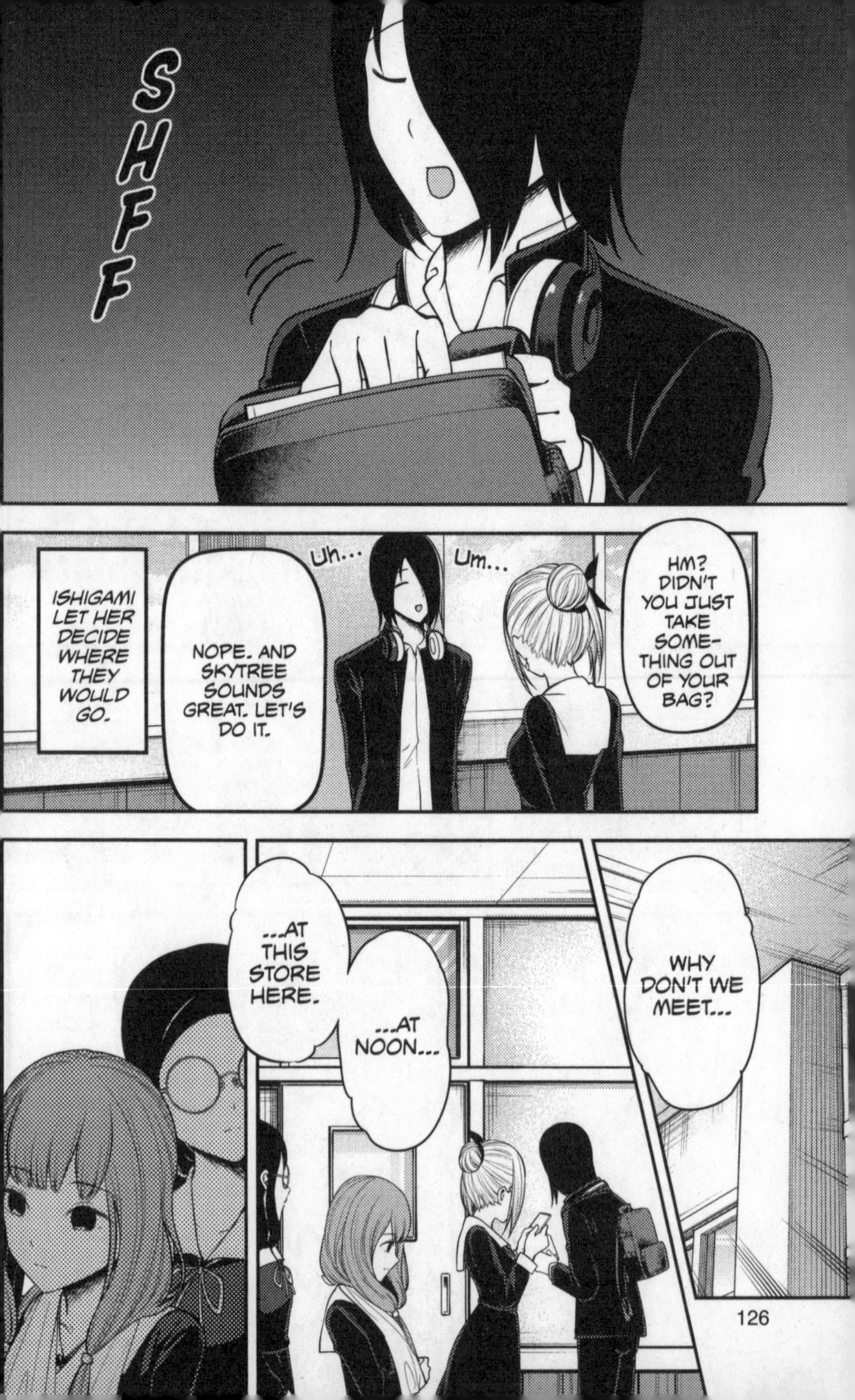
SHFF
HM? DIDN'T YOU JUST TAKE SOME-THING OUT OF YOUR BAG?
Um...
Uh...
NOPE. AND SKYTREE SOUNDS GREAT. LET'S DO IT.
ISHIGAMI LET HER DECIDE WHERE THEY WOULD GO.
WHY DON'T WE MEET...
...AT NOON...
...AT THIS STORE HERE.

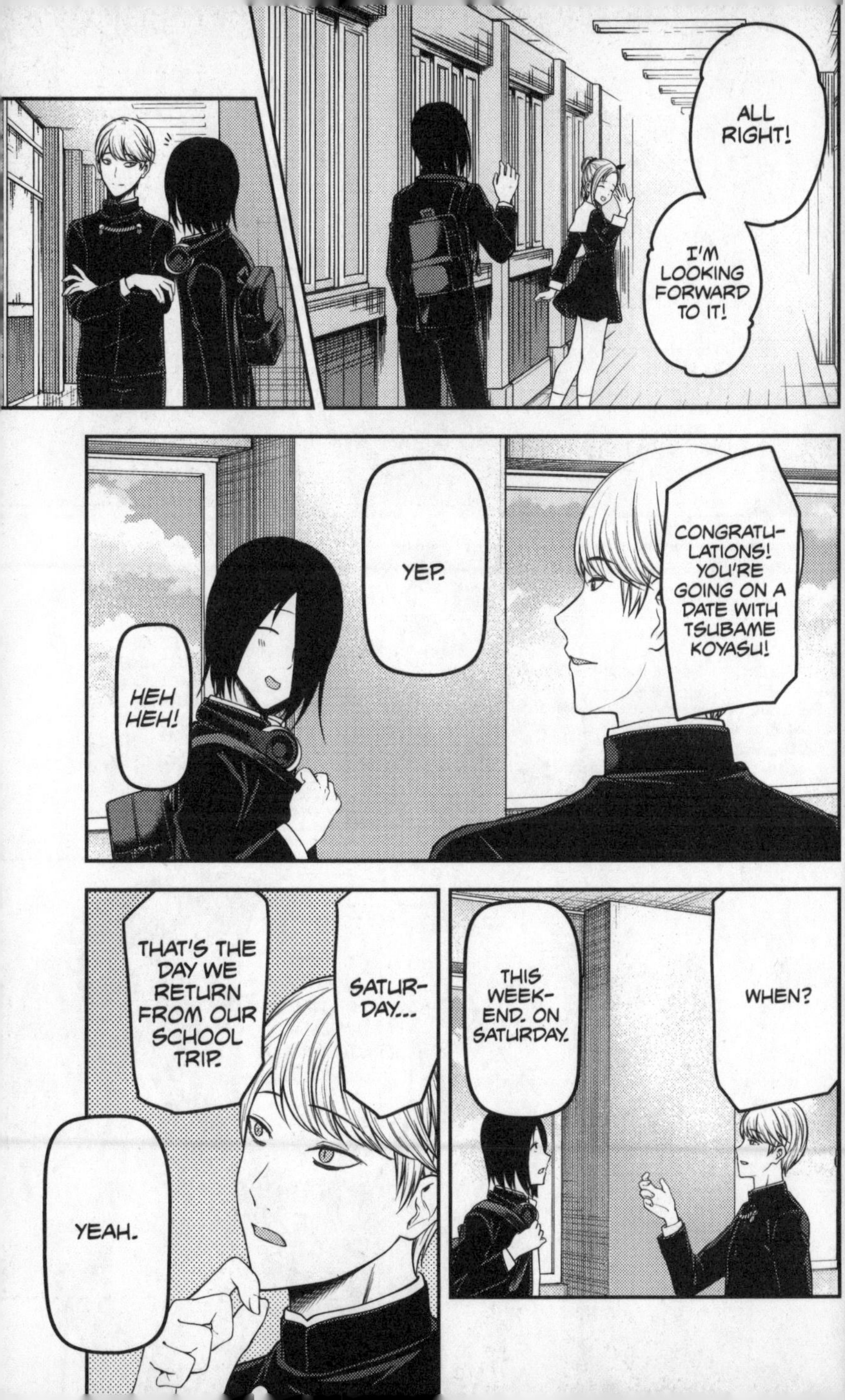
ALL RIGHT!
I'M LOOKING FORWARD TO IT!
CONGRATULATIONS! YOU'RE GOING ON A DATE WITH TSUBAME KOYASU!
YEP.
HEH HEH!
WHEN?
THIS WEEKEND. ON SATURDAY.
SATURDAY...
THAT'S THE DAY WE RETURN FROM OUR SCHOOL TRIP.
YEAH.

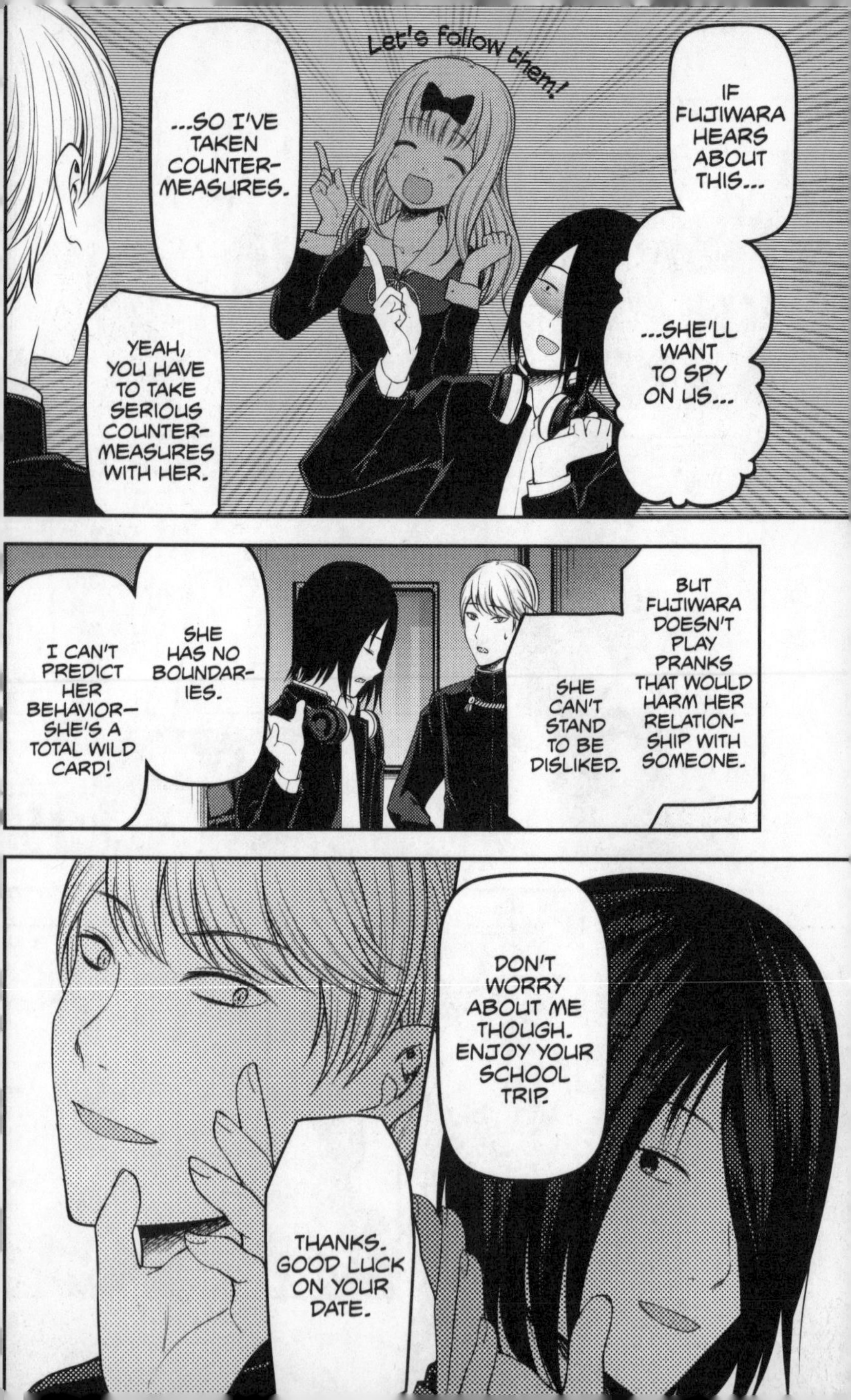
IF FUJIWARA HEARS ABOUT THIS...
...SHE'LL WANT TO SPY ON US...
Let's follow them!
...SO I'VE TAKEN COUNTER-MEASURES.
YEAH, YOU HAVE TO TAKE SERIOUS COUNTER-MEASURES WITH HER.
BUT FUJIWARA DOESN'T PLAY PRANKS THAT WOULD HARM HER RELATION-SHIP WITH SOMEONE.
SHE CAN'T STAND TO BE DISLIKED.
SHE HAS NO BOUNDAR-IES.
I CAN'T PREDICT HER BEHAVIOR—SHE'S A TOTAL WILD CARD!
DON'T WORRY ABOUT ME THOUGH. ENJOY YOUR SCHOOL TRIP.
THANKS. GOOD LUCK ON YOUR DATE.

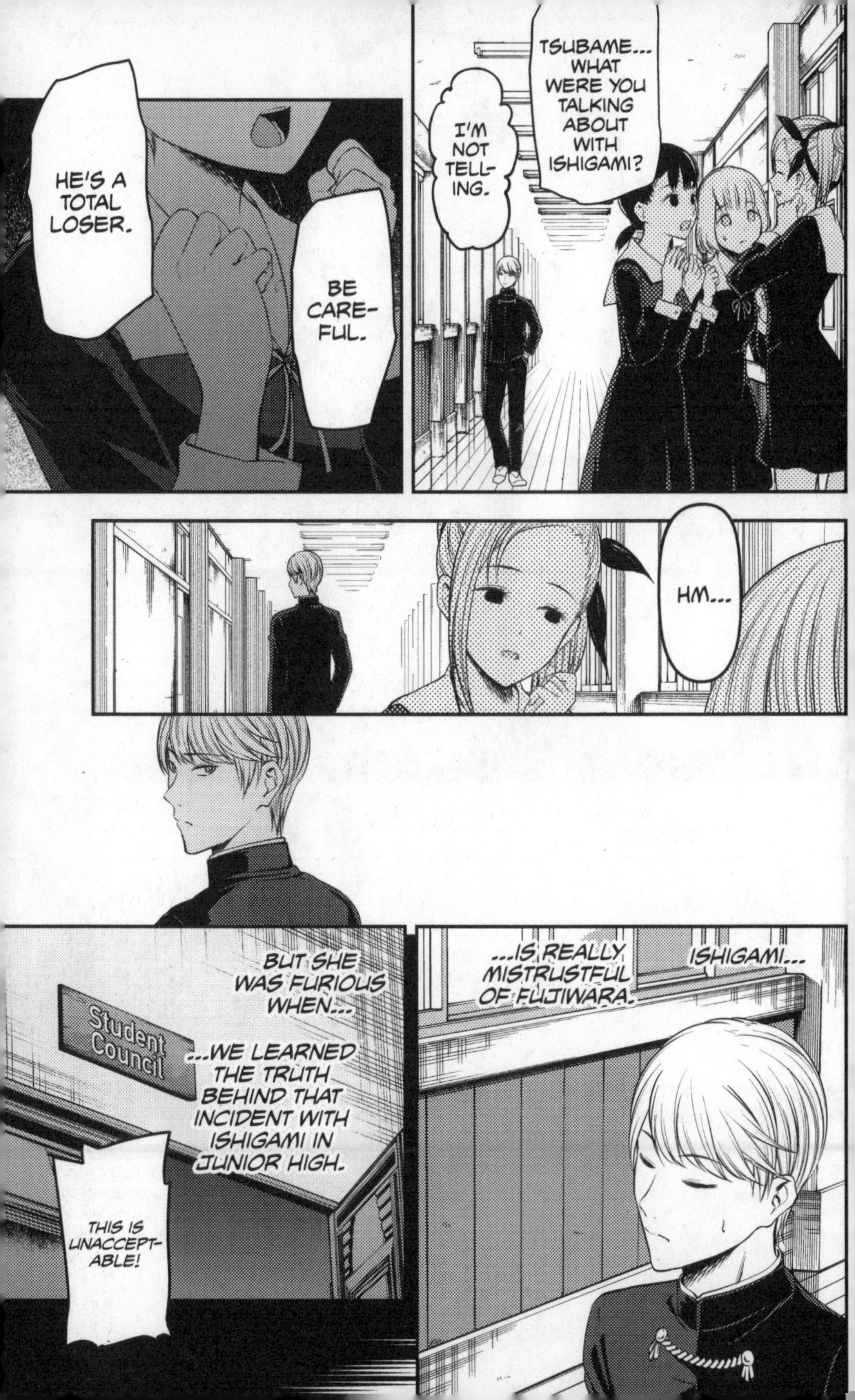
TSUBAME... WHAT WERE YOU TALKING ABOUT WITH ISHIGAMI?
I'M NOT TELLING.
HE'S A TOTAL LOSER.
BE CAREFUL.
HM...
ISHIGAMI...
...IS REALLY MISTRUSTFUL OF FUJIWARA.
BUT SHE WAS FURIOUS WHEN...
Student Council
...WE LEARNED THE TRUTH BEHIND THAT INCIDENT WITH ISHIGAMI IN JUNIOR HIGH.
THIS IS UNACCEPTABLE!

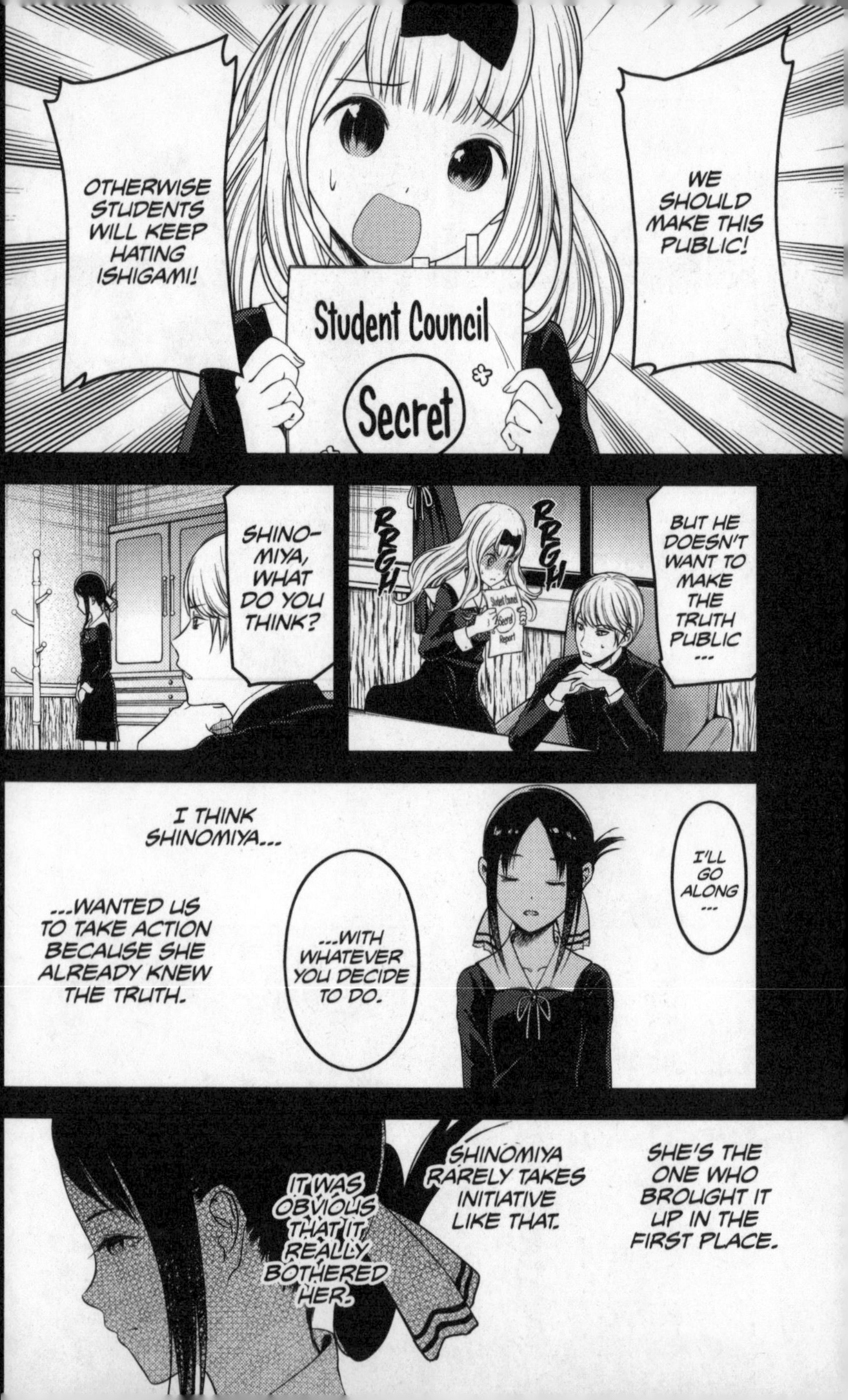
WE SHOULD MAKE THIS PUBLIC!
OTHERWISE STUDENTS WILL KEEP HATING ISHIGAMI!
Student Council
Secret
BUT HE DOESN'T WANT TO MAKE THE TRUTH PUBLIC...
RRGH
RRGH
Student Council Secret Report
SHINOMIYA, WHAT DO YOU THINK?
I'LL GO ALONG...
...WITH WHATEVER YOU DECIDE TO DO.
I THINK SHINOMIYA...
...WANTED US TO TAKE ACTION BECAUSE SHE ALREADY KNEW THE TRUTH.
SHE'S THE ONE WHO BROUGHT IT UP IN THE FIRST PLACE.
SHINOMIYA RARELY TAKES INITIATIVE LIKE THAT.
IT WAS OBVIOUS THAT IT REALLY BOTHERED HER.

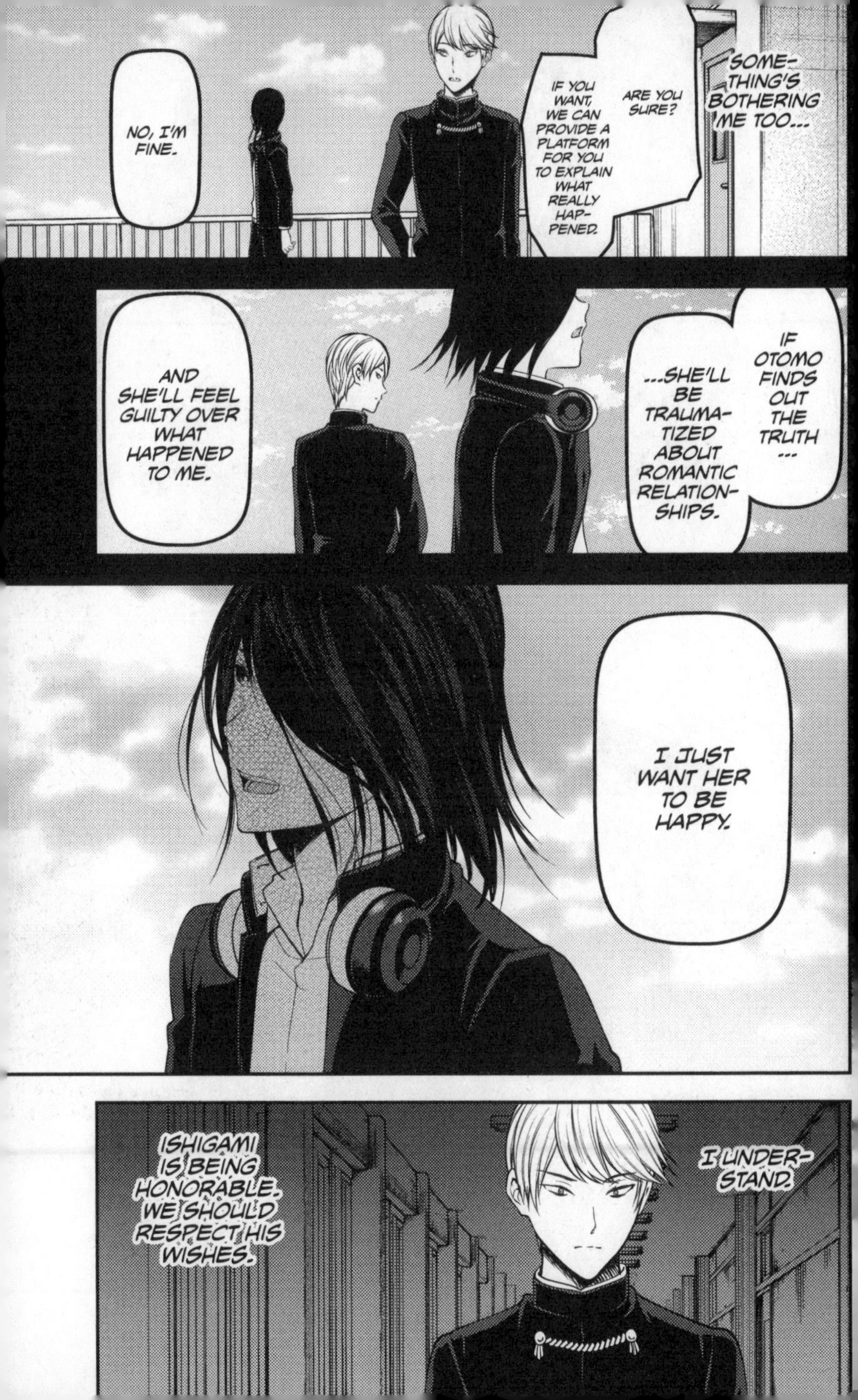
SOMETHING'S BOTHERING ME TOO...
ARE YOU SURE?
IF YOU WANT, WE CAN PROVIDE A PLATFORM FOR YOU TO EXPLAIN WHAT REALLY HAPPENED.
NO, I'M FINE.
IF OTOMO FINDS OUT THE TRUTH---
...SHE'LL BE TRAUMATIZED ABOUT ROMANTIC RELATIONSHIPS.
AND SHE'LL FEEL GUILTY OVER WHAT HAPPENED TO ME.
I JUST WANT HER TO BE HAPPY.
I UNDERSTAND.
ISHIGAMI IS BEING HONORABLE. WE SHOULD RESPECT HIS WISHES.

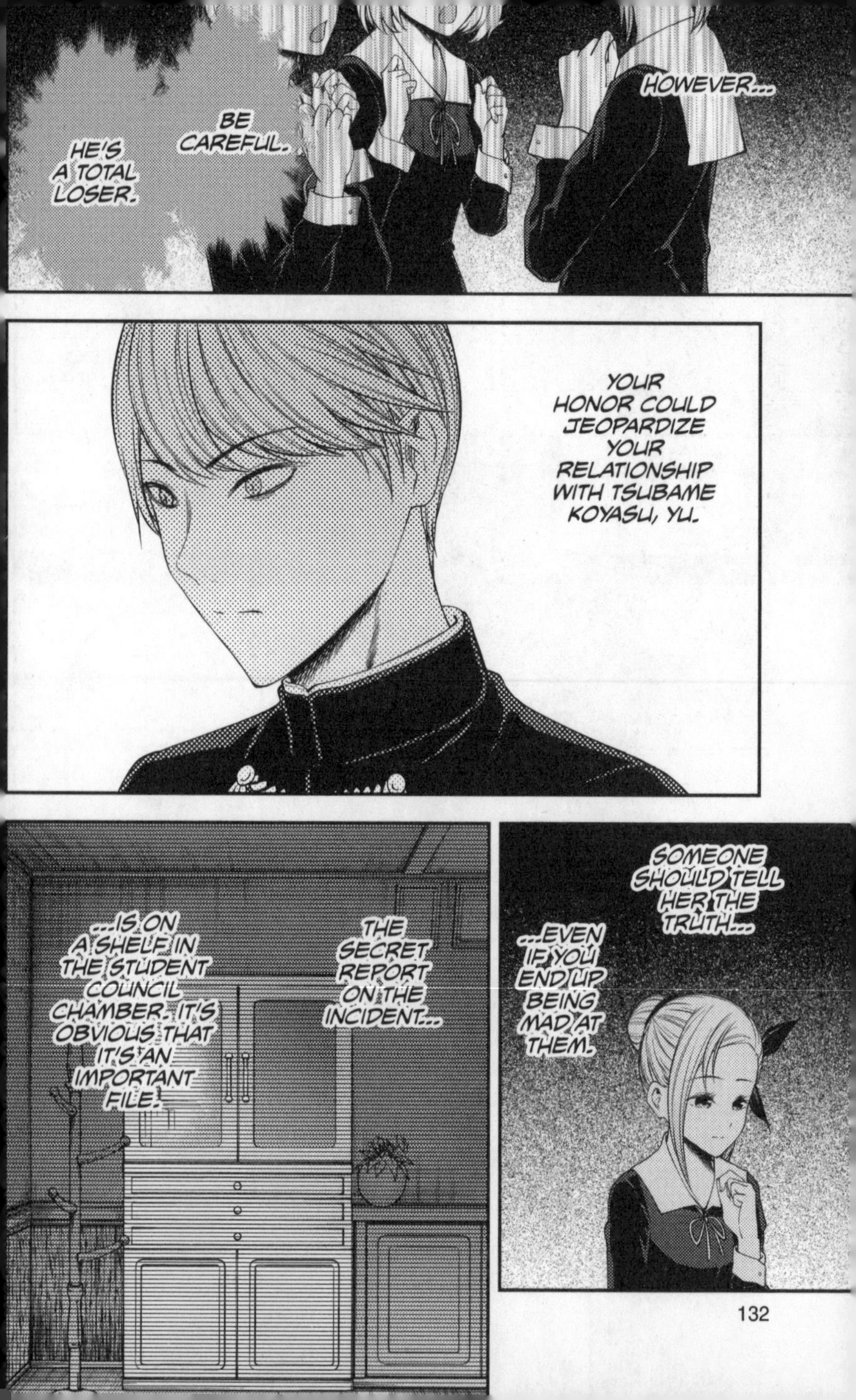
HOWEVER...
BE CAREFUL.
HE'S A TOTAL LOSER.
YOUR HONOR COULD JEOPARDIZE YOUR RELATIONSHIP WITH TSUBAME KOYASU, YU.
SOMEONE SHOULD TELL HER THE TRUTH...
...EVEN IF YOU END UP BEING MAD AT THEM.
THE SECRET REPORT ON THE INCIDENT...
...IS ON A SHELF IN THE STUDENT COUNCIL CHAMBER. IT'S OBVIOUS THAT IT'S AN IMPORTANT FILE.

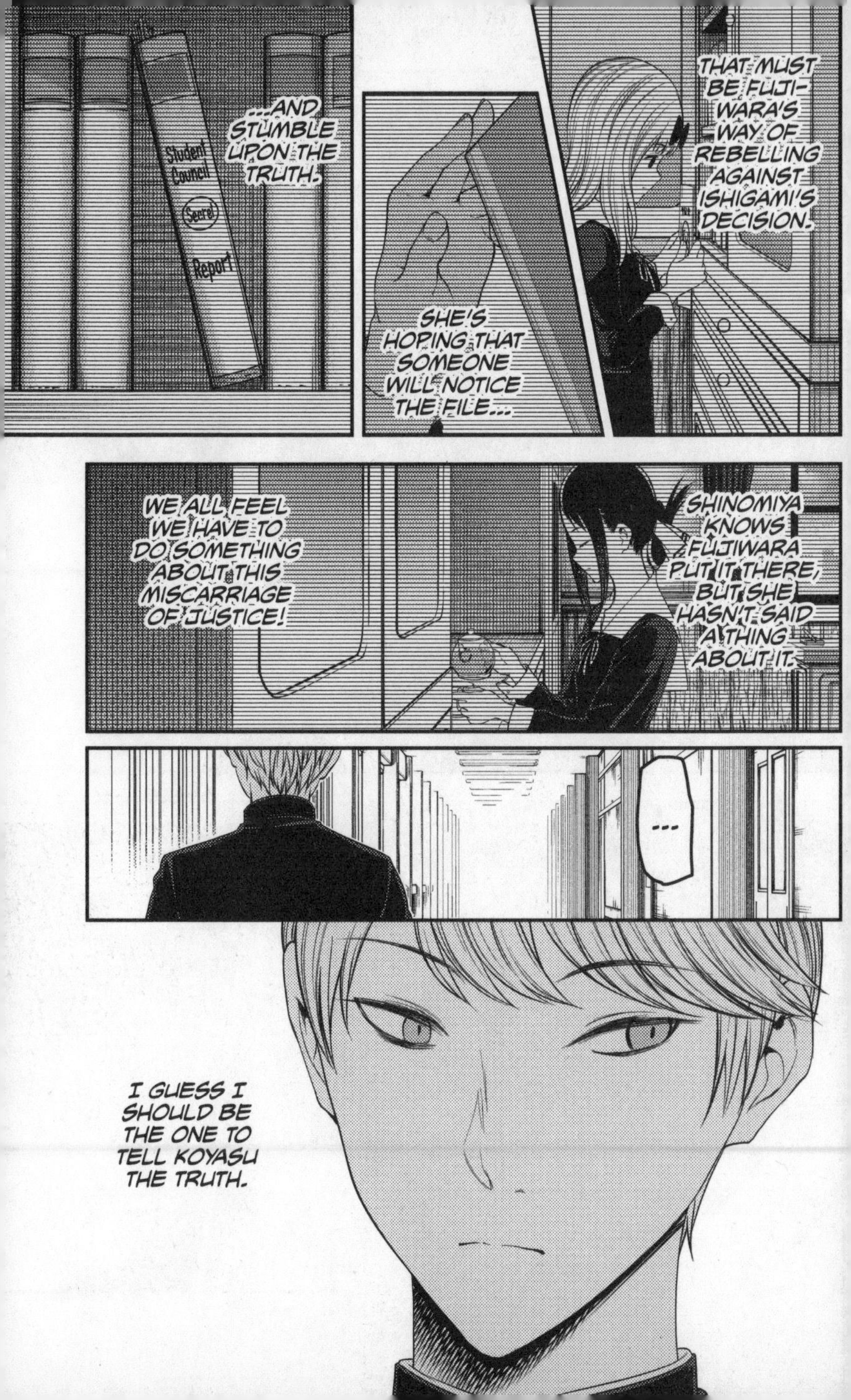
THAT MUST BE FUJI-WARA'S WAY OF REBELLING AGAINST ISHIGAMI'S DECISION.
SHE'S HOPING THAT SOMEONE WILL NOTICE THE FILE...
Student Council Secret Report
...AND STUMBLE UPON THE TRUTH.
SHINOMIYA KNOWS FUJIWARA PUT IT THERE, BUT SHE HASN'T SAID A THING ABOUT IT.
WE ALL FEEL WE HAVE TO DO SOMETHING ABOUT THIS MISCARRIAGE OF JUSTICE!
...
I GUESS I SHOULD BE THE ONE TO TELL KOYASU THE TRUTH.

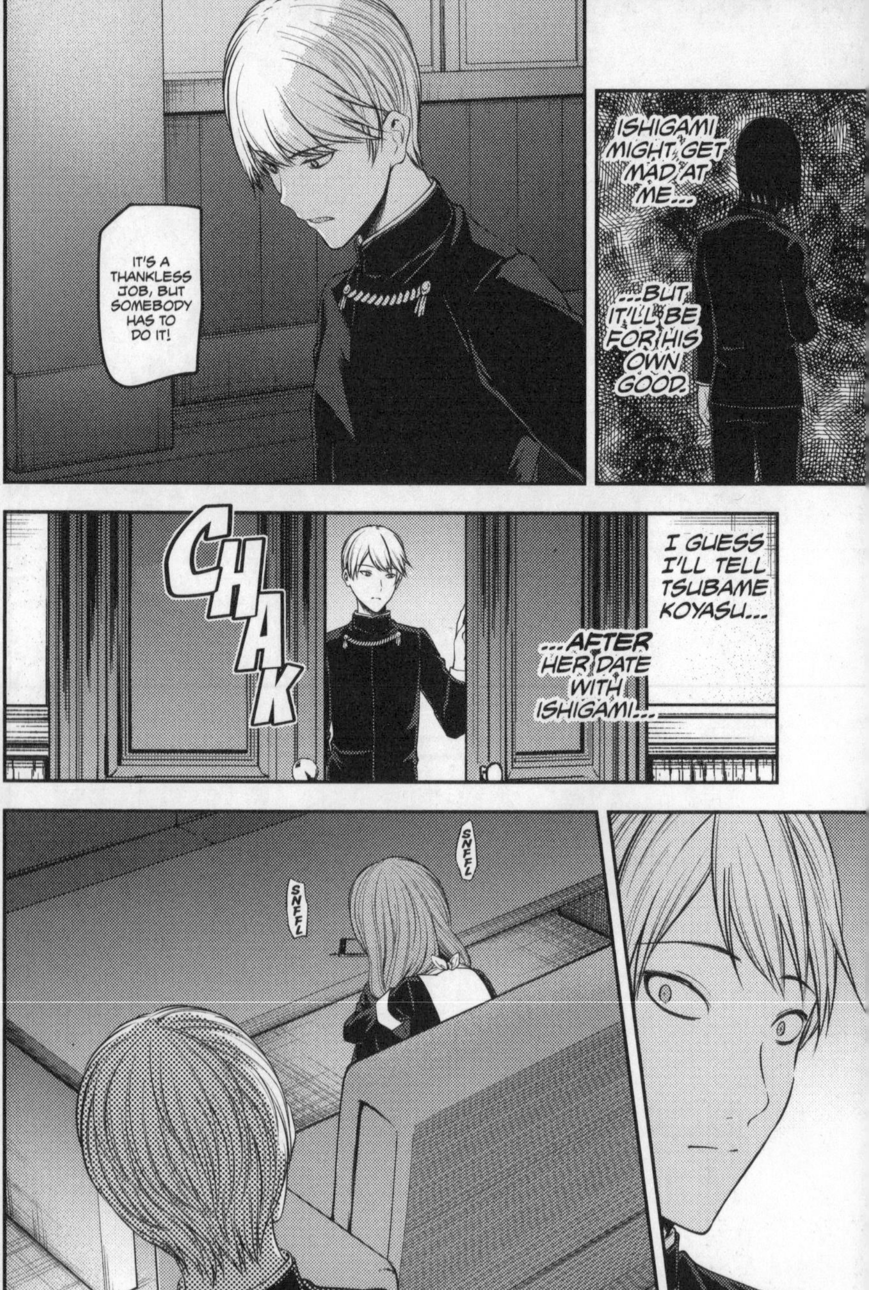
ISHIGAMI MIGHT GET MAD AT ME...
...BUT IT'LL BE FOR HIS OWN GOOD.
IT'S A THANKLESS JOB, BUT SOMEBODY HAS TO DO IT!
I GUESS I'LL TELL TSUBAME KOYASU...
...AFTER HER DATE WITH ISHIGAMI...
CHAK
SNFFL
SNFFL

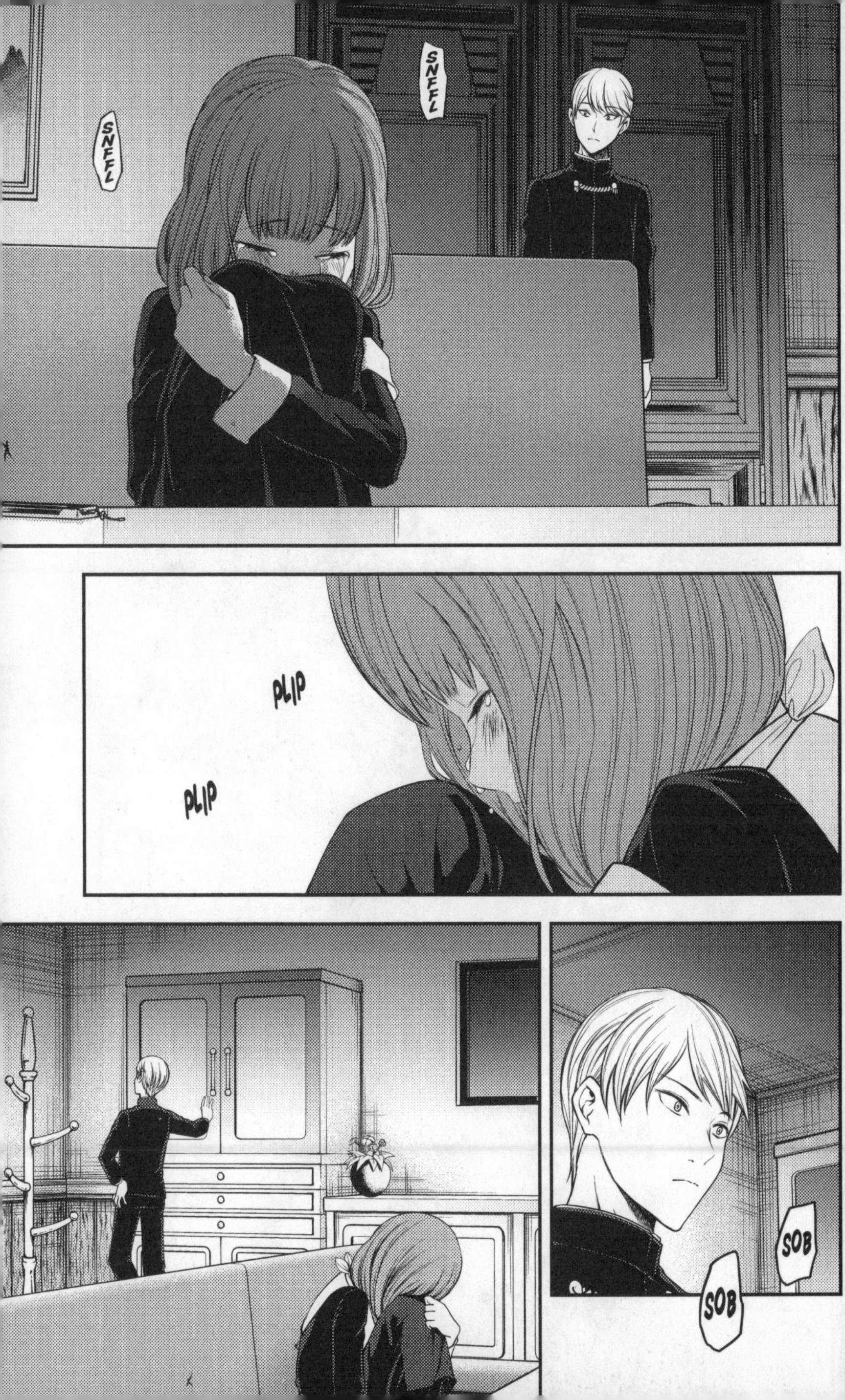
SNFFL
SNFFL
PLIP
PLIP
SOB
SOB

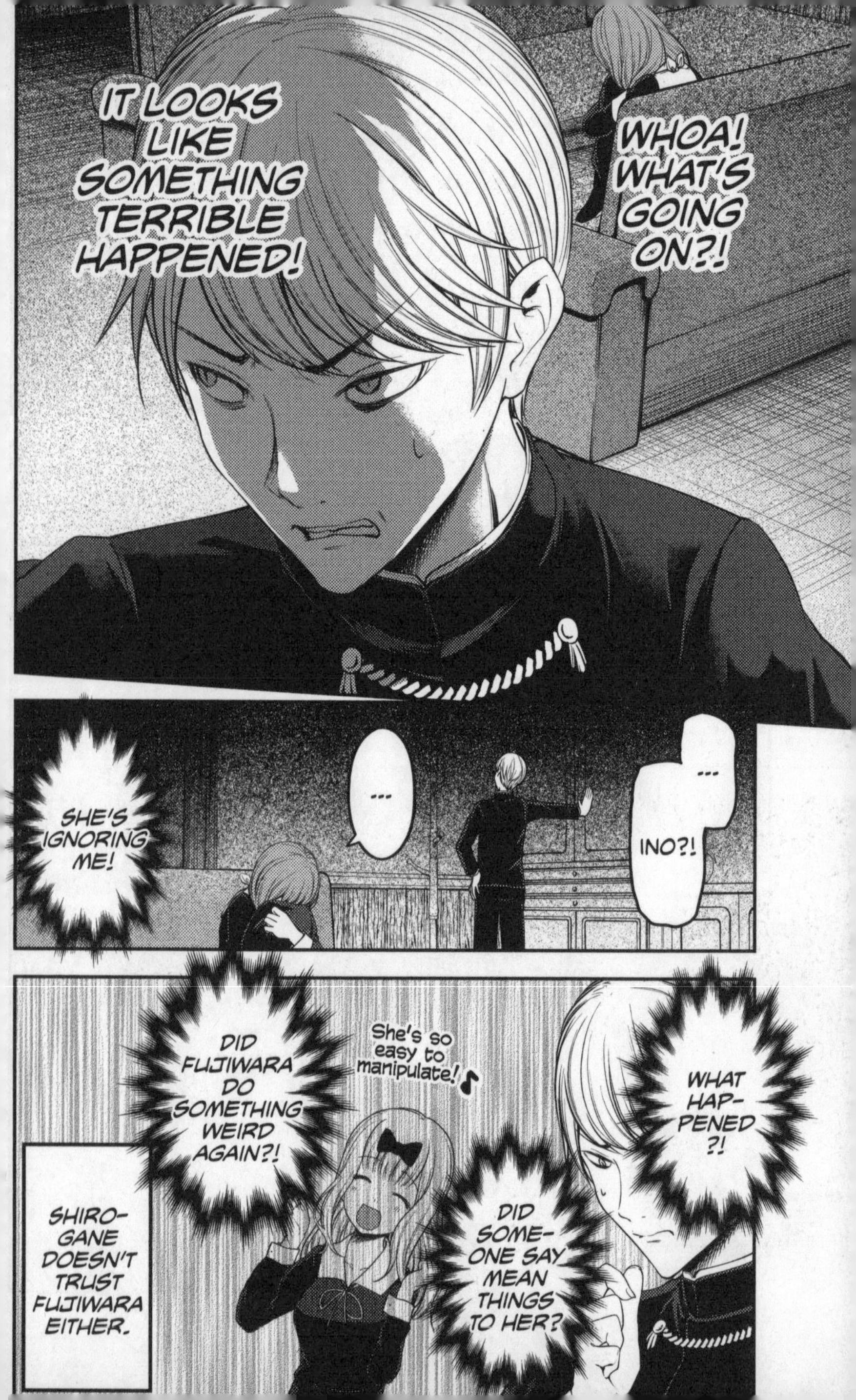
WHOA! WHAT'S GOING ON?!
IT LOOKS LIKE SOMETHING TERRIBLE HAPPENED!
...
INO?!
...
SHE'S IGNORING ME!
WHAT HAP-PENED?!
DID SOME-ONE SAY MEAN THINGS TO HER?
She's so easy to manipulate! ♪
DID FUJIWARA DO SOMETHING WEIRD AGAIN?!
SHIRO-GANE DOESN'T TRUST FUJIWARA EITHER.

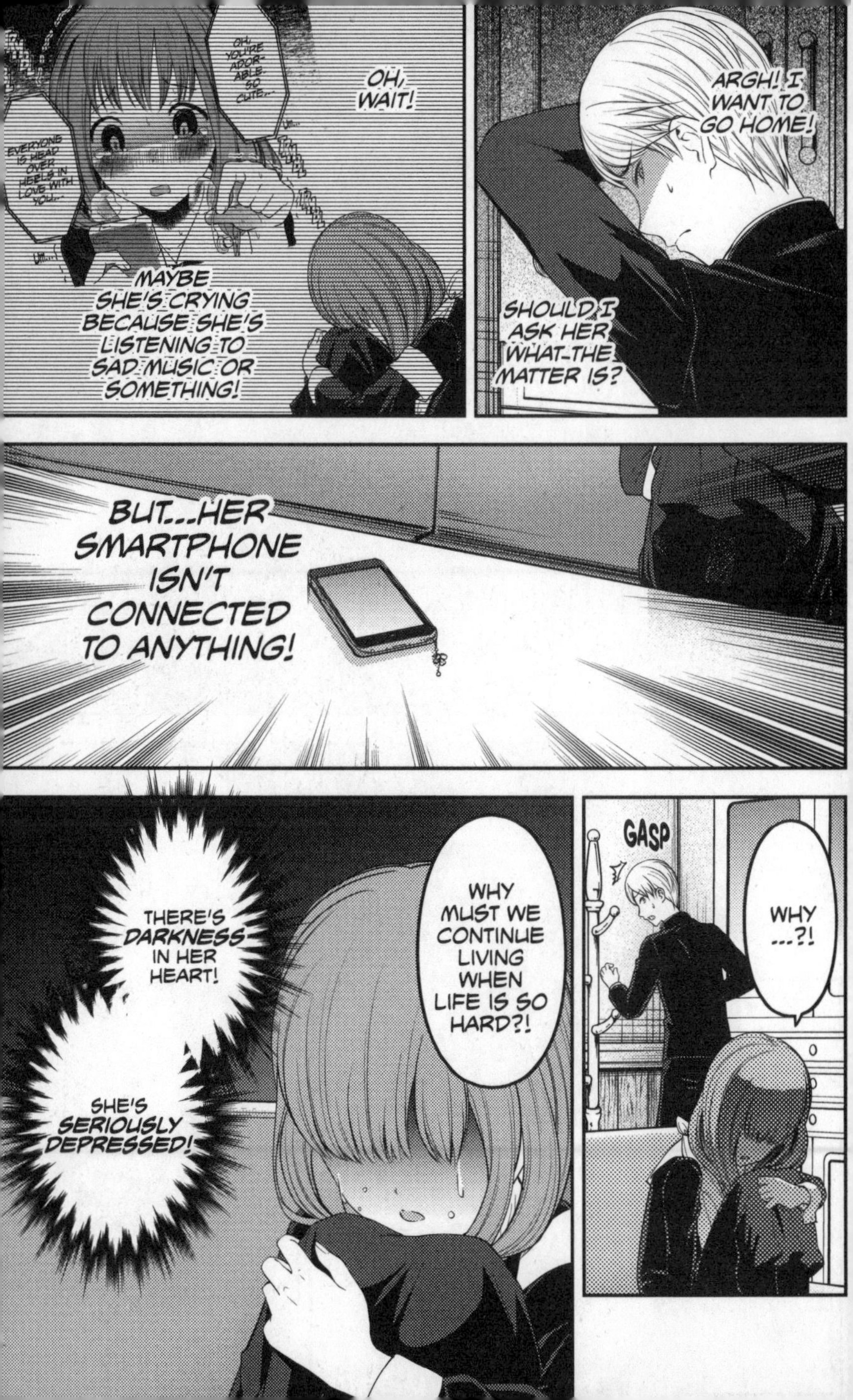
ARGH! I WANT TO GO HOME!
SHOULD I ASK HER WHAT THE MATTER IS?
OH, YOU'RE ADORABLE. SO CUTE...
OH, WAIT!
EVERYONE IS HEAD OVER HEELS IN LOVE WITH YOU...
Um...
Um...
MAYBE SHE'S CRYING BECAUSE SHE'S LISTENING TO SAD MUSIC OR SOMETHING!
BUT...HER SMARTPHONE ISN'T CONNECTED TO ANYTHING!
GASP
WHY...?!
WHY MUST WE CONTINUE LIVING WHEN LIFE IS SO HARD?!
THERE'S DARKNESS IN HER HEART!
SHE'S SERIOUSLY DEPRESSED!

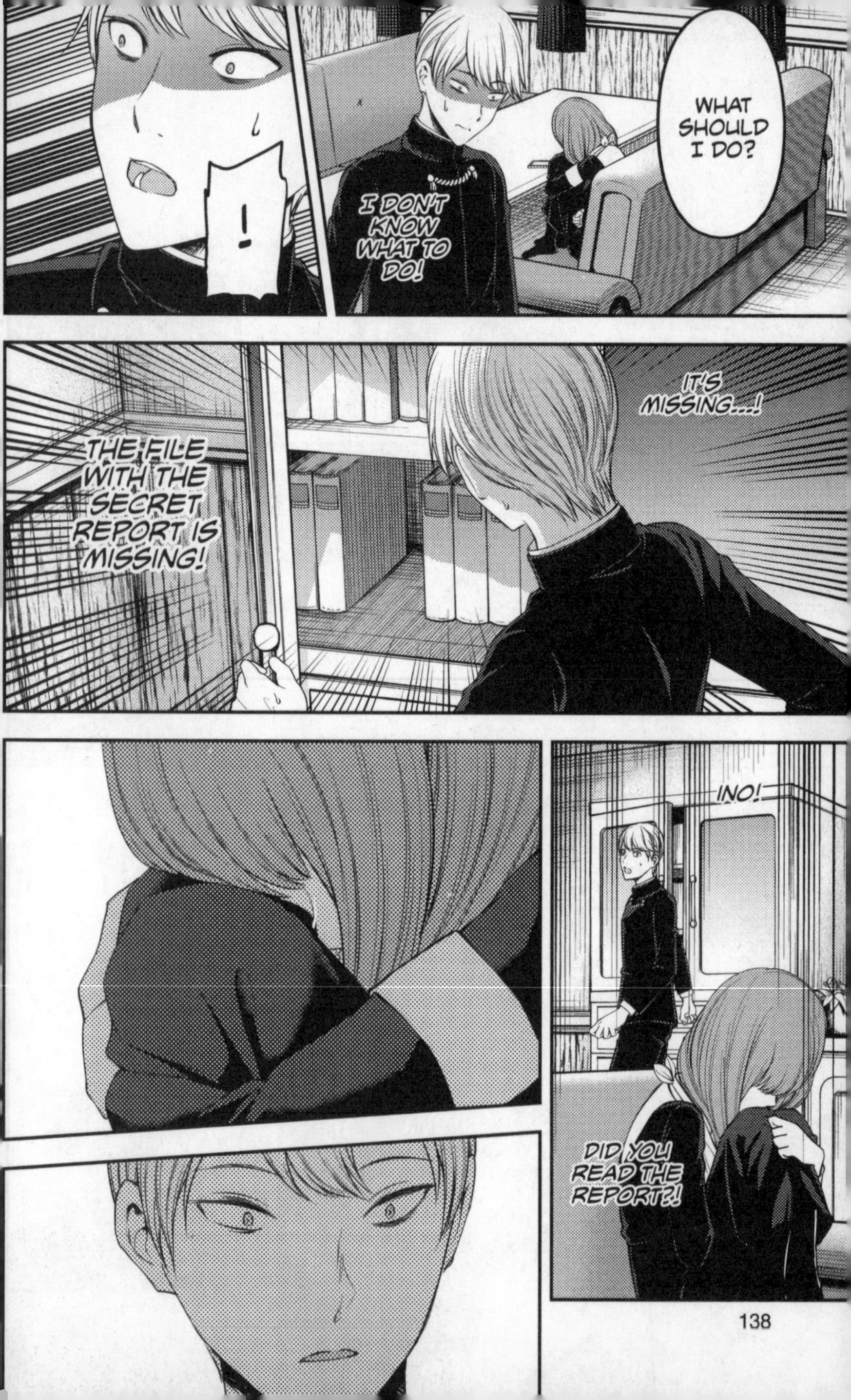
WHAT SHOULD I DO?
I DON'T KNOW WHAT TO DO!
!
IT'S MISSING...!
THE FILE WITH THE SECRET REPORT IS MISSING!
INO!
DID YOU READ THE REPORT?!

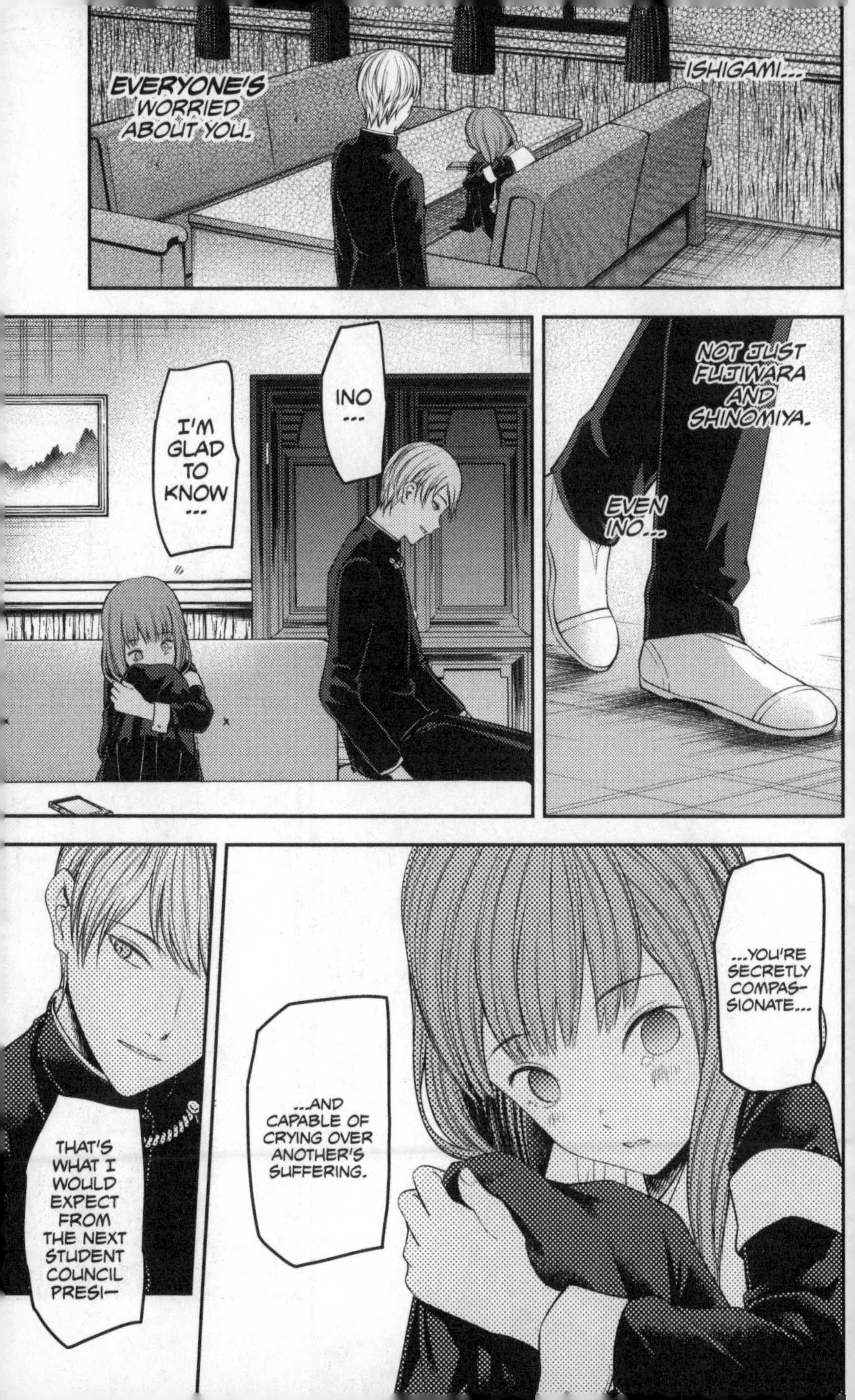
ISHIGAMI...
EVERYONE'S WORRIED ABOUT YOU.
NOT JUST FUJIWARA AND SHINOMIYA.
EVEN INO...
INO...
I'M GLAD TO KNOW...
...YOU'RE SECRETLY COMPASSIONATE...
...AND CAPABLE OF CRYING OVER ANOTHER'S SUFFERING.
THAT'S WHAT I WOULD EXPECT FROM THE NEXT STUDENT COUNCIL PRESI—

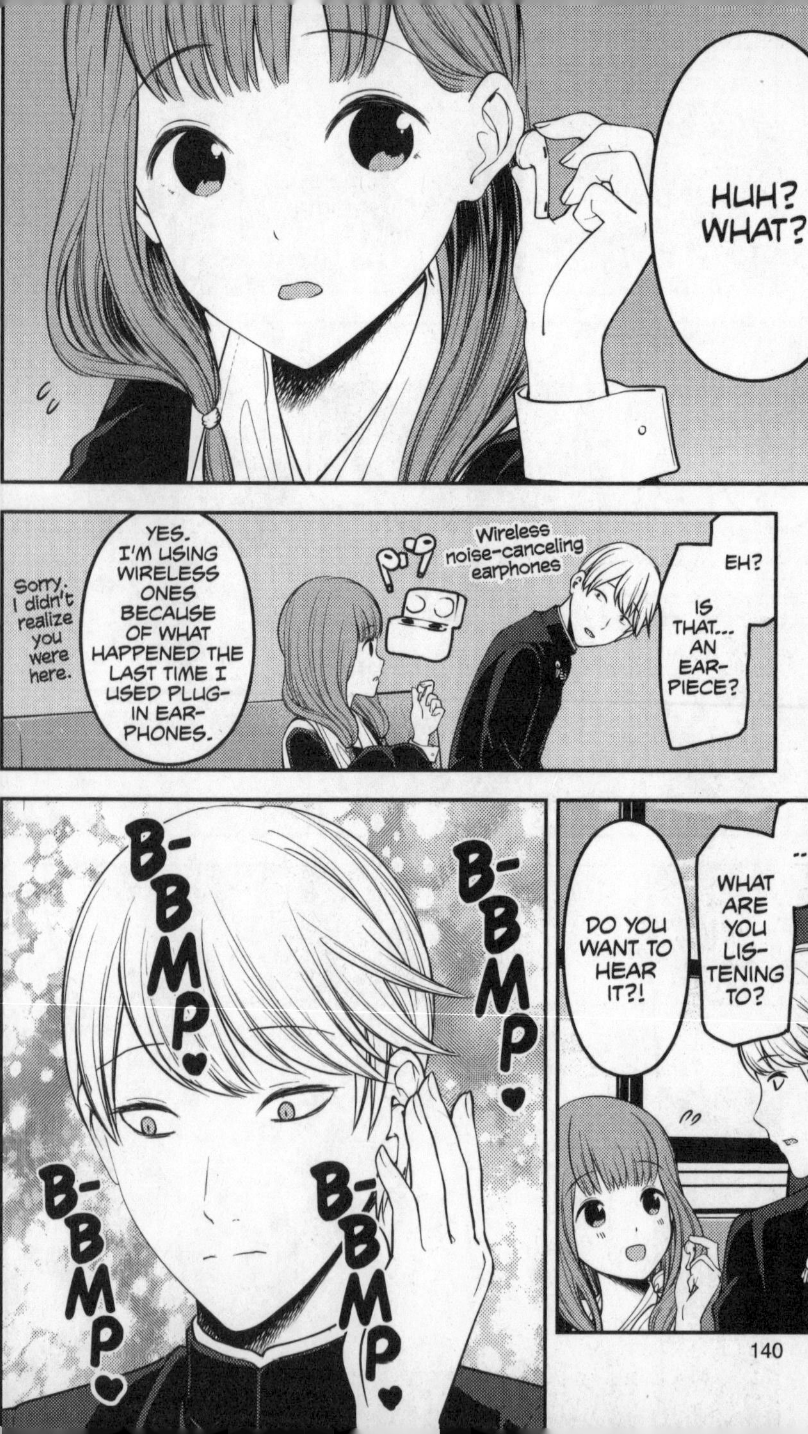
HUH? WHAT?
EH?
IS THAT... AN EARPIECE?
Wireless noise-canceling earphones
YES. I'M USING WIRELESS ONES BECAUSE OF WHAT HAPPENED THE LAST TIME I USED PLUG-IN EARPHONES.
Sorry. I didn't realize you were here.
...
WHAT ARE YOU LISTENING TO?
DO YOU WANT TO HEAR IT?!
B-BBMP.
B-BBMP.
B-BBMP.
B-BBMP.

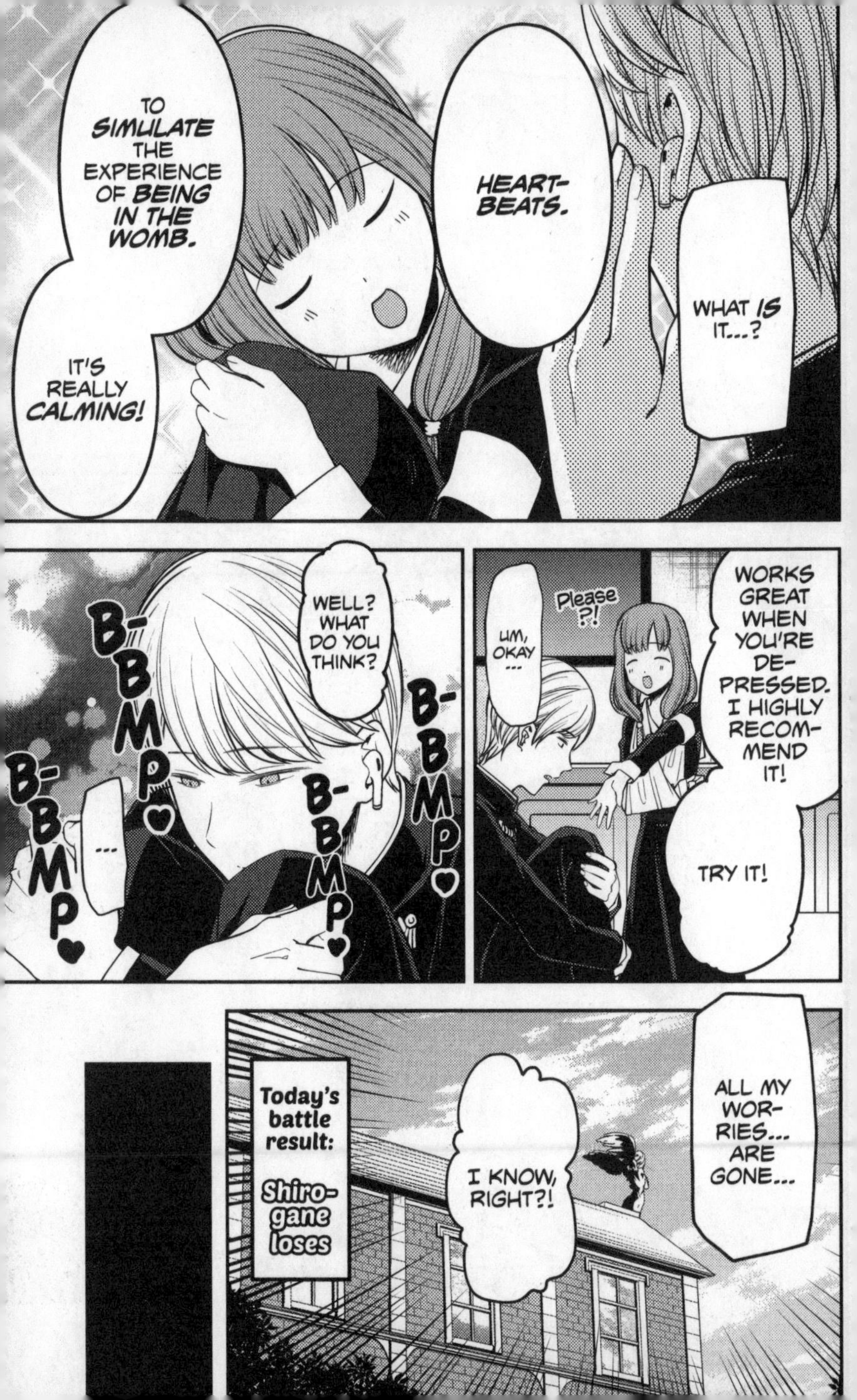
WHAT IS IT...?
HEART-BEATS.
TO SIMULATE THE EXPERIENCE OF BEING IN THE WOMB.
IT'S REALLY CALMING!
WORKS GREAT WHEN YOU'RE DE-PRESSED. I HIGHLY RECOM-MEND IT!
Please?!
UM, OKAY...
TRY IT!
WELL? WHAT DO YOU THINK?
B-BMP♥
B-BMP♥
B-BMP♥
...
B-BMP♥
ALL MY WOR-RIES... ARE GONE...
I KNOW, RIGHT?!
Today's battle result:
Shiro-gane loses

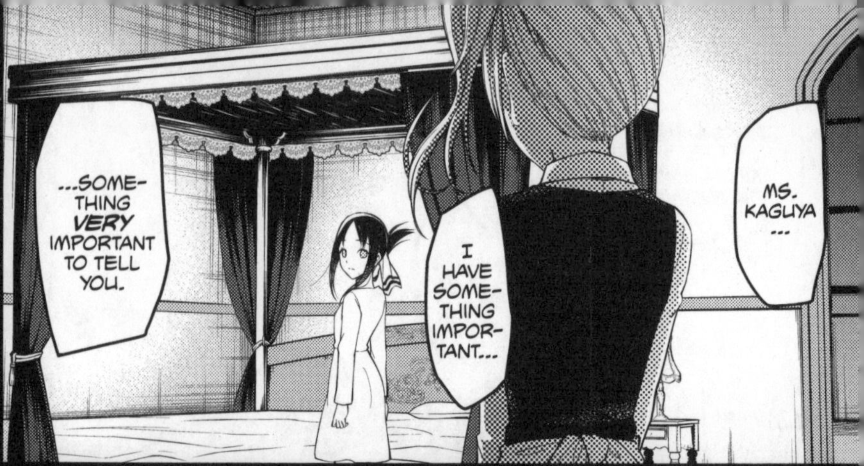
MS. KAGUYA ...
I HAVE SOMETHING IMPORTANT...
...SOMETHING VERY IMPORTANT TO TELL YOU.

THE NEXT STORY ARC IS ABOUT THE SCHOOL TRIP!

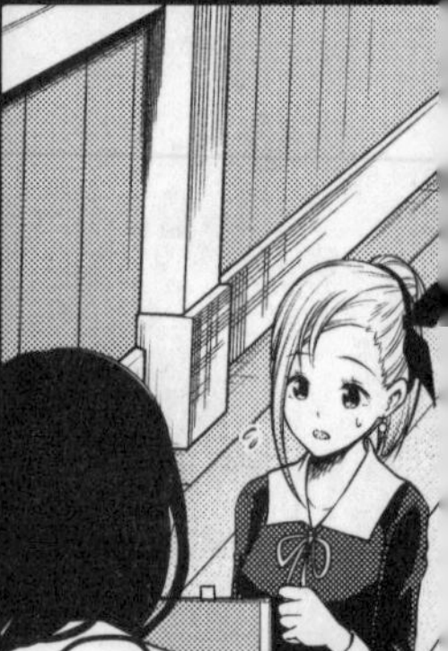
WHAT'S THAT?

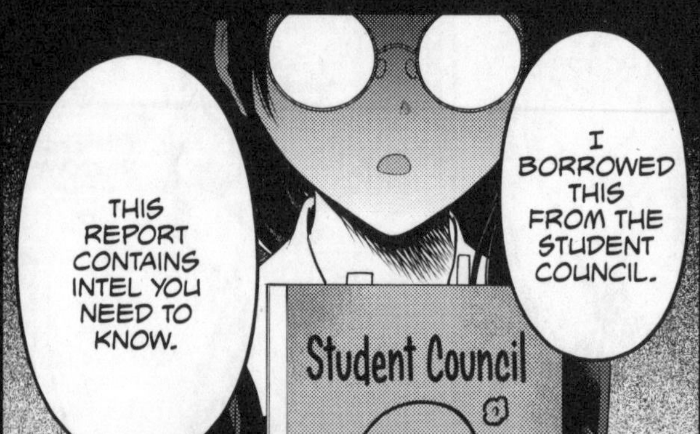
I BORROWED THIS FROM THE STUDENT COUNCIL.
THIS REPORT CONTAINS INTEL YOU NEED TO KNOW.
Student Council Secret Report! ~Complete Edition~

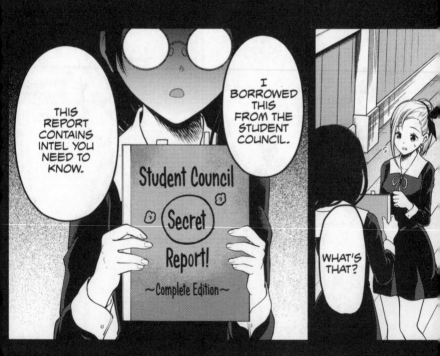

AND THUS...THE SECRET-IS-NO-LONGER-A-SECRET CHAPTER BEGINS!

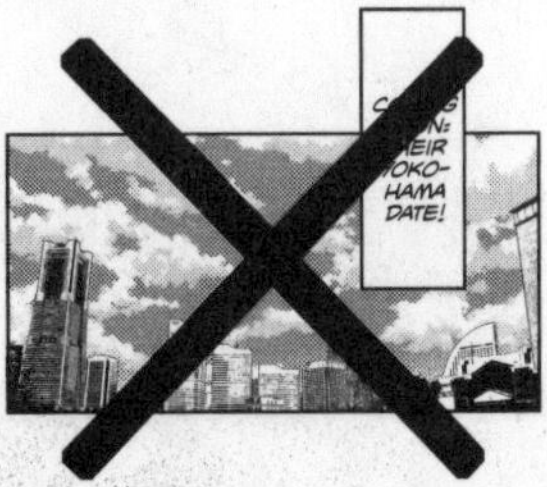
HAMA DATE!
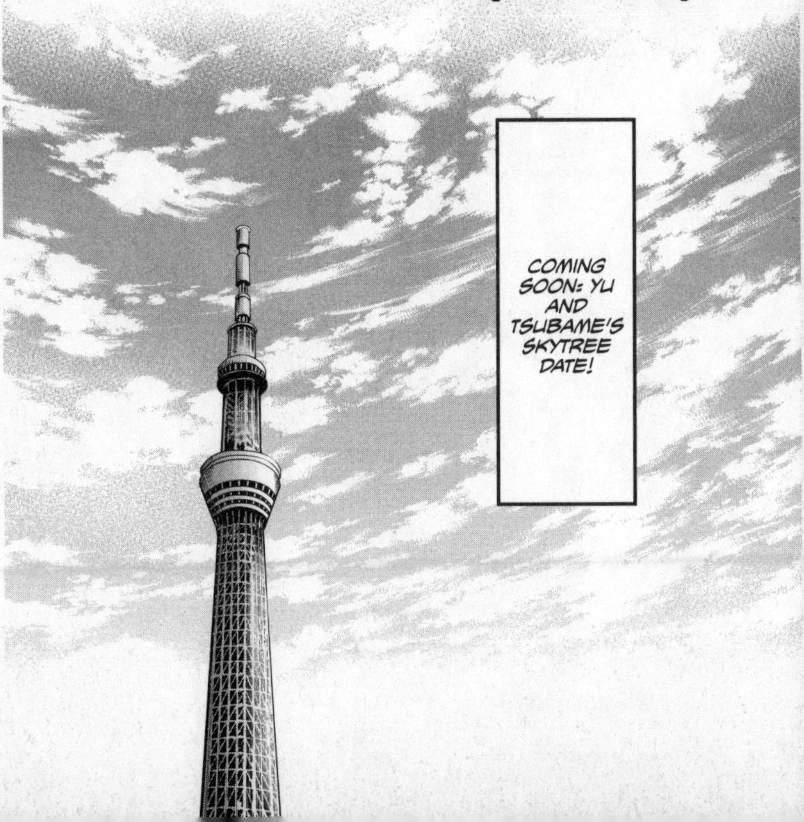
COMING SOON: YU AND TSUBAME'S SKYTREE DATE!

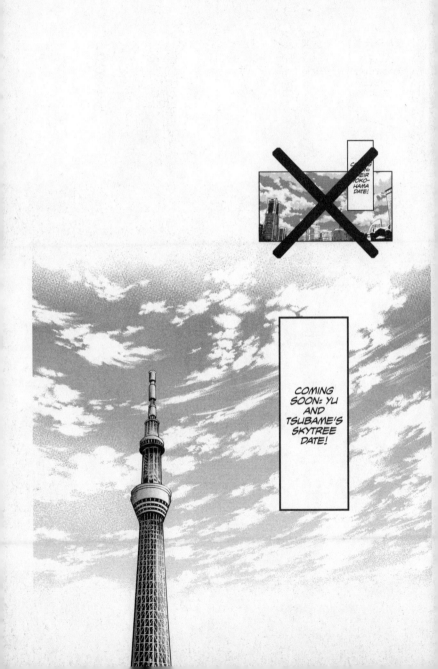

KAGUYA-SAMA
LOVE IS WAR

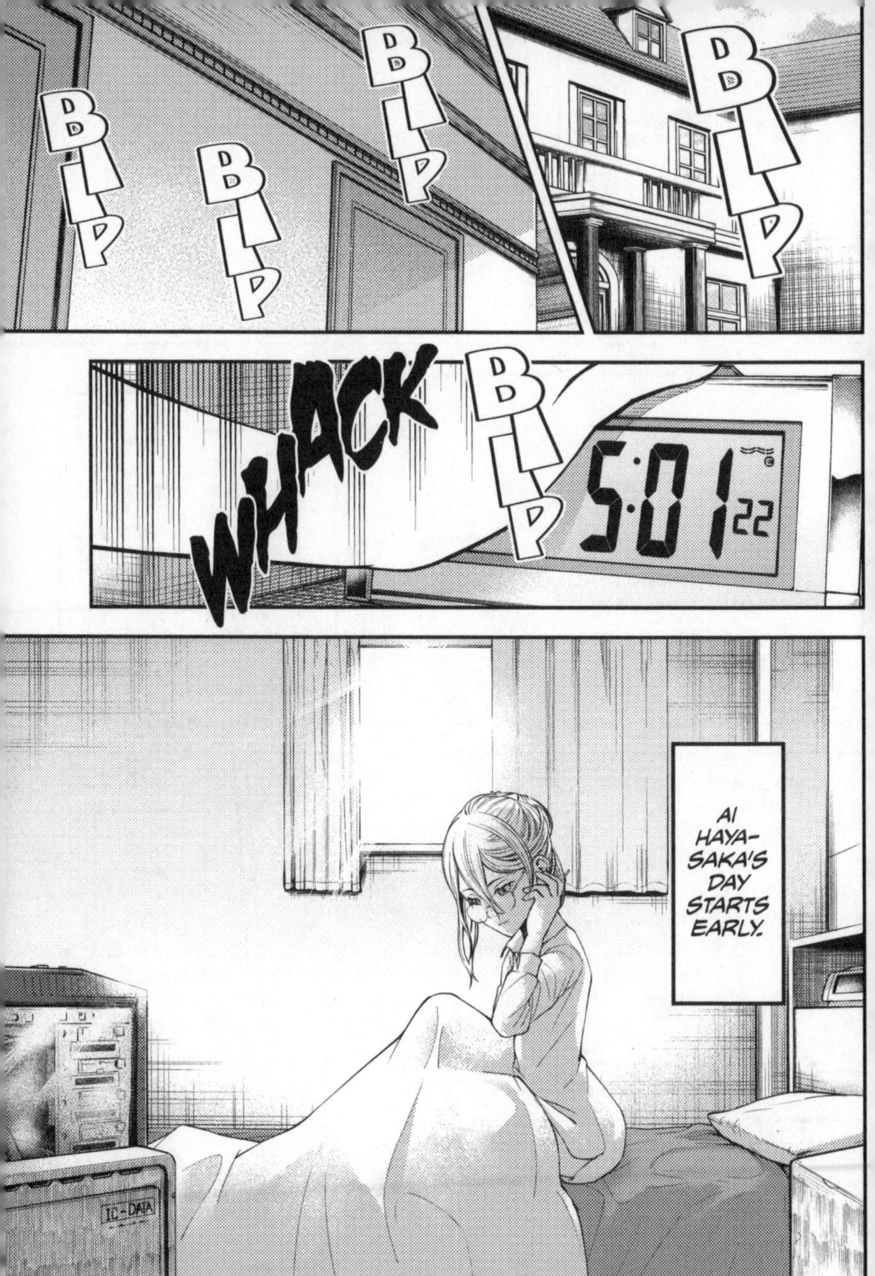
BLIP
BLIP
BLIP
BLIP
BLIP
WHACK
5:01 22
AI HAYASAKA'S DAY STARTS EARLY.

Battle 179 Ai Hayasaka's Morning Routine

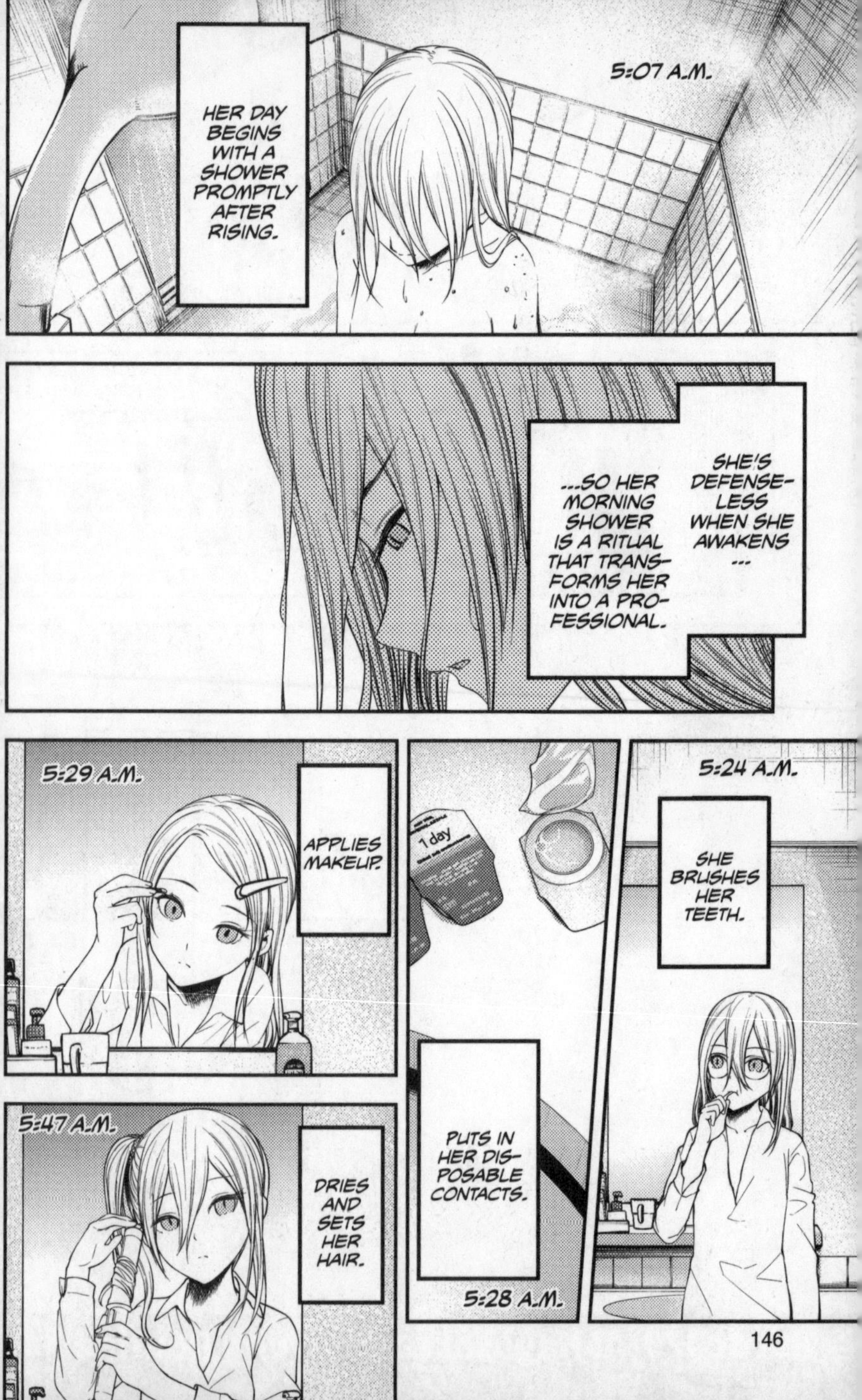
5:07 A.M.
HER DAY BEGINS WITH A SHOWER PROMPTLY AFTER RISING.
SHE'S DEFENSE-LESS WHEN SHE AWAKENS...
...SO HER MORNING SHOWER IS A RITUAL THAT TRANS-FORMS HER INTO A PRO-FESSIONAL.
5:24 A.M.
SHE BRUSHES HER TEETH.
1 day
PUTS IN HER DIS-POSABLE CONTACTS.
5:28 A.M.
5:29 A.M.
APPLIES MAKEUP.
5:47 A.M.
DRIES AND SETS HER HAIR.

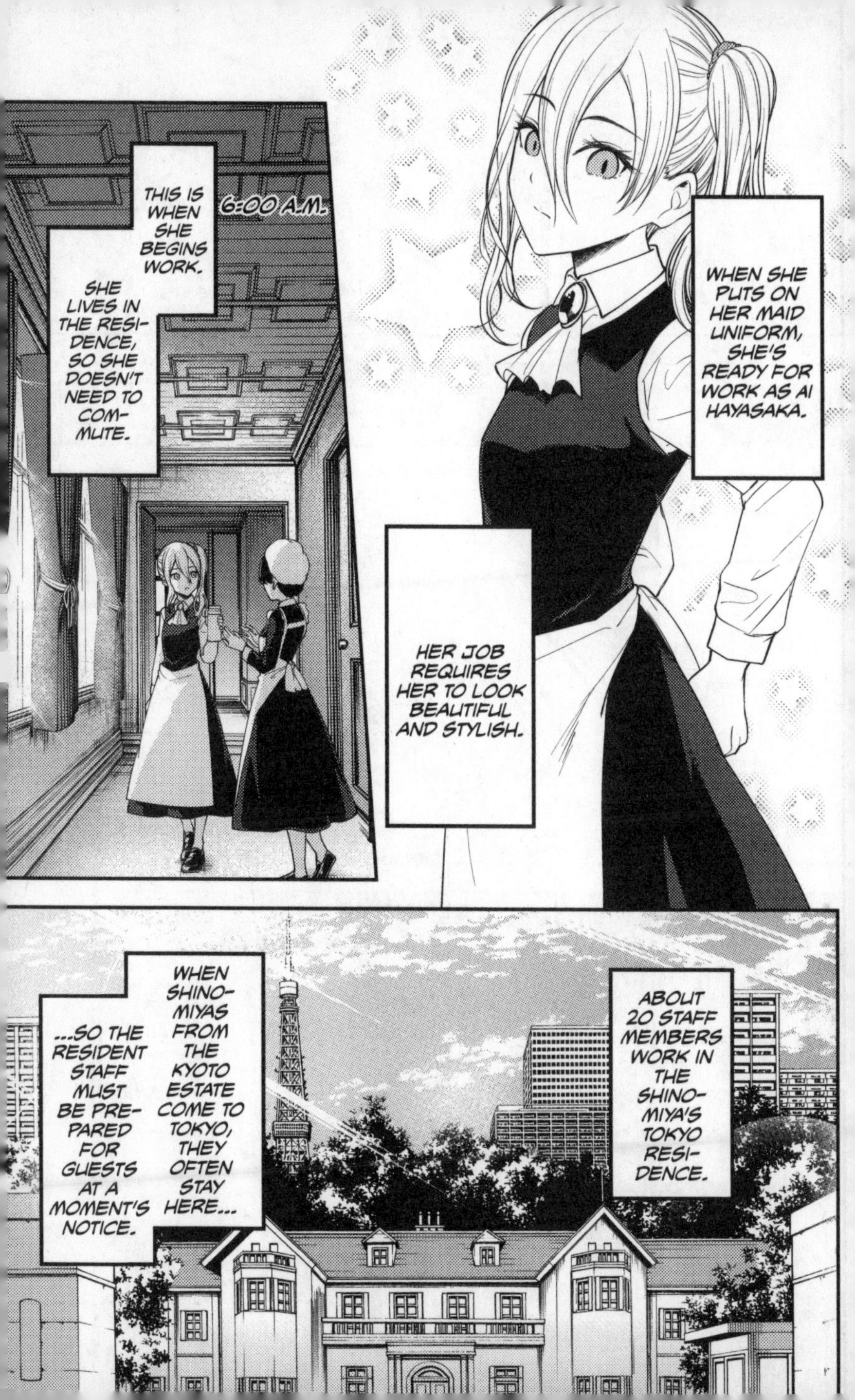
WHEN SHE PUTS ON HER MAID UNIFORM, SHE'S READY FOR WORK AS AI HAYASAKA.
HER JOB REQUIRES HER TO LOOK BEAUTIFUL AND STYLISH.
6:00 A.M.
THIS IS WHEN SHE BEGINS WORK.
SHE LIVES IN THE RESI-DENCE, SO SHE DOESN'T NEED TO COM-MUTE.
ABOUT 20 STAFF MEMBERS WORK IN THE SHINO-MIYA'S TOKYO RESI-DENCE.
WHEN SHINO-MIYAS FROM THE KYOTO ESTATE COME TO TOKYO, THEY OFTEN STAY HERE...
...SO THE RESIDENT STAFF MUST BE PRE-PARED FOR GUESTS AT A MOMENT'S NOTICE.

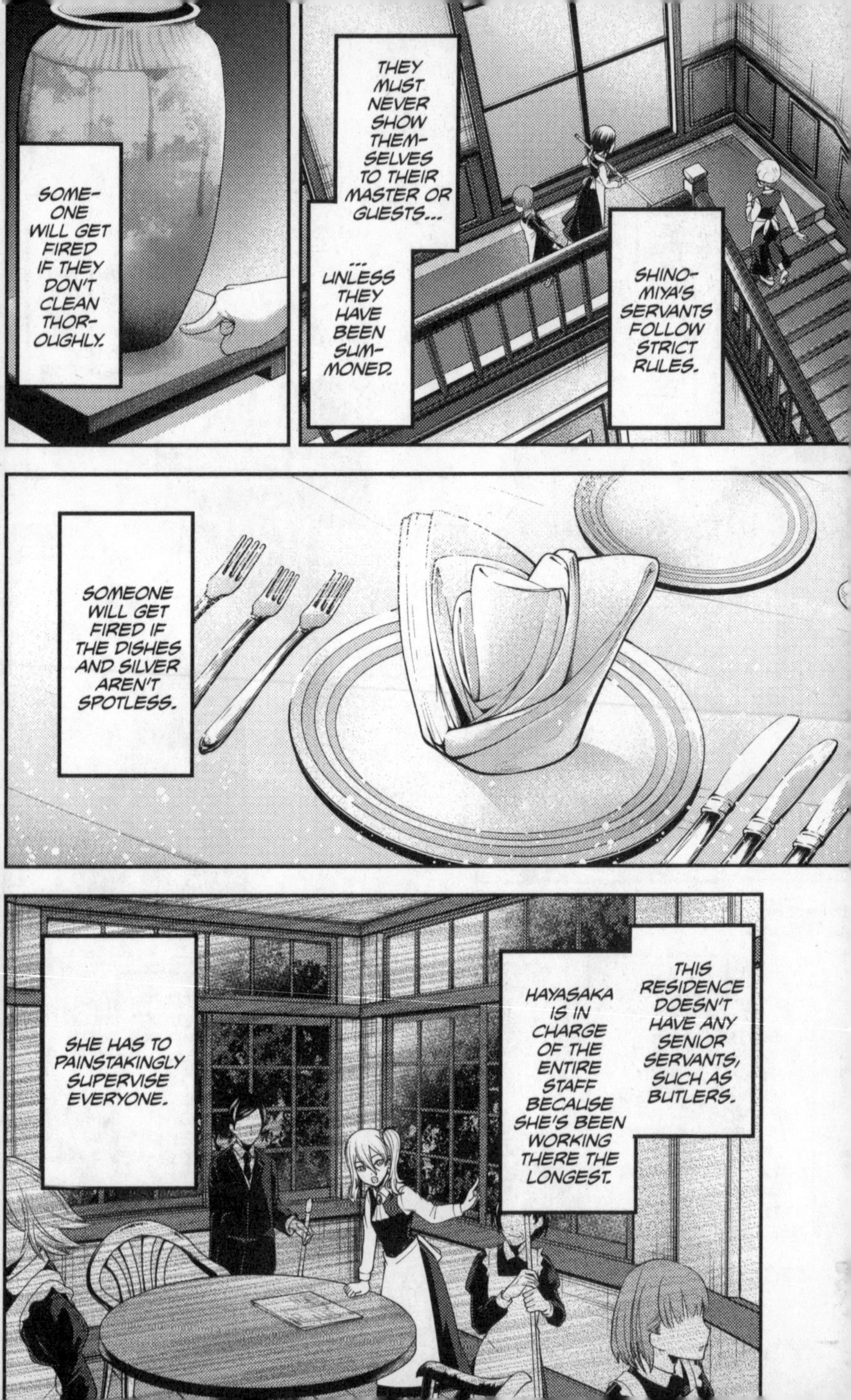
SHINO-MIYA'S SERVANTS FOLLOW STRICT RULES.
THEY MUST NEVER SHOW THEM-SELVES TO THEIR MASTER OR GUESTS...
...UNLESS THEY HAVE BEEN SUM-MONED.
SOME-ONE WILL GET FIRED IF THEY DON'T CLEAN THOR-OUGHLY.
SOMEONE WILL GET FIRED IF THE DISHES AND SILVER AREN'T SPOTLESS.
THIS RESIDENCE DOESN'T HAVE ANY SENIOR SERVANTS, SUCH AS BUTLERS.
HAYASAKA IS IN CHARGE OF THE ENTIRE STAFF BECAUSE SHE'S BEEN WORKING THERE THE LONGEST.
SHE HAS TO PAINSTAKINGLY SUPERVISE EVERYONE.

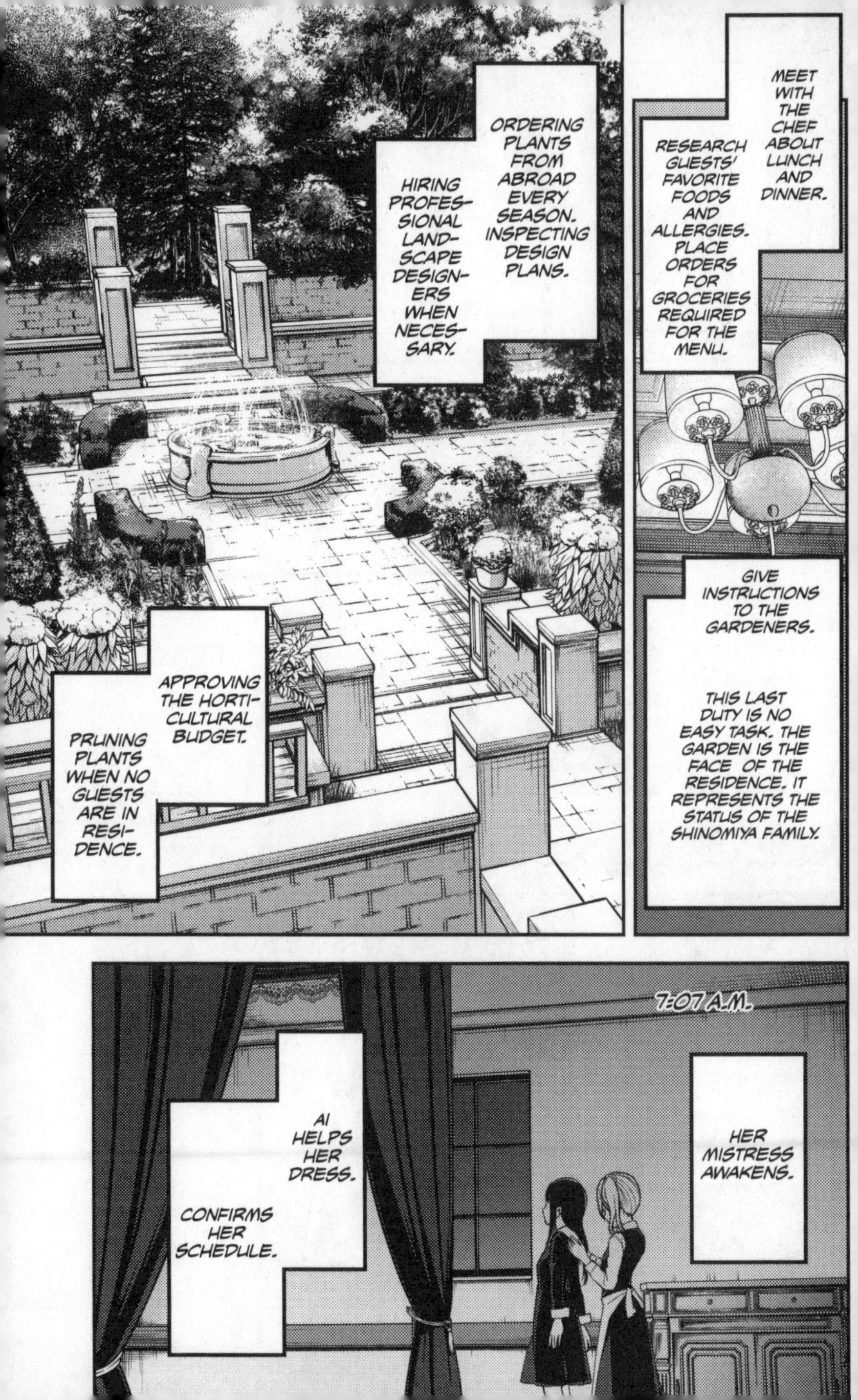
MEET WITH THE CHEF ABOUT LUNCH AND DINNER.
RESEARCH GUESTS' FAVORITE FOODS AND ALLERGIES. PLACE ORDERS FOR GROCERIES REQUIRED FOR THE MENU.
GIVE INSTRUCTIONS TO THE GARDENERS.
THIS LAST DUTY IS NO EASY TASK. THE GARDEN IS THE FACE OF THE RESIDENCE. IT REPRESENTS THE STATUS OF THE SHINOMIYA FAMILY.
ORDERING PLANTS FROM ABROAD EVERY SEASON. INSPECTING DESIGN PLANS.
HIRING PROFES-SIONAL LAND-SCAPE DESIGNER-ERS WHEN NECES-SARY.
APPROVING THE HORTI-CULTURAL BUDGET.
PRUNING PLANTS WHEN NO GUESTS ARE IN RESI-DENCE.
7:07 A.M.
HER MISTRESS AWAKENS.
AI HELPS HER DRESS.
CONFIRMS HER SCHEDULE.

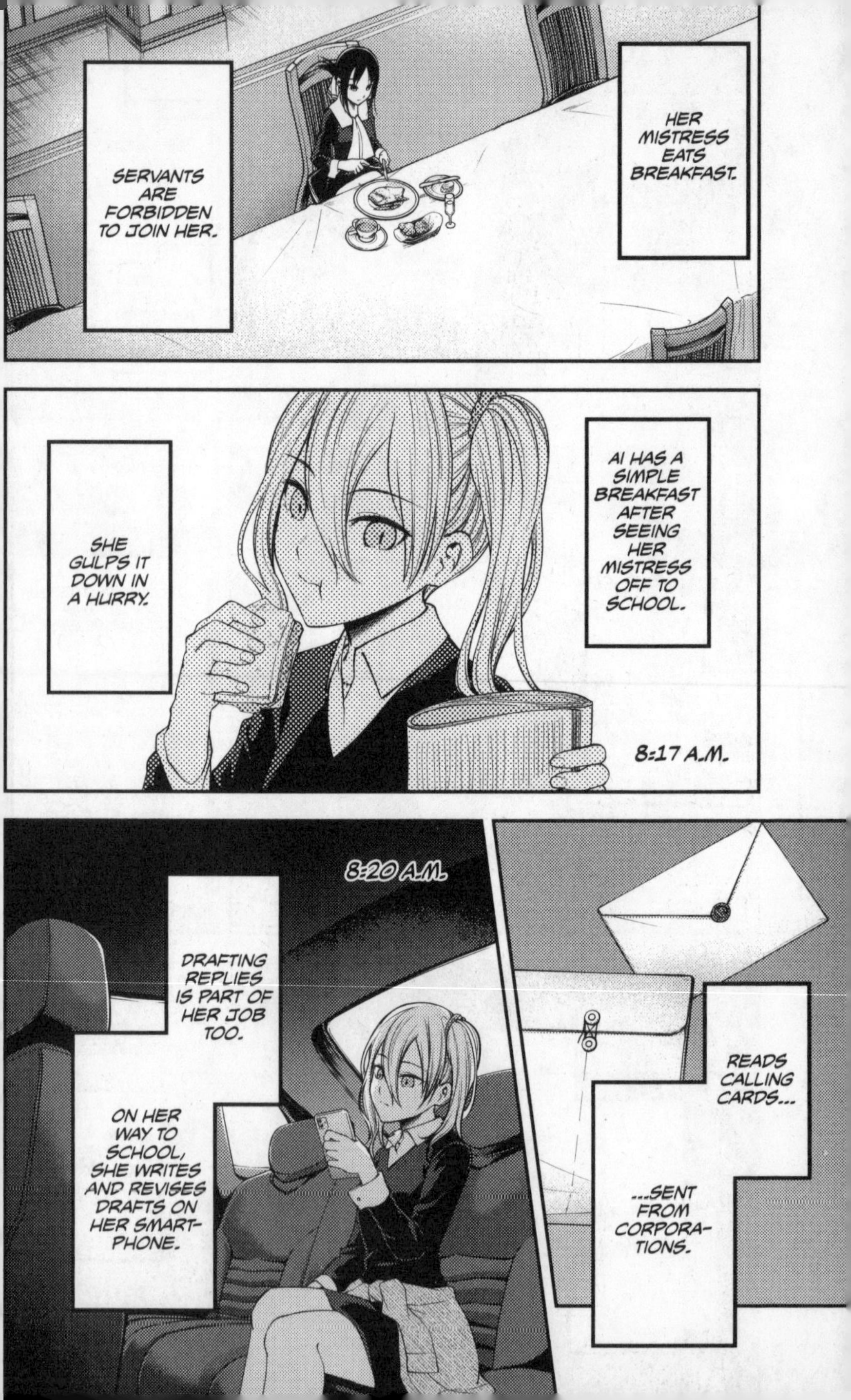
HER MISTRESS EATS BREAKFAST.
SERVANTS ARE FORBIDDEN TO JOIN HER.
AI HAS A SIMPLE BREAKFAST AFTER SEEING HER MISTRESS OFF TO SCHOOL.
SHE GULPS IT DOWN IN A HURRY.
8:17 A.M.
READS CALLING CARDS...
...SENT FROM CORPORATIONS.
8:20 A.M.
DRAFTING REPLIES IS PART OF HER JOB TOO.
ON HER WAY TO SCHOOL, SHE WRITES AND REVISES DRAFTS ON HER SMARTPHONE.

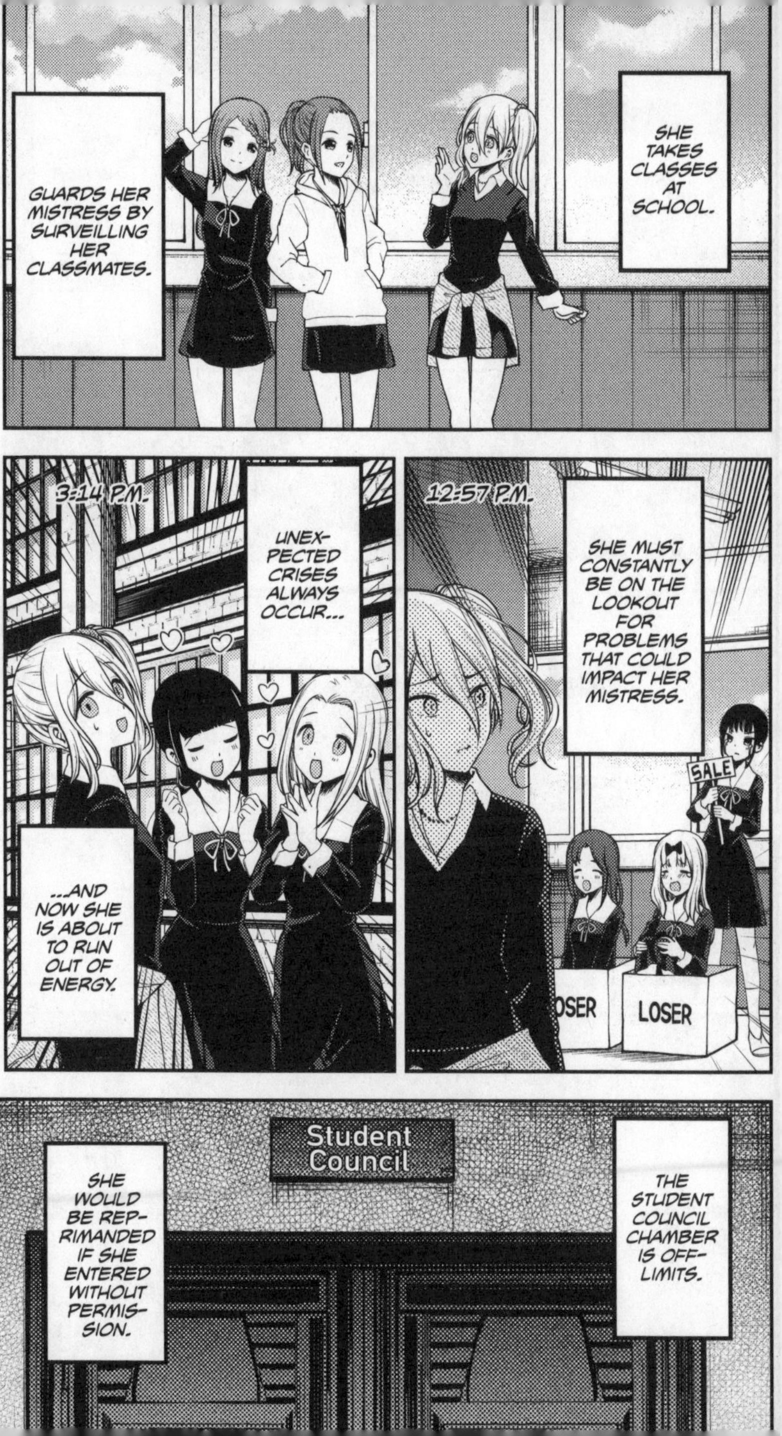
SHE TAKES CLASSES AT SCHOOL.
GUARDS HER MISTRESS BY SURVEILLING HER CLASSMATES.
12:57 P.M.
SHE MUST CONSTANTLY BE ON THE LOOKOUT FOR PROBLEMS THAT COULD IMPACT HER MISTRESS.
SALE
LOSER
3:14 P.M.
UNEXPECTED CRISES ALWAYS OCCUR...
...AND NOW SHE IS ABOUT TO RUN OUT OF ENERGY.
THE STUDENT COUNCIL CHAMBER IS OFF-LIMITS.
Student Council
SHE WOULD BE REPRIMANDED IF SHE ENTERED WITHOUT PERMISSION.

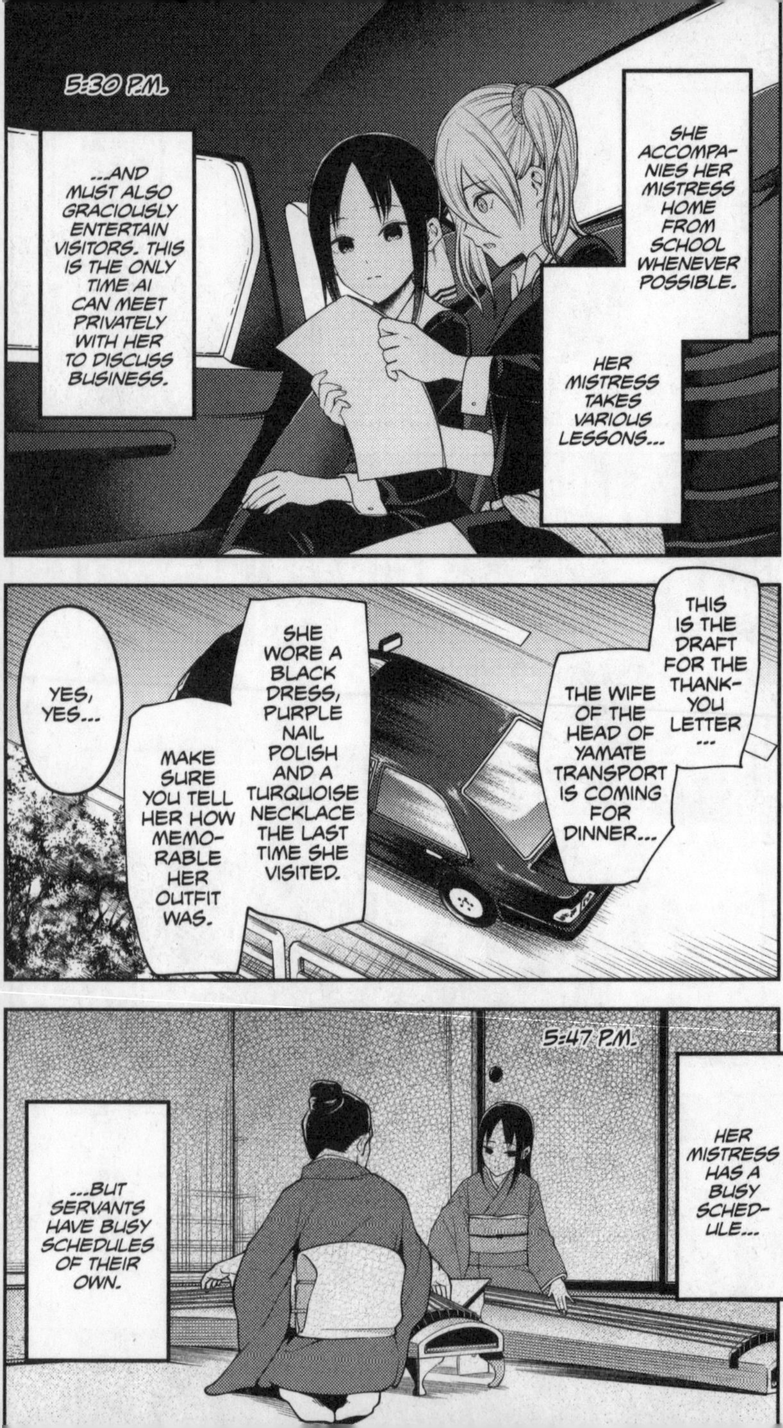
5:30 P.M.
SHE ACCOMPANIES HER MISTRESS HOME FROM SCHOOL WHENEVER POSSIBLE.
HER MISTRESS TAKES VARIOUS LESSONS...
...AND MUST ALSO GRACIOUSLY ENTERTAIN VISITORS. THIS IS THE ONLY TIME AI CAN MEET PRIVATELY WITH HER TO DISCUSS BUSINESS.
THIS IS THE DRAFT FOR THE THANK-YOU LETTER...
THE WIFE OF THE HEAD OF YAMATE TRANSPORT IS COMING FOR DINNER...
SHE WORE A BLACK DRESS, PURPLE NAIL POLISH AND A TURQUOISE NECKLACE THE LAST TIME SHE VISITED.
MAKE SURE YOU TELL HER HOW MEMORABLE HER OUTFIT WAS.
YES, YES...
5:47 P.M.
HER MISTRESS HAS A BUSY SCHEDULE...
...BUT SERVANTS HAVE BUSY SCHEDULES OF THEIR OWN.

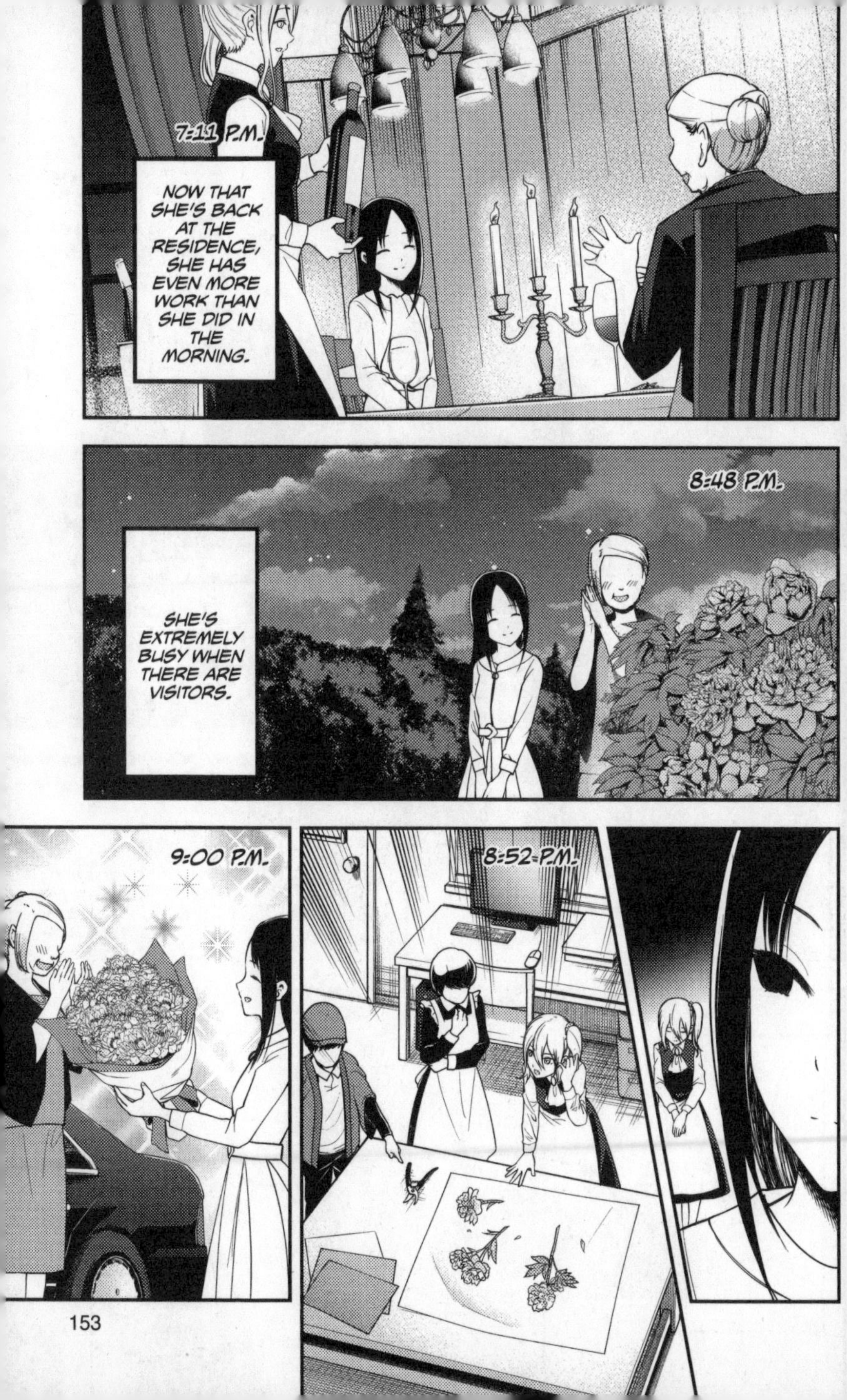
7:11 P.M.
NOW THAT SHE'S BACK AT THE RESIDENCE, SHE HAS EVEN MORE WORK THAN SHE DID IN THE MORNING.
8:48 P.M.
SHE'S EXTREMELY BUSY WHEN THERE ARE VISITORS.
8:52 P.M.
9:00 P.M.

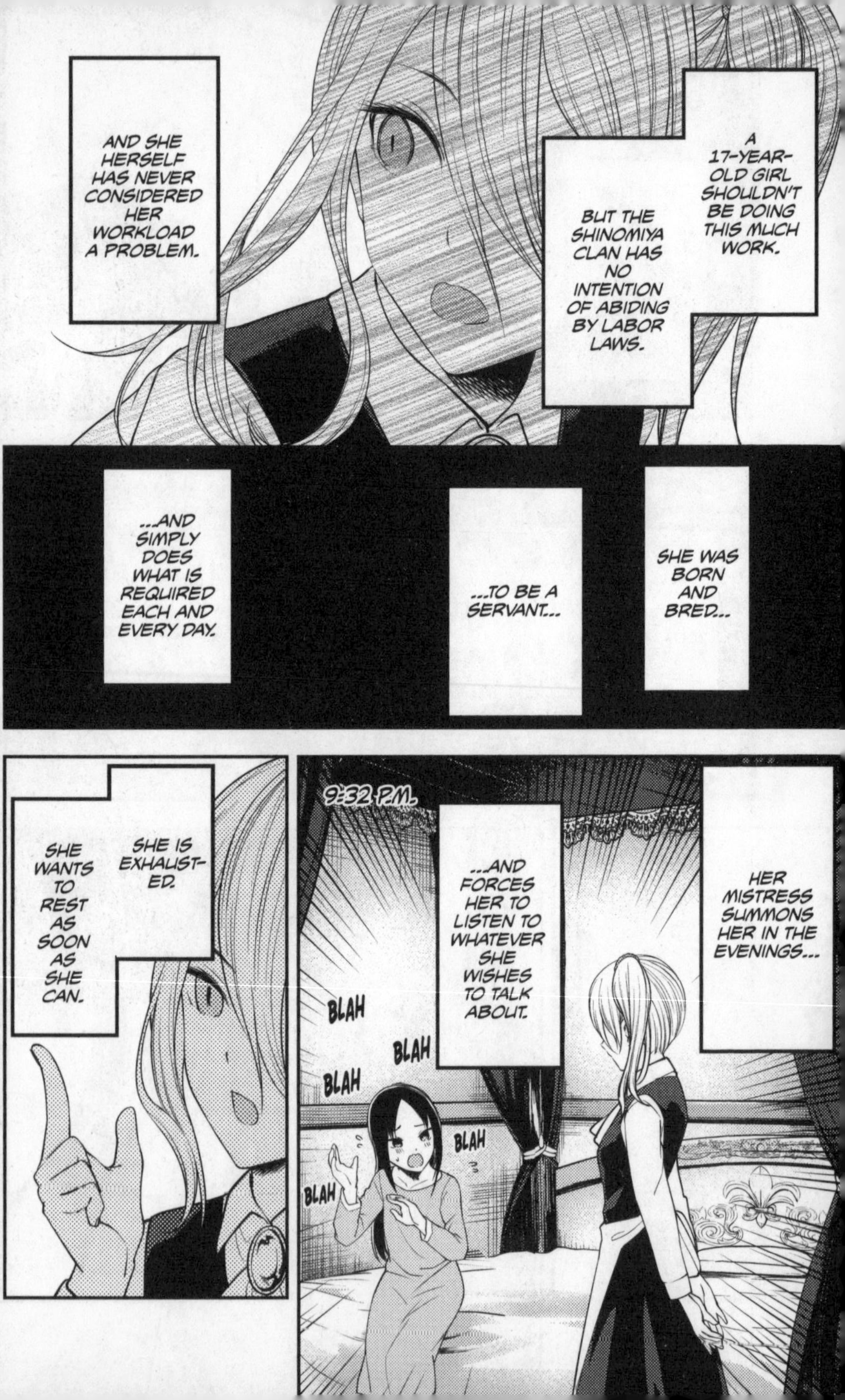
A 17-YEAR-OLD GIRL SHOULDN'T BE DOING THIS MUCH WORK.
BUT THE SHINOMIYA CLAN HAS NO INTENTION OF ABIDING BY LABOR LAWS.
AND SHE HERSELF HAS NEVER CONSIDERED HER WORKLOAD A PROBLEM.
SHE WAS BORN AND BRED...
...TO BE A SERVANT...
...AND SIMPLY DOES WHAT IS REQUIRED EACH AND EVERY DAY.
9:32 P.M.
HER MISTRESS SUMMONS HER IN THE EVENINGS...
...AND FORCES HER TO LISTEN TO WHATEVER SHE WISHES TO TALK ABOUT.
BLAH
BLAH
BLAH
BLAH
BLAH
SHE IS EXHAUST-ED.
SHE WANTS TO REST AS SOON AS SHE CAN.

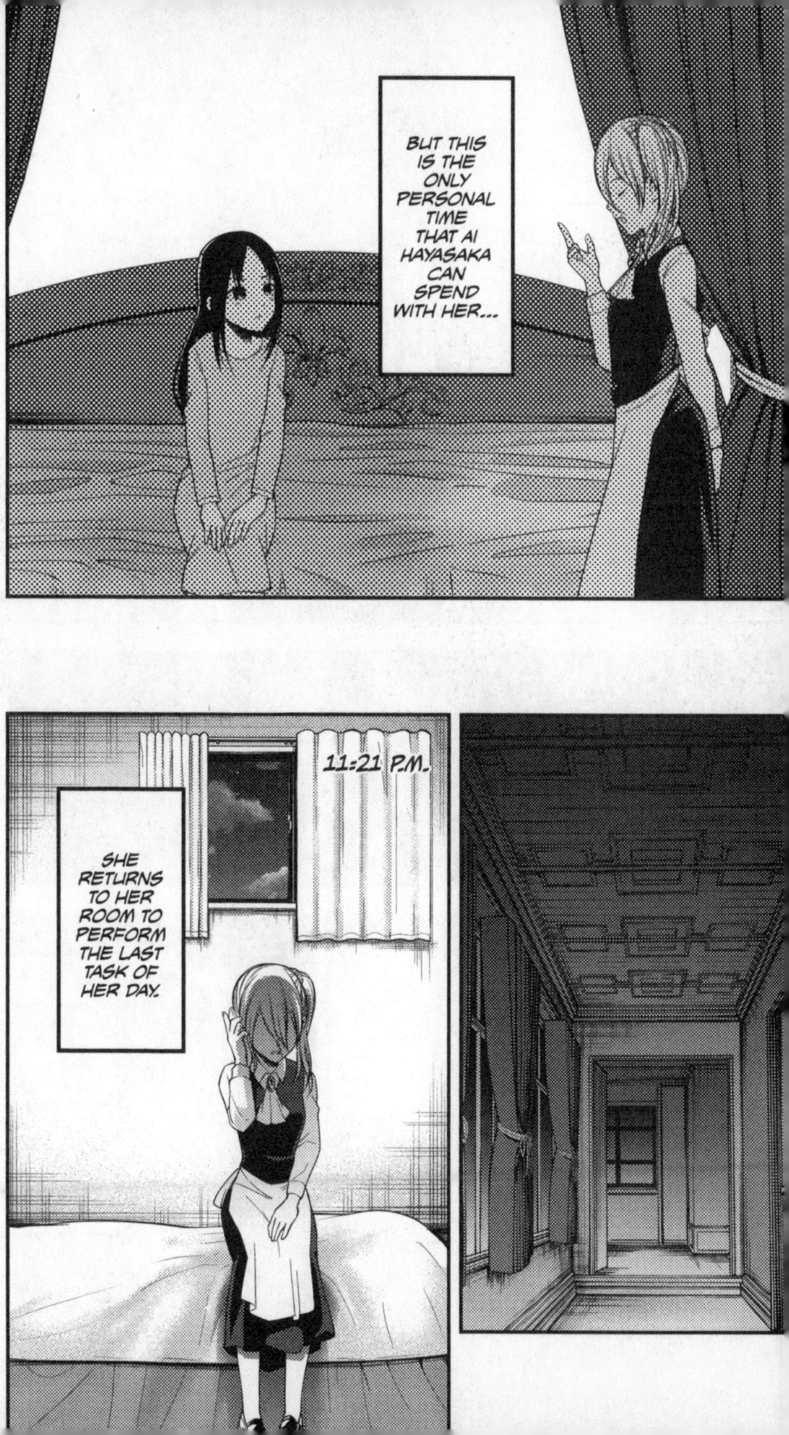
BUT THIS IS THE ONLY PERSONAL TIME THAT AI HAYASAKA CAN SPEND WITH HER...
11:21 P.M.
SHE RETURNS TO HER ROOM TO PERFORM THE LAST TASK OF HER DAY.

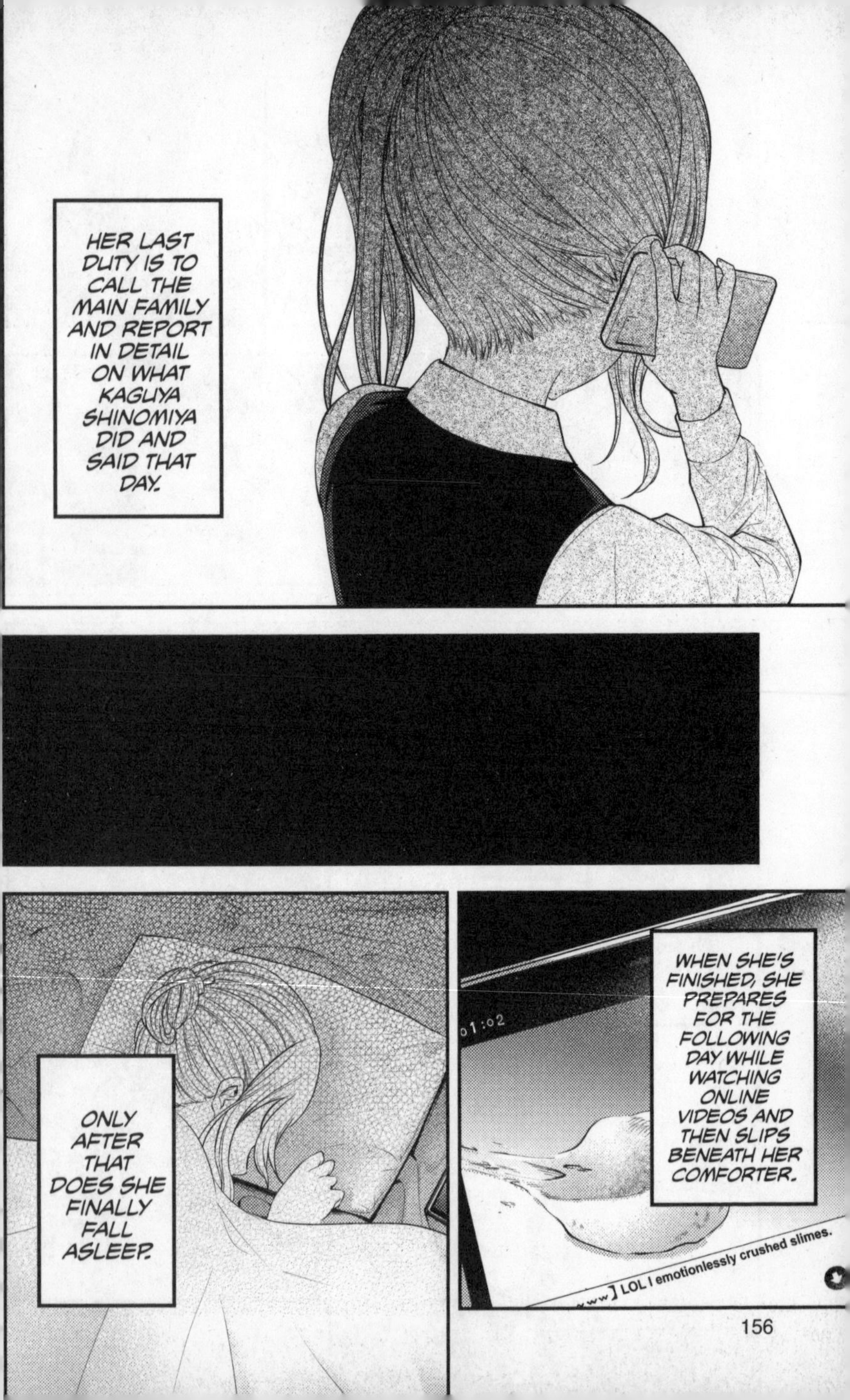
HER LAST DUTY IS TO CALL THE MAIN FAMILY AND REPORT IN DETAIL ON WHAT KAGUYA SHINOMIYA DID AND SAID THAT DAY.
WHEN SHE'S FINISHED, SHE PREPARES FOR THE FOLLOWING DAY WHILE WATCHING ONLINE VIDEOS AND THEN SLIPS BENEATH HER COMFORTER.
01:02
www] LOL I emotionlessly crushed slimes.
ONLY AFTER THAT DOES SHE FINALLY FALL ASLEEP.

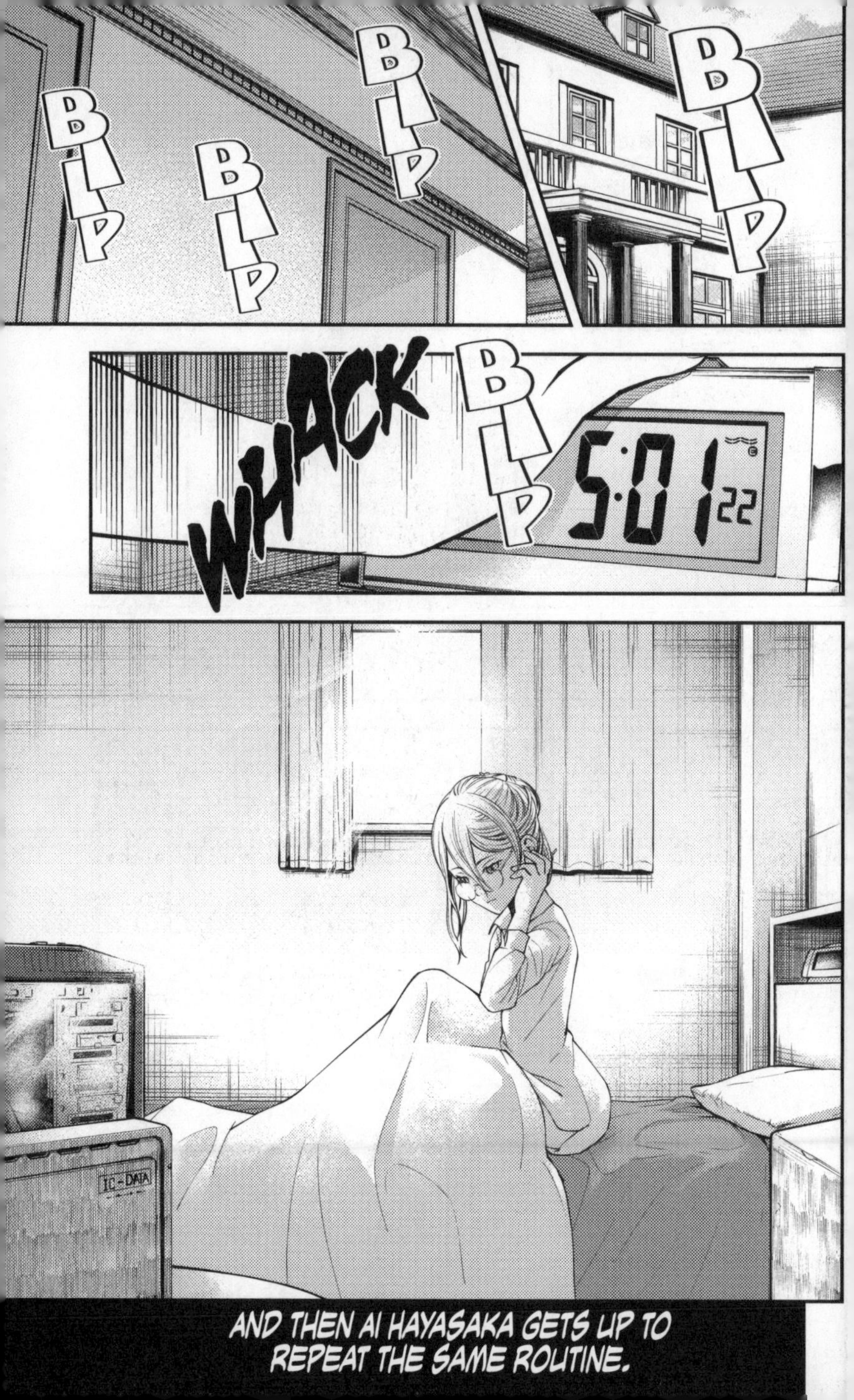
BIP
BIP
BIP
BIP
BIP
WHACK
5:01 22
AND THEN AI HAYASAKA GETS UP TO REPEAT THE SAME ROUTINE.

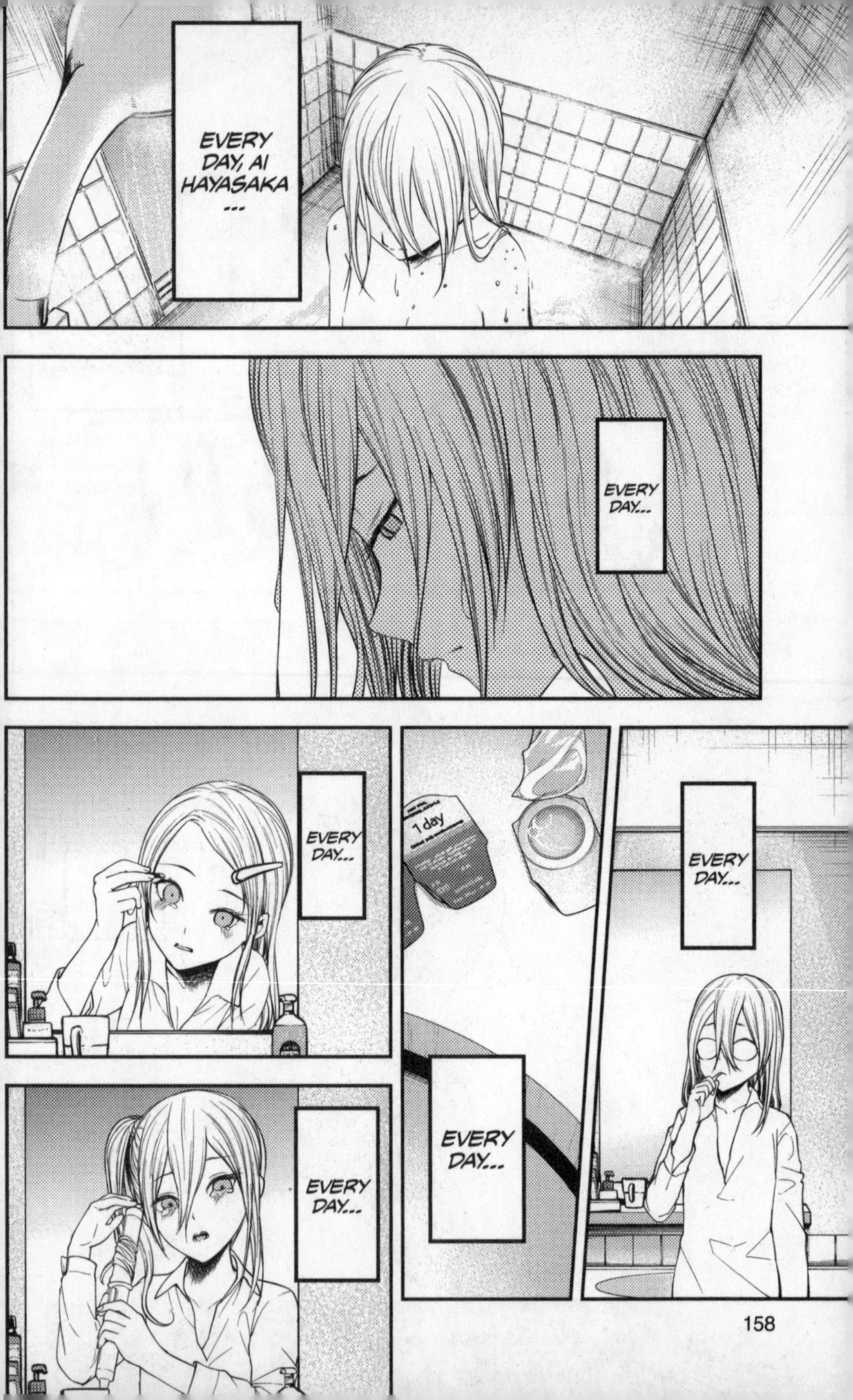
EVERY DAY, AI HAYASAKA ...
EVERY DAY...
EVERY DAY...
1 day
EVERY DAY...
EVERY DAY...
EVERY DAY...

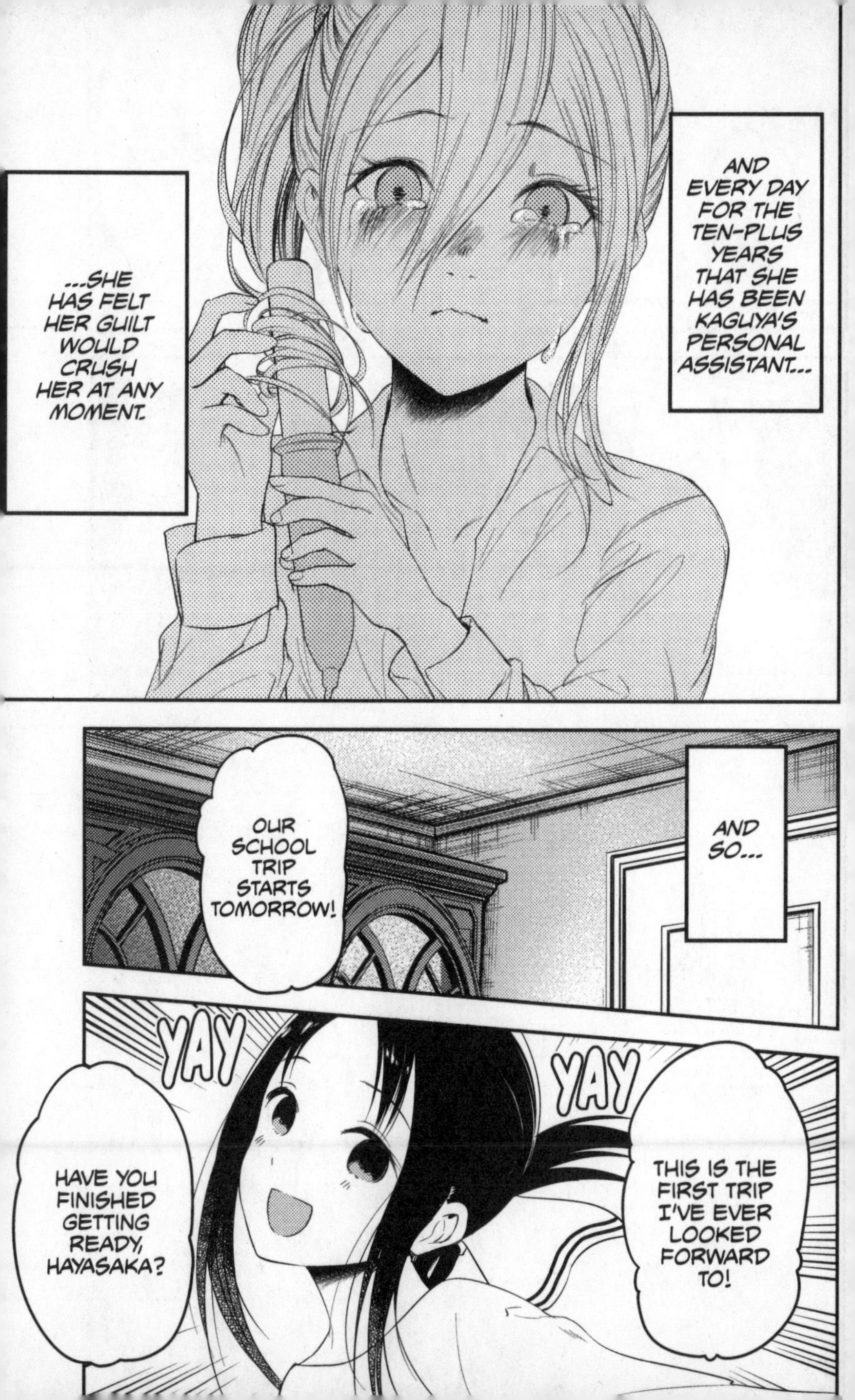
AND EVERY DAY FOR THE TEN-PLUS YEARS THAT SHE HAS BEEN KAGUYA'S PERSONAL ASSISTANT...
...SHE HAS FELT HER GUILT WOULD CRUSH HER AT ANY MOMENT.
AND SO...
OUR SCHOOL TRIP STARTS TOMORROW!
YAY
YAY
THIS IS THE FIRST TRIP I'VE EVER LOOKED FORWARD TO!
HAVE YOU FINISHED GETTING READY, HAYASAKA?

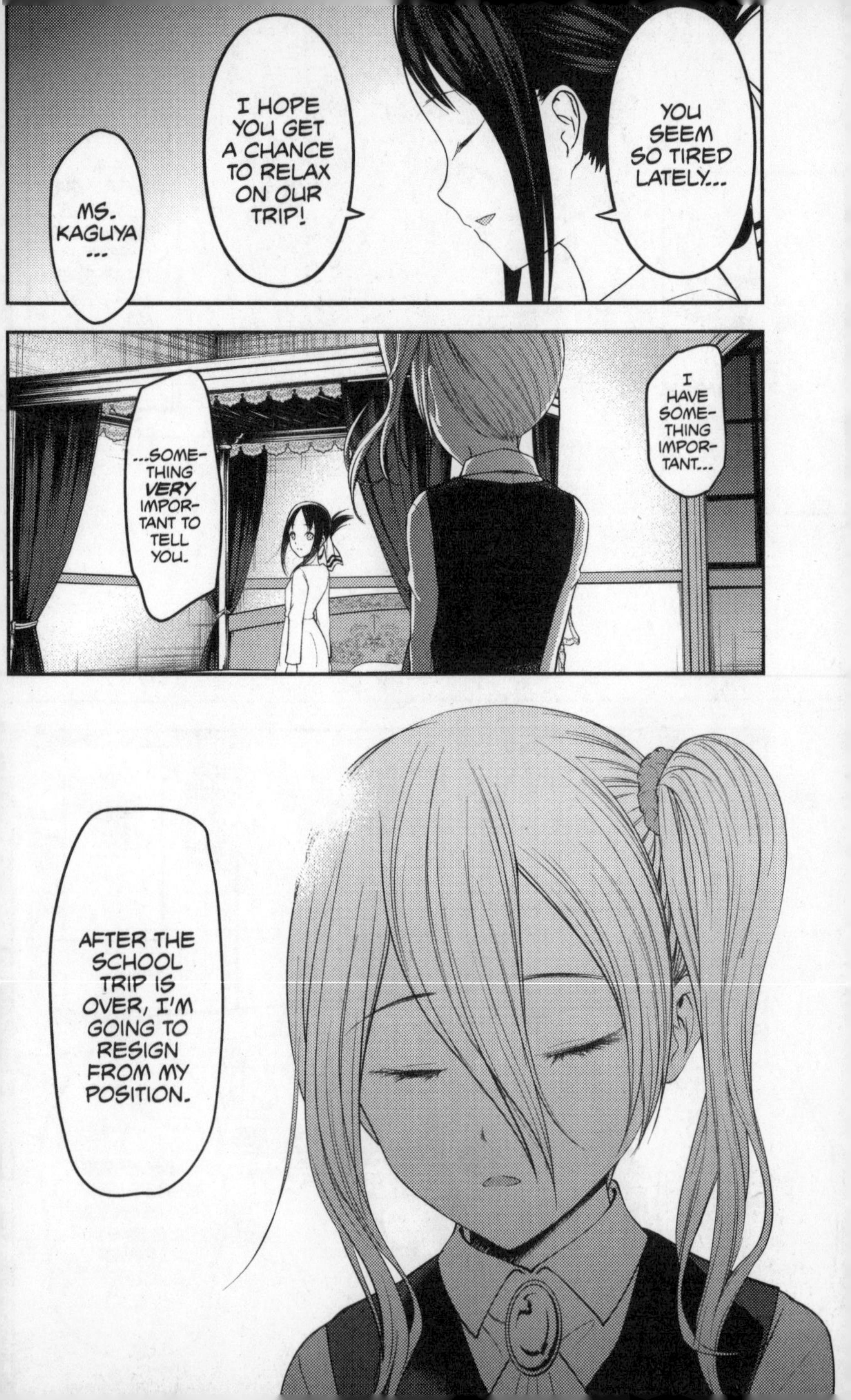
YOU SEEM SO TIRED LATELY...
I HOPE YOU GET A CHANCE TO RELAX ON OUR TRIP!
MS. KAGUYA...
I HAVE SOMETHING IMPORTANT...
...SOMETHING *VERY* IMPORTANT TO TELL YOU.
AFTER THE SCHOOL TRIP IS OVER, I'M GOING TO RESIGN FROM MY POSITION.

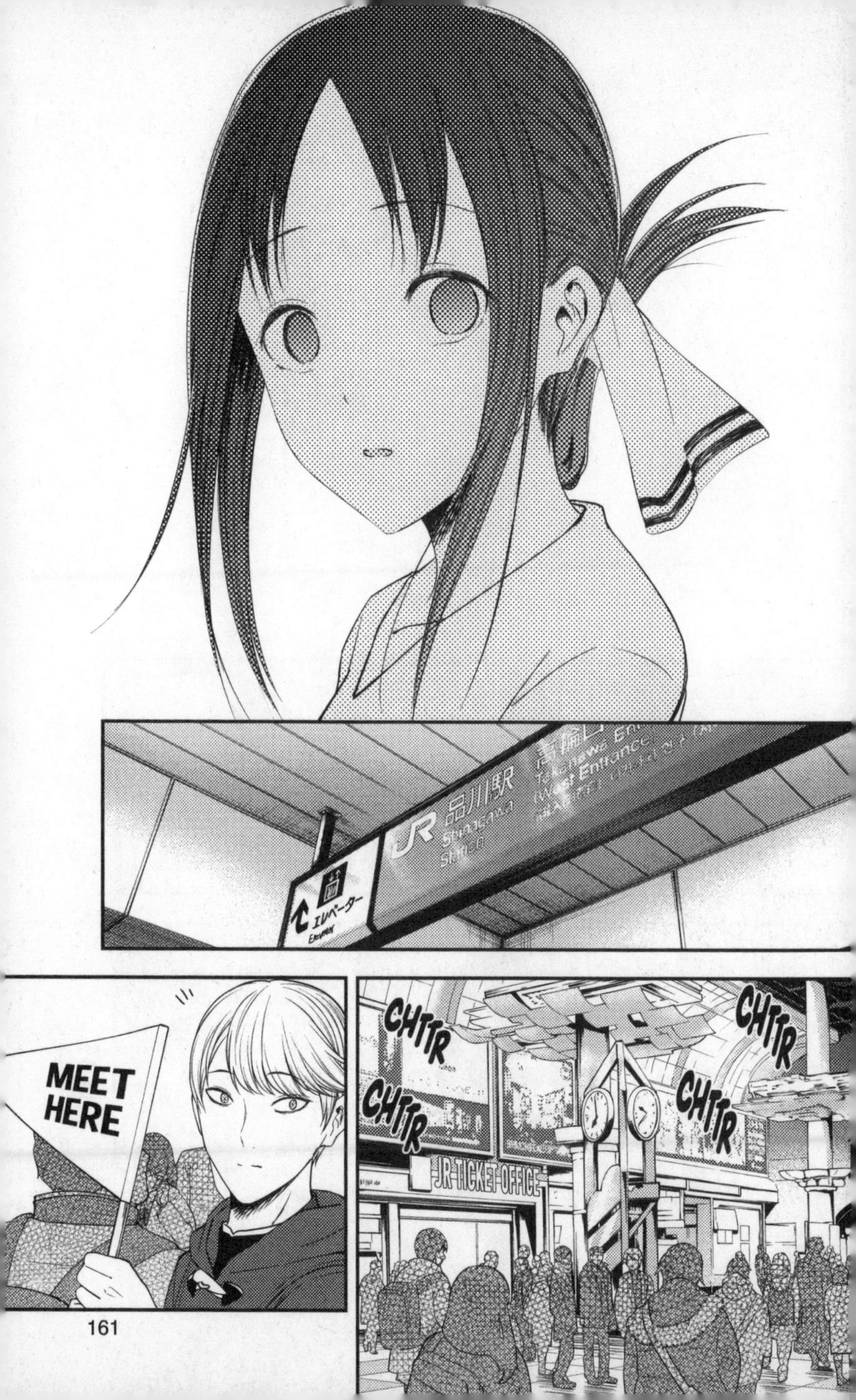
JR
品川駅
Shinagawa Station
(West Entrance)
エレベーター
CHTTR
CHTTR
CHTTR
CHTTR
JR TICKET OFFICE
MEET HERE

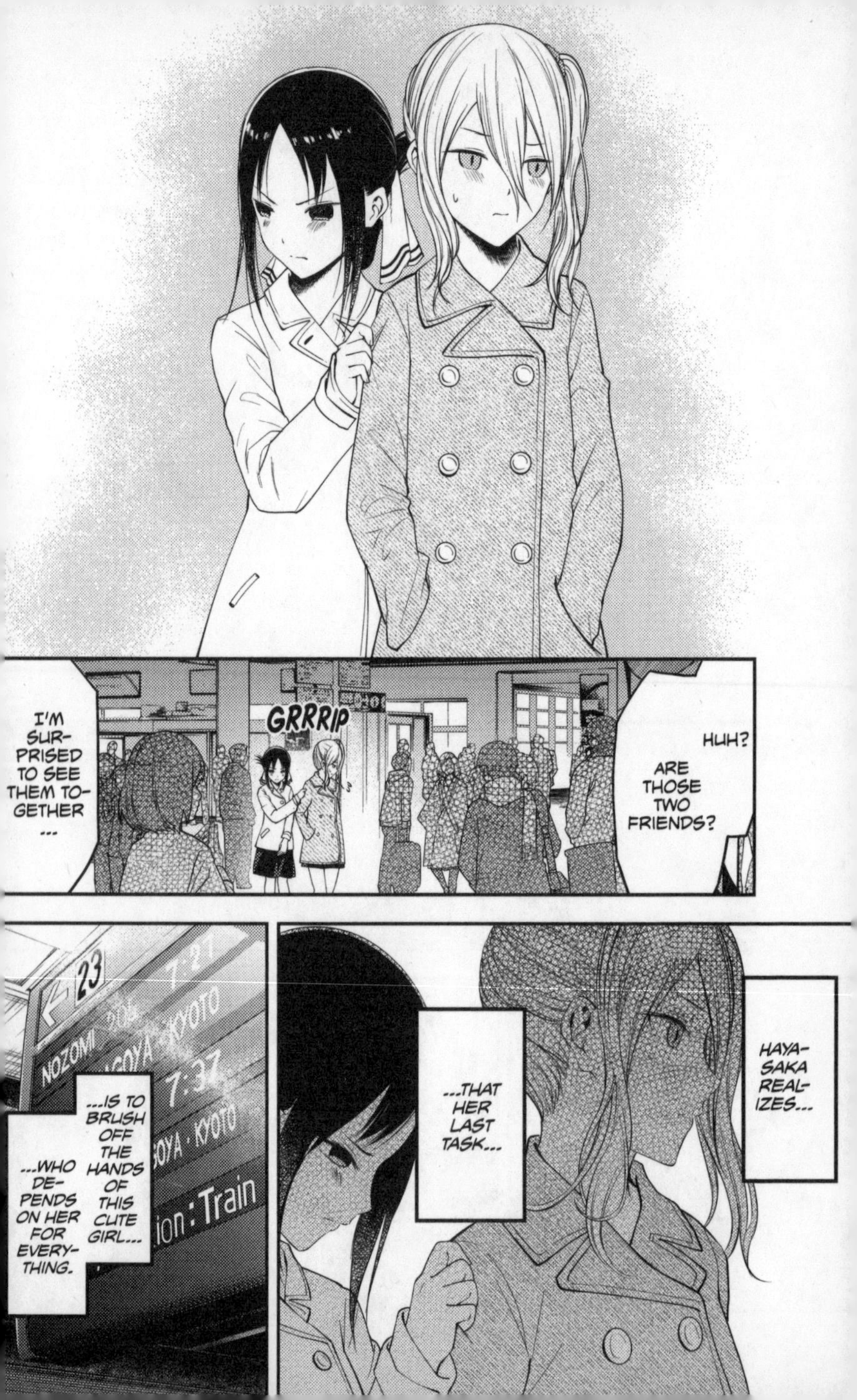
HUH?
ARE THOSE TWO FRIENDS?
GRRRIP
I'M SURPRISED TO SEE THEM TOGETHER...
HAYASAKA REALIZES...
...THAT HER LAST TASK...
23
NOZOMI
7:27
KYOTO
7:37
...IS TO BRUSH OFF THE HANDS OF THIS CUTE GIRL...
...WHO DEPENDS ON HER FOR EVERYTHING.

KAGUYA-SAMA

LOVE IS WAR

Battle 180 Miyuki Shirogane Wants to Go Places

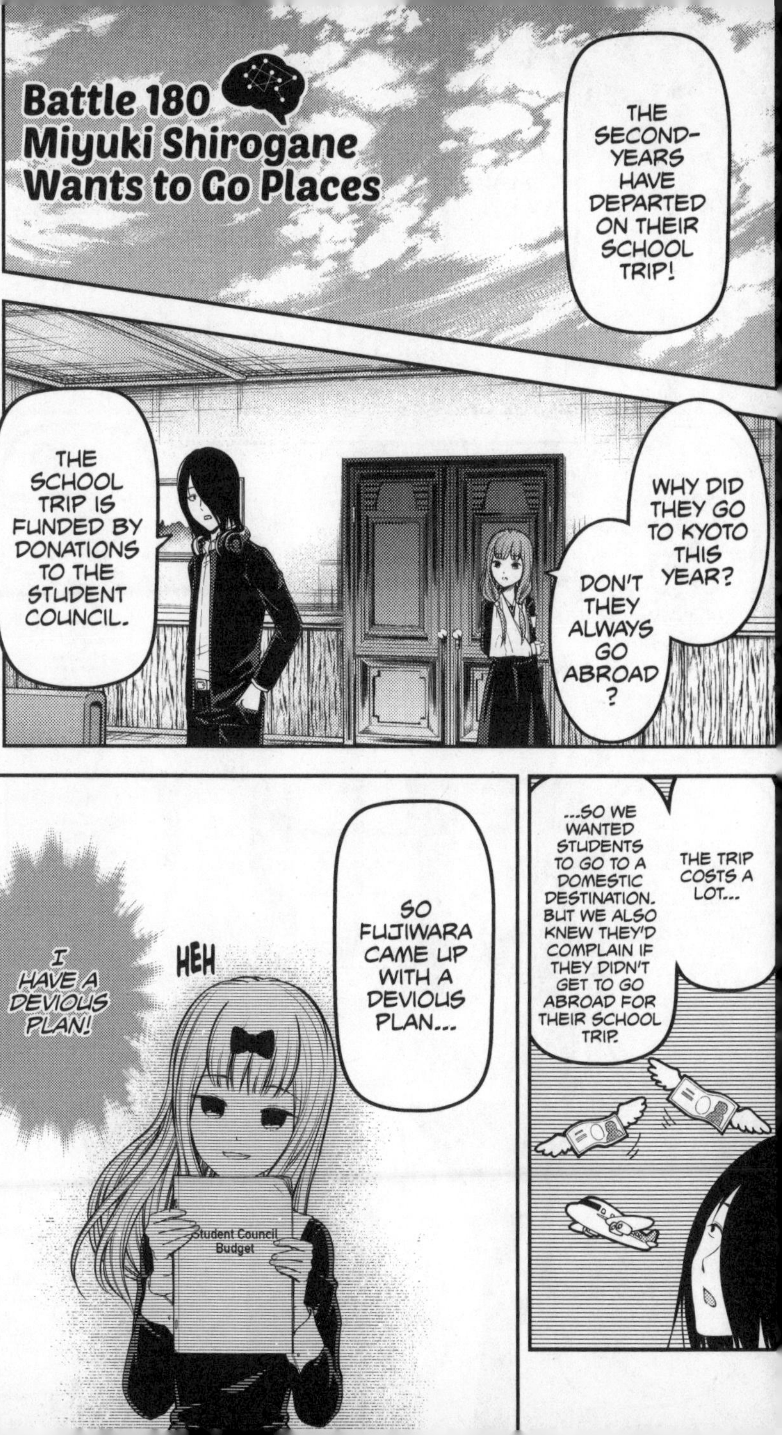
THE SECOND-YEARS HAVE DEPARTED ON THEIR SCHOOL TRIP!
WHY DID THEY GO TO KYOTO THIS YEAR?
DON'T THEY ALWAYS GO ABROAD?
THE SCHOOL TRIP IS FUNDED BY DONATIONS TO THE STUDENT COUNCIL.
THE TRIP COSTS A LOT...
...SO WE WANTED STUDENTS TO GO TO A DOMESTIC DESTINATION. BUT WE ALSO KNEW THEY'D COMPLAIN IF THEY DIDN'T GET TO GO ABROAD FOR THEIR SCHOOL TRIP.
SO FUJIWARA CAME UP WITH A DEVIOUS PLAN...
HEH
I HAVE A DEVIOUS PLAN!
Student Council Budget

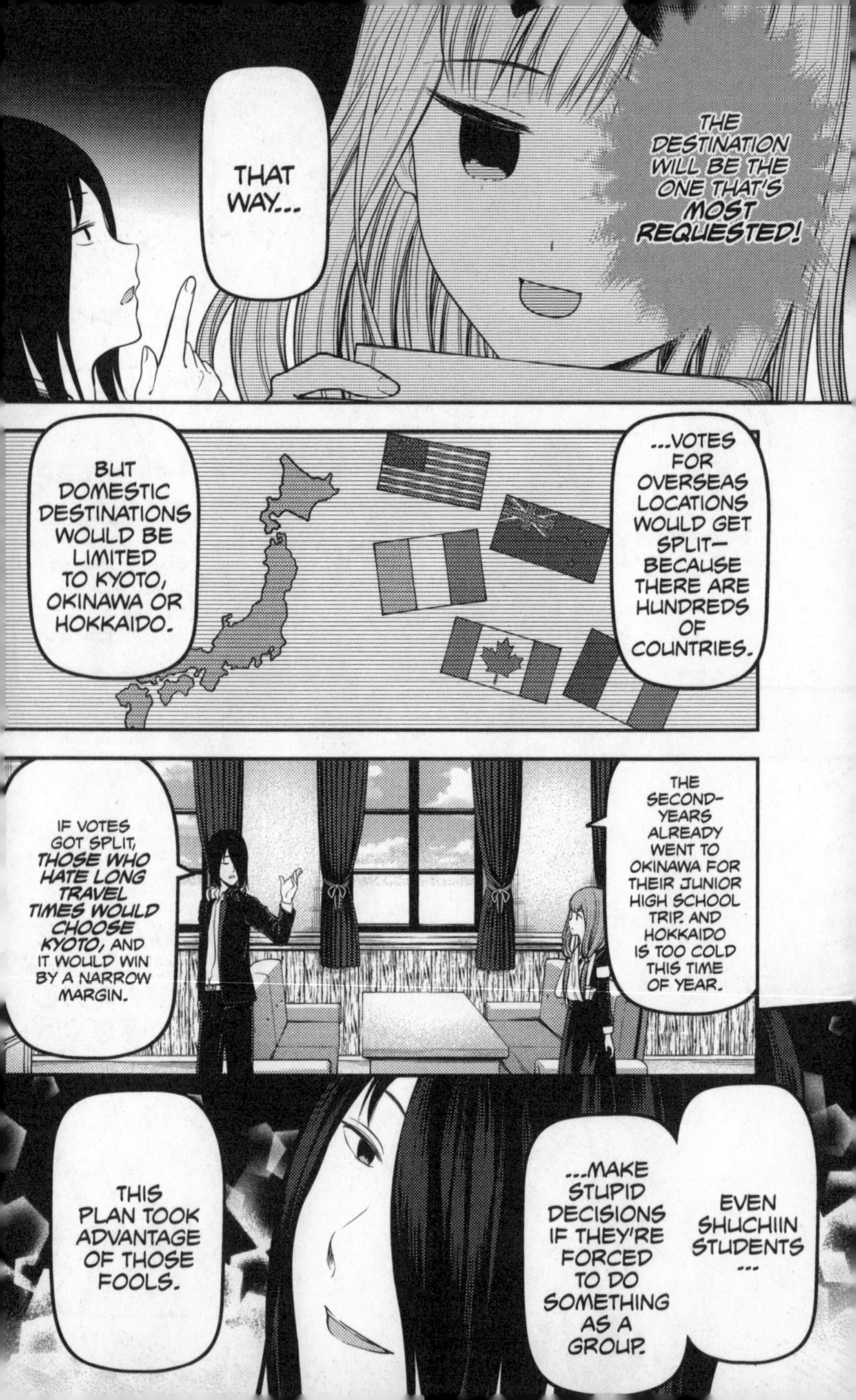
THE DESTINATION WILL BE THE ONE THAT'S MOST REQUESTED!
THAT WAY...
...VOTES FOR OVERSEAS LOCATIONS WOULD GET SPLIT—BECAUSE THERE ARE HUNDREDS OF COUNTRIES.
BUT DOMESTIC DESTINATIONS WOULD BE LIMITED TO KYOTO, OKINAWA OR HOKKAIDO.
THE SECOND-YEARS ALREADY WENT TO OKINAWA FOR THEIR JUNIOR HIGH SCHOOL TRIP. AND HOKKAIDO IS TOO COLD THIS TIME OF YEAR.
IF VOTES GOT SPLIT, THOSE WHO HATE LONG TRAVEL TIMES WOULD CHOOSE KYOTO, AND IT WOULD WIN BY A NARROW MARGIN.
EVEN SHUCHIIN STUDENTS...
...MAKE STUPID DECISIONS IF THEY'RE FORCED TO DO SOMETHING AS A GROUP.
THIS PLAN TOOK ADVANTAGE OF THOSE FOOLS.

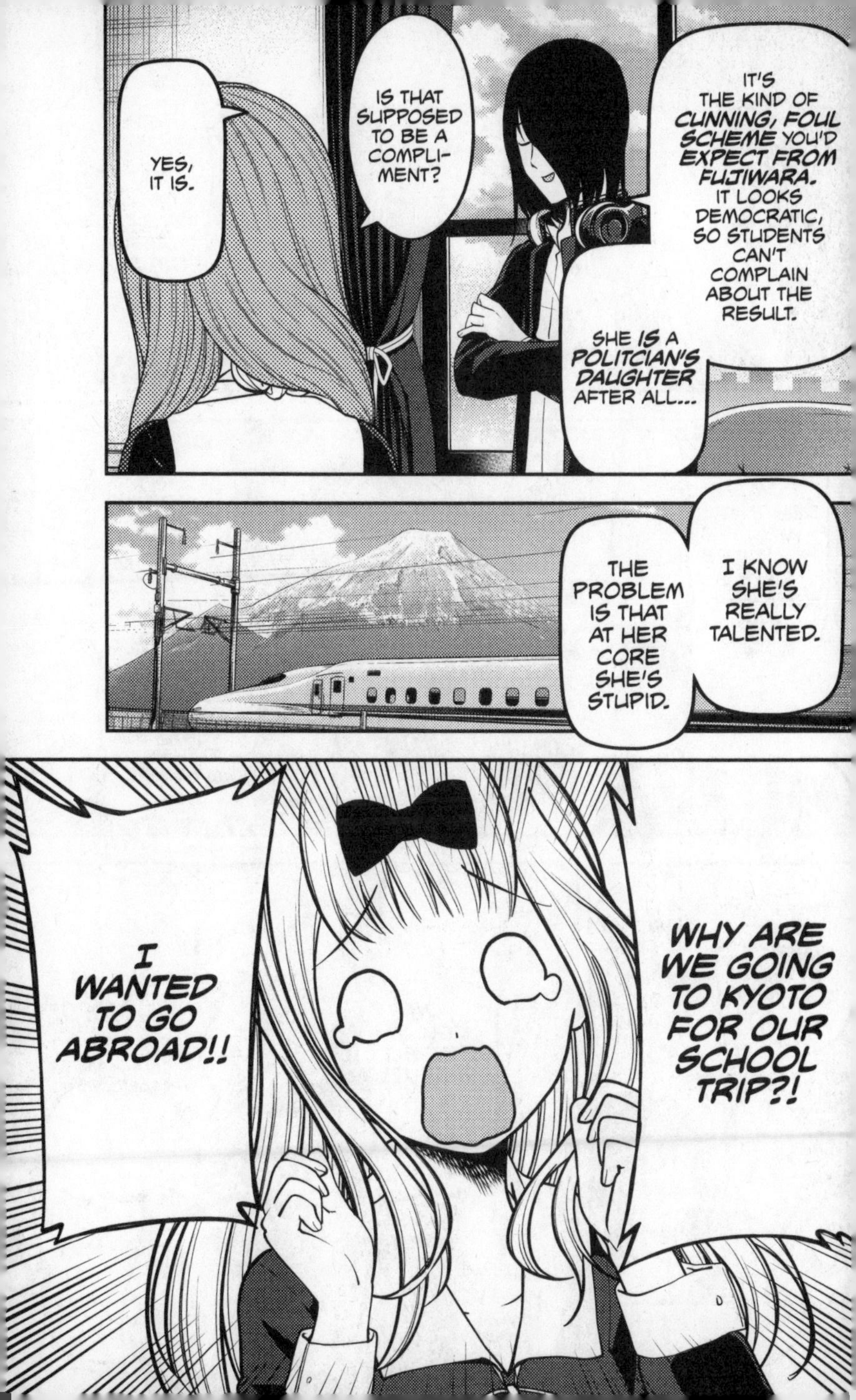
IT'S THE KIND OF CUNNING, FOUL SCHEME YOU'D EXPECT FROM FUJIWARA. IT LOOKS DEMOCRATIC, SO STUDENTS CAN'T COMPLAIN ABOUT THE RESULT.
SHE IS A POLITCIAN'S DAUGHTER AFTER ALL...
IS THAT SUPPOSED TO BE A COMPLIMENT?
YES, IT IS.
I KNOW SHE'S REALLY TALENTED.
THE PROBLEM IS THAT AT HER CORE SHE'S STUPID.
WHY ARE WE GOING TO KYOTO FOR OUR SCHOOL TRIP?!
I WANTED TO GO ABROAD!!

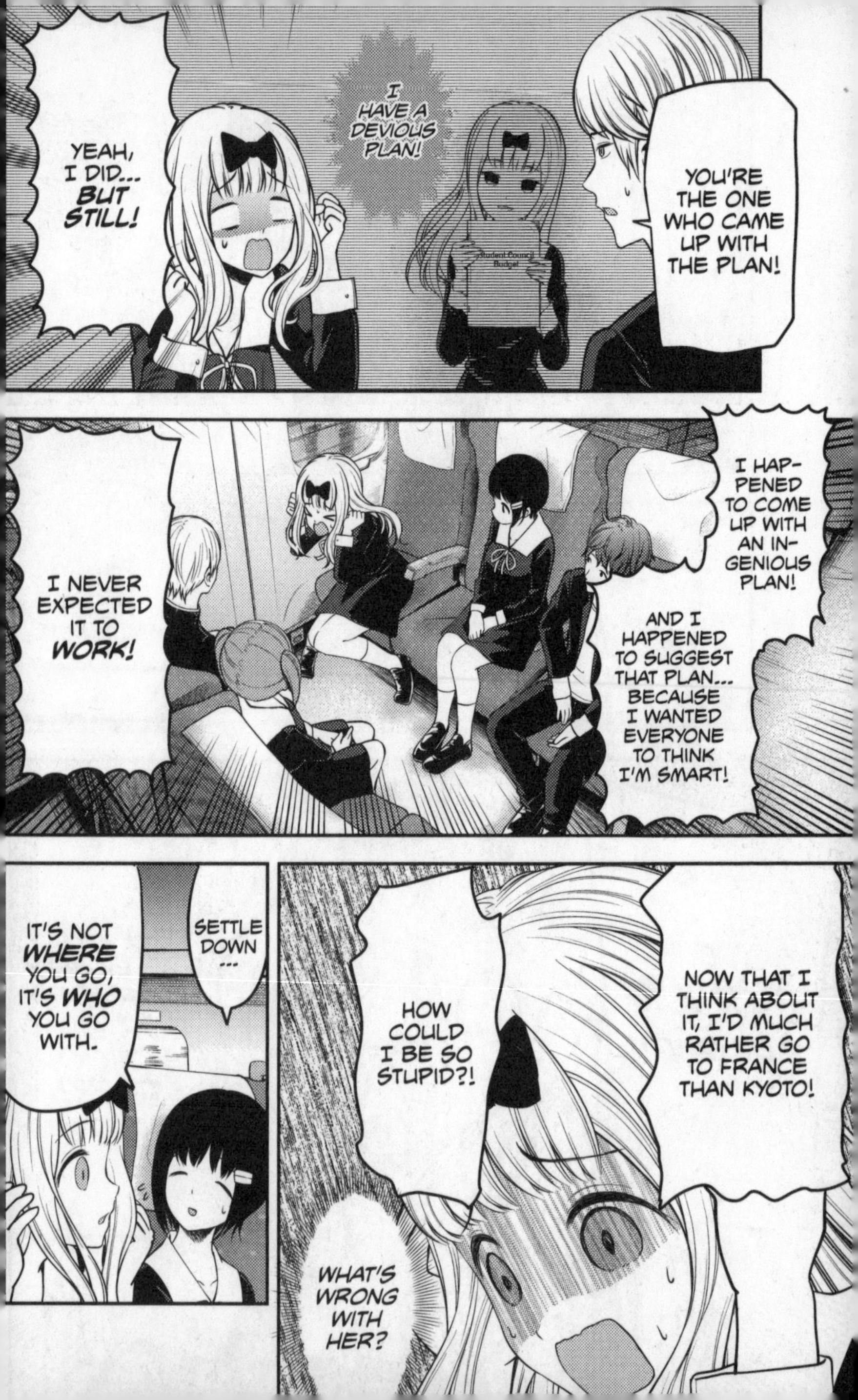
YOU'RE THE ONE WHO CAME UP WITH THE PLAN!
I HAVE A DEVIOUS PLAN!
Student Council Budget
YEAH, I DID... **BUT STILL!**
I HAPPENED TO COME UP WITH AN INGENIOUS PLAN!
AND I HAPPENED TO SUGGEST THAT PLAN... BECAUSE I WANTED EVERYONE TO THINK I'M SMART!
I NEVER EXPECTED IT TO **WORK!**
NOW THAT I THINK ABOUT IT, I'D MUCH RATHER GO TO FRANCE THAN KYOTO!
HOW COULD I BE SO STUPID?!
WHAT'S WRONG WITH HER?
SETTLE DOWN...
IT'S NOT **WHERE** YOU GO, IT'S **WHO** YOU GO WITH.

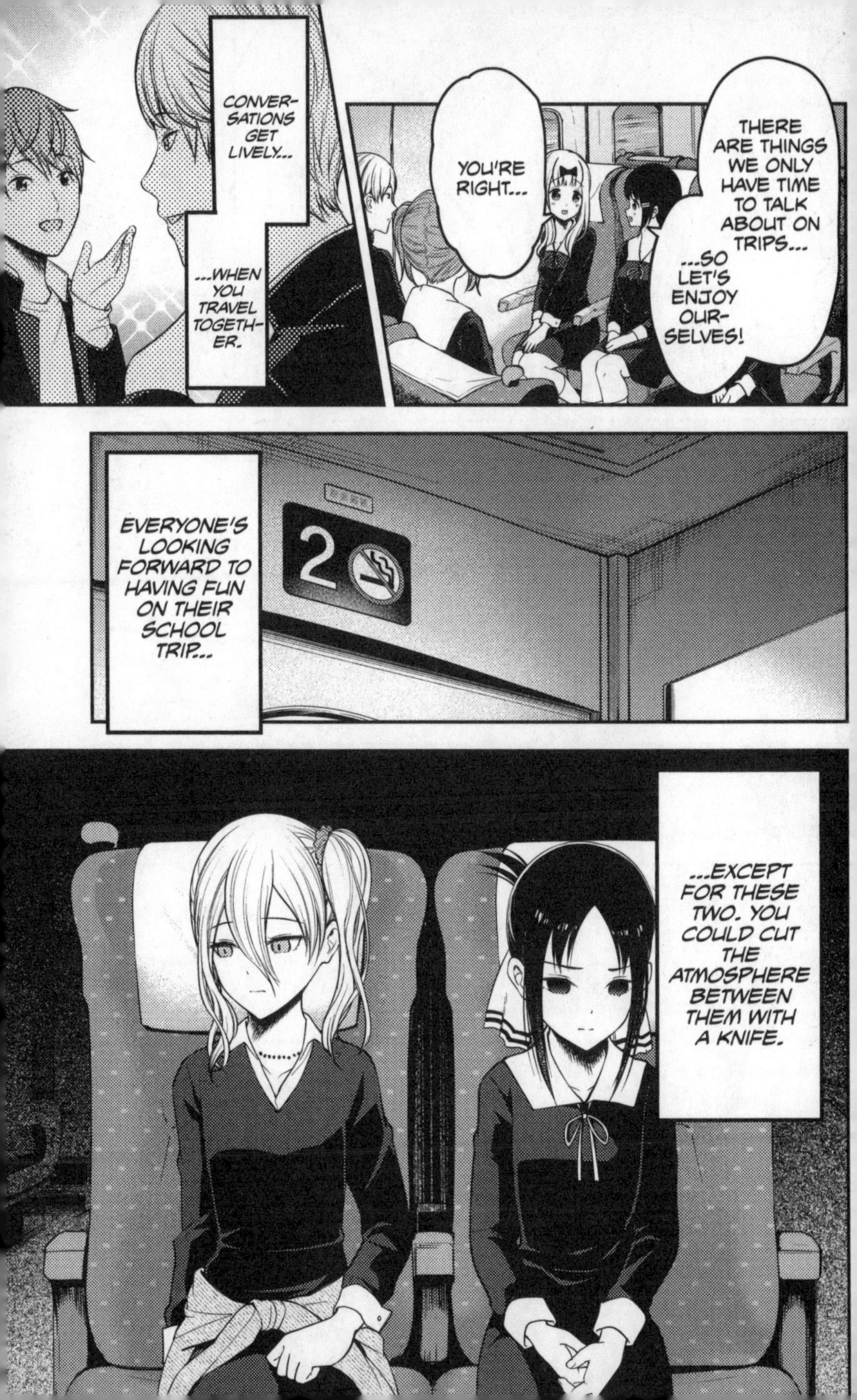
THERE ARE THINGS WE ONLY HAVE TIME TO TALK ABOUT ON TRIPS...
...SO LET'S ENJOY OURSELVES!
YOU'RE RIGHT...
CONVERSATIONS GET LIVELY...
...WHEN YOU TRAVEL TOGETHER.
EVERYONE'S LOOKING FORWARD TO HAVING FUN ON THEIR SCHOOL TRIP...
2
...EXCEPT FOR THESE TWO. YOU COULD CUT THE ATMOSPHERE BETWEEN THEM WITH A KNIFE.

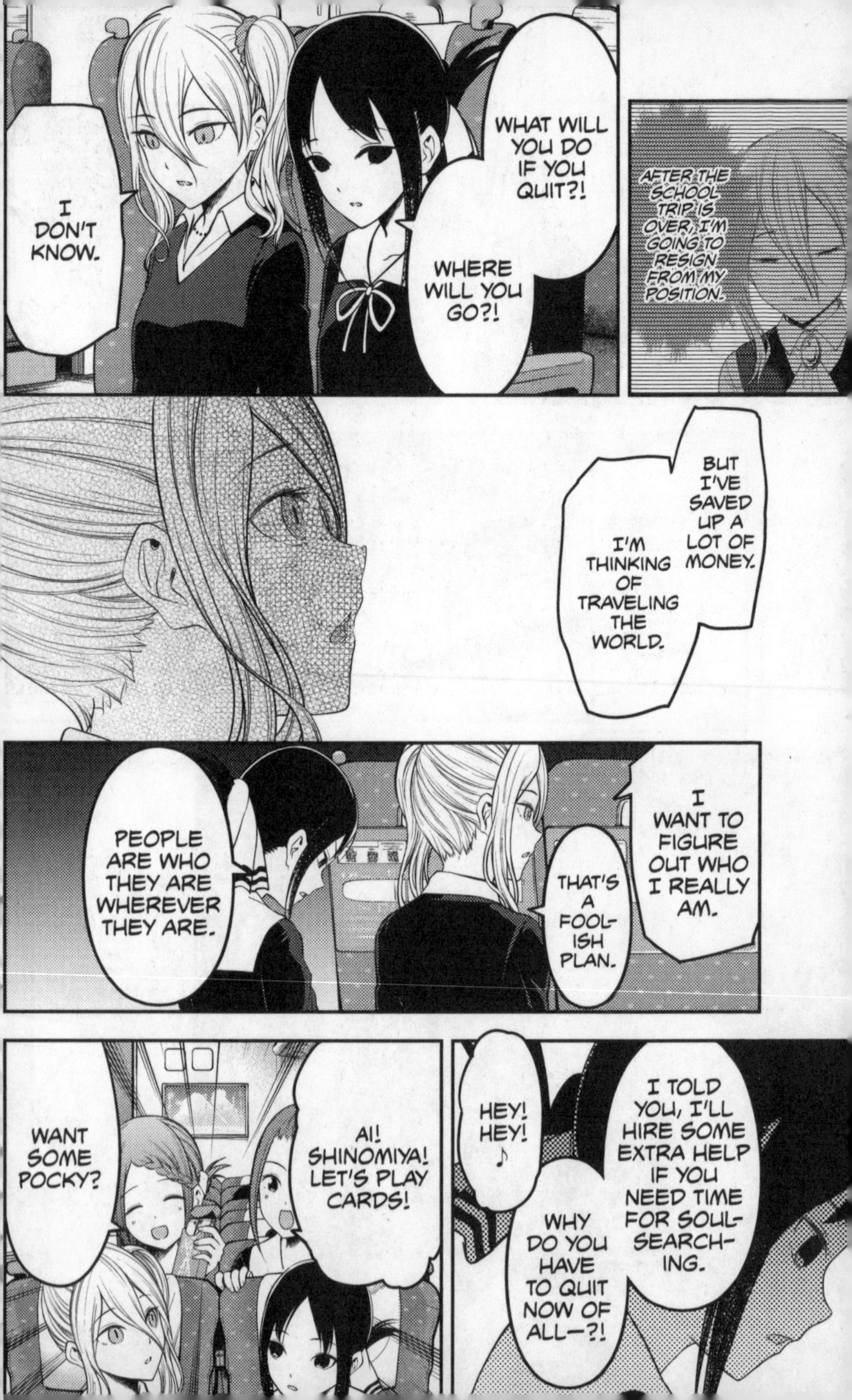
AFTER THE SCHOOL TRIP IS OVER, I'M GOING TO RESIGN FROM MY POSITION.
WHAT WILL YOU DO IF YOU QUIT?!
WHERE WILL YOU GO?!
I DON'T KNOW.
BUT I'VE SAVED UP A LOT OF MONEY.
I'M THINKING OF TRAVELING THE WORLD.
I WANT TO FIGURE OUT WHO I REALLY AM.
THAT'S A FOOLISH PLAN.
PEOPLE ARE WHO THEY ARE WHEREVER THEY ARE.
I TOLD YOU, I'LL HIRE SOME EXTRA HELP IF YOU NEED TIME FOR SOUL-SEARCHING.
HEY! HEY! ♪
WHY DO YOU HAVE TO QUIT NOW OF ALL—?!
AI! SHINOMIYA! LET'S PLAY CARDS!
WANT SOME POCKY?

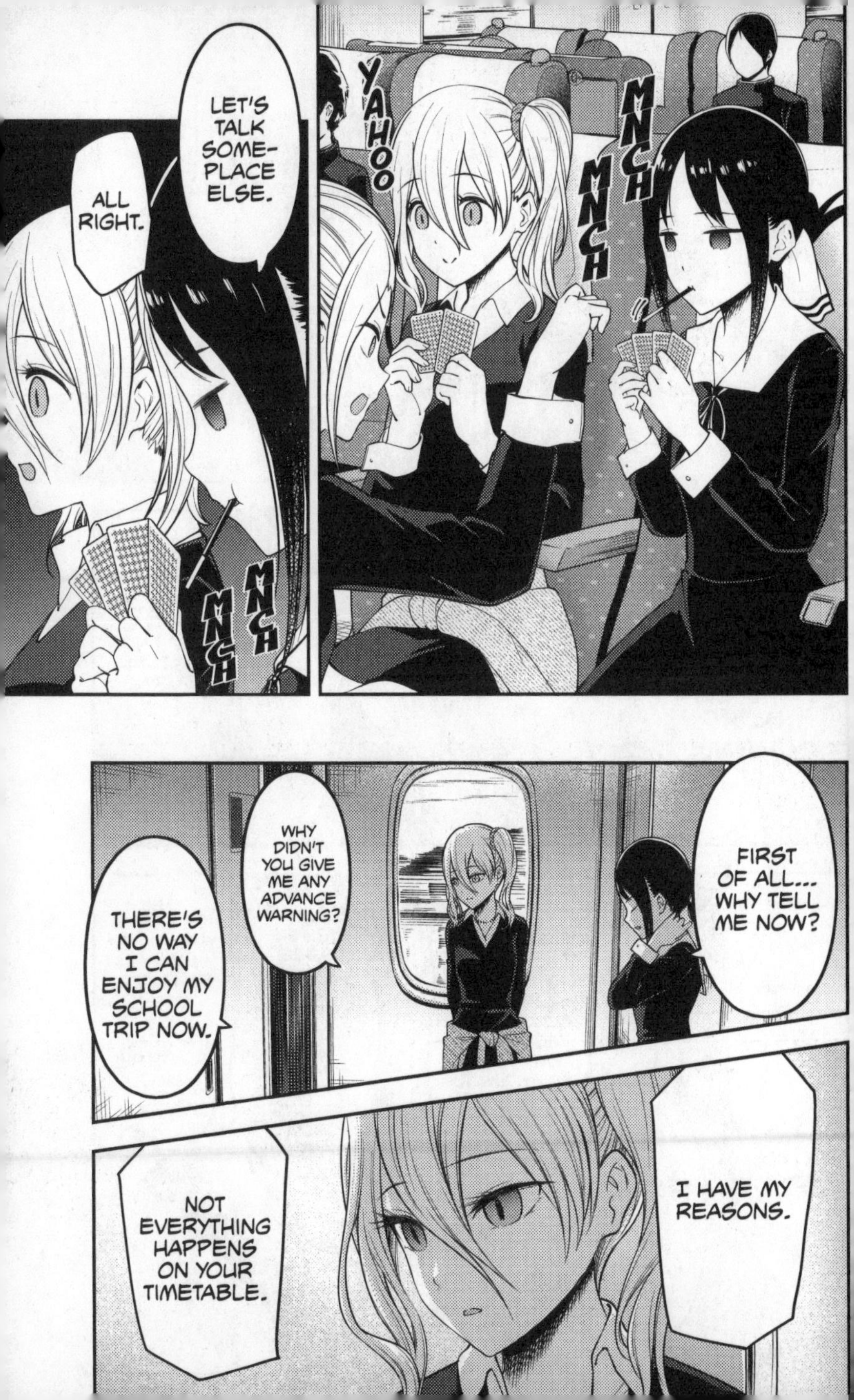
YAHOO
MNCH MNCH
LET'S TALK SOME-PLACE ELSE.
ALL RIGHT.
MNCH MNCH
FIRST OF ALL... WHY TELL ME NOW?
WHY DIDN'T YOU GIVE ME ANY ADVANCE WARNING?
THERE'S NO WAY I CAN ENJOY MY SCHOOL TRIP NOW.
I HAVE MY REASONS.
NOT EVERYTHING HAPPENS ON YOUR TIMETABLE.

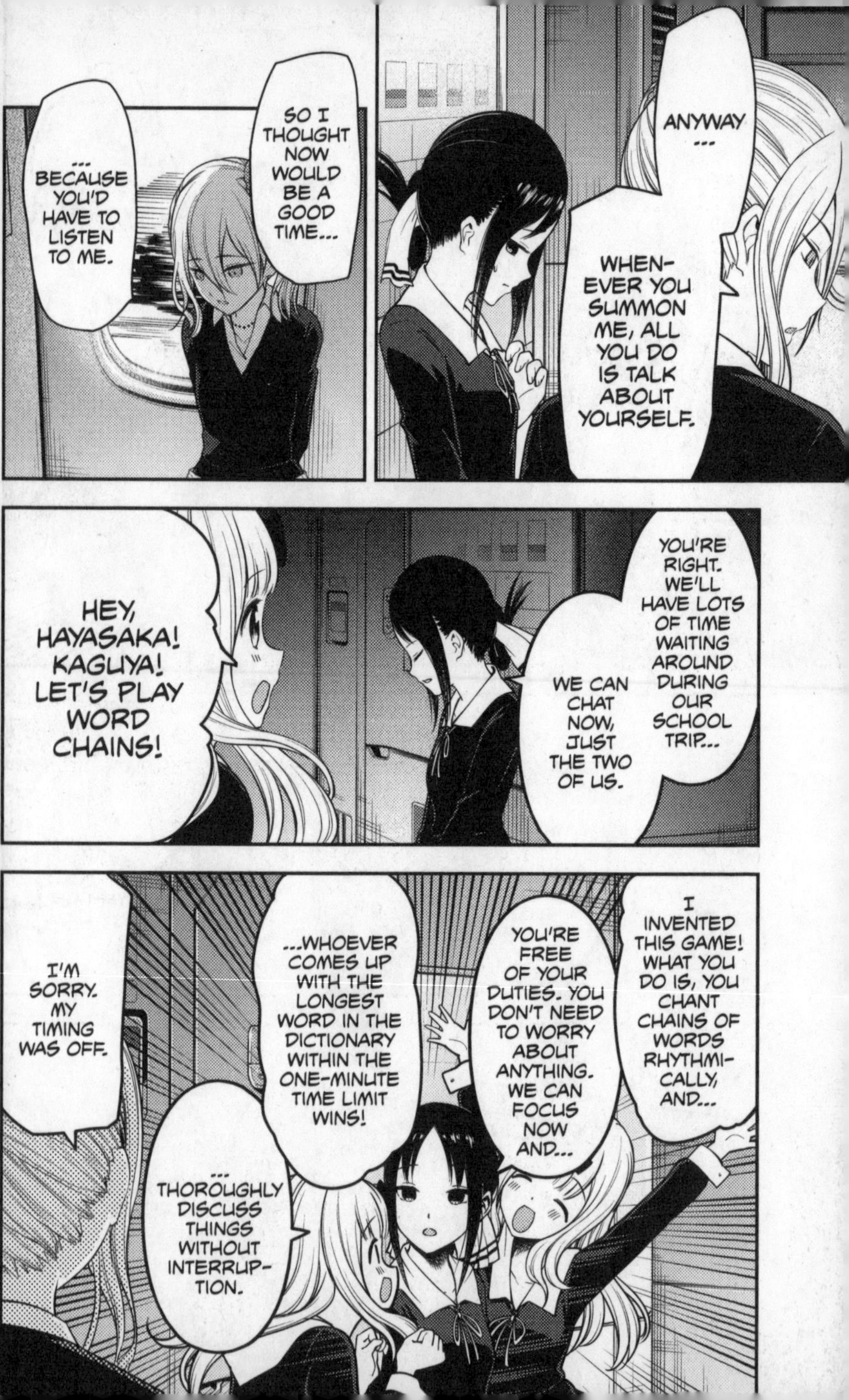
ANYWAY...
WHENEVER YOU SUMMON ME, ALL YOU DO IS TALK ABOUT YOURSELF.
SO I THOUGHT NOW WOULD BE A GOOD TIME...
...BECAUSE YOU'D HAVE TO LISTEN TO ME.
YOU'RE RIGHT. WE'LL HAVE LOTS OF TIME WAITING AROUND DURING OUR SCHOOL TRIP...
WE CAN CHAT NOW, JUST THE TWO OF US.
HEY, HAYASAKA! KAGUYA! LET'S PLAY WORD CHAINS!
I INVENTED THIS GAME! WHAT YOU DO IS, YOU CHANT CHAINS OF WORDS RHYTHMICALLY, AND...
YOU'RE FREE OF YOUR DUTIES. YOU DON'T NEED TO WORRY ABOUT ANYTHING. WE CAN FOCUS NOW AND...
...WHOEVER COMES UP WITH THE LONGEST WORD IN THE DICTIONARY WITHIN THE ONE-MINUTE TIME LIMIT WINS!
...THOROUGHLY DISCUSS THINGS WITHOUT INTERRUPTION.
I'M SORRY. MY TIMING WAS OFF.

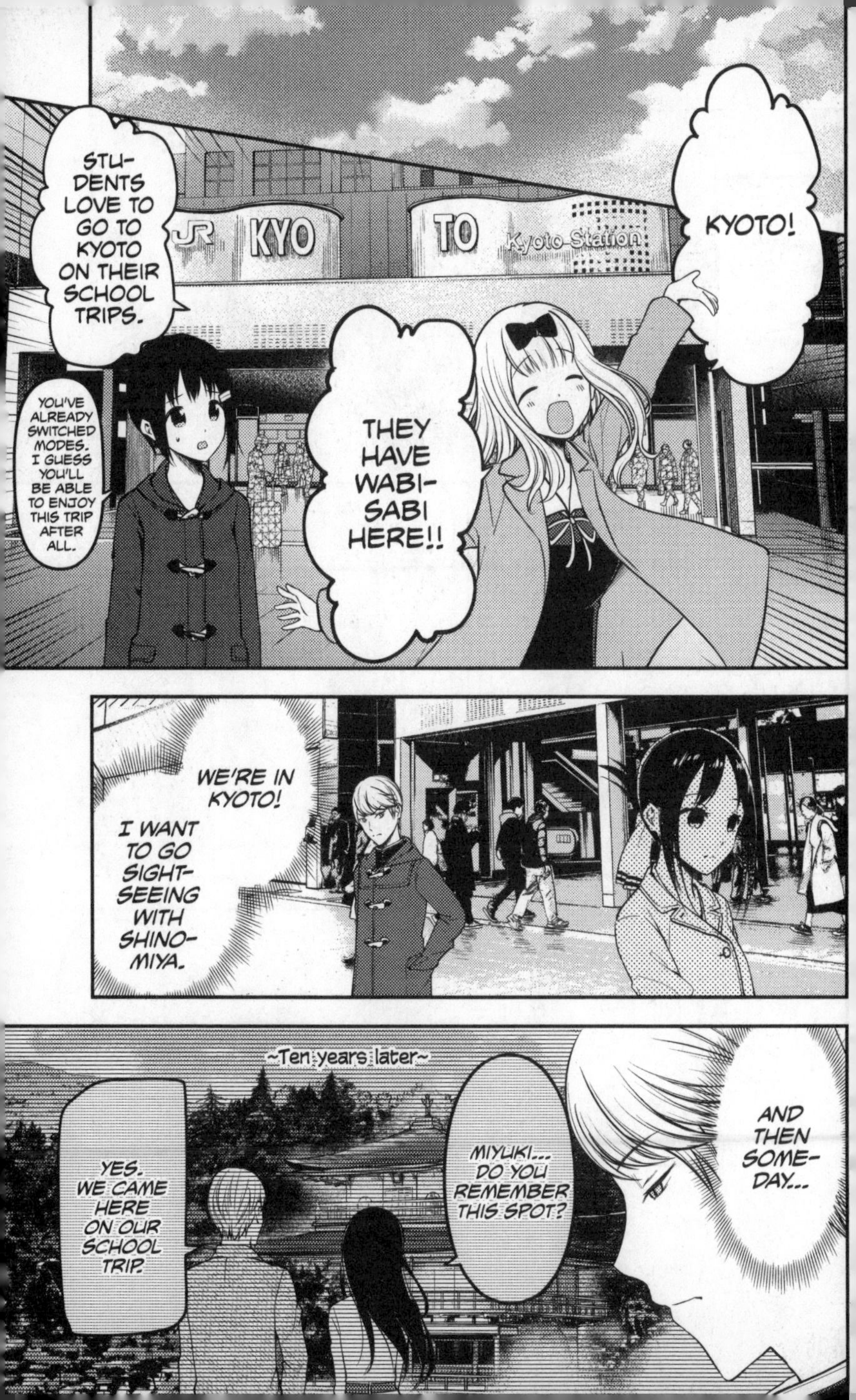
KYOTO!
JR KYO TO Kyoto Station
THEY HAVE WABI-SABI HERE!!
STUDENTS LOVE TO GO TO KYOTO ON THEIR SCHOOL TRIPS.
YOU'VE ALREADY SWITCHED MODES. I GUESS YOU'LL BE ABLE TO ENJOY THIS TRIP AFTER ALL.
WE'RE IN KYOTO!
I WANT TO GO SIGHTSEEING WITH SHINOMIYA.
~Ten years later~
AND THEN SOMEDAY...
MIYUKI... DO YOU REMEMBER THIS SPOT?
YES. WE CAME HERE ON OUR SCHOOL TRIP.

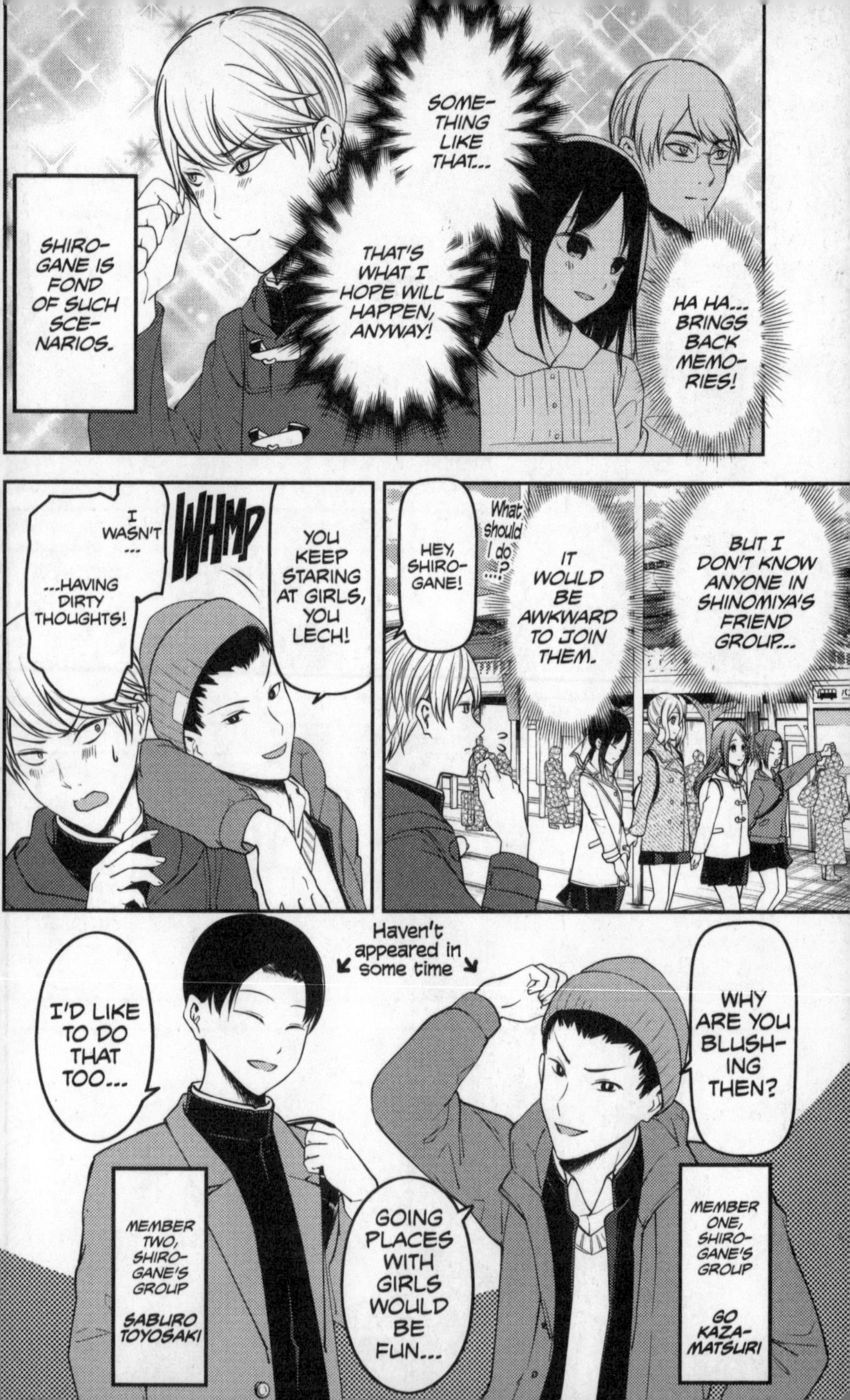
SOMETHING LIKE THAT...
THAT'S WHAT I HOPE WILL HAPPEN, ANYWAY!
HA HA... BRINGS BACK MEMORIES!
SHIROGANE IS FOND OF SUCH SCENARIOS.
BUT I DON'T KNOW ANYONE IN SHINOMIYA'S FRIEND GROUP...
IT WOULD BE AWKWARD TO JOIN THEM.
What should I do...?
HEY, SHIROGANE!
YOU KEEP STARING AT GIRLS, YOU LECH!
WHMP
I WASN'T... ...HAVING DIRTY THOUGHTS!
WHY ARE YOU BLUSHING THEN?
MEMBER ONE, SHIROGANE'S GROUP
GO KAZAMATSURI
Haven't appeared in some time
I'D LIKE TO DO THAT TOO...
GOING PLACES WITH GIRLS WOULD BE FUN...
MEMBER TWO, SHIROGANE'S GROUP
SABURO TOYOSAKI

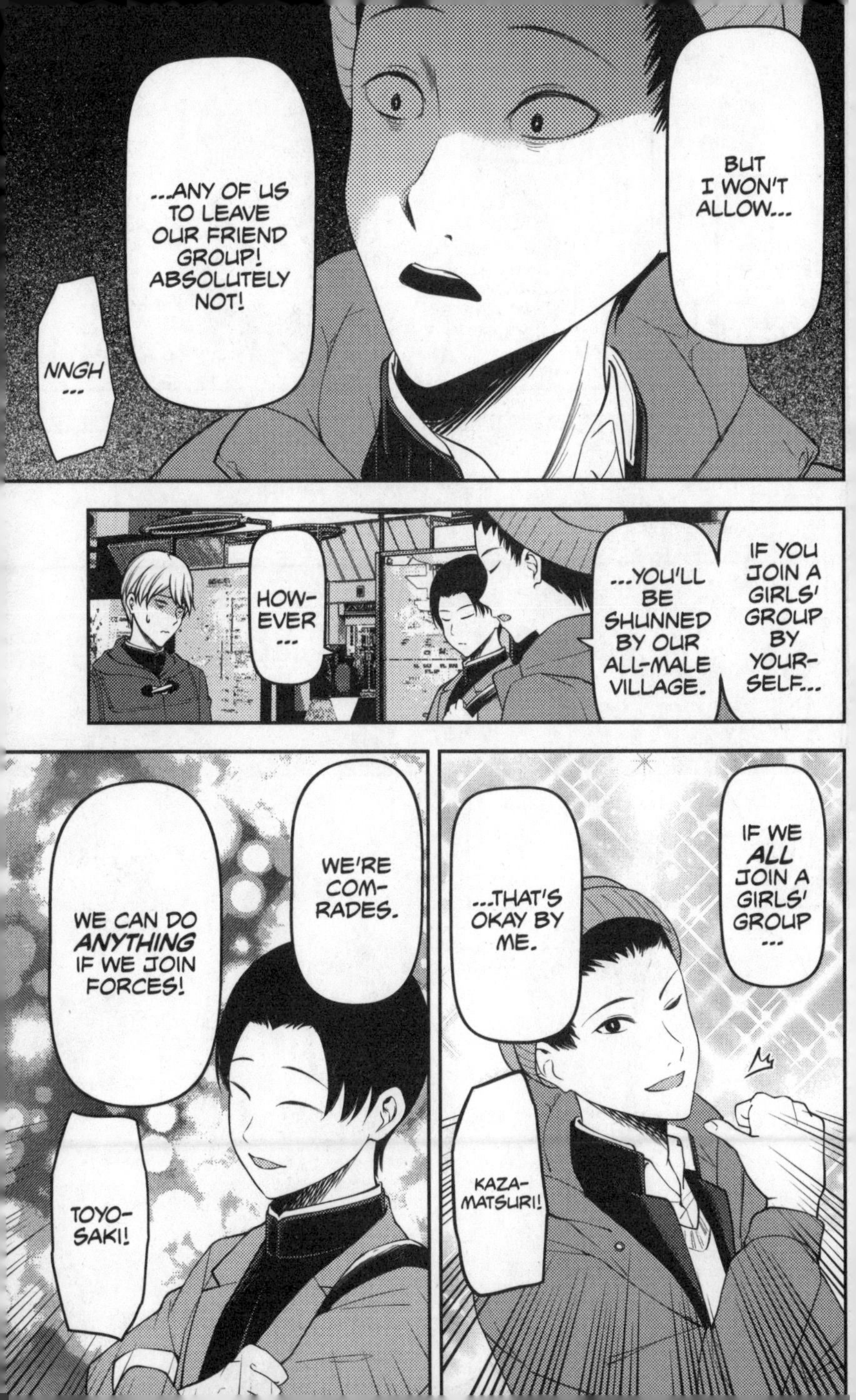
BUT I WON'T ALLOW...
...ANY OF US TO LEAVE OUR FRIEND GROUP! ABSOLUTELY NOT!
NNGH...
IF YOU JOIN A GIRLS' GROUP BY YOURSELF...
...YOU'LL BE SHUNNED BY OUR ALL-MALE VILLAGE.
HOWEVER...
IF WE ALL JOIN A GIRLS' GROUP...
...THAT'S OKAY BY ME.
KAZAMATSURI!
WE'RE COMRADES.
WE CAN DO ANYTHING IF WE JOIN FORCES!
TOYOSAKI!

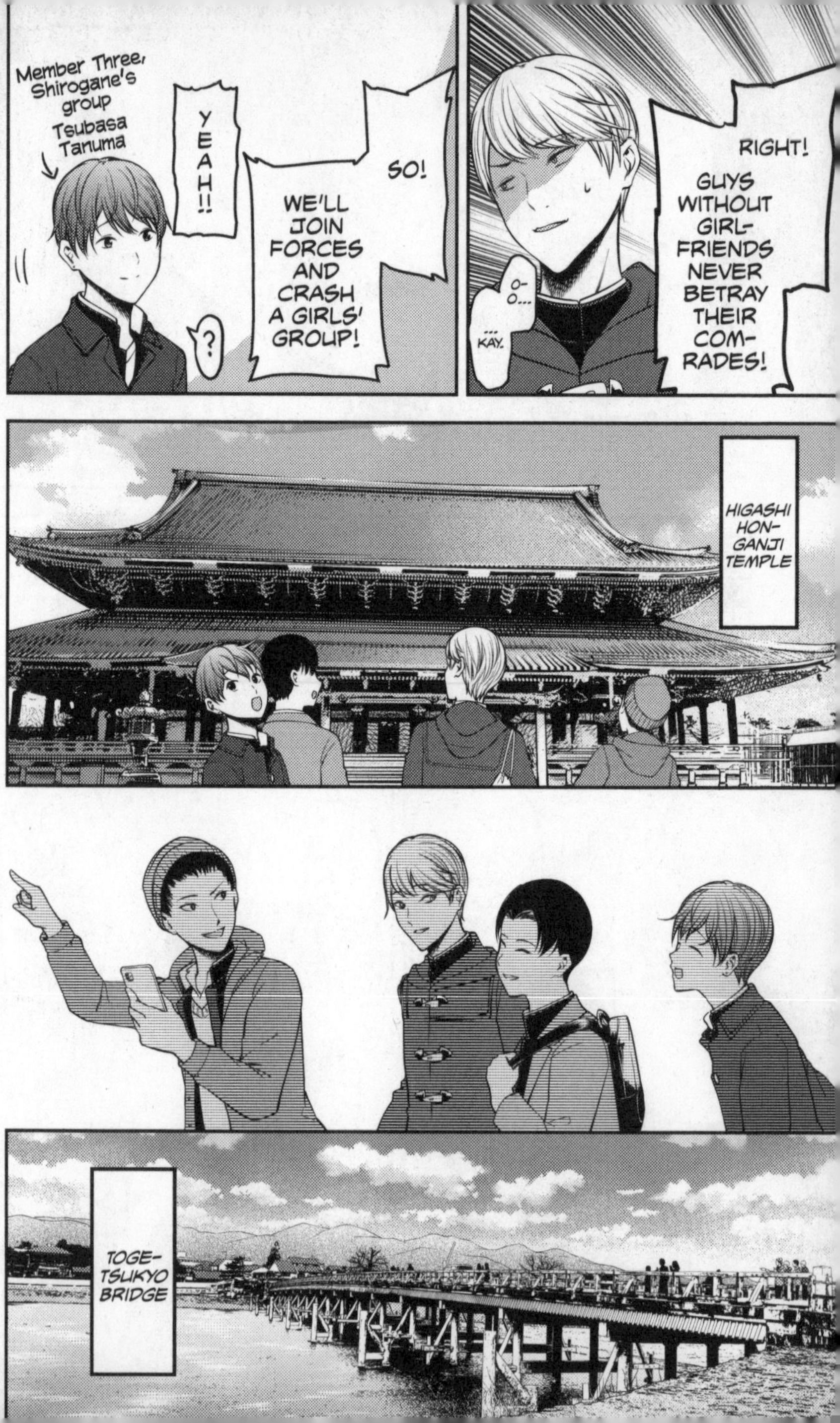
RIGHT!
GUYS WITHOUT GIRL-FRIENDS NEVER BETRAY THEIR COM-RADES!
O-O... ...KAY.
SO!
WE'LL JOIN FORCES AND CRASH A GIRLS' GROUP!
YEAH!!
?
Member Three, Shirogane's group Tsubasa Tanuma
HIGASHI HON-GANJI TEMPLE
TOGE-TSUKYO BRIDGE

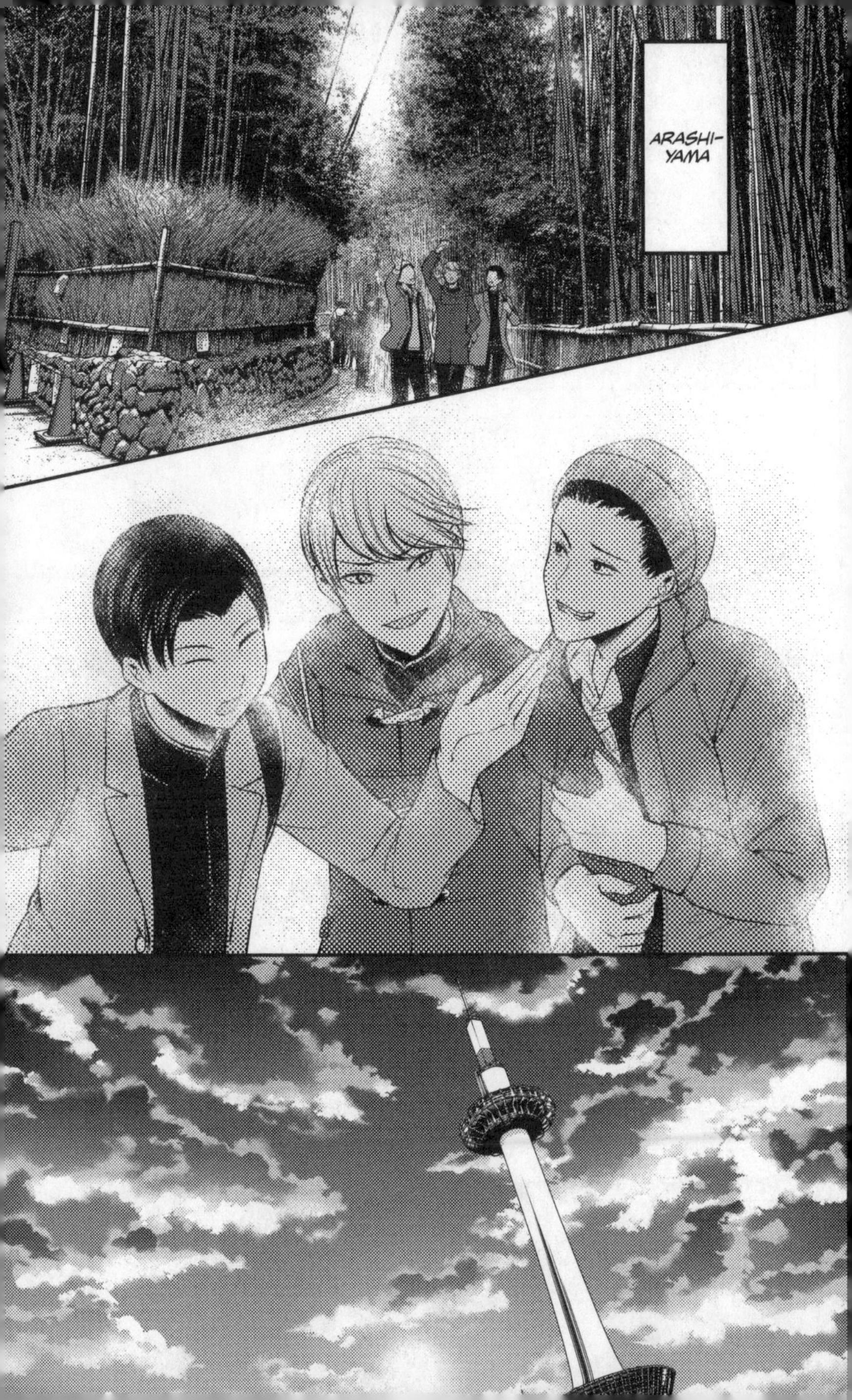
ARASHI-
YAMA

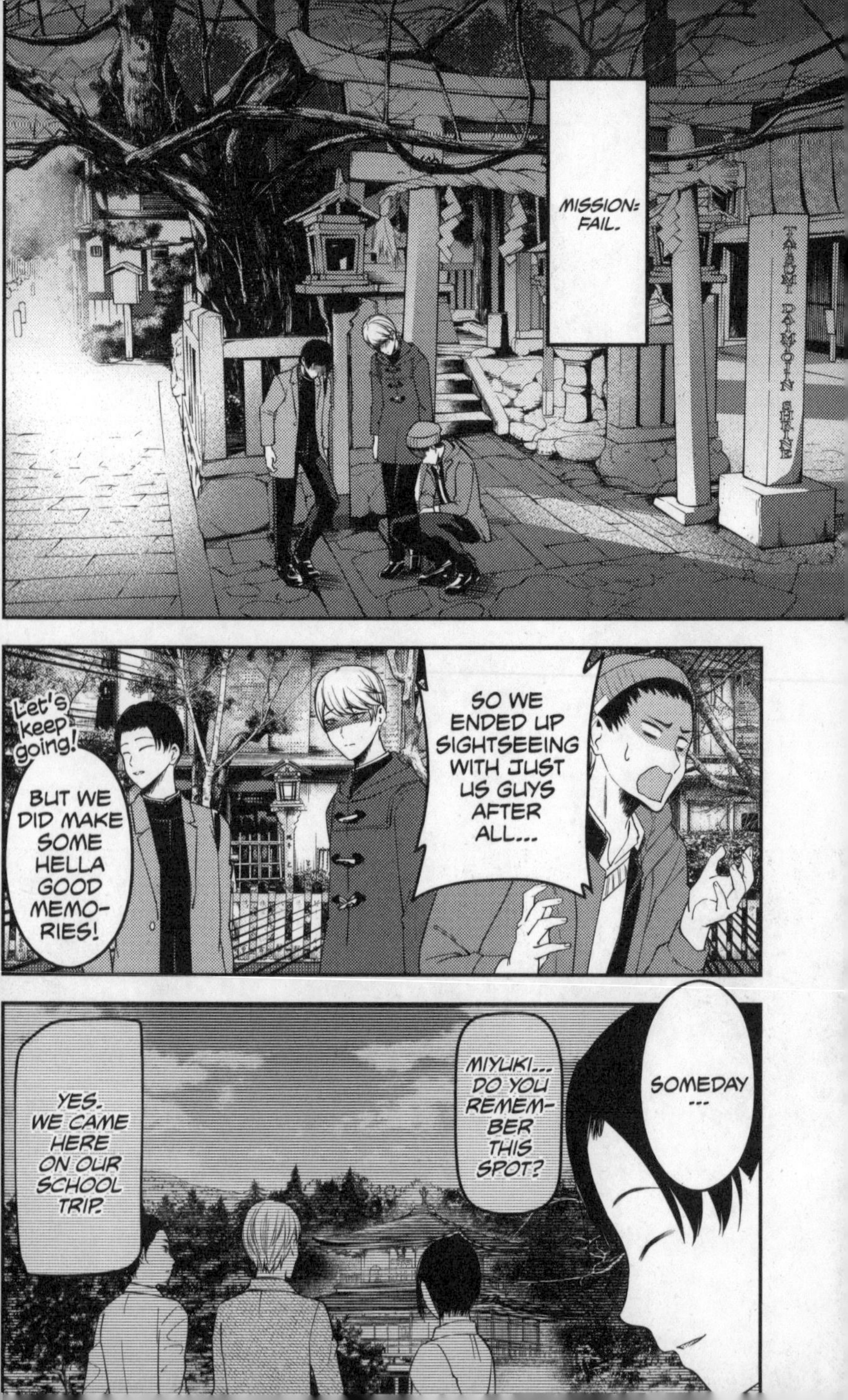
MISSION: FAIL.
SO WE ENDED UP SIGHTSEEING WITH JUST US GUYS AFTER ALL...
Let's keep going!
BUT WE DID MAKE SOME HELLA GOOD MEMORIES!
SOMEDAY ---
MIYUKI... DO YOU REMEMBER THIS SPOT?
YES. WE CAME HERE ON OUR SCHOOL TRIP.

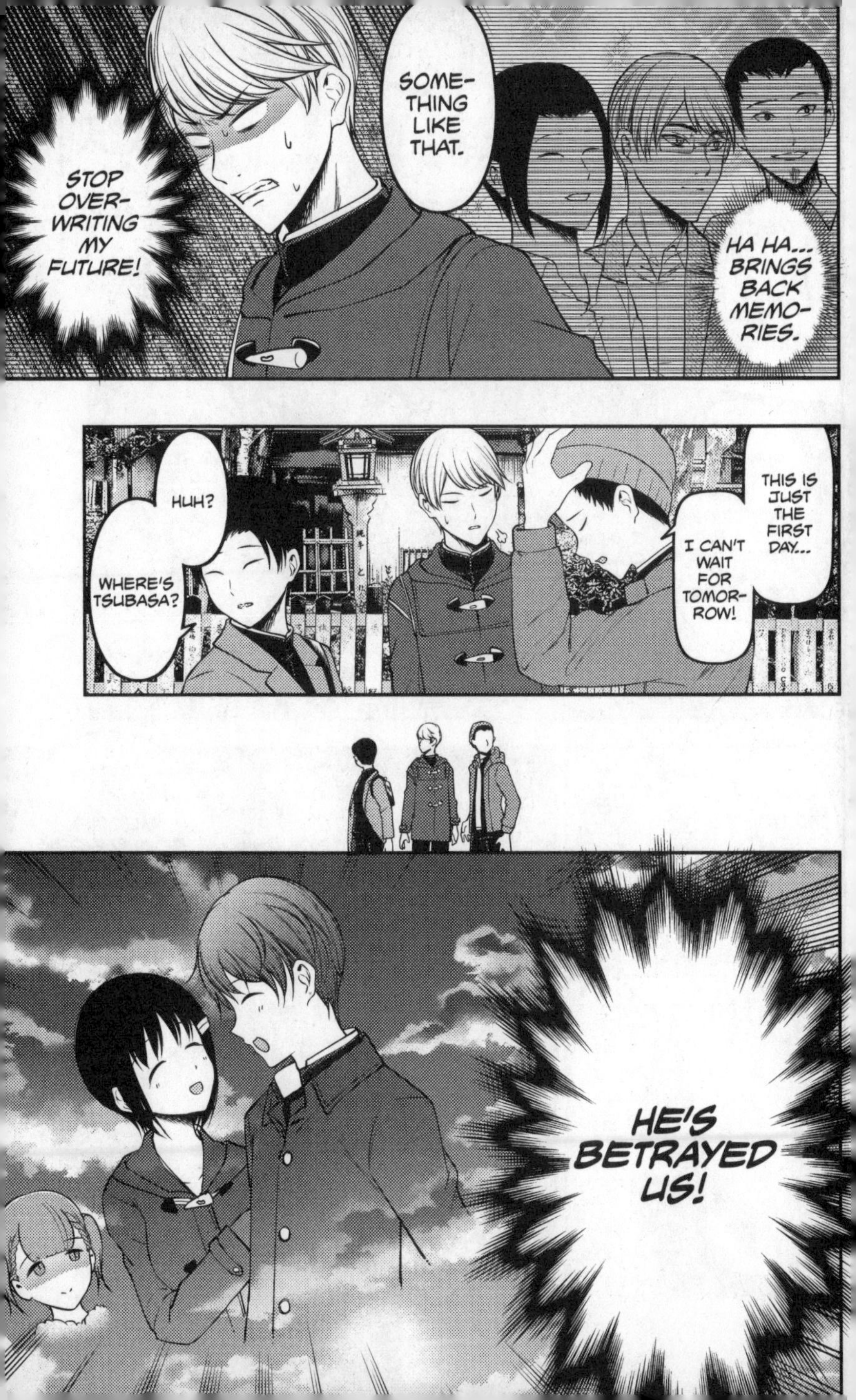
SOME-THING LIKE THAT.
HA HA... BRINGS BACK MEMO-RIES.
STOP OVER-WRITING MY FUTURE!
THIS IS JUST THE FIRST DAY...
I CAN'T WAIT FOR TOMOR-ROW!
HUH?
WHERE'S TSUBASA?
HE'S BETRAYED US!

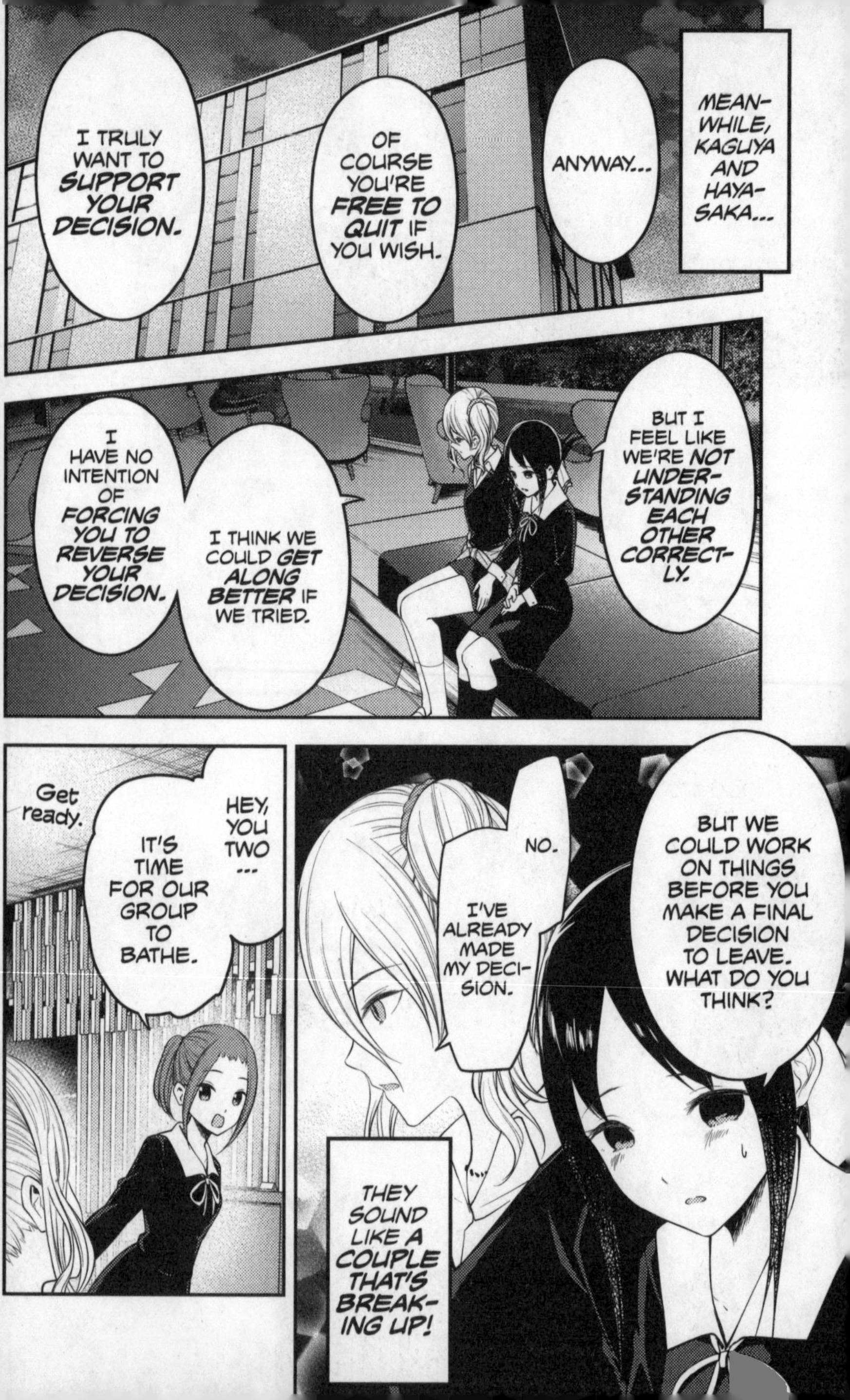
MEANWHILE, KAGUYA AND HAYASAKA...
ANYWAY...
OF COURSE YOU'RE FREE TO QUIT IF YOU WISH.
I TRULY WANT TO SUPPORT YOUR DECISION.
BUT I FEEL LIKE WE'RE NOT UNDERSTANDING EACH OTHER CORRECTLY.
I THINK WE COULD GET ALONG BETTER IF WE TRIED.
I HAVE NO INTENTION OF FORCING YOU TO REVERSE YOUR DECISION.
BUT WE COULD WORK ON THINGS BEFORE YOU MAKE A FINAL DECISION TO LEAVE. WHAT DO YOU THINK?
NO.
I'VE ALREADY MADE MY DECISION.
THEY SOUND LIKE A COUPLE THAT'S BREAKING UP!
HEY, YOU TWO...
IT'S TIME FOR OUR GROUP TO BATHE.
Get ready.

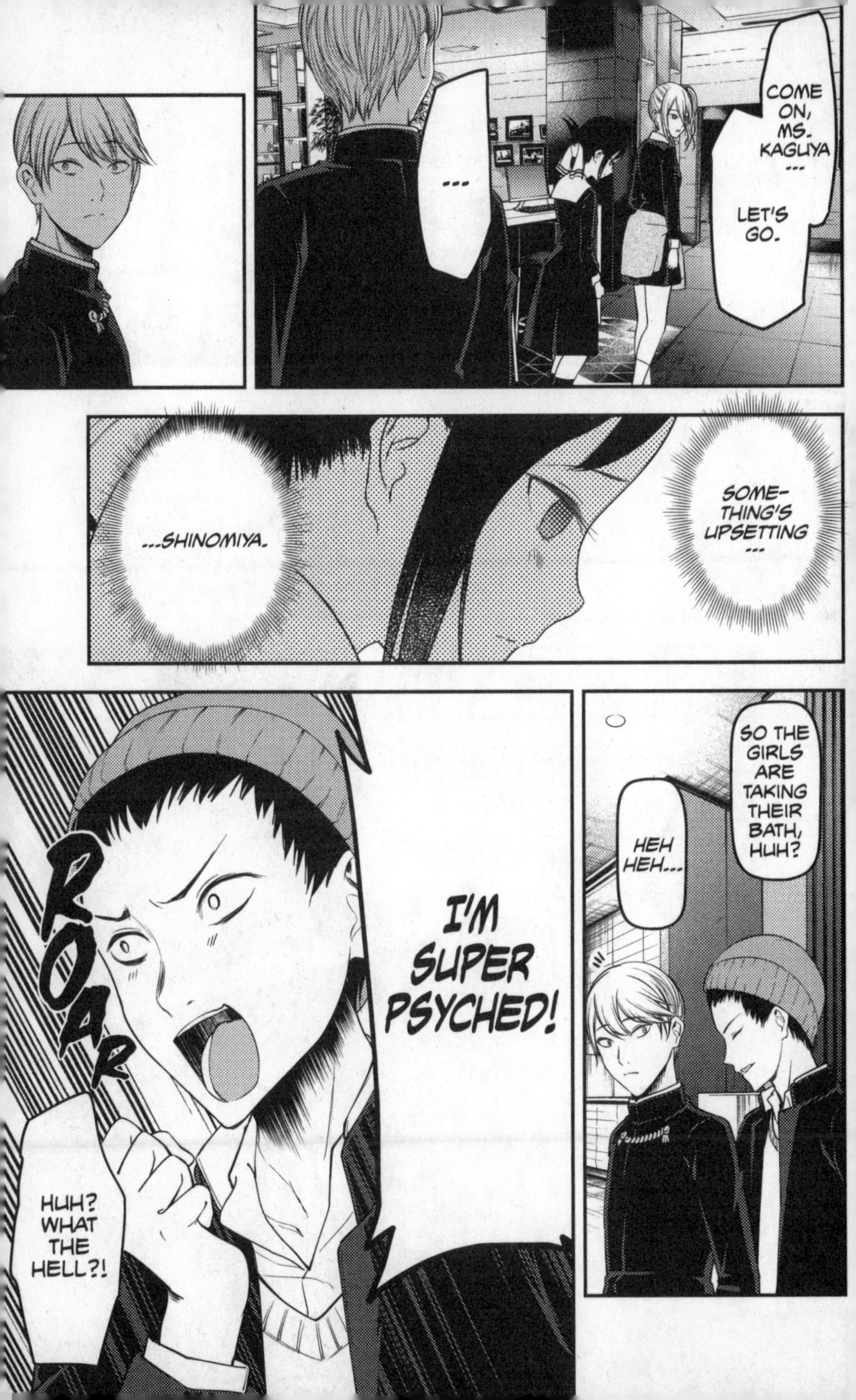
COME ON, MS. KAGUYA...
LET'S GO.
...
SOME-THING'S UPSETTING...
...SHINOMIYA.
SO THE GIRLS ARE TAKING THEIR BATH, HUH?
HEH HEH...
I'M SUPER PSYCHED!
ROAR
HUH? WHAT THE HELL?!

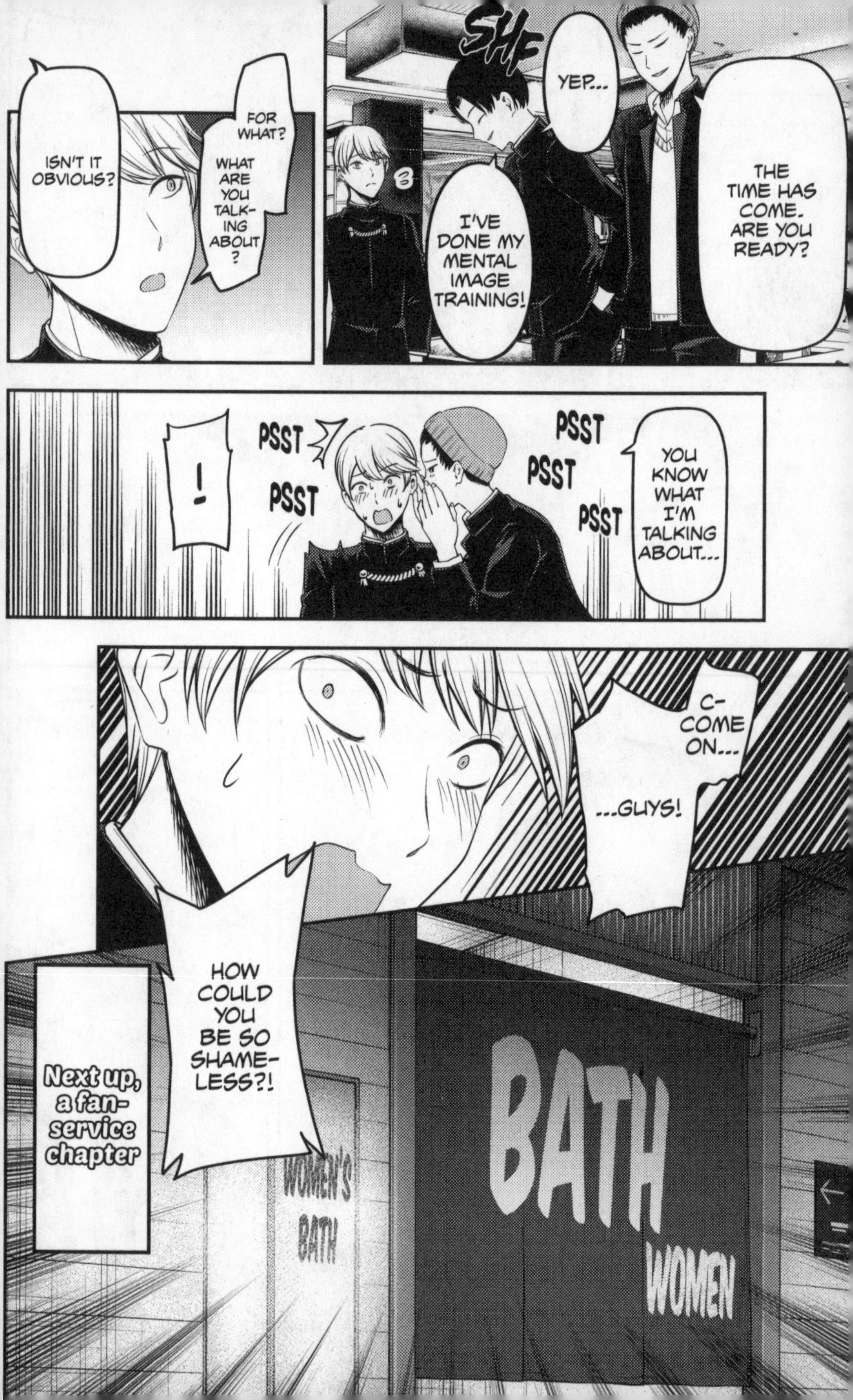
SHF
THE TIME HAS COME. ARE YOU READY?
YEP...
I'VE DONE MY MENTAL IMAGE TRAINING!
FOR WHAT?
WHAT ARE YOU TALKING ABOUT?
ISN'T IT OBVIOUS?
YOU KNOW WHAT I'M TALKING ABOUT...
PSST
PSST
PSST
PSST
PSST
!
C-COME ON...
...GUYS!
HOW COULD YOU BE SO SHAME-LESS?!
BATH
WOMEN
WOMEN'S BATH
Next up, a fan-service chapter

Groups

Year 2, Class A
Shinomiya, Hayasaka, Hinokuchi and Suruga

Year 2, Class B
Shirogane, Tanuma, Kazamatsuri and Toyosaki
Fujiwara and friends
Kashiwagi and Shijo and their classmates

Year 2, Class C
Kose, Kino and their classmates

Taking care of business back at school
Ino and Ishigami

KAGUYA-SAMA

LOVE IS WAR

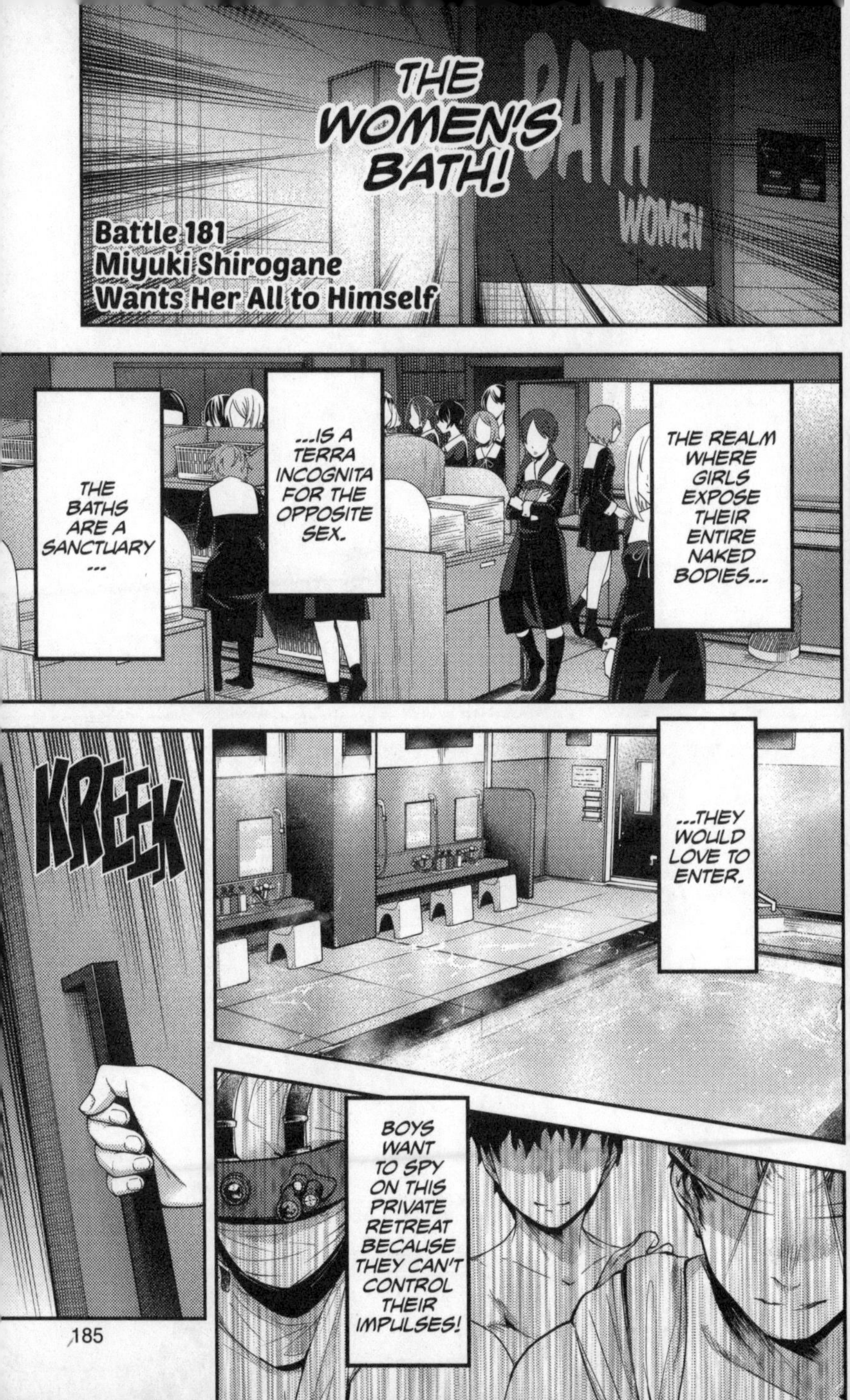
THE WOMEN'S BATH!
BATH
WOMEN
Battle 181
Miyuki Shirogane Wants Her All to Himself
THE REALM WHERE GIRLS EXPOSE THEIR ENTIRE NAKED BODIES...
...IS A TERRA INCOGNITA FOR THE OPPOSITE SEX.
THE BATHS ARE A SANCTUARY ...
...THEY WOULD LOVE TO ENTER.
BOYS WANT TO SPY ON THIS PRIVATE RETREAT BECAUSE THEY CAN'T CONTROL THEIR IMPULSES!
KREEK

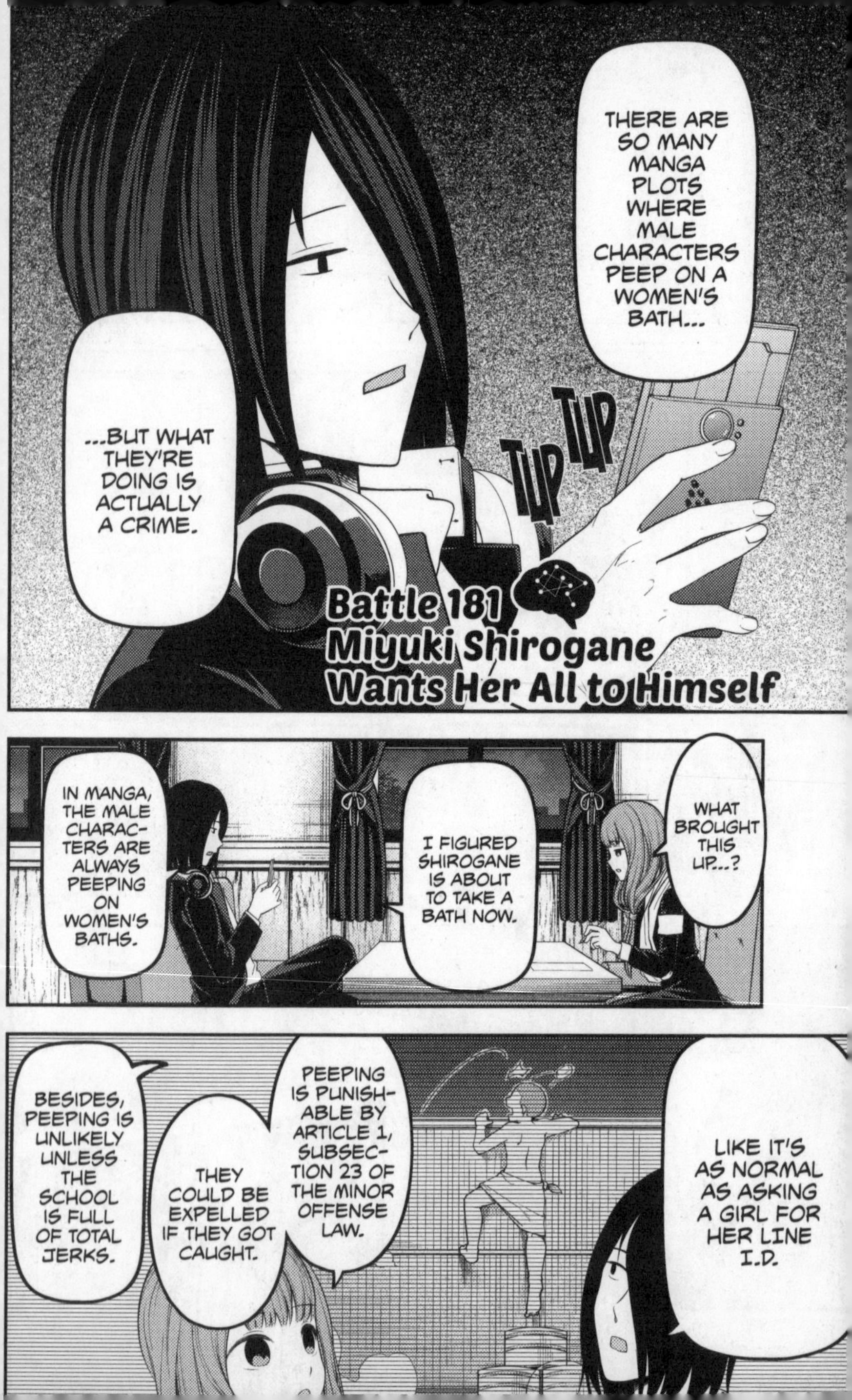
THERE ARE SO MANY MANGA PLOTS WHERE MALE CHARACTERS PEEP ON A WOMEN'S BATH...
...BUT WHAT THEY'RE DOING IS ACTUALLY A CRIME.
TUP TUP
Battle 181 Miyuki Shirogane Wants Her All to Himself
WHAT BROUGHT THIS UP...?
I FIGURED SHIROGANE IS ABOUT TO TAKE A BATH NOW.
IN MANGA, THE MALE CHARAC-TERS ARE ALWAYS PEEPING ON WOMEN'S BATHS.
LIKE IT'S AS NORMAL AS ASKING A GIRL FOR HER LINE I.D.
PEEPING IS PUNISH-ABLE BY ARTICLE 1, SUBSEC-TION 23 OF THE MINOR OFFENSE LAW.
THEY COULD BE EXPELLED IF THEY GOT CAUGHT.
BESIDES, PEEPING IS UNLIKELY UNLESS THE SCHOOL IS FULL OF TOTAL JERKS.

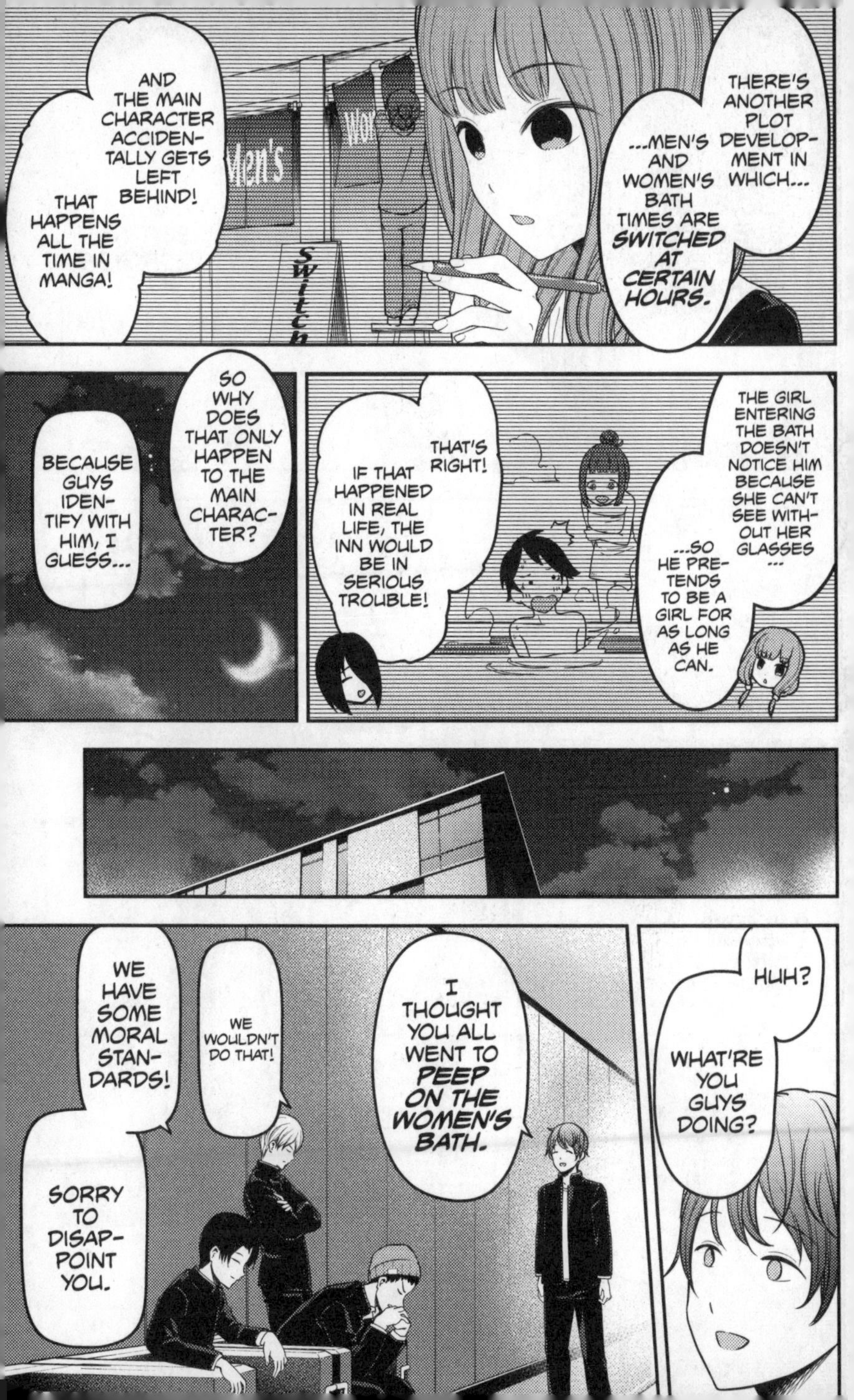
THERE'S ANOTHER PLOT DEVELOPMENT IN WHICH...
...MEN'S AND WOMEN'S BATH TIMES ARE SWITCHED AT CERTAIN HOURS.
Men's
AND THE MAIN CHARACTER ACCIDENTALLY GETS LEFT BEHIND!
THAT HAPPENS ALL THE TIME IN MANGA!
THE GIRL ENTERING THE BATH DOESN'T NOTICE HIM BECAUSE SHE CAN'T SEE WITHOUT HER GLASSES...
...SO HE PRETENDS TO BE A GIRL FOR AS LONG AS HE CAN.
THAT'S RIGHT!
IF THAT HAPPENED IN REAL LIFE, THE INN WOULD BE IN SERIOUS TROUBLE!
SO WHY DOES THAT ONLY HAPPEN TO THE MAIN CHARACTER?
BECAUSE GUYS IDENTIFY WITH HIM, I GUESS...
HUH?
WHAT'RE YOU GUYS DOING?
I THOUGHT YOU ALL WENT TO PEEP ON THE WOMEN'S BATH.
WE WOULDN'T DO THAT!
WE HAVE SOME MORAL STANDARDS!
SORRY TO DISAPPOINT YOU.

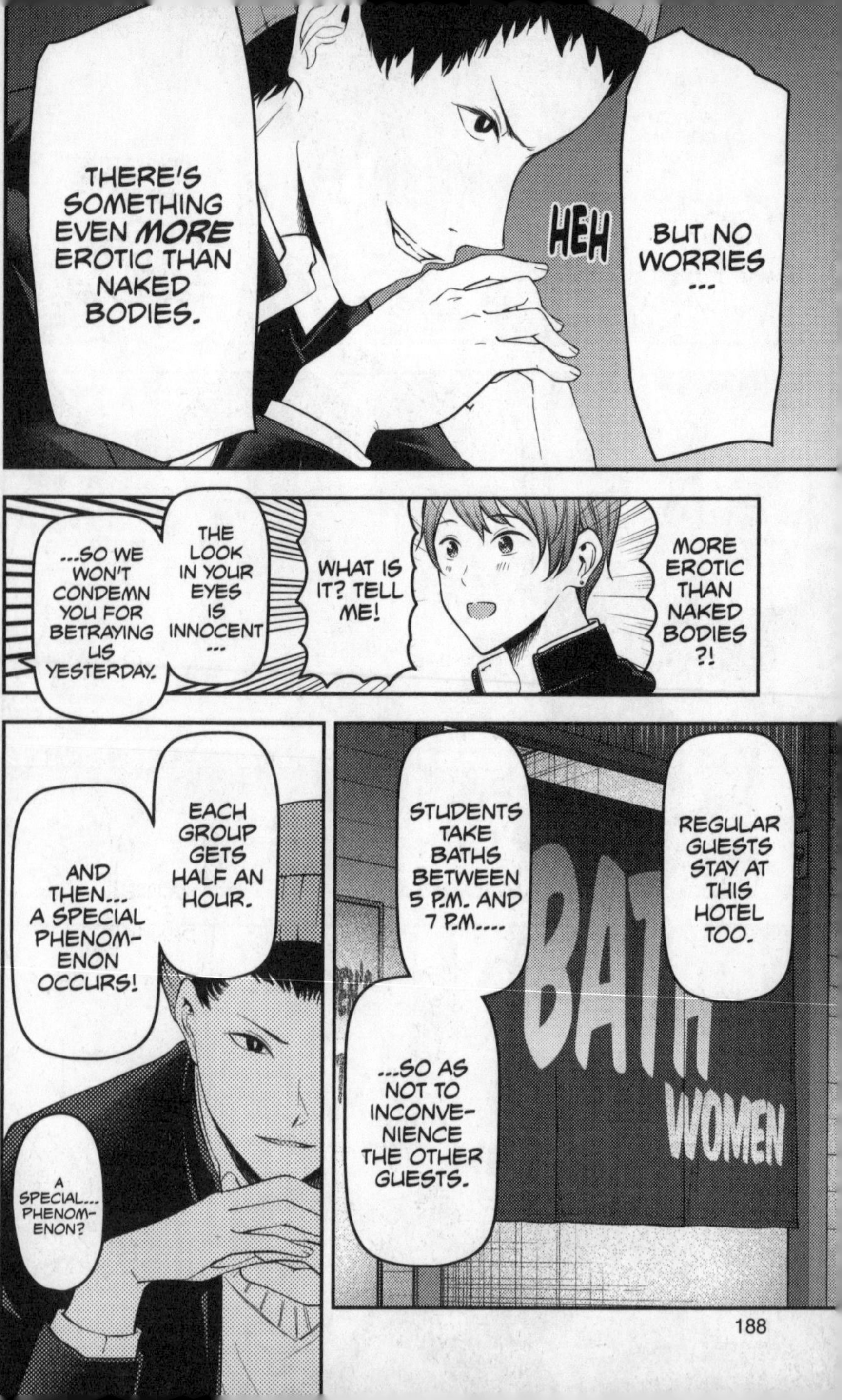
BUT NO WORRIES ...
HEH
THERE'S SOMETHING EVEN MORE EROTIC THAN NAKED BODIES.
MORE EROTIC THAN NAKED BODIES?!
WHAT IS IT? TELL ME!
THE LOOK IN YOUR EYES IS INNOCENT ...
...SO WE WON'T CONDEMN YOU FOR BETRAYING US YESTERDAY.
REGULAR GUESTS STAY AT THIS HOTEL TOO.
STUDENTS TAKE BATHS BETWEEN 5 P.M. AND 7 P.M....
...SO AS NOT TO INCONVENIENCE THE OTHER GUESTS.
BATH
WOMEN
EACH GROUP GETS HALF AN HOUR.
AND THEN... A SPECIAL PHENOMENON OCCURS!
A SPECIAL... PHENOMENON?

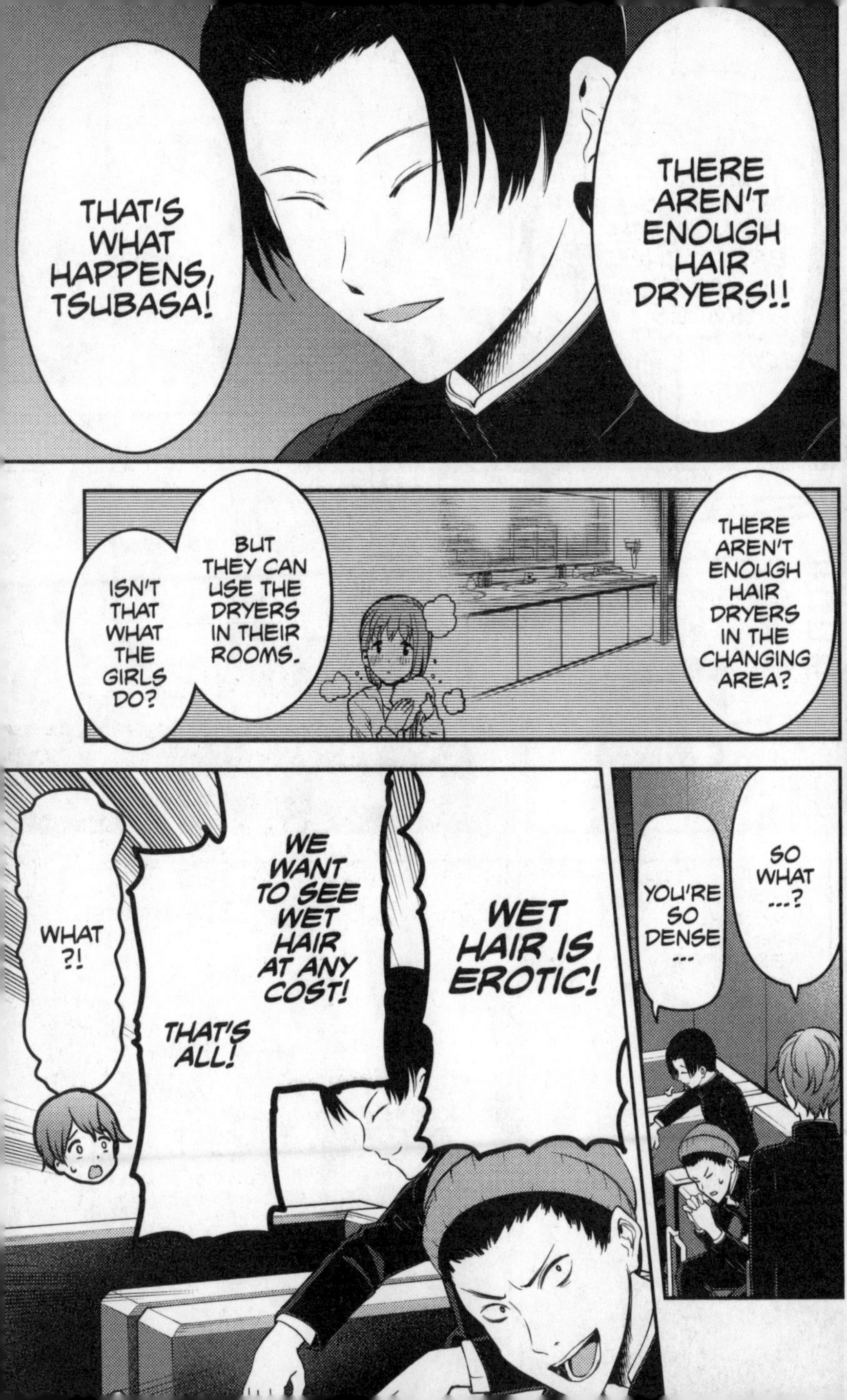
THERE AREN'T ENOUGH HAIR DRYERS!!
THAT'S WHAT HAPPENS, TSUBASA!
THERE AREN'T ENOUGH HAIR DRYERS IN THE CHANGING AREA?
BUT THEY CAN USE THE DRYERS IN THEIR ROOMS.
ISN'T THAT WHAT THE GIRLS DO?
SO WHAT ...?
YOU'RE SO DENSE ...
WET HAIR IS EROTIC!
WE WANT TO SEE WET HAIR AT ANY COST!
THAT'S ALL!
WHAT ?!

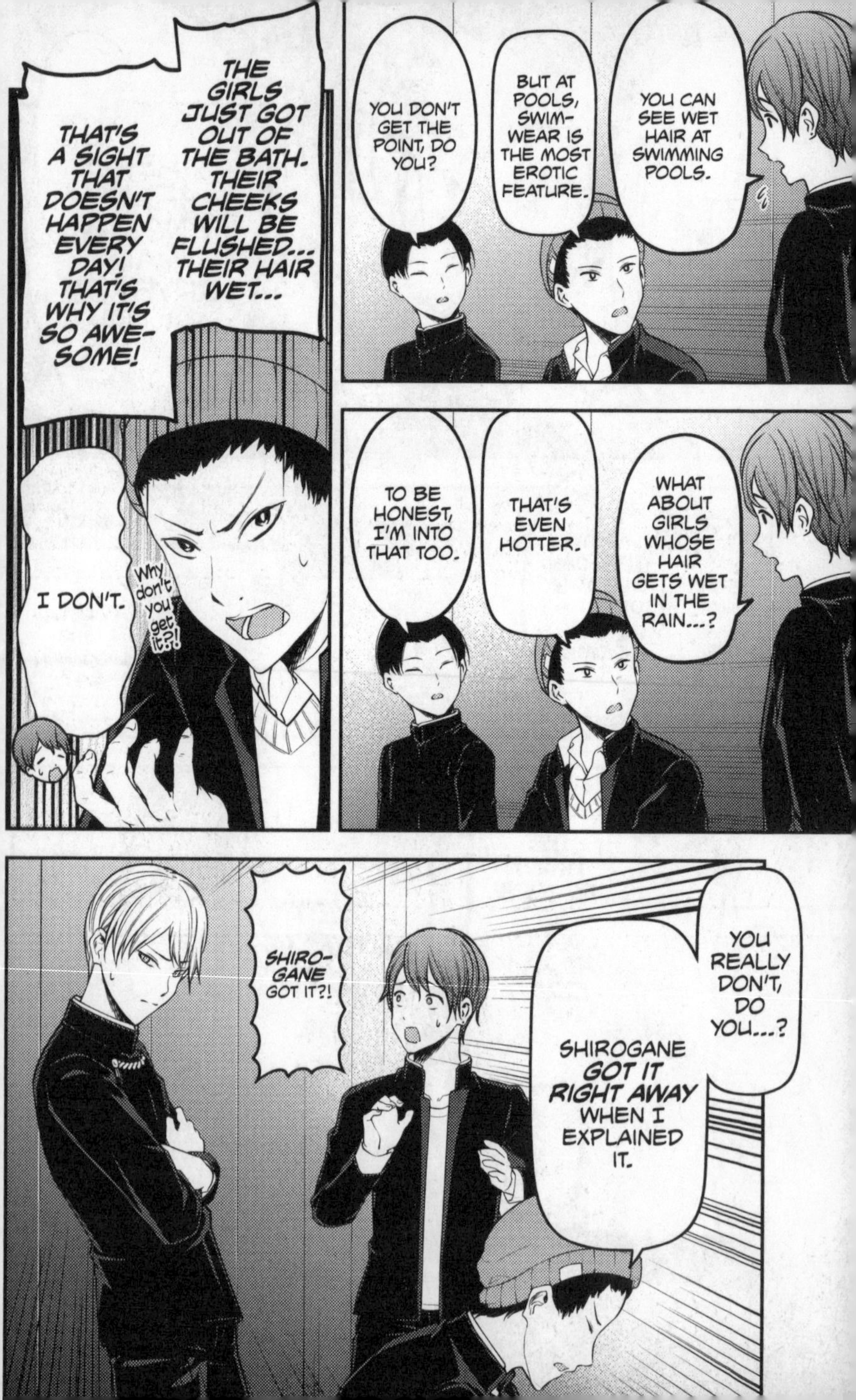
YOU CAN SEE WET HAIR AT SWIMMING POOLS.
BUT AT POOLS, SWIM-WEAR IS THE MOST EROTIC FEATURE.
YOU DON'T GET THE POINT, DO YOU?
WHAT ABOUT GIRLS WHOSE HAIR GETS WET IN THE RAIN...?
THAT'S EVEN HOTTER.
TO BE HONEST, I'M INTO THAT TOO.
THE GIRLS JUST GOT OUT OF THE BATH. THEIR CHEEKS WILL BE FLUSHED... THEIR HAIR WET...
THAT'S A SIGHT THAT DOESN'T HAPPEN EVERY DAY! THAT'S WHY IT'S SO AWE-SOME!
Why don't you get it?!
I DON'T.
YOU REALLY DON'T, DO YOU...?
SHIROGANE GOT IT RIGHT AWAY WHEN I EXPLAINED IT.
SHIROGANE GOT IT?!

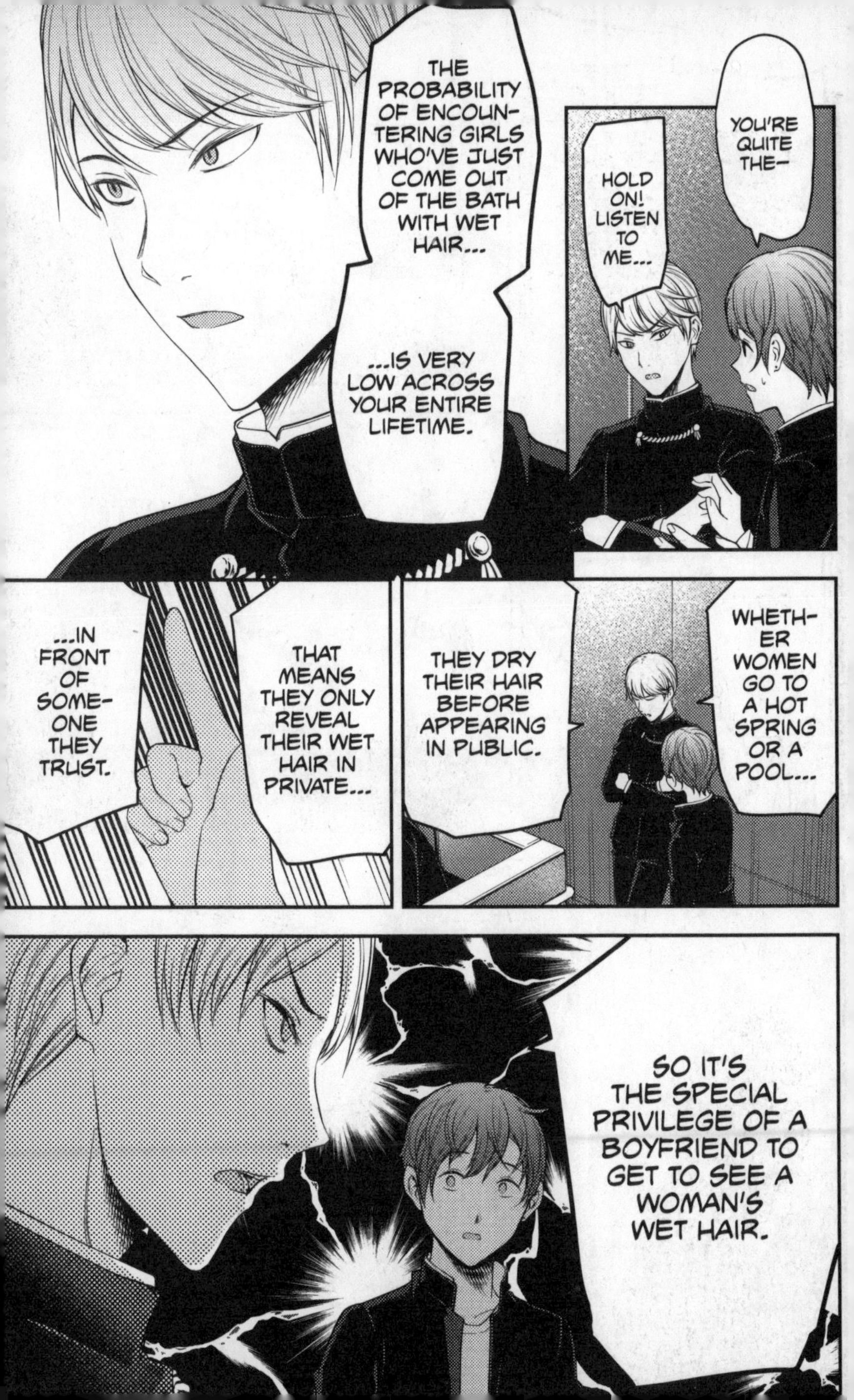
YOU'RE QUITE THE—
HOLD ON! LISTEN TO ME...
THE PROBABILITY OF ENCOUNTERING GIRLS WHO'VE JUST COME OUT OF THE BATH WITH WET HAIR...
...IS VERY LOW ACROSS YOUR ENTIRE LIFETIME.
WHETHER WOMEN GO TO A HOT SPRING OR A POOL...
THEY DRY THEIR HAIR BEFORE APPEARING IN PUBLIC.
THAT MEANS THEY ONLY REVEAL THEIR WET HAIR IN PRIVATE...
...IN FRONT OF SOMEONE THEY TRUST.
SO IT'S THE SPECIAL PRIVILEGE OF A BOYFRIEND TO GET TO SEE A WOMAN'S WET HAIR.

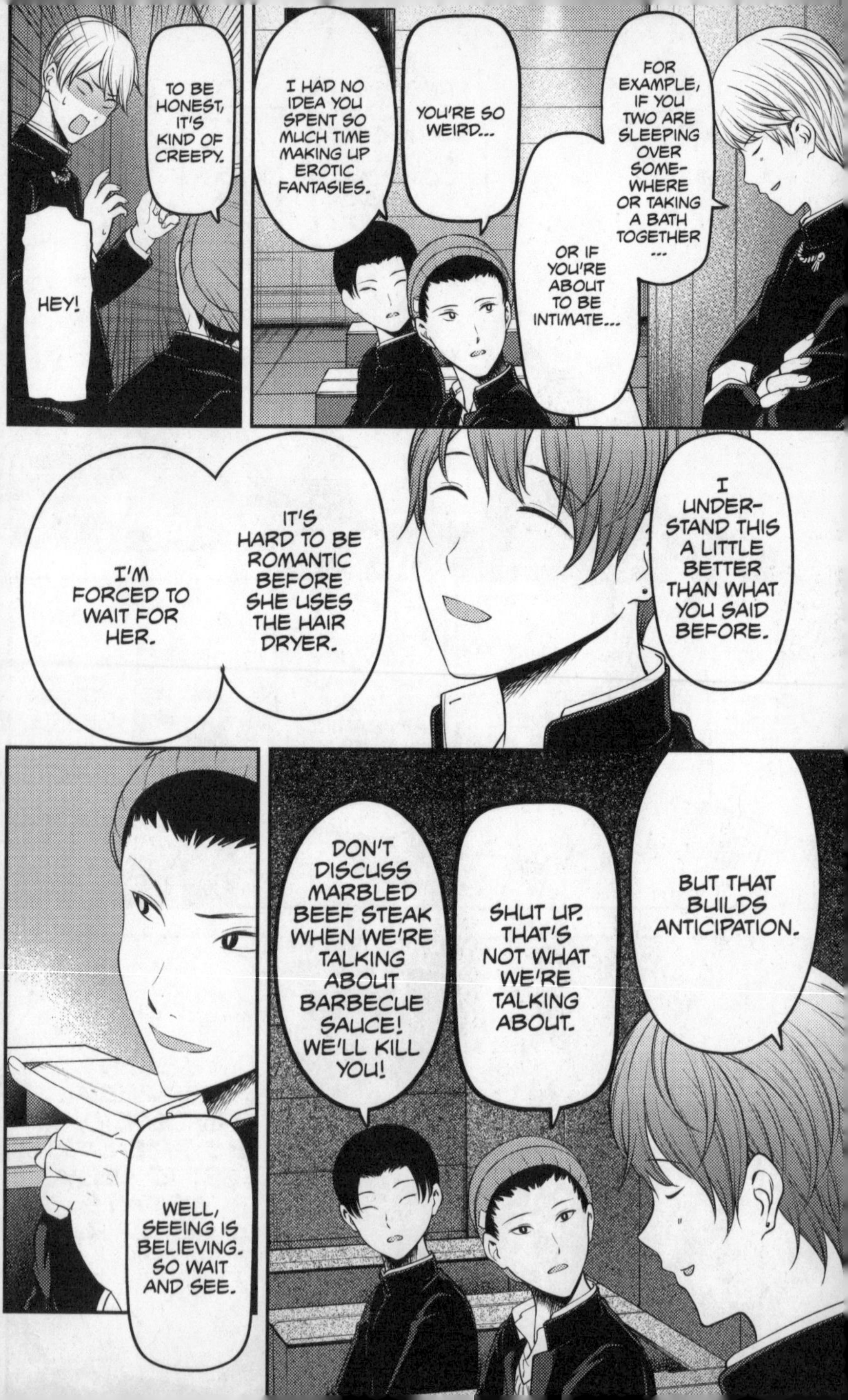
FOR EXAMPLE, IF YOU TWO ARE SLEEPING OVER SOMEWHERE OR TAKING A BATH TOGETHER...
OR IF YOU'RE ABOUT TO BE INTIMATE...
YOU'RE SO WEIRD...
I HAD NO IDEA YOU SPENT SO MUCH TIME MAKING UP EROTIC FANTASIES.
TO BE HONEST, IT'S KIND OF CREEPY.
HEY!
I UNDERSTAND THIS A LITTLE BETTER THAN WHAT YOU SAID BEFORE.
IT'S HARD TO BE ROMANTIC BEFORE SHE USES THE HAIR DRYER.
I'M FORCED TO WAIT FOR HER.
BUT THAT BUILDS ANTICIPATION.
SHUT UP. THAT'S NOT WHAT WE'RE TALKING ABOUT.
DON'T DISCUSS MARBLED BEEF STEAK WHEN WE'RE TALKING ABOUT BARBECUE SAUCE! WE'LL KILL YOU!
WELL, SEEING IS BELIEVING. SO WAIT AND SEE.

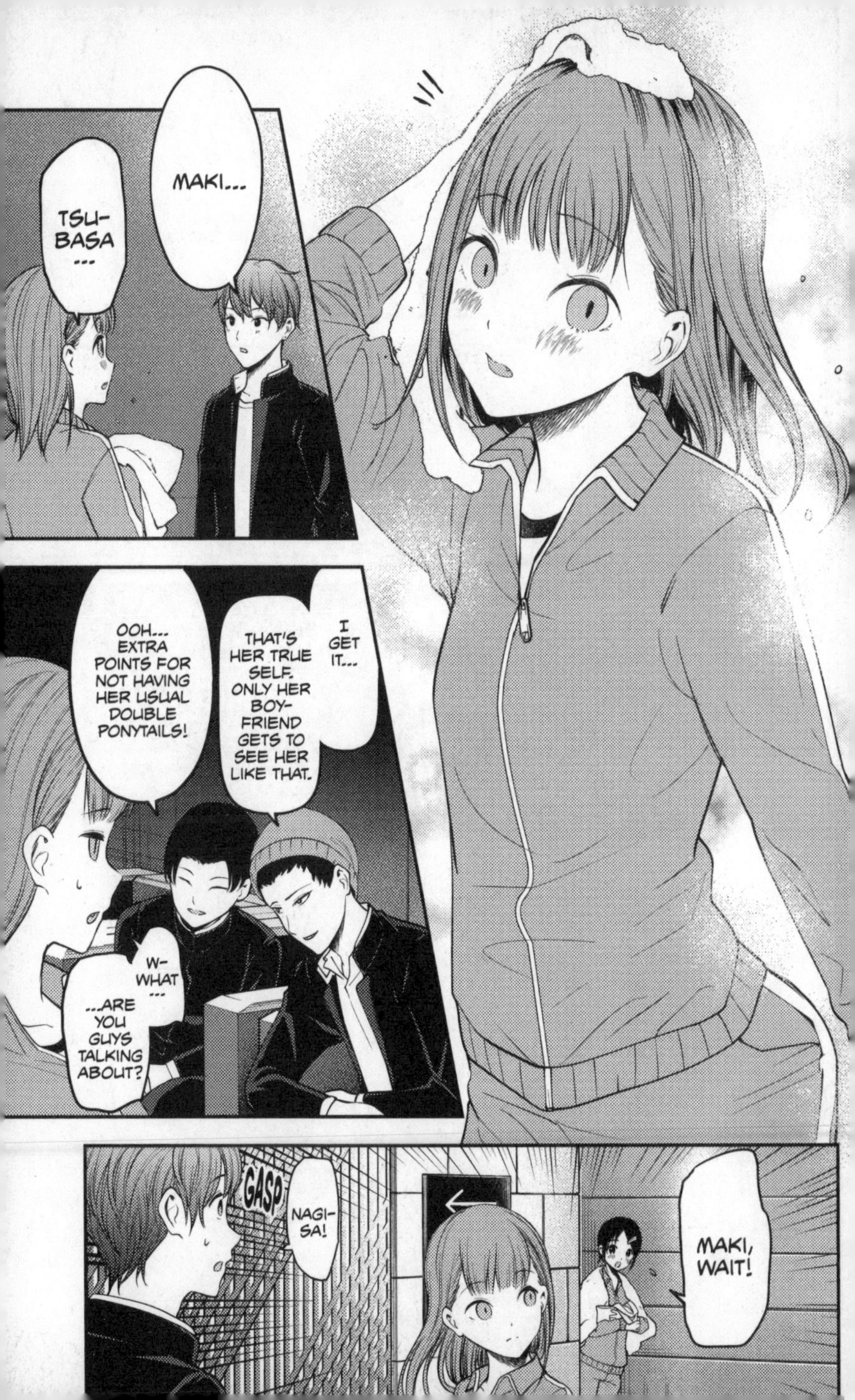
MAKI...
TSU-BASA...
I GET IT...
THAT'S HER TRUE SELF. ONLY HER BOY-FRIEND GETS TO SEE HER LIKE THAT.
OOH... EXTRA POINTS FOR NOT HAVING HER USUAL DOUBLE PONYTAILS!
W-WHAT...
...ARE YOU GUYS TALKING ABOUT?
MAKI, WAIT!
NAGI-SA!
GASP

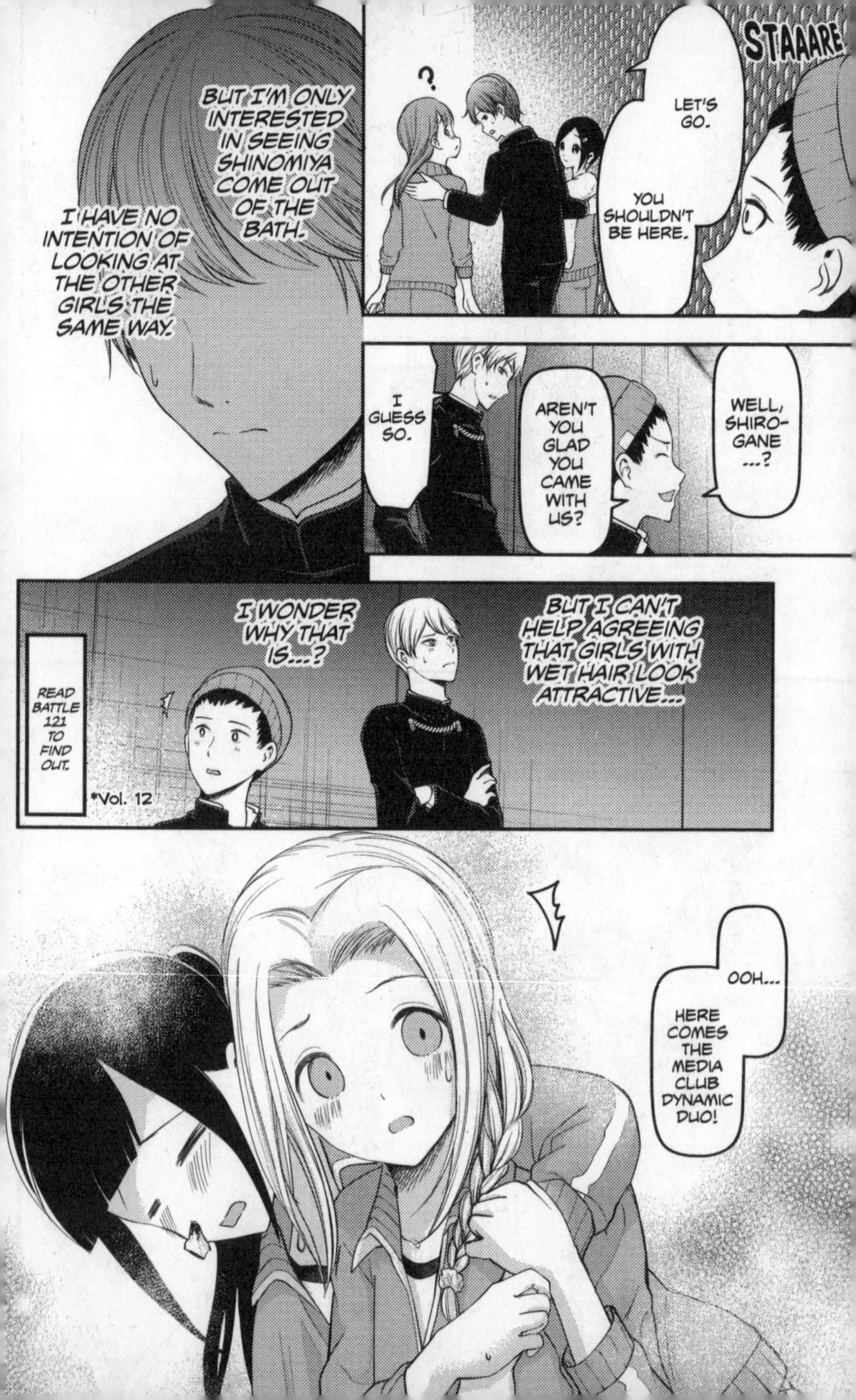
STAAARE
LET'S GO.
YOU SHOULDN'T BE HERE.
WELL, SHIRO-GANE...?
AREN'T YOU GLAD YOU CAME WITH US?
I GUESS SO.
BUT I'M ONLY INTERESTED IN SEEING SHINOMIYA COME OUT OF THE BATH.
I HAVE NO INTENTION OF LOOKING AT THE OTHER GIRLS THE SAME WAY.
BUT I CAN'T HELP AGREEING THAT GIRLS WITH WET HAIR LOOK ATTRACTIVE...
I WONDER WHY THAT IS...?
READ BATTLE 121 TO FIND OUT.
*Vol. 12
OOH...
HERE COMES THE MEDIA CLUB DYNAMIC DUO!

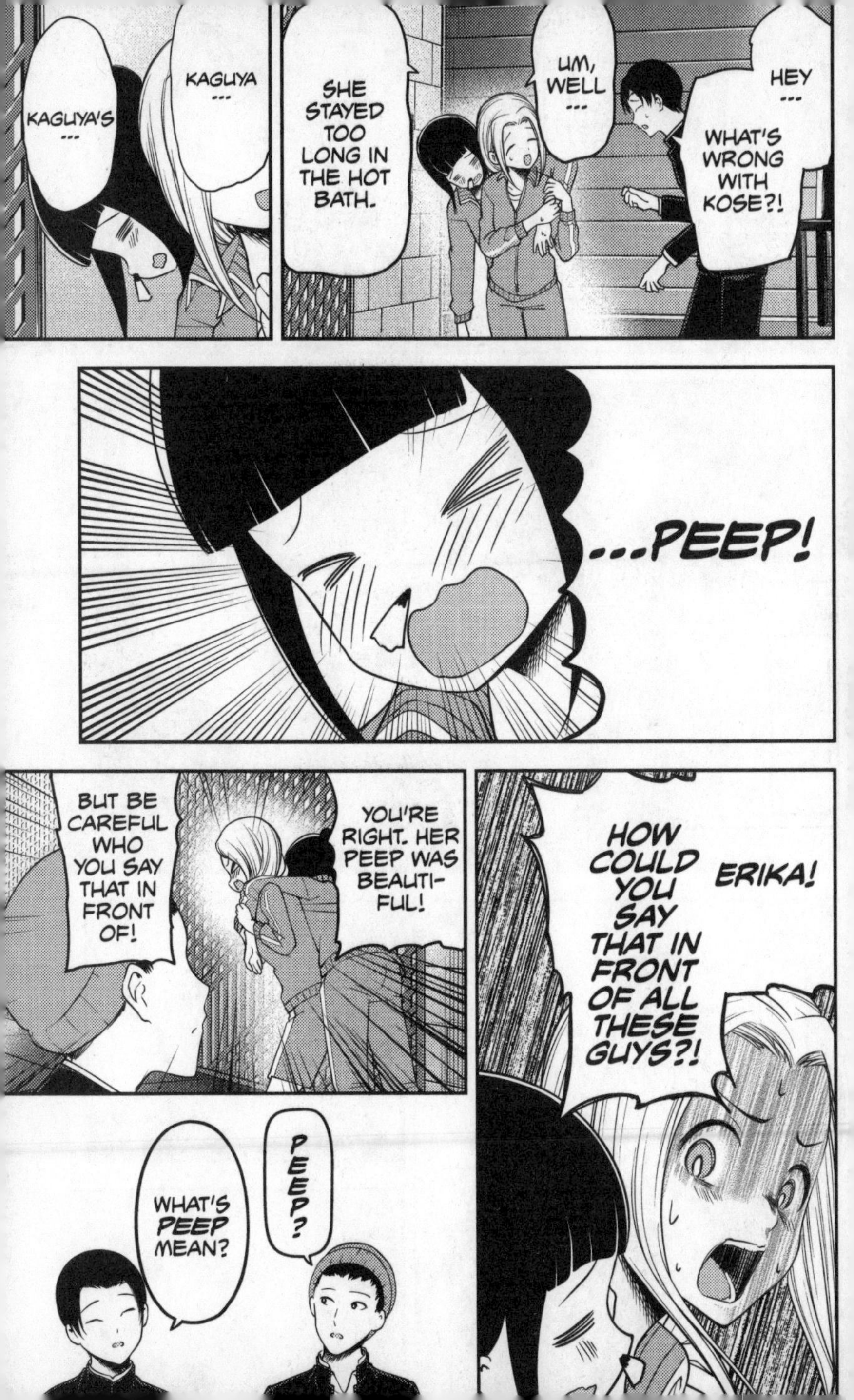
HEY... WHAT'S WRONG WITH KOSE?!
UM, WELL...
SHE STAYED TOO LONG IN THE HOT BATH.
KAGUYA...
KAGUYA'S...
...PEEP!
ERIKA!
HOW COULD YOU SAY THAT IN FRONT OF ALL THESE GUYS?!
YOU'RE RIGHT. HER PEEP WAS BEAUTI-FUL!
BUT BE CAREFUL WHO YOU SAY THAT IN FRONT OF!
PEEP?
WHAT'S PEEP MEAN?

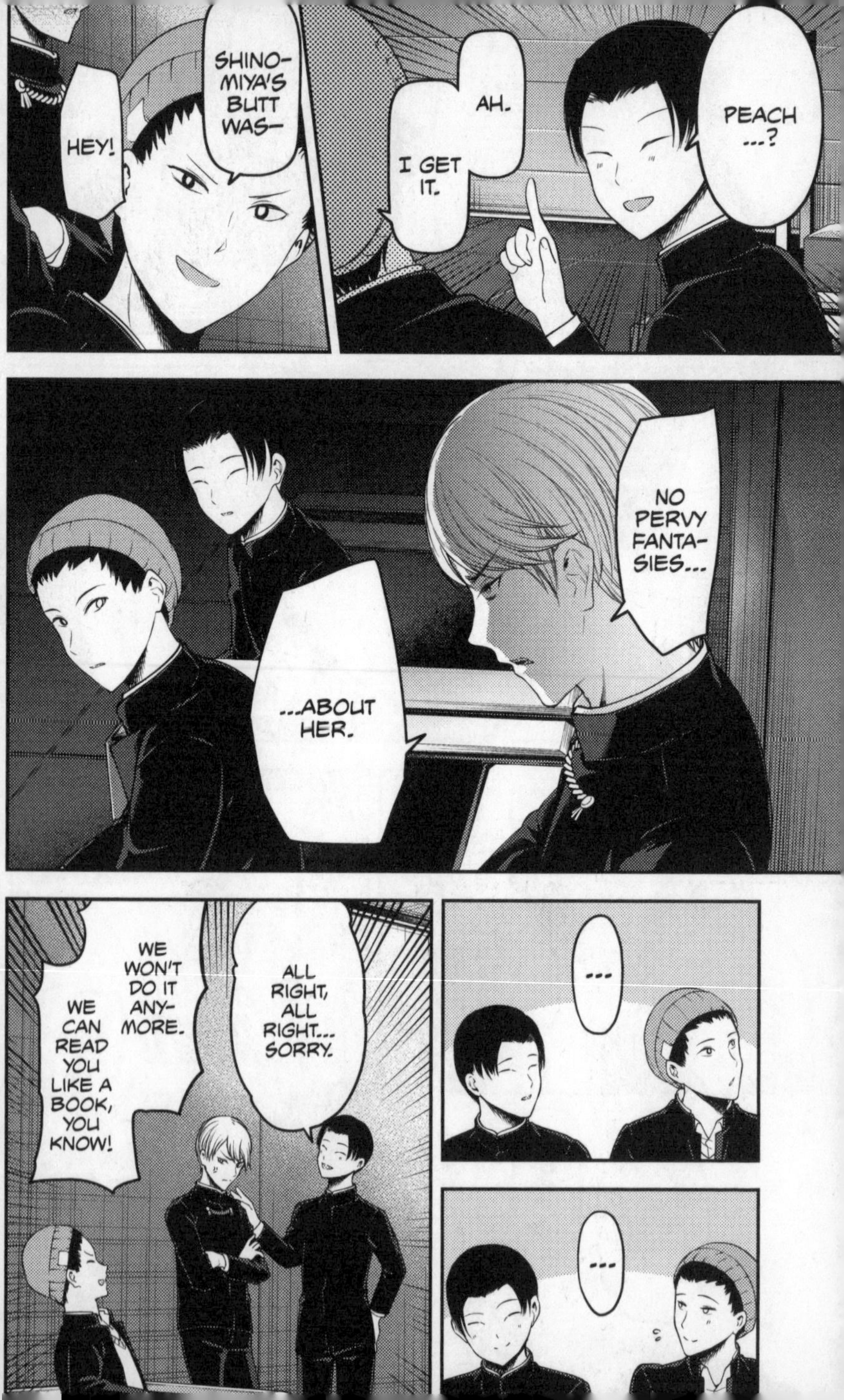
PEACH ...?
AH.
I GET IT.
SHINO-MIYA'S BUTT WAS—
HEY!
NO PERVY FANTA-SIES...
...ABOUT HER.
...
...
ALL RIGHT, ALL RIGHT... SORRY.
WE WON'T DO IT ANY-MORE.
WE CAN READ YOU LIKE A BOOK, YOU KNOW!

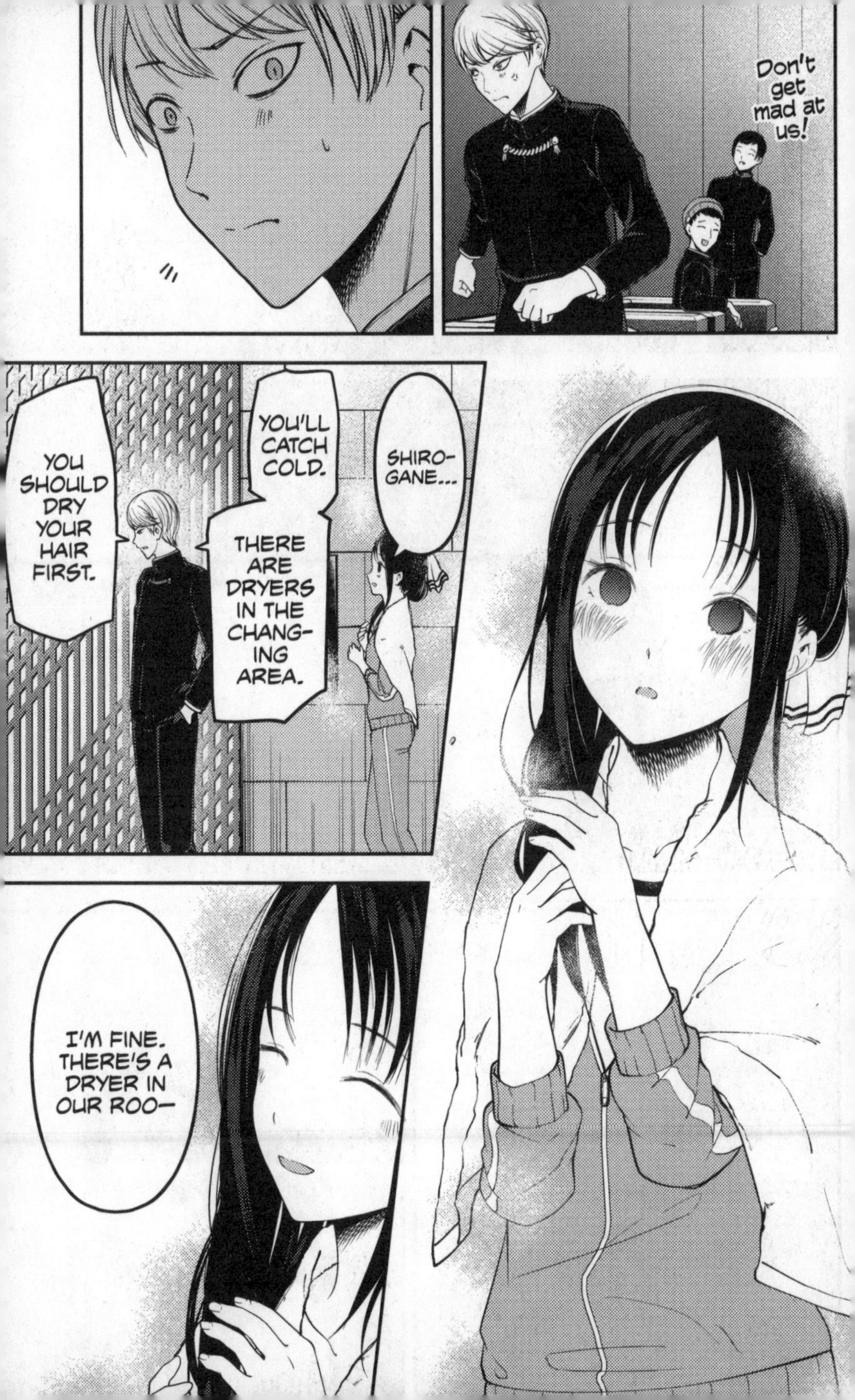
Don't get mad at us!
SHIRO-GANE...
YOU'LL CATCH COLD.
THERE ARE DRYERS IN THE CHANGING AREA.
YOU SHOULD DRY YOUR HAIR FIRST.
I'M FINE. THERE'S A DRYER IN OUR ROO—

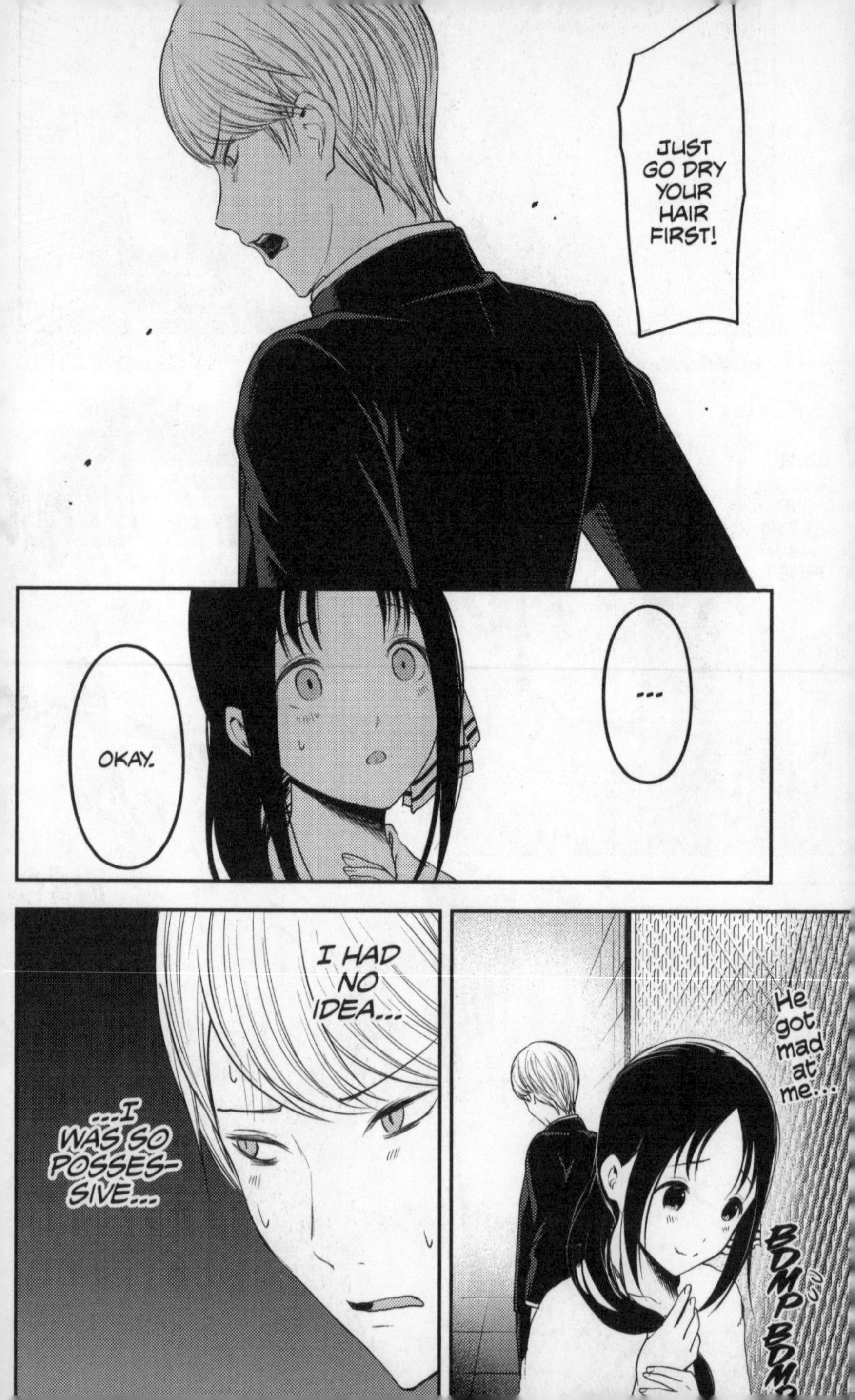
JUST GO DRY YOUR HAIR FIRST!
...
OKAY.
He got mad at me...
BDMP BDMP
I HAD NO IDEA...
...I WAS SO POSSES-SIVE...

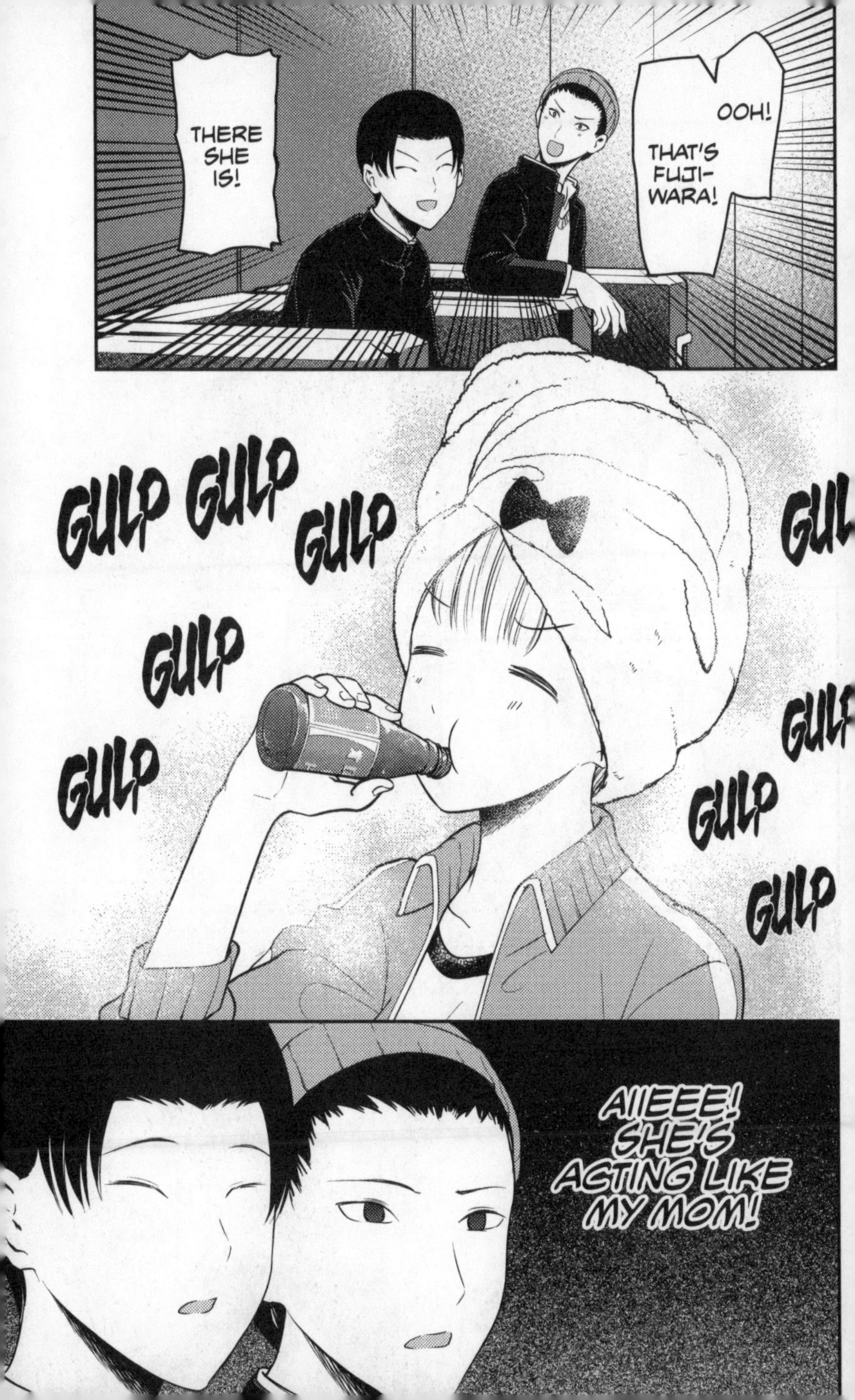
OOH! THAT'S FUJI-WARA!
THERE SHE IS!
GUL
GULF
GULP
GULP
GULP GULP
GULP
GULP
GULP
AIIEEE! SHE'S ACTING LIKE MY MOM!

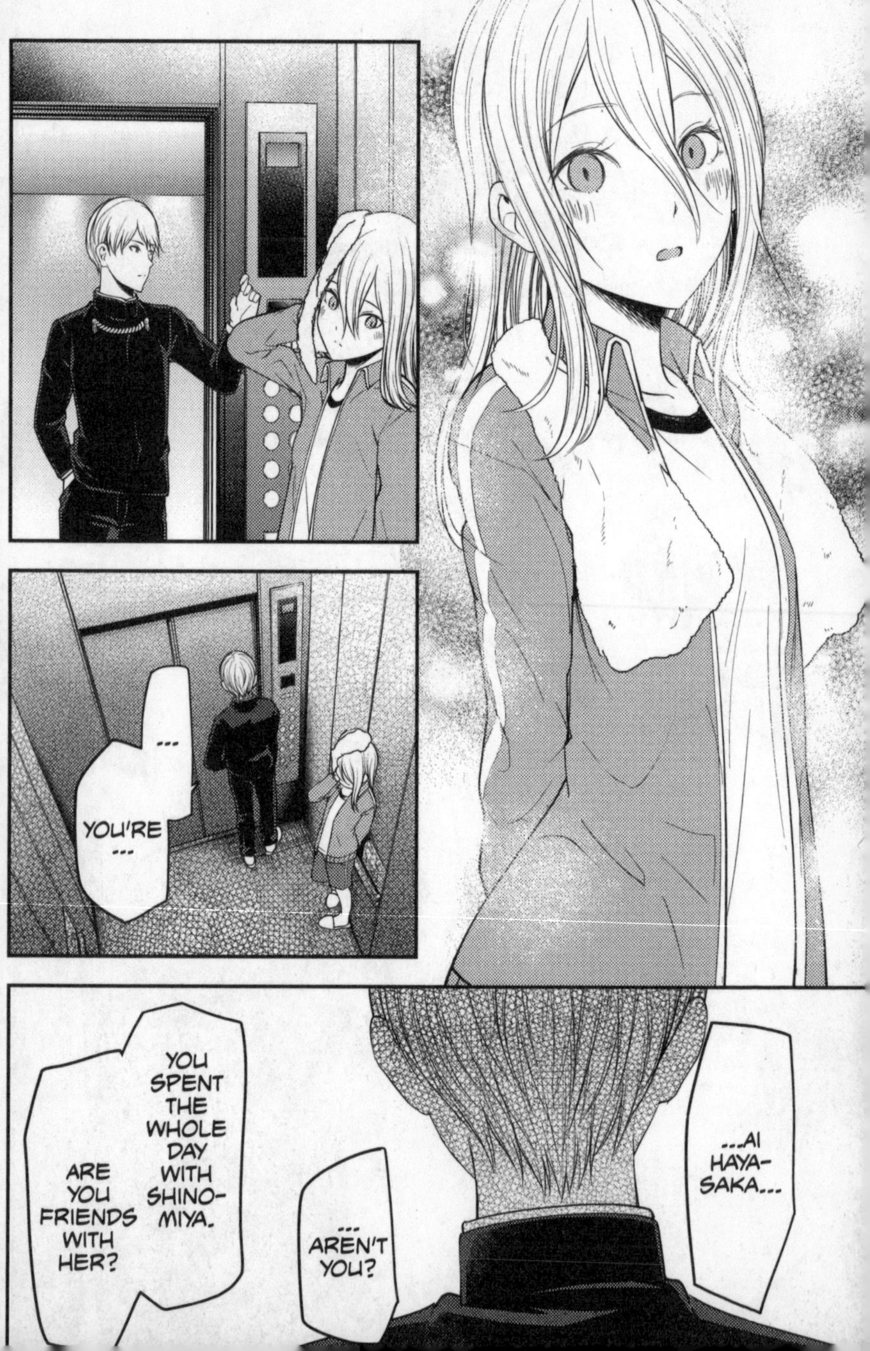
...
YOU'RE ...
...AI HAYA-SAKA...
...AREN'T YOU?
YOU SPENT THE WHOLE DAY WITH SHINO-MIYA.
ARE YOU FRIENDS WITH HER?

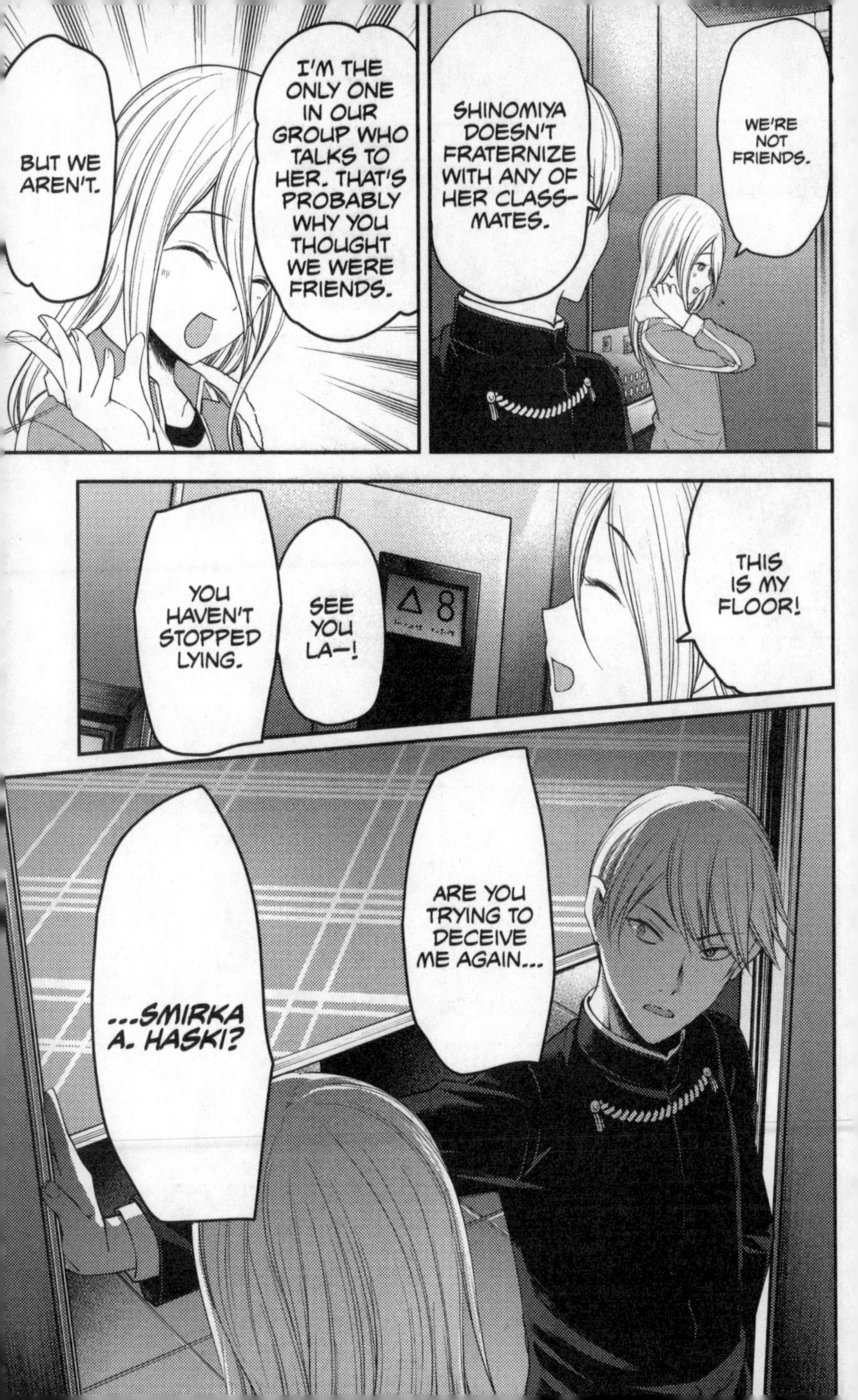
WE'RE NOT FRIENDS.
SHINOMIYA DOESN'T FRATERNIZE WITH ANY OF HER CLASS-MATES.
I'M THE ONLY ONE IN OUR GROUP WHO TALKS TO HER. THAT'S PROBABLY WHY YOU THOUGHT WE WERE FRIENDS.
BUT WE AREN'T.
THIS IS MY FLOOR!
SEE YOU LA—!
YOU HAVEN'T STOPPED LYING.
ARE YOU TRYING TO DECEIVE ME AGAIN...
...SMIRKA A. HASKI?

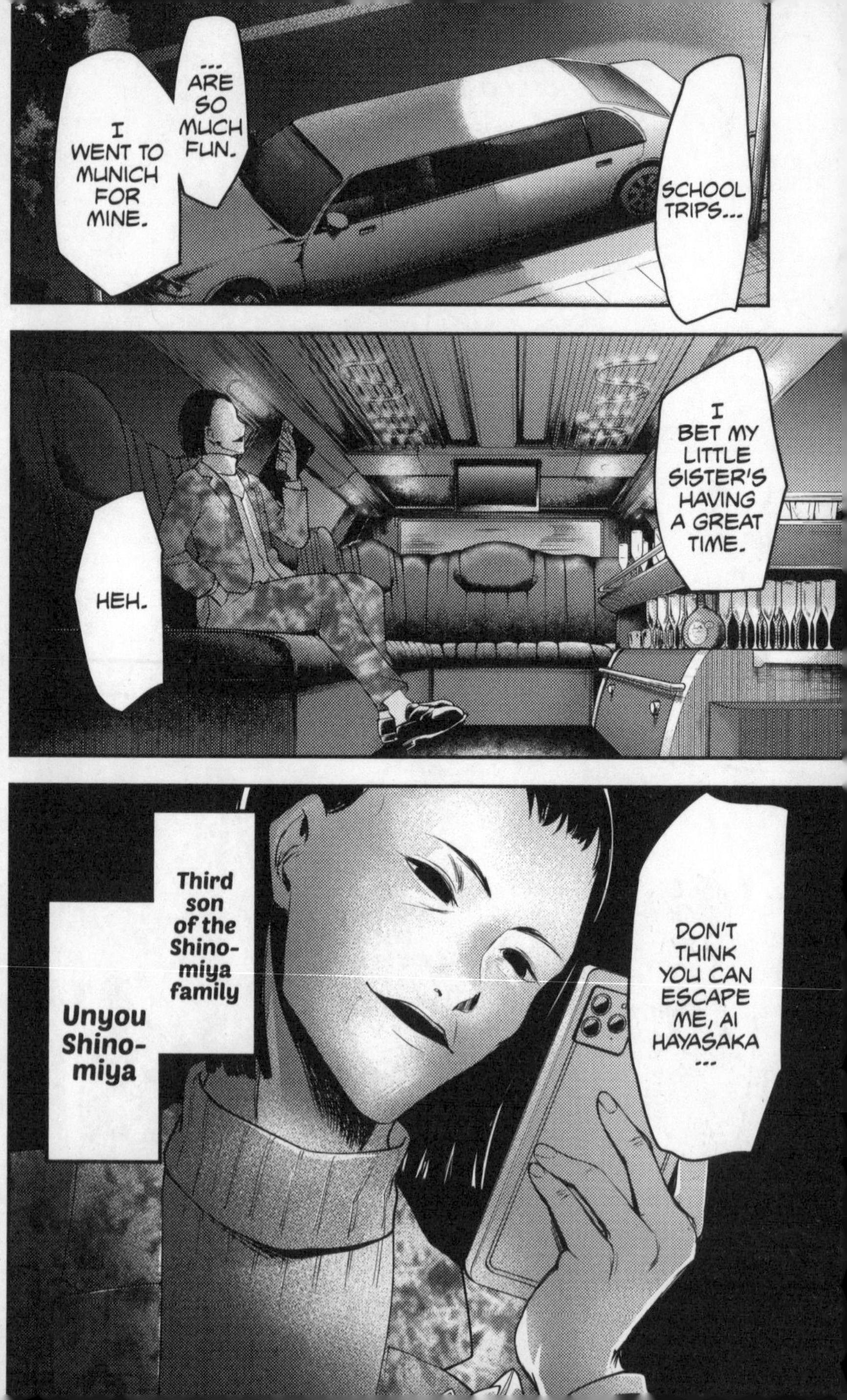
SCHOOL TRIPS...
...ARE SO MUCH FUN.
I WENT TO MUNICH FOR MINE.
I BET MY LITTLE SISTER'S HAVING A GREAT TIME.
HEH.
DON'T THINK YOU CAN ESCAPE ME, AI HAYASAKA...
Third son of the Shinomiya family
Unyou Shinomiya

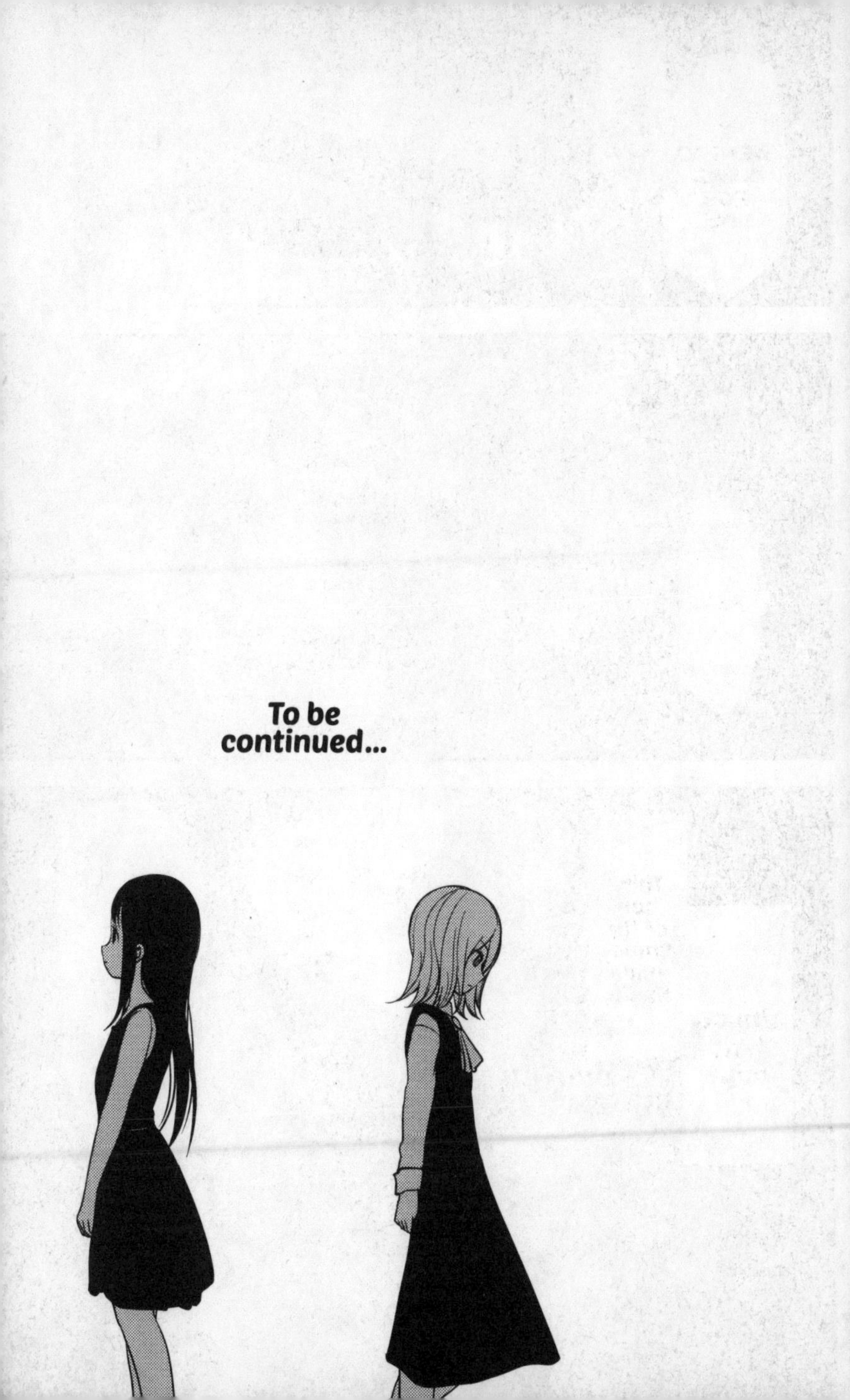
To be continued...

SOMETIMES YOU NEED TO LIE TO AVOID HAVING TO LIE...

AKA AKASAKA

Aka Akasaka got his start as an assistant to Jinsei Kataoka and Kazuma Kondou, the creators of *Deadman Wonderland*. His first serialized manga was an adaptation of the light novel series *Sayonara Piano Sonata*, published by Kadokawa in 2011. *Kaguya-sama: Love Is War* began serialization in *Miracle Jump* in 2015 but was later moved to *Weekly Young Jump* in 2016 due to its popularity.

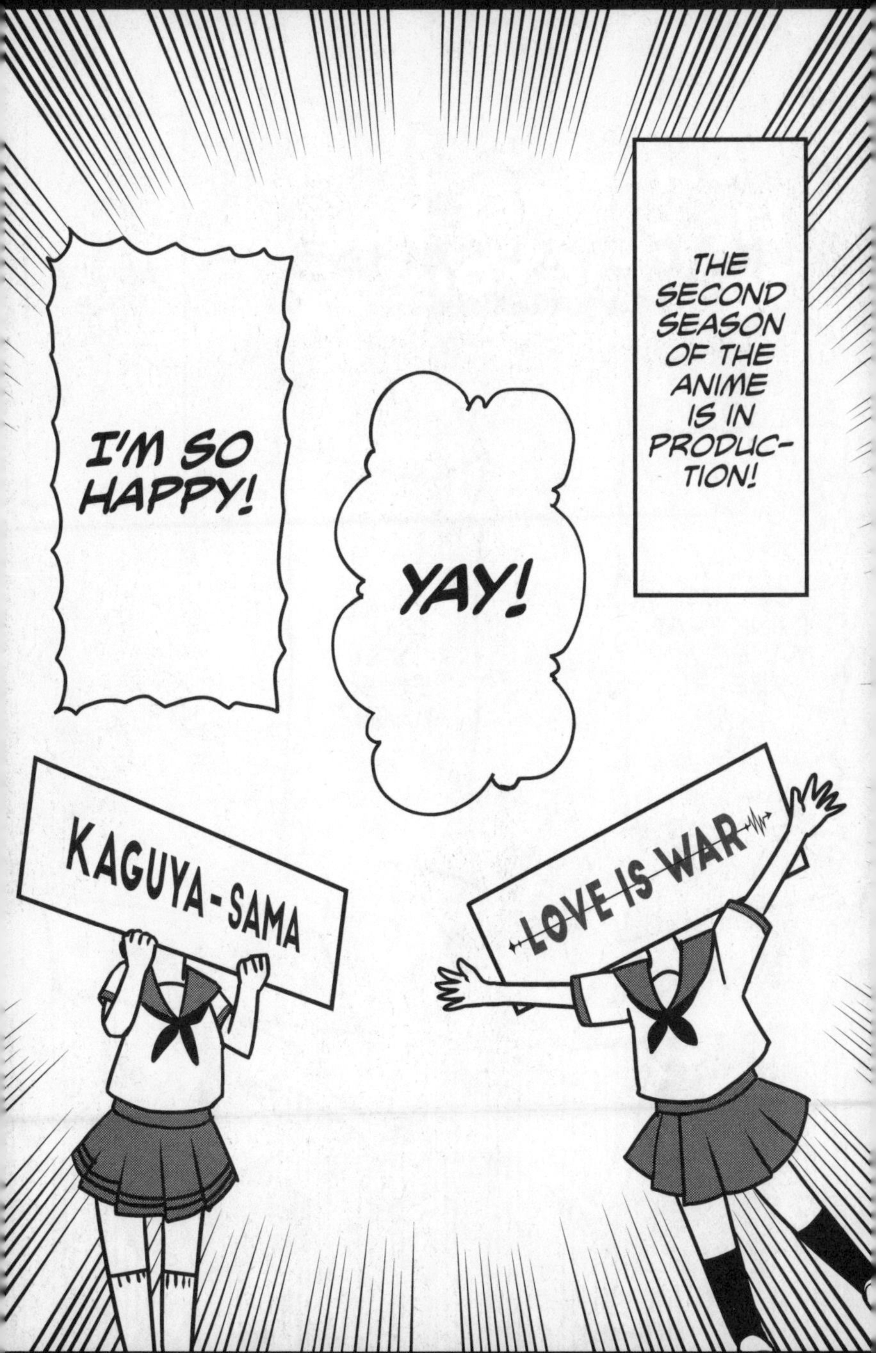
THE SECOND SEASON OF THE ANIME IS IN PRODUC-TION!
YAY!
I'M SO HAPPY!
LOVE IS WAR
KAGUYA-SAMA

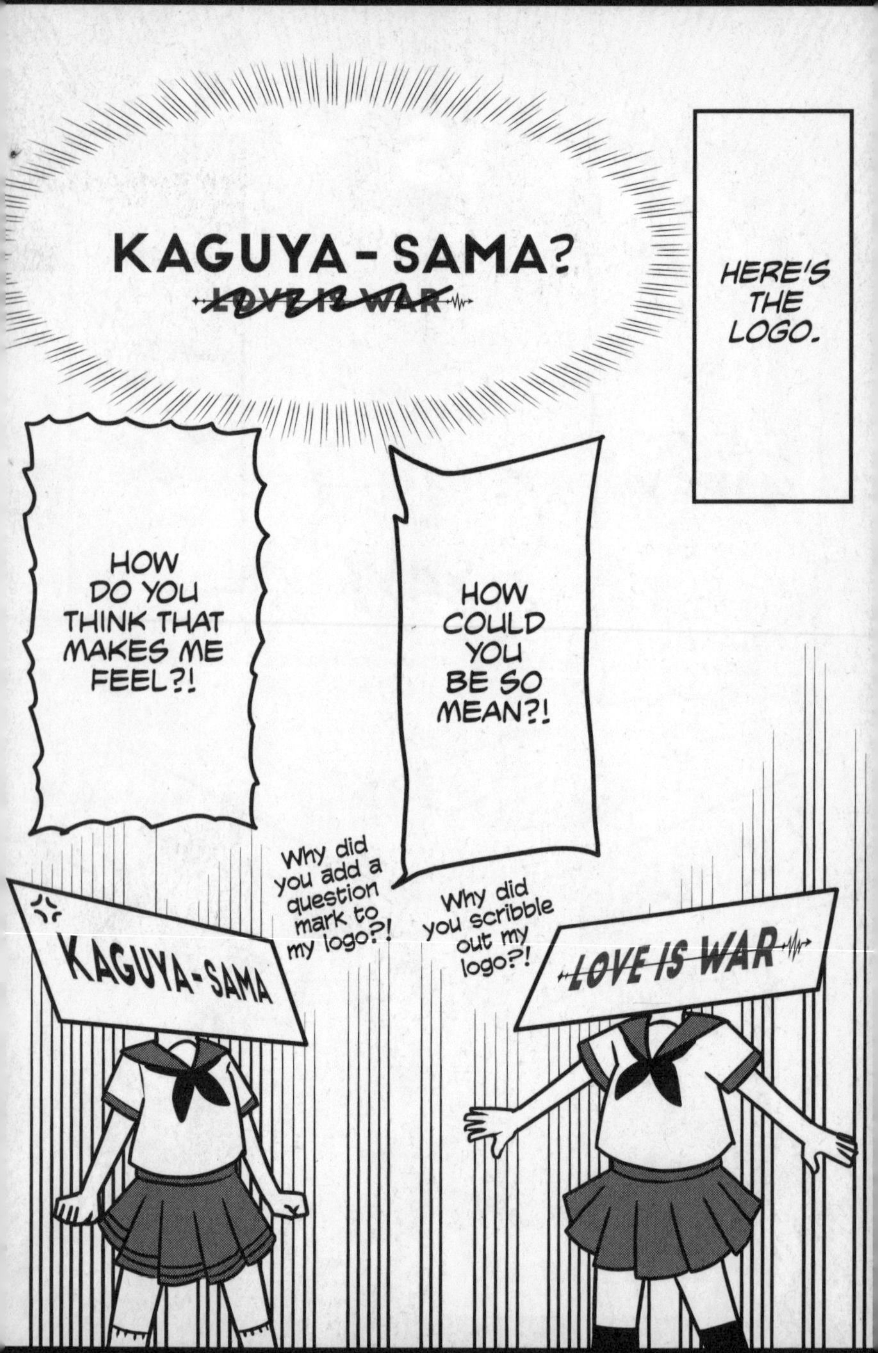
HERE'S THE LOGO.
KAGUYA-SAMA?
LOVE IS WAR
HOW COULD YOU BE SO MEAN?!
HOW DO YOU THINK THAT MAKES ME FEEL?!
LOVE IS WAR
Why did you scribble out my logo?!
Why did you add a question mark to my logo?!
KAGUYA-SAMA

KAGUYA-SAMA
LOVE IS WAR

SHONEN JUMP MANGA EDITION

18

STORY AND ART BY
AKA AKASAKA

Translation/Tomo Kimura
English Adaptation/Annette Roman
Touch-Up Art & Lettering/Steve Dutro
Cover & Interior Design/Alice Lewis
Editor/Annette Roman

KAGUYA-SAMA WA KOKURASETAI~TENSAITACHI NO REN'AI ZUNO SEN~
© 2015 by Aka Akasaka
All rights reserved.
First published in Japan in 2015 by SHUEISHA Inc., Tokyo.
English translation rights arranged by SHUEISHA Inc.

Printed in Canada

Published by VIZ Media, LLC
P.O. Box 77010
San Francisco, CA 94107

10 9 8 7 6 5 4 3 2 1
First printing, February 2021

COMING NEXT VOLUME

19

KAGUYA-SAMA
LOVE IS WAR

19

STORY & ART BY
AKA AKASAKA

Will this romantic comedy turn into a thriller? Two warring factions in Kaguya's family are trying to force her personal assistant, Ai, to abandon Kaguya and serve them. While Miyuki tries to save Ai from getting kidnapped, she sends an urgent message to Kaguya to meet her at the place where their relationship began—but Kaguya can't figure out where that is! Meanwhile, as Yu and Tsubame grow closer, Miko grows more jealous, and different student council factions clash over whom Yu should date!

You're never too old to become a YouTube sensation.